HIGHER BUSINESS MANAGEMENT

PETER HAGAN
ALISTAIR B WYLIE
ANNE BECK

Hodder Gibson
2A Christie Street, Paisley, PA1 1NB

ACKNOWLEDGEMENTS

The publishers would like to thank the following individuals, institutions and companies for permission to reproduce photographs in this book. Every effort has been made to trace ownership of copyright. The publishers would be happy to make arrangements with any copyright holder whom it has not been possible to contact:

Alan Wylie page 227: Corbis Bill Varie page 222, Helen King page 228, R W Jones pages 214 and 219 and The Scotsman page 42; Equal Opportunities Commission page 235; Hodder & Stoughton page 156; Life File Andrew Ward pages 48 bottom and 212; PA Photos pages 230 and 238; Science Photo Library Colin Cuthbert page 47, Martin F Chillmaid page 48 top.

Illustrated by Peters and Zabransky Ltd.

Index provided by Indexing Specialists.

Orders: please contact Bookpoint Ltd, 130 Milton Park, Abingdon, Oxon OX14 4SB. Telephone: (44) 01235 827720. Fax: (44) 01235 400454. Lines are open from 9.00–6.00, Monday to Saturday, with a 24 hour message answering service. You can also order through our website www.hodderheadline.co.uk.

British Library Cataloguing in Publication Data
A catalogue record for this title is available from the British Library

ISBN 0 340 84902 9

Published by Hodder Gibson, 2a Christie Street, Paisley PA1 1NB.
Tel: 0141 848 1609; Fax: 0141 889 6315; email: hoddergibson@hodder.co.uk

First published 2003
Impression number   10 9 8 7 6 5 4 3 2 1
Year   2009 2008 2007 2006 2005 2004 2003

ISBN 0 340 81120 X

Published by Hodder Gibson, 2a Christie Street, Paisley PA1 1NB.
Tel: 0141 848 1609; Fax: 0141 889 6315; email: hoddergibson@hodder.co.uk

First Published 2003
Impression number   10 9 8 7 6 5 4 3 2 1
Year   2009 2008 2007 2006 2005 2004 2003
With Answers

Copyright © 2003 Peter Hagan, Alistair B Wylie and Anne Beck.

Typeset by J&L Composition, Filey, North Yorkshire. Printed for Hodder Gibson, 2a Christie Street, Paisley, PA1 1NB, Scotland, UK

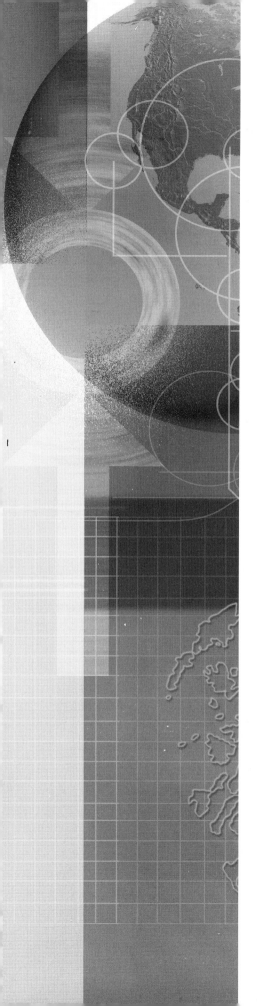

UNIT 1 • BUSINESS ENTERPRISE   7

CONTENTS

3

UNIT 2 • BUSINESS DECISION AREAS   102

CONTENTS

4

CONTENTS

UNIT 3 • EXTERNAL ASSESSMENT 269

CONTENTS

CHAPTER ONE

UNIT:1 BUSINESS ENTERPRISE

BUSINESS IN CONTEMPORARY SOCIETY

This chapter is covered at both Intermediate 2 and Higher levels. The course content for both levels is very similar. At *Intermediate level 2* we will look at:

INTERMEDIATE LEVEL 2

- How wealth is created by the production and consumption (buying and using) of goods and services.
- How these goods and services satisfy the needs of the consumer.
- The 3 sectors of activity – primary, secondary and tertiary.
- The different types of business organisations in our society.
- The various methods of obtaining finance for each of the organisations.
- The objectives of organisations and how they relate to these different types of organisation.
- The role of the entrepreneur.
- The stakeholders of organisations and their importance and relationships to the organisations.
- The changes in the business environment including the size of firms, the importance of both multi-nationals and small businesses; the factors which cause these changes including political, socio-cultural, and economic; and the importance of change to survival.

At *Higher* level we will look at:

HIGHER LEVEL

- The production of goods and services.
- What resources are used by business.
- The factors of production – land, labour, capital

and enterprise – and how they are used to produce goods and services to satisfy the wants of the customer.
- How organisations grow.

We will also be looking at the different sectors of activity – primary, secondary and tertiary (services) sectors.

TOPIC ONE: The role of business in society

 ### WHAT IS BUSINESS ACTIVITY?

Business activity is something that we don't think about very much, but every day we use the goods and services produced by hundreds of different businesses, either directly or indirectly. For example, when you go to buy a burger, how many different businesses are involved in the production of the burger you bought?

It is easy to identify the outlet where you bought the burger, but who supplied the burger chain with the bun, the burger and all the other ingredients: the packaging, the power to cook the burger, the transportation, etc? Who provided the bakery with the ingredients to bake the bun? Who grew the wheat? The list goes on and on.

Then there are all the government services which we expect to be associated with food production. Who takes away the waste? Who inspects the premises to make sure they conform to standards that will ensure that we come to no harm from eating the burger? Who makes sure that the burger chain pays the taxes on profits and VAT? All these different businesses or organisations are involved in allowing us to spend £1 or so on buying a burger.

We can describe business activity as the production of goods and services to give people what they want. What we want as consumers is a wide variety of quality goods and services at prices that we can afford. We would find it very difficult to provide these goods and services for ourselves, so we expect businesses to provide them for us, at a price that will allow them to continue providing these goods and services.

We all have many different wants: food, clothing, shelter, entertainment, travel, etc. We get these through the activities of business.

QUESTION

Q1 Identify as many different types of business organisations as you can that are involved in producing a new music CD.

DEFINITION OF 'BUSINESS ACTIVITY'

Business activity is any activity which provides us with goods and services to satisfy our wants. The **output** of business activity is the **goods** and **services** we want.

Goods

Goods are things we can see and touch, such as clothes, DVD players, cars, food, etc. They are described as tangible products and are split into two categories: **durable goods** and **non-durable goods**.

Durable goods are those we can use again and again, like computers, CD players, etc. They have a reasonable life span. Some will be expensive, like cars, while others, like pencils, will be cheap. They will not last forever, but we would expect them to stand up to a lot of use. Non-durable goods are things we can normally use only once, like food, drinks, newspapers, etc.

Services

Services are things that are done for us. They can be described as non-tangible products. The service industries make up the largest part of our modern economy in Scotland, with the majority of employees working in services. Some of our main traditional service industries are things like banking, insurance, tourism, education and health. However, in recent years there has been a rapid growth in employment in call centres across Scotland, with the biggest growth being in the Highlands.

CASE STUDY — Call centres

The number of people employed in call centres in Scotland has increased by over 200% in the past five years, with more than 46,000 Scots now employed there. Finance and telecommunications have the biggest share of the market, however travel and leisure are also big users of call centres, and public bodies are now increasing the number of their call centres. It is estimated that by 2008 around 70,000 jobs in Scotland will be in the call centre industry.

Telephone Service Centres, a Falkirk-based company providing services to blue chip companies, has operations across Scotland, in Dunoon, Falkirk, Greenock and Rothesay, with further plans for a new centre in Aviemore. Last year it announced a £3.3 million expansion at Larbert near Falkirk and the employment of a further 700 workers to add to its existing workforce of around 1000.

Visit *www.scotland.gov.uk* to find details of the public-sector call centres that have been set up.

QUESTION 2

Explain why there has been a growth in employment in call centres in Scotland, and state the reasons why it is important that Scotland continues to attract these jobs.

In order to produce goods and services, businesses need to use resources. These resources are the **inputs** for business activity, with the goods and services that they produce being the **outputs**.

These resources are what we call the **factors of production**. These are the resources that business needs to produce goods and services. They are:

● Land — **This is all the natural resources, such as oil, water, and the land itself. It includes everything that can be extracted from the land and sea, grown on the land or produced in the atmosphere. It also includes sunshine which is used with solar panels to create energy.**

● Labour — **All organisations need people to work for them. Some will only need a few; many, like local government, will need thousands. Labour is the people required to make the organisation work. It includes all their physical and mental effort.**

● Capital — **These are the man-made resources. Elsewhere, capital will be described as the money invested in an organisation, however here we use it as an economic term to describe factories, machines, lorries, tools, etc. They have all been created or produced from natural resources, and are needed to produce goods and services.**

CHAPTER:One

TOPIC ONE

● Enterprise – **This could be described as the most important factor of production because, without it, production would not take place. Enterprise is the human effort and will to provide goods and services. The entrepreneur is the person who brings together all the other resources and takes the risks to produce the goods or services.**

CASE STUDY

Entrepreneurs

We would often think of Richard Branson as being a good example of an entrepreneur, and we would be right. However, Scotland has many entrepreneurs of its own. Tom Farmer, the founder of Kwik-Fit, took risks in starting up in his business. The resulting company now employs thousands of workers across Scotland, the UK and Europe. The richest man in Scotland is Sir John Wood, who set up the Wood Group as a supplier to the oil industry. It now carries out a wide range of engineering work across the world. It is easy to see these people as entrepreneurs, however, the owner of the local corner shop and the local council opening up a new school are also entrepreneurs, in that they bring together the factors of production to produce services.

QUESTION

Q3 Identify a local business organisation and describe each of the factors of production it uses in order to operate.

WEALTH CREATION

The wealth of a country is measured by how many goods and services the country can produce. So the more business activity there is, and the more goods and services that are produced, the wealthier a country is. Therefore, the more we produce, the better off we can become.

CYCLE OF BUSINESS

The cycle of business can be described as the constant production of goods and services to satisfy the wants of consumers.

In order to survive and enjoy life, we have certain things that we want or need. The needs are simple; we need food, clothing, shelter and warmth to survive. Our wants can be very complicated and varied, depending on our individual character and interests. We all have different tastes, for example.

It is the role of business to identify these wants, and then produce goods and services to satisfy them. However, people living in a modern economy are always looking for newer, more advanced goods and services, so businesses have to then identify and satisfy these new wants. This constant creation of new wants stimulates business to supply more goods and services, and so we have this cycle of new wants and new production.

UNIT 1

In reality, it is even more complicated than that. Most consumers don't know everything that they will want in the future, so business has to try to anticipate what they will buy in the future. For example, it can take up to five years to develop a new car, so car producers have to try to work out what it is we will want in the future from our cars. With billions of pounds being spent on developing a new car, there is a huge risk involved.

In many instances consumers do not know that they want a product before it is actually produced. How many mobile phone users would have said 10 years ago that they would find it useful, or that they would feel the need to replace it every year or so?

SECTORS OF INDUSTRIAL ACTIVITY

There are three sectors of industry:

Primary sector

Businesses that are involved in exploiting or extracting the natural resources (e.g. farming, mining, fishing and oil exploration).

Secondary sector

Businesses that are involved in manufacturing and construction. They take the natural resources produced in the primary sector and change them into things we can use (e.g. car manufacture, building firms).

Tertiary (services) sector

Businesses that are involved in providing services rather than goods, such as banking and tourism.

QUESTION

Q4 For each of the sectors of industry indentify three local business that operate in that sector.

All economies start out in the primary sector, and as an economy grows it moves through each of the sectors. This process is called **de-industrialisation**, which the Scottish economy has gone through during the last 30 years. Although Scotland still has important primary and secondary sectors, the numbers employed in these sectors has declined dramatically over this time.

Many of our manufacturing industries, like ship-building, steel-making, and car manufacture, have been greatly reduced in size or have disappeared entirely, and service industries are much more important to our economy.

For example, as we have seen, there has been significant growth in employment in call centres and also e-commerce businesses.

TOPIC TWO: Types of business organisation

At both **Intermediate 2** and **Higher** levels we will look at the different types of business organisation in our society. This includes:

- the self-employed
- private limited companies
- public limited companies
- voluntary organisations
- charities
- public corporations
- government-funded service providers
- local authority-funded providers.

At **Higher** level we will also look at international aspects of the business organisation and multi-national companies.

This topic is assessed internally at **both** levels and further information and guidance can be found at the end of the chapter.

Organisations are made up of people working together, using resources, to produce goods and services by changing inputs into outputs. Business organisations exist to satisfy consumers' wants by making and providing goods and services.

There are two main types of business organisation: **private sector** and **public sector** organisations.

PRIVATE SECTOR ORGANISATIONS

The basic aim or objective of most private sector organisations is to make a profit. Profits are achieved when the income from sales exceeds the expenditure on costs. Voluntary and charity organisations' basic aim is to raise money for good causes, or to provide services that would not be provided otherwise.

The most common types of private business organisations are:

- sole traders
- partnerships
- limited companies.

We will also look at franchises.

Sole traders

A sole trader is a business which is owned and managed by one person (e.g. small shops, hairdressers, trades people).

- **It is very simple to set up.**
- **You get to make all the decisions.**
- **You get to keep all the profits.**

There are no legal formalities to go through to set up in business as a sole trader. You can simply start trading. As the person in charge of the business and the only owner, you get to make all of the business decisions, and can run it to suit your own needs; also, there is no one else to have to share the profits with.

DISADVANTAGES
- **Borrowing from the bank is more difficult, and it may charge higher rates of interest on loans to sole traders.**

- **The sole trader has unlimited liability, so if the business is not successful and runs up debts, the owner could lose not only the business but his/her home, car and possessions to pay off these business debts, and if this still wasn't enough they could be made bankrupt by the courts.**

- **Sole traders have to run their businesses without help. Taking holidays or falling ill would mean that there is no income, but the costs continue.**

A sole trader used to be the most popular form of business, however, the disadvantages make it far less attractive than it used to be. Probably the most important factor is the unlimited liability involved. The prospect of losing everything is often not worth the risk. When you consider that over 80% of new businesses fail within the first year or so of operation, it is easy to see why. Coupled with this is the fact that it is now much easier and cheaper to set up a limited company.

Partnerships

A partnership is a business which is owned and controlled by two or more people but less than 20 (except for legal and accountancy firms which are allowed more). Again, it is usually a small business, but is the type of organisation preferred by the professions.

Partnerships are groups of two or more people who join together to set up in business. They own and control the business together. Legal and accountancy firms are allowed to have as many partners as they wish, however, other partnerships are usually restricted to a maximum of 20 partners. As well as solicitors and accountants, doctors, dentists, architects and other professional businesses are common partnership private business organisations. It was popular in the past for the trades, for example a plumber and an electrician setting up in business together, but for the same reasons as sole traders, these small businesses usually now opt for a private limited company set-up.

Partnerships should have a legal agreement stating how profits are to be shared, who has what responsibilities, how much money they are allowed to draw from the business, etc.

ADVANTAGES
- **The partners can share the responsibilities involved in running the business, so taking holidays or falling ill will not be so much of a problem.**

CHAPTER:One

TOPIC
TWO

- **Partners can specialise** (e.g. a plumber and an electrician).

- **More money can be invested in the business because there are more owners.**

- **The partners also have unlimited liability (except for certain types of sleeping partners).**

- **There may be arguments between the partners on how to run the business.**

- **Partners can leave or new partners can be taken on, which can upset the running of the business.**

Limited companies

Most new businesses now prefer to set up as a limited company rather than a sole trader or a partnership. The costs involved have decreased and it is becoming much simpler. For example, you can now set up a new limited company on the Internet. Limited companies, as their name suggests, have limited liability. They can lose only the money or capital they have in the business, not any of their personal possessions. The **shareholders** (a minimum of two are required by law) are those people who own a share of the business, in the form of share certificates, and so are the owners of the business.

There are two types of limited company:

- **public limited companies – plc**
- **private limited companies – Ltd.**

To become a limited company you must register your company with the Registrar of Companies and complete two legal documents – **memorandum of association** and **articles of association**. These set out the aims of the business, how it will be run and how it will be financed.

The profits are shared out in the form of dividends, each shareholder receiving a certain amount for each of the share certificates they own in the business.

The main difference between the two is that plcs are allowed to sell their shares to the public through the stock exchange. Private limited companies can't; they can only sell to individuals who are invited to buy shares with the full agreement of the existing shareholders.

- **Shareholders have** limited liability. **If the business fails they lose only the amount of money they have invested.**

- *For private limited companies only*, **they do not have to disclose most of the information that public limited companies have to provide to the public, such as their annual reports.**

- *For public limited companies only*, **because the shares can be bought and sold at any time, people are more willing to invest, the business can raise money by selling more shares to the public for big projects, and this means they find it easier to plan, develop and expand.**

● **All companies must be registered with the Registrar of Companies. This means that they have to disclose some financial information, which the public and their competitors can see.**

● **Big organisations can be very difficult to manage properly or well due to diseconomies of scale.**

● **It is more difficult to keep workers happy and well motivated in a big organisation.**

● **There are costs involved in setting up and administering the legal requirements placed on limited companies.**

The majority of big firms are public limited companies, like BP, British Airways and Stagecoach.

QUESTION

Q5

For each of the following examples, identify which would be the best type of business organisation to use. Justify your decison for each.

(a) Firm of solicitors.
(b) Window cleaner.
(c) Garage repair and sales.

Franchises

Franchises are arrangements where one business pays for the right to run under the trading name of another. For example, many of McDonald's branches are operated as franchises.

The person or firm who owns and runs the business is called the **franchisee**. The firm that owns the name is called the **franchiser**.

For McDonald's, the franchisee buys the right to open a restaurant and trade as McDonald's, but has to run the business the way they are told to by McDonald's.

ADVANTAGES

● **McDonald's can open more branches and sell more meals without having to buy additional premises or recruit, train and pay staff.**

● **The new business gets the existing well-established name and reputation of McDonald's with all their brand products, and will therefore attract a lot of customers immediately.**

● **The new business will be helped and supported by McDonald's, including benefiting from their advertising and their established processes for quality.**

● **Product innovation can be shared among all the franchisees. For example, one franchisee thought up the 'Egg McMuffin' and shared the successful recipe with all the others.**

DISADVANTAGES

● **McDonald's reputation depends upon how good the franchisees are. If there is one piece of bad publicity about a single product or branch, it will affect all the branches.**

- The franchise agreement allows McDonald's to tell the franchisee exactly how to run the business and they have to buy all their supplies from them.

- The franchisee has to pay part of his/her profits or a percentage of sales to McDonald's.

The voluntary sector

Voluntary sector organisations do not aim to make profits, but to raise money for good causes, or to provide services to the public which would not be provided otherwise, or not be provided well. Any profits that charities make are used to help people. They are formed by people sharing similar beliefs or concerns who then become members of the charity.

Charities have to be registered with the Charity Commissioners who watch over their activities. To be recognised as a charity, the organisation has to have one or more of the following as its main objectives:

- **to relieve poverty**
- **to advance education**
- **to advance religion**
- **to carry out activities beneficial to the community.**

Once it has been recognised as a charity it is given 'charitable status' which means it does not have to pay some taxes such as VAT.

PUBLIC SECTOR ORGANISATIONS

Public sector organisations are set up and owned by the government to provide services to the public. These are services which the private sector could not provide very well or could not provide at all. Making a profit is not always that important, however keeping within the budget (money from the government) that they are allocated is very important.

Public corporations

Public corporations are businesses which are owned and run by the government for us. Examples include the BBC and Royal Mail. The government appoints a chairman and board of directors to run the business on its behalf.

There used to be many more public corporations but these were 'privatised' (sold on the stock market), such as British Telecom, BP and the gas and electricity companies.

The most recent example of privatisation is air traffic control; the government sold a 50% share to private business. The argument is that private business can raise capital for new developments and improvements to services much more easily and more efficiently than the government can. Government spending comes from taxation, so if the government wanted to improve services it would either have to raise taxes or reduce spending elsewhere, which would mean less money spent on things like health or education.

Government-funded service providers

The government provides us with some services, such as the National Health Service, Social Security and Defence. These are services which the private sector would be unlikely to offer to the public in ways that the government or the public would find acceptable.

Although there has been a huge growth in private medical insurance in recent years, it is very dependent on the ability to pay. All political parties in the UK agree that free health care should be available to all at the point of delivery. Families should not have to worry about the costs of operations or medical treatment. Some charges are made for prescriptions, dental treatment and glasses, but only where the individuals can afford to pay.

These service providers are financed by the government in order to carry out its policies in these areas. Each year they are given a set amount of money to spend. Each usually has its own appointed government Minister who has supervisory control and provides guidelines to managers as to how the service should be run. The managers then make many of the decisions as to how the money could be best spent to meet the government objectives.

Local authorities

Local authorities provide us with services such as education, housing, leisure and recreation, and street lighting. They get their money from council tax, government grants, and from fees for things like using facilities at sports centres.

Local authorities either set up their own departments to provide these services or they 'contract out' to private companies who receive a fee for providing them, such as cleaning or meals for schools. The local authority has to do this, as national government legislation insists that some services have to be put out to 'compulsory tendering', where private companies are invited to bid for the work. Those who offer the best value for money are given the contract for a number of years.

Bear Scotland

Recently Bear Scotland was awarded the contract for upkeep of the national road network in Scotland, where previously it had been provided by the local authorities. Although this move was very unpopular, the government decided that Bear Scotland could provide a better value for money service.

QUESTION 6

Which of the following services are provided by government and are publicly funded? You should also identify whether they are provided by local or national (Scottish or UK) government.

(a) University education.
(b) Local bus service.
(c) Water supply.
(d) Sheltered housing.
(e) Letter postal service.

TOPIC THREE: The role of the entreprenuer

At **Intermediate 2** and **Higher** levels we will be looking at how the entrepreneur:

- **Identifies business opportunities**
- **combines the factors of production**
- **brings new ideas (innovation)**
- **takes the risks.**

This topic is **not** assessed internally at Higher level, but **is** assessed at Intermediate 2 level. Guidance and advice on how to prepare for assessment can be found at the end of this chapter.

The entrepreneur is the person who combines the factors of production to produce goods or services. Or, to put it another way, the entrepreneur is the person who brings together the workers and the natural and man-made resources and organises them to produce goods and services which we need or want.

Without someone taking on the role of the entrepreneur, nothing would be produced. He or she will identify an opportunity to provide new goods or services, or to provide existing goods or services cheaper or in a better way. This could involve identifying a new market for existing products, such as sports clothing for casual wear, as was the case with John Boyle and Sports Division. He made many millions out of the venture, but also provided employment for thousands of staff, before he sold his operation to JJB Sports.

Stagecoach, which is now a large international company, started out by offering very cheap bus journeys from Glasgow to London which proved very popular and profitable.

 **Dyson**

Dyson is a successful multinational company founded by James Dyson to produce innovative products that use new technology. The Dyson vacuum cleaner was developed because James Dyson noticed that his vacuum cleaner lost suction very quickly as soon as the dust bag started to fill. He realised that the bag was a design fault for the effective operation of the vacuum cleaner, and set about finding an alternative. His solution, the 'dual cyclone' cleaner, is now sold all over the world and is the most popular cleaner in western Europe, Australia and New Zealand. The DC07 is the latest model, proving that continuing investment in innovation, even with the risks involved, is central to the role of the entrepreneur.

 Visit **www.dyson.com** for more information on the entrepreneur James Dyson.

In all cases these entrepreneurs used their own money or borrowed money to put all the necessary resources together. They are 'risk takers'; they can stand to lose everything if the idea doesn't work.

UNIT 1

TOPIC FOUR: Factors affecting the operation of business and Business as a dynamic activity

 Several factors exist which can affect the operation of any organisation. Generally, the majority of factors may be seen as negative but several can be identified as being positive. The factors include:

- socio–cultural
- technological
- economic
- political
- sources of finance and assistance
  - local enterprise companies
  - banks
  - local authorities
  - grants and allowances
  - trade fairs
  - advice and courses for small businesses
  - European Union (EU) grants

- methods of growth
  - horizontal integration
  - vertical integration
  - diversification
  - mergers and take-overs
  - demerger
  - divestment
- competitive environment
  - national
  - international.

We will now look at each of these factors in turn.

SOCIO–CULTURAL FACTORS

Socio–cultural factors acknowledge the fickleness of the consumer and changes in the needs and wants of the population. Items that are 'in fashion' one year are rarely still 'in fashion' the following year. Consumers are generally regarded as being fickle and prone to impulsive buying.

Tastes change quickly and consumers are rarely loyal to one particular brand or product. They tend to be influenced to a much greater extent by special offers or new features.

Furthermore, changes in the population lead to changes in items that are purchased by consumers. The population trend for most of the more economically developed countries shows that over the next few decades there will be a greater proportion of elderly and retired people in the general population because of advances in medicine and the fact that we are all living longer. This means that there will be a 'knock-on effect' to organisations as their products and services may have to alter to suit the needs of this changing population.

TECHNOLOGICAL FACTORS

Technological factors are especially relevant today as most organisations rely heavily on the use of information technology in their everyday operation.

Information technology has evolved into Information and Communication Technology (ICT) and the pace of change is phenomenal. The majority of businesses are investing heavily in ICT to improve their operation. However, there is a downside to the use of modern technology. The pace of change is such that hardware and software that was up to date just last year is now already out of date. This means that there is a great cost involved for businesses. Money which did not require to be spent a decade ago is now dominating the buying decisions of many businesses.

The increase in the use of technology is not an option for many companies as they could easily go out of business as their competitors race ahead through the use of new technologies. Maintaining a competitive advantage is essential to stay ahead of the competition. All of these factors place an added strain on the business.

ECONOMIC FACTORS

Economic factors affecting the operation of businesses may take several forms. One economic factor which is outwith the control of any organisation is the state of the economy. This is a factor which greatly affects the operation of the business and over which the business has no control.

The national and international competitive environment is an area over which the organisation can exert some control. This could be in the form of an advertising campaign or through competitive pricing policy.

Another economic factor which may impact on an organisation is a pressure group. Pressure groups can exert a negative influence on organisations to the extent that the organisation may have to alter its plans or change a course of action in order to meet the demands of its consumers. An example of an environmental pressure group is Greenpeace.

POLITICAL FACTORS

Political factors which could affect the operation of business include the implementation of government policies. For example, the government has strict policies on the sale of weapons and arms to certain countries. This acts as a restriction on the size of market that a weapon manufacturing company is able to target.

SOURCES OF FINANCE AND ASSISTANCE
Local enterprise companies (LECs)

Local enterprise companies have existed for many years now and they are a valuable source of information for many new companies in the process of starting up as well as providing information to established companies.

They have access to a wide range of expertise and information including sources of finance, e.g. grants, that can be applied for by businesses.

TASK ONE HIGHER AND INTERMEDIATE

If you have access to the Internet, visit the website of Scottish Enterprise (*www.scotent.co.uk*) and write a short report (200 words) on the services that they are able to offer to local businesses.

Banks

Banks (high street and commercial) are a valuable source of information and finance to businesses.

Banks have access to the latest information and many years of expertise in dealing with the individual needs of businesses. They are not only able to offer finance solutions to business but can assist in the planning process and give general financial advice.

TASK TWO HIGHER AND INTERMEDIATE

If you have access to the Internet, visit the websites of some of the more well-known banks and compile a short report on the services that they offer to business. Is there a difference between the banks and the services that they offer? Is there one bank that is clearly better than all the others? Your report should be in the region of 250 words.

You may wish to use the following sites:

www.bankofscotland.co.uk
www.rbs.co.uk
www.halifax.co.uk

Local authorities

Local authorities can be a source of assistance to businesses although it would not usually be in the field of finance.

Local authorities may be keen to help business set up in their area if there is an existing need for that particular type of business. Assistance may be in the form of a grant (this may or may not need to be repaid at a later date) or in the form of subsidised accommodation.

TASK THREE HIGHER AND INTERMEDIATE

If you have access to the Internet, visit your local authority's website and see if it has information on assistance available to companies setting up in the area.

For example, the website for Glasgow City Council is *www.glasgow.gov.uk*

Grants and allowances

Financial assistance may be available from either central or local government in the form of grants and allowances. There will typically be two areas that will attract grants and allowances:

- the set-up of a new business
- the relocation of an existing business to an area of need.

Grants may or may not have to be repaid by the business at a later date. It is usual for an allowance not to have to be repaid. Where grants have to be repaid at a later date, this will usually be at a very favourable rate of interest.

Trade fairs

Trade fairs are often organised at a local level by enterprise companies and at a national level by other national organisations or even by central government departments themselves. They are a useful way of bringing together businesses from different areas of one country or from different countries, enabling agreements for exports and imports to be agreed.

Advice and courses for small businesses

Small businesses are not usually able to take advantage of the kind of staff training that is available in larger organisations, for reasons such as a lack of expertise and small staff numbers. Local enterprise companies, central and local government and other businesses are a vital source of advice for small businesses.

The areas of information technology, employment law and accounting are all essential areas where knowledge and advice are often required by small businesses. Local enterprise companies often run business seminars to share good practice and disseminate information. Specialised training companies are able to offer training sessions and consultancy on many other areas of business operation.

European Union (EU) grants

EU grants are available to businesses that meet specific criteria for application. The amounts and types of grants available change depending on identified areas of need within the European Union countries.

METHODS OF GROWTH

Horizontal and vertical integration

Companies may grow and develop in different ways and this can have an effect on their operation. Integration of companies occurs when organisations combine to become larger and more powerful.

Horizontal integration occurs when two companies which operate at the same stage of production merge into one. Reasons for this include:

- **an attempt to dominate the market in which they operate**

- **a desire to become stronger and therefore more resistant to future take-over**

- **more efficient operation.**

Vertical integration occurs when two companies which operate at different stages of production decide to merge into one. Advantages to be gained here include:

- **more efficient operation**

- **acquisition of production process at a different stage, reducing the need to 'contract out' work.**

Diversification

Diversification is often a business's response to a change in its market or may be used as an opportunity to enter new markets. Richard Branson's company, Virgin, is a good example of a company which has diversified successfully. Virgin operates businesses as diverse as aeroplanes, trains, personal investment, soft drinks, alcoholic drinks and music stores all over the world.

Stagecoach is a good example of a Scottish company which has diversified and continued to grow very rapidly over the past 20 years. Read the short overview that follows.

Stagecoach, founded in Perth, Scotland, in 1980 with just two buses, is now one of the world's biggest rail and bus groups, operating around 20,000 vehicles and with more than 40,000 employees worldwide, and revenues last year of more than £2 billion.

Still headquartered in Scotland, Stagecoach Group plc has four main divisions: Stagecoach UK Bus, Coach USA, Stagecoach Rail and Overseas Bus. About half of the group's employees are in the UK and half overseas, and a quarter of the company is American.

In the UK, Stagecoach UK Bus is one of the biggest bus operators, headquartered in Perth, with 12 companies running a network stretching from Devon to the Highlands of Scotland.

Stagecoach also runs the biggest UK rail franchise, with 1700 trains a day on South West Trains into London Waterloo, and the smallest, with Island Line on the Isle of Wight.

Stagecoach is also partner with Virgin Rail on the key West Coast and Cross Country long-distance rail routes, and it runs Sheffield Supertram.

The company's acquisition of Coach USA in the summer of 1999 made Stagecoach Group the second-largest coach and bus operator in the vast North American market, with businesses in 38 US states and Canada. Headquartered in Houston, Texas, Coach USA runs commuters into Manhattan, cruise passengers from airport to ship in Florida, and tourists around the streets of New York and San Francisco, as well as a host of tour and charter, sightseeing, airport shuttle, convention and taxi services.

Stagecoach Group is also the largest bus operator in New Zealand, the second-largest bus operator in Hong Kong with Citybus; and also runs buses in mainland China and Australia.

In April 1993 the company was floated on the London Stock Exchange. Stagecoach's businesses provide a broad portfolio of transport interests with a good exposure to both the UK and international transport markets. Other investments include a 23.3% stake in Road King, a toll operating company in China, and *thetrainline.com*, a joint venture with Virgin Group.

Stagecoach is committed to building a substantial international transport business and is encouraged by the UK government's commitment to public transport and greater usage. (taken from *www.stagecoach.com*)

Diversification is the result of the take-over or merger of different firms operating in different markets. The reasons for this include:

- **growth and development**
- **spread of risk in case one area of the business fails**
- **acquisition of assets**
- **collection of new knowledge and experience.**

Mergers and take-overs

Mergers and take-overs can often lead to a combination of both negative and positive factors affecting the operation of a business.

A **merger** occurs when two businesses agree to join forces and act as one business.

A **take-over**, however, arises from one business buying another business. This purchase often occurs under duress and in a predatory manner.

Mergers are generally viewed as being good for both companies involved as well as the customers that they serve. Sometimes they do have a negative effect in that they can lead to down-sizing and job losses.

Take-overs are usually viewed as being bad for the company being taken over and good for customers. They are usually regarded as a cause of job losses and having a negative impact on the company which has been taken over.

Demerger

Demerger occurs when two companies which have previously joined forces decide to part company and operate individually once more. This kind of situation will have an impact on how the businesses are operated.

Divestment

Divestment involves selling off one or more subsidiary companies originally belonging to the parent company.

COMPETITIVE ENVIRONMENT

Finally, the competitive environment acts as both a positive and a negative influence on the operation of business. A positive influence can be seen in the example of a business sector where healthy competition results in the production of new products which benefit the consumer. Conversely, a negative influence is demonstrated by the example of the effect that new companies entering an existing market can have on the companies already established in that particular sector. As an example, consider the effect that Camelot's operation of the National Lottery has had on companies such as Littlewood's Pools; huge redundancies and site closures. There is also added pressure on companies today as the UK is part of the European Union. Organisations may be under threat from competition not only from within their own country but also from other countries within the EU.

To summarise, you should remember that not all factors which affect business are negative. Many factors are positive and all should be considered in relation to the organisation that they affect.

Businesses must be dynamic (i.e. be able to react to changes in the environment) if they are to survive and develop. Pressure to change may come from within or outwith the business.

Whisky company take-over bid

Burn Stewart Distillers says it has received an approach which may lead to an offer being made for the company.

The company specialises in producing supermarket own-label Scotch whisky.

Burn Stewart, which is based at East Kilbride, near Glasgow, also produces a range of other spirits including gin and vodka.

'The board and its financial advisers, Noble Grossart Ltd, strongly advise shareholders to take no action in respect of their shareholdings', Burn Stewart states.

'The board will keep its shareholders informed of all significant developments', the company added.

Advance says UK Alliance Trusts should merge

Vulture fund Advance UK Trust is urging Dundee-based Alliance Trust to merge with its sister company, Second Alliance Trust.

Its decision to press for such a move follows the £560m Second Alliance's ejection last week from the FTSE All-Share index — and consequently the Mid-250 index — because of lack of trading in this trust's shares.

The £1.7bn Alliance Trust, the largest Scottish investment trust and among the few biggest in the UK, holds the same investments as Second Alliance. The two trusts have identical boards, and Advance said their combination seemed like a 'no-brainer'.

Advance UK, based in London, also highlighted its belief that several Scottish investment houses should join forces to create a single investment trust.

Advance UK tries to make money by forcing corporate change — including mergers and liquidations — in the investment trust sector. Such activity, or its prospect, cuts the discount.

(*www.insider.co.uk*)

CASE STUDY

James Thin book shops bought over for £2 million

Bookseller James Thin has seen 12 of its shops sold off after Oxford-based Blackwells announced it has agreed to the take-over of the troubled chain.

The academic bookseller has agreed to pay 'in excess of £2 million' for the stores at universities around the UK, including Thin's flagship store on South Bridge, Edinburgh.

The group said there were no plans for redundancies at any of the branches.

Chief executive Philip Blackwell said: 'As a long-established family firm, we believe Blackwell's is the natural successor to carry forward Thin's bookselling legacy.'

Ainslie Thin, chairman of James Thin, added: 'The Scottish community should be very relieved at this happy outcome, which I greatly welcome.'

As well as the South Bridge branch, the Edinburgh stores are at the city's university – at Buccleuch Street and King's Buildings – Heriot-Watt and Napier Universities, Queen Margaret University College, the Edinburgh Academy, Fettes College and Merchiston Castle School.

The other stores are in St Andrews, Huddersfield University and Crichton College in Dumfries.

Blackwell's deal comes less than a month after fellow bookseller Ottakar's snapped up eight James Thin stores in a £1.6 million deal. Edinburgh-based James Thin, which was founded in 1848, went into voluntary administration in January.

(*www.insider.co.uk*)

Examples of **internal** pressures include:

- **change of management**
- **the introduction of new technology**
- **a change in the company's financial position.**

Examples of **external** pressures include:

- Political/legal – **Changes in the government may bring about changes in legislation that adversely affect the operation of the business. This is especially relevant within the EU where all member countries are subject to Europe-wide legislation.**

- Economic – **Within the EU, companies are subject to economic competition, not only from rivals within their own country but also from companies across Europe.**

UNIT 1

- Social – **Business must try to anticipate the future needs and wants of the consumer and thereby stay ahead of the competition. Mistakes in anticipating what the customer wants or unexpected contributory factors can have negative effects on the success of the business.**

- Technological – **Changes in technology such as the continuing development of the Internet and e-business are costly to business. There may be a reluctance for businesses to get involved where the benefits of the technology are unproven or the financial cost is high.**

Business as a dynamic activity – Squarepeg Consulting Ltd

The Dot-Com entrepreneurial skills of Reality's Chris Gorman have rubbed off on two of his former senior employees who have set their sights on transforming offline business into effective digital economy solutions through a new, plain speaking e-solutions company set up in Edinburgh.

Having amassed an unprecedented 20 years' Internet experience between them, former Reality account directors, Beth Edberg and James Varga – co-directors of new e-business solutions organisation, Squarepeg Consulting – have set their sights on cutting a swathe through the techno-babble associated with e-solutions, by offering their clients practical advice in plain English.

Beth commented, 'Squarepeg is positioned to be a resource for business which can rely on us to be at the cutting edge of new technologies and the digital market place. We are there to make sense of everything within the context of practical e-business solutions.' Squarepeg has already realised 50% of their projected revenue for 2001 which puts them in a position to turnover £500,000 in their first year of trading. Current clients include London-based Hostmark, a pan-European internet data centre organisation.

(***www.insider.co.uk***)

QUESTION

Q7

(a) **State three factors which can affect the operation of business.**
(b) **Give one example of a socio–cultural factor.**
(c) **Give one example of an economic factor.**
(d) **Give one example of a political factor.**
(e) **Explain the terms 'merger' and 'demerger'.**
(f) **List and explain at least three sources of finance and advice to business.**
(g) **What is divestment?**

CHAPTER:One

TOPIC FOUR

TOPIC FIVE: Business objectives

All businesses must have objectives. These objectives will differ from organisation to organisation and will often depend on the type of organisation. Objectives identify the specific goals of the organisation, how they are to be achieved and the eventual result.

Objectives may be split in any organisation and identified as being either:

- general
- specific.

General objectives are those objectives which are determined by the top layer of management in the organisation. They outline the general goals and aims of the organisation and may not necessarily identify how these are to be achieved at a departmental level.

Specific objectives are made in the light of general objectives and are more focused in their nature. They identify how the general objectives of the organisation can be achieved through the performance of each department within the organisation.

Business objectives will differ according to the organisation in question. However, the main business objectives can be identified as:

- survival
- growth and development
- profit
- social responsibility
- provision of a service.

Each of these objectives is fundamental to the continued existence of an organisation. For many organisations, the objective of maximising profits will be their primary goal, however this does not apply to all organisations. For example, a charity does not have profit as its main objective. Charities exist to provide a service to those in need and the provision of the services required would be amongst their main objectives.

SURVIVAL

All businesses, given a choice, would like to survive into the future. Survival is one of the main business objectives but it is dependent on the business objectives of profit (maximisation) and growth.

GROWTH AND DEVELOPMENT

While it is not a pre-requisite for survival that a business should grow, it is necessary for all businesses to develop if they wish to survive.

It is unrealistic for a business to expect that its products and customer base need never be altered. Any business that adopts this attitude to the market will not survive in the long term. Survival is dependent on the development of the business and its staff and the re-invention and evolution of its products.

UNIT: 1

PROFIT (MAXIMISATION)

Commercial organisations are all concerned with making profits. A profitable business means money for its owners and stakeholders.

Profit maximisation is not enough for the continued success of the business. The growth and development of the business as a whole are also important.

SOCIAL RESPONSIBILITY

Many businesses nowadays are concerned with how the public perceives them and how they treat the environment. This is called social responsibility and is an area of concern for all businesses.

Social responsibility can cover the following areas:

- **working conditions**
- **treatment of the environment**
- **business associations.**

Businesses that are not socially responsible may find that they attract the interest of pressure groups, have their products boycotted by consumers and are not an attractive proposition for investors.

PROVISION OF A SERVICE

Most businesses provide some type of product or service, however there are some types of organisations for which the provision of a service is their main concern. That is to say, they may not be concerned with profits or growth but only in providing a service to their customers.

The typical type of organisation that is concerned with providing a service will be a charity.

Other business objectives which may be identified include:

- **innovation**
- **market position**
- **management performance and development**
- **productivity**
- **physical and financial resources**
- **public responsibility**
- **employee performance and relations**
- **environmental concerns**
- **maximise use of available resources**
- **public profile.**

The job of management is to run businesses for the long term. Real success is measured by the increased value created for shareholders. Companies that prosper also remember that they have no right to the loyalty of customers – they earn it through the best strategies, products and service, delivered by outstanding people. HBOS is that sort of business.

The financial services industry is hugely competitive, but fast moving with new ways of doing business and new channels opening up all the time. An era of substantial value creation for shareholders derived primarily from customer inertia is rapidly being replaced by one of consumer led competition. In everything we do we seek to take our business closer to that consumer.

In many areas we act as a new entrant in other people's markets. We are aggressive and bold with new products and make no apology for striving to deliver better value to our competitors' customers than they are prepared to do. The strategy for HBOS is, therefore, to use our strengths and focus on making sure we deliver the best performance of any in our peer group.

It is comparatively simple:

Everywhere we drive existing businesses much harder and seek to realise their full potential. We seek to be more productive, sell more, and hold on to our customers by giving them real value and superb service.

The UK's most comprehensive new channel strategy is seeing HBOS make major investments in the new ways in which customers will want to trade with us. Business by phone and on the Internet is now a substantial part of our distribution mix and HBOS has advanced product capability in these growth areas.

Knowing what to do and having the resource to do it is the easiest part of most strategies. Being better than anyone else at what you do requires outstanding management. Everywhere in the HBOS group, external management talent has been added to strengthen the HBOS team. I believe this team will win. This business is about growth.

(*www.insider.co.uk*)

QUESTION

Identify two business objectives of HBOS from the case study.

QUESTION

How do the business objectives of an organisation like the British Broadcasting Corporation (BBC – a public funded organisation) differ from an organisation like Scottish Television (a commercial television company). Your answer should be in the region of 100 words.

(a) What do objectives help to identify?
(b) What two categories can objectives be split into?
(c) State three main business objectives.

TOPIC SIX: Stakeholders in business

Stakeholders in business are those people who have a key interest in the business. Their interest as a stakeholder will differ according to the type of business in which they have an interest.

Stakeholders in business may include:

- owners
- employees
- customers
- banks
- investors
- local government
- suppliers

- management
- members
- committees
- donors
- taxpayers
- community
- shareholders.

Stakeholders have an effect on all businesses as they may be able to exert control over or influence decisions which have to be made. The degree to which they are able to exercise their influence will be determined by their degree of involvement or relative interest in the company.

For example, within a public limited company, a shareholder in possession of 35% of the shares in a company will be regarded as a greater stakeholder when compared to an employee holding 1% of the shares.

The amount of influence that a stakeholder can exert on a company will also be determined by the circumstances under which the influence is exerted. For example, a company may usually regard its owners as the key stakeholders in the business. However, imagine the scenario where a company is polluting the local environment. In this case, the local community may be able to exert a great deal of pressure and hold greater influence compared to the owners even although the local community is not a major stakeholder.

Examples of the different aims that stakeholders have in an organisation include:

- customers interested in obtaining the best prices and the highest quality
- employees concerned about job security and future prospects
- suppliers wishing to receive payment for their goods as soon as possible.

CHAPTER:One

TOPIC SIX

Examples of the influence that stakeholders can exert on organisations include:

- **lending institutions having the power to grant or refuse applications for loans**

- **managers making decisions on a day-to-day basis**

- **the community as a whole persuading a business to carry out its wishes**

- **shareholders exerting their right to vote at the annual general meeting of a limited company.**

CASE STUDY

Podium: The impact of communicating your intangible assets by Siobhan Mathers

Since 1998 the Department of Trade and Industry (DTI) has been consulting on an overhaul of company law, which is likely to make its way on to the statute books next year. Unsurprisingly, the government claims that this will cut red tape and make UK business more competitive by simplifying reporting requirements.

Yet a core element of the DTI proposals is an obligation to report on qualitative, intangible assets such as skills and knowledge of employees, and reputation. Will this simplify matters by providing standards for what is now a voluntary process, or is it more evidence of the bureaucratic hand of the nanny state? Is this transparency in action or information overload?

The proposed revision to operating and financial reviews (OFRs) stems from changes in the ways in which companies do business, coupled with increasing stakeholder expectations of good corporate conduct and transparency. A hefty 49% of Scots were categorised as corporate responsibility activists in a recent MORI survey, compared to 19% across the UK. It seems that we have little faith in the politicians who represent us, yet even less confidence in the companies who manage our money, process our food and manufacture our cars.

Changing perceptions of companies are seen as key motivators in the 'no logo' society. If a company doesn't communicate strongly what it's about, who it employs and why, whom it trades with and where, it is increasingly likely that it will be subjected to unwanted scrutiny. If the answers do not look good, the company will face questions in Holyrood, London, Brussels and beyond. It will suffer non-governmental organisations (NGOs), Internet campaigns; local direct action; and, if the worst comes to the worst, consumer boycotts. So is the government just trying to shield the UK corporate world from exposure to such risks, or is it fuelling the risks?

Social, environmental and ethical reporting have become commonplace for the big corporates, but new requirements would stretch the aspects covered and the size of companies affected. For example, one suggested threshold for companies having to comply is a turnover in excess of £50 million; this would apply to approximately the top 200 Scottish companies as ranked by turnover. For many of these, addressing the requirements of the OFR will be new territory.

There is no doubt that intangible assets such as people, brands and stakeholder relations are assuming ever-increasing importance; a healthy balance sheet will now have to include qualitative as well as quantitative reassurance to shareholders.

A company ill at ease with its stakeholders is now likely to make the market and individual shareholders nervous. Increasingly sceptical and sophisticated consumers want their values reflected in their actions.

UNIT 1

Market analysts are increasingly looking for a coherent corporate social responsibility (CSR) strategy as an indicator of the broader wellbeing of the company.

The final report of the DTI's company law steering group recommends that preliminary announcements be published on the Internet immediately after release to markets and annual reports should be put on the company website within four months of the end of the financial year.

The Internet has already opened up a new front on which corporate reputation must be managed. OFRs will strengthen the need for companies to be constantly on their guard against the likes of politicians, NGOs, trade unions and the press. But it will also present opportunities for companies to engage positively with stakeholders. From this perspective the OFR requirements could be seen as government helping companies to manage risk.

So it seems that the DTI's OFR proposals would clarify reporting requirements and extend scope rather than impose a new burden on business. An increasing number of companies already share information on intangible assets and implement stakeholder management strategies on a voluntary basis; the proposals are likely to have most impact on medium-sized companies that have not yet had to formulate CSR and communications strategies.

(*www.sundayherald.co.uk*)

QUESTION 11

(a) What is a stakeholder in business?
(b) Give three examples of stakeholders in business.
(c) What kind of influence may stakeholders be able to exert on business?
(d) Complete the following table by inserting an example for each type of business. The first row has been completed as an example.

TYPE OF ORGANISATION	EXAMPLE OF STAKEHOLDER	EXAMPLE OF INFLUENCE
sole trader	owner	owner's motivation to succeed
partnership		
private limited company		
public limited company		
voluntary organisation		
charity		
public corporation		
government-funded service provider		
local government-funded provider		

CHAPTER SUMMARY

- Business activity is the production of goods and services to satisfy consumer needs.

- The factors of production are land (natural resources), labour (the mental and physical effort of people), capital (man-made resources), and enterprise (the activity of entrepreneurs).

- Entrepreneurs bring together the factors of production to produce goods and services; they are risk takers and come up with the ideas.

- Wealth creation is achieved through the production of goods and services – the more a country produces, the wealthier it will be.

- The cycle of business identifies the production of goods and services to satisfy people's wants and needs, only for them to come up with new wants for business to satisfy.

- The sectors of industry are the primary (extraction and agricultural industries), secondary (manufacturing industries) and tertiary (service industries).

- Private sector organisations are profit-making; they include sole traders, partnerships and private and public limited companies.

- Public sector organisations are government-funded either nationally, such as the Benefits Agency, or locally such as education departments.

- The voluntary sector is made up of organisations producing goods and services for the benefit of their members or for the benefit of society, such as charities.

At the end of this chapter you should be able to:

- Identify the factors affecting the operation of business in relation to the impact on the organisation.

- List different sources of finance and assistance available to business at local and national levels.

- Describe different methods of growth.

- Discuss the competitive environment in which business operates.

- Identify different types of stakeholders.

- Discuss the influence of different types of stakeholders on business.

You should be aware of the following main business objectives:

- Survival.

- Growth and development.

- Profit.

- Social responsibility.

- Provision of a service.

PREPARATION FOR ASSESSMENT

This section of the course covers both Intermediate 2 and Higher levels, and the questions can be used for both. The difference will be in the depth of answer. Assessment is also at both levels.

HIGHER ASSESSMENT

PC (a) – Comparision of the types of business organisation in the UK and their organisational objectives

For the actual assessments at Higher level, you should be able to compare the types of business organisation in the UK. You will need to know how each type of business is owned and controlled, plus how each is financed (dealt with later in this chapter). This will probably mean that you will have to pick an example from the publicly funded sector and one from the privately funded sector. There is also the possibility that you will be asked to pick one from the voluntary sector as well.

Try the following question and then check your answer with the solution given.

QUESTION

Compare three different types of business organisation in the UK in terms of ownership and control. (6 marks)

Remember, in the actual assessment you will also be asked to compare how they are financed. You should ensure that you include at least one **publicly funded** and at least one **privately funded** organisation in your answer.

One mark will be given for each comparison of ownership, and one mark for comparison of control. To earn the mark, you must clearly show that you understand the differences between them.

SOLUTION

Stagecoach is a privately owned business. Its type of business organisation is a public limited company whose shares can be bought and sold on the stock market. The owners of the business are the shareholders, who in return for their investment receive a share of the profits by way of a dividend. They are controlled by the Board of Directors who represent the shareholders, and by senior managers, appointed by the Board to make decisions on a day-to-day basis.

Your local authority or council is an example of a publicly funded organisation. It is owned by the local taxpayers rather than shareholders, who vote for members of the council to run the authority on their behalf.

The SSPCA is a charity operating in the voluntary sector. It does not have any owners as such, but those who make donations, or provide sponsorship, or become members of the society will operate in the role of owners. Control of the charity will lie with the full-time employees/ managers who are appointed to run the charity, along with the members who will have some form of voting rights.

PC (b) – Comparison of the relative influence of key stakeholders on different types of organisation is accurate

Here you will need to identify different stakeholders for different organisations, and then describe how they can influence the organisation. For example, employees of a plc can take different forms of industrial action to influence the decisions the company makes, such as how much they will pay the employees. On the other hand, a local authority will have to take account of the people in the local community when deciding whether or not to close a local school.

The number you will be asked to identify will depend on the assessment you are given, however, you should be able to identify at least three stakeholders for each organisation.

PC (c) – Interpretation of factors affecting the operation of business enterprise is accurate in terms of their impact on an organisation

Here you will have to explain how each of the external factors of socio-cultural, technological, economic, political, and competitive environment, can affect the operation of a business. You should be able to give an example of one for each. For example, the fact that women now have far more economic power than ever before means that marketing and production have to be aimed to meet women's needs as much as men's.

INTERMEDIATE 2 ASSESSMENT

PC (a) – Explanation of different types of business organisation is accurate and refers to types of ownership and methods of obtaining finance

This assessment will ask you to describe the various types of business organisation with reference to how they are owned and how they can obtain finance. What exactly you will be asked will depend on which assessment you are given.

You could be given three types of organisation and then asked how each of them is owned. For example, a sole trader is a person working for themselves; they make all the decisions for the business and keep all the profits.

You will then be asked to explain how the sole trader is financed. You should explain that the sole trader would use their own money to set up the business; they may need a loan from the bank or a mortgage, depending on the cost of setting up. Once the business is established they could re-invest some of the profits from the business or add more of their own money. They could get a bank loan, however sole traders will find this more difficult than other types of business as they are seen to be more risky.

PC (b) – Objectives of business organisations are correctly explained and accurately related to different types of business organisation

Here you will be asked to identify different objectives for different organisations. for example, a voluntary organisation would have 'to provide a service' as one of its objectives, whereas a public limited company may have 'profit maximisation'.

PC (c) – Explanation of the role of the entrepreneur is accurate and related to specific examples of entrepreneurial activity

Here you are asked to describe the role of the entrepreneur and give examples. What you answer will depend on the assessment you are given, however, your answer should include: The entrepreneur is the person who comes up with the business idea, brings together the factors of production, and takes the risks. You will then be asked to identify an entrepreneur. There are a large number of examples and you could mention Tom Farmer who founded Quick-Fit.

PC (d) – Description of major internal and external stakeholders is accurate in terms of their relationship to an organisation

Here you will be asked to say who the stakeholders are and what their relationship to the organisation is. For example, the shareholders have invested money in the organisation, and will want a good return for their investment. Be careful because you can only use shareholders for public and private limited companies.

PC (e) – Explanation of factors which can cause change in the business environment is accurate and includes relevant examples drawn from the current situation in the UK

Here you are asked to write about what causes change in businesses. This could include internal or external factors. Internal factors could include developing new products, and you would have to give an example of a new product which has changed the way the organisation operates. An example could be Dyson's new washing machine.

An example of an external factor could be new laws passed to give part-time workers the same rights as full-time workers, and you could write that the banks now have to offer cheap borrowing to part-time workers as well as full-time employees.

CHAPTER:One

CHAPTER (TWO)

UNIT:1 BUSINESS ENTERPRISE

BUSINESS INFORMATION AND INFORMATION & IT IN BUSINESS

This chapter of the book covers *Business Information* at *Intermediate level 2* and *Information & IT* at *Higher* level. There is a high degree of overlap between these two areas but each topic will be clearly identified as relating to the appropriate level.

The topics covered in this chapter are as follows:

INTERMEDIATE LEVEL 2
- Sources of information:
  - primary
  - secondary
  - internal
  - external.
- Costs and benefits of different sources of information.
- Types of information:
  - written
  - oral
  - pictorial
  - graphical
  - numerical.
- Uses of information in business:
  - monitoring and control
  - decision-making
  - measuring performance
  - identifying new business opportunities.
- Types of IT:
  - mini computers
  - personal computers
  - multimedia
  - telecommunications, eg video conferencing, e-mail.
- Uses of IT:
  - decision-making
  - provision of information
  - maintenance of records
  - communications.
- Costs and benefits of IT.
- Effects of IT.

HIGHER LEVEL
- Sources of information:
  - primary
  - secondary
  - internal
  - external.
- Types of information:
  - qualitative
  - quantitative.
- The value of information:
  - accuracy
  - timeliness
  - completeness
  - appropriateness
  - availability
  - cost
  - objectivity
  - conciseness.

- Examples of IT:
  - characteristics and uses of current examples of IT:
    - mainframe
    - mini computer
    - networks – LAN, WAN
  - telecommunications technology
  - e-mail
  - multimedia
  - CD-ROMs
  - the Internet.
- IT in business:
  - uses of IT
  - costs and benefits of IT.

- Business software:
  - characteristics and uses of business software:
    - word processing
    - spreadsheets
    - database
    - presentation
    - desk top publishing
    - decision-making packages
  - data protection legislation
  - costs and benefits of software.

TOPIC ONE: Sources of information

 All businesses rely on information in order to operate effectively and efficiently and to make good business decisions.

Information can come from four different sources:

- **primary**
- **secondary**
- **internal**
- **external.**

Primary information is usually information which has been collected by the business itself. This type of information is very important. The characteristics of primary information are that it should be free from bias or distortion and must be able to be traced to its original source. Businesses will use primary information as a basis for making informed decisions on the running of the business.

Examples of primary information include market research, customer complaints, financial data, customer questionnaires, feedback and other statistics prepared by the business. Another characteristic of primary information is that it is usually expensive to obtain, however it is the most reliable and useful source of information available to a business.

Secondary information is a cheaper source of information when compared to primary information. The reason that it is cheaper is because it may not be ideally suited to the purpose required by the business, may be less reliable and may have been skewed to meet a particular need. It may not be possible to trace the original source of this information and, for this reason alone, secondary information may not be the most suitable information for a business to use in making important decisions.

Examples of secondary information include any kind of published information: market surveys published by third parties, newspapers, magazines, journals, reports from analysts, financial reports and information collected from the Internet.

Internal information is information that is sourced from within the business. This could be financial data or information on customers. All internal information should be verifiable and reliable.

External information is information that is sourced from outwith the business. This could be government statistics, market research by third parties, consumer test reports, income statistics and demographics. This type of information is helpful to all businesses as it gives useful information on the operating environment for the business and can provide information on the business's direct competitors. The only downside to this type of information is that it is not generally verifiable.

QUESTION

Q1

(a) What is primary information?
(b) What is secondary information?
(c) What is internal information?
(d) What is external information?

TOPIC SUMMARY

● Information is important to all businesses, particularly for decision-making.

● Primary information is collected by the business and is verifiable.

● Secondary information is collected from third parties and is not usually traceable to source.

● Internal information is collected from within the business.

● External information is collected from sources outwith the business.

● Generally, the more expensive the information, the more reliable and verifiable it should be.

TOPIC TWO: Costs and benefits of different sources of information

The following table provides a useful summary of some of the costs and benefits of different sources of information:

TYPE OF INFORMATION	COSTS	BENEFITS
Primary	Expensive to obtain	Reliable, verifiable
Secondary	Less expensive than primary	Gives a wider view than primary information since it takes into account external influences. Wider variety of sources compared to primary
Internal	No financial costs	Reliable, verifiable
External	May have a financial cost	More sources available compared to primary

TOPIC THREE: Types of information

Information can be presented in a variety of different formats:

- **written**
- **oral**
- **pictorial**
- **graphical**
- **numerical.**

Written information may be presented on paper or on a computer screen, e.g. via e-mail or on the Internet. Written communication of information remains one of the most popular forms of presenting information.

Oral information is information communicated by voice. Where this information is not recorded for future use, its value may be diminished and its reliability called into question.

Pictorial information is information displayed in the form of a photograph or picture. Sometimes, a picture or sign can communicate information more quickly and effectively than written information, e.g. road signs.

Graphical information is often used to display complex data in an easy-to-understand format which is pleasing to the eye. It is of particular use where comparisons have to be made or where there is a comparison over a period of time. Here is an example of a company's sales performance forecast for the year 2002:

IMAGE 1.
A road sign

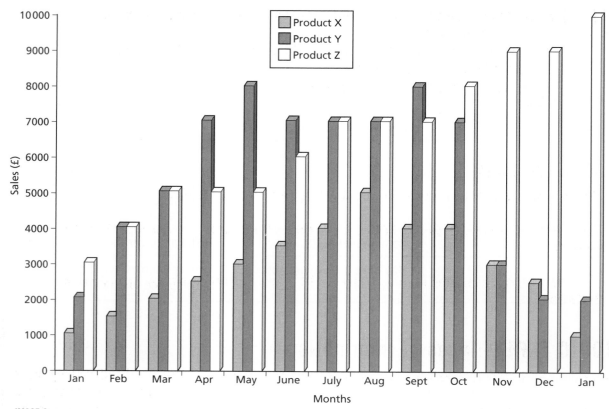

Product X, Y, Z Sales for 2002

IMAGE 2.
Sales performance forecast

Numerical information is any form of information that is presented as numbers rather than text, for example the business's financial results.

TOPIC FOUR: Types of information

There are two types of information that can be used by businesses in the decision-making process:

● qualitative
● quantitative.

Qualitative information is information that is descriptive in nature and may also include people's personal judgements or opinions.

Quantitative information is information that is both definable and measurable and is usually expressed numerically. It is often used for the purposes of comparison, e.g. to compare the performance of one business with that of another or to compare the performance of the business over a period of time.

BUSINESS ENTERPRISE

(a) Choose two different sources of information. Describe these sources and give an example of each one.

(b) Identify at least one cost and one benefit of the sources of information chosen in your answer to Question 1.

(c) List at least three different types of information.

TOPIC SUMMARY

● Sources of information include primary, secondary, internal and external.

● Types of information include qualitative, quantitative, written, oral, pictorial, graphical and numerical.

● There are various costs and benefits which can be associated with each type and source of information.

TOPIC FIVE: The value of information

Any information that is to be used by business as part of its operation and decision-making must be of actual value to the business. Good and reliable information is required in order to make correct and informed decisions. The value of information to any business cannot be underestimated and it is important to remember that not all information will be of use to a business.

Many business decisions will be affected by the quality of the information that is available in order to make the decision. Large quantities of information are useless if the information contained is not of a suitable quality. It is preferable to have a small amount of reliable, high-quality and verifiable information rather than a large quantity of unreliable, poor-quality and non-verifiable information.

High-quality information should display the following characteristics:

● Accuracy – **This is important because decisions which are based on inaccurate information will lead to an incorrect outcome.**

● Timeliness – **Information for decision-making must be available when it is required by the business and must be up-to-date and reliable. Late and out-of-date information will lead to the wrong decisions being made.**

● Completeness – **Any information that is to be used for decision-making in the business must be complete. The use of incomplete information will not provide a true picture and will lead to inaccurate decisions being made.**

- Appropriateness – **The information used by the business must be appropriate to the situation in which it is being applied. If irrelevant or inappropriate information is used, there is an increased risk that the wrong decision will be made.**
- Availability – **Information required by the business for decision-making must be readily available. In certain instances, it may be necessary to use substitute information of a lower quality. This may be preferable to having access to no information at all.**

- Cost – **The collection and storage of information for the business must be cost-effective. Where the purchase or gathering of information is not cost-effective, its collection and use must be called into question.**

- Objectivity – **All information used in the decision-making process should be objective, i.e. free from bias. It should not contain subjective and personal opinions.**

- Conciseness – **Information used for decision-making should be concise and straight to the point. Over-fussy presentation and too much information may hide the key points.**

All good quality information should meet each of the eight criteria listed. Fast access to high-quality, concise information is of greater importance to business than access to huge quantities of lower-quality information which also may have to be sorted.

The value of information that is collected by the business will also be influenced by the purpose for which the information is to be used. For example, a business will be more willing to pay more money for important information that it requires to make an important decision which could potentially make it a lot of money in the future, compared to, say, information about the latest tax regulations relating to its particular business sector.

TASK ONE HIGHER

'Most information is useless, regardless of its source, type or value. In fact, it is usually out-of-date by the time I receive it!'

Discuss the above quote in the context of sources, types and values of information. Your answer should be in the region of 250 words.

QUESTION Q3

(a) List at least five characteristics of good information.
(b) Complete the table on page 45 by answering whether the source of information linked to the purpose required is either high or low value and give a reason for your answer. The first one has been completed for you.

SOURCE	PURPOSE	HIGH/LOW?	REASON
Personal Computing magazine	To decide which computer to buy	High	Information source is specific to the need and is from a reliable source
The Internet	To find the latest weather forecast		
The Scotsman newspaper	To decide how to cast your vote at the next election		
Magazine advert for a new snack food	To decide whether or not to buy it		
Conversation overheard on the bus	To predict the winner of the Snooker World Championships		
Scottish Qualifications Authority	To find out students' exam results from last year		
Telephone banking service	To find out the balance on your account		
Horoscope in a magazine	To find out what will happen to you in the future		
Person standing next to you on the train station platform	To find out when the next train is due to arrive		

TOPIC SUMMARY

High-quality information should have the following characteristics:

- **accuracy**
- **timeliness**
- **completeness**
- **appropriateness**
- **availability**
- **cost**
- **objectivity**
- **conciseness.**

TOPIC SIX: Uses of information in business

 Information may be used by a business for a variety of different purposes. The main categories to be considered are:

- **monitoring and control**
- **decision-making**

- measuring performance
- identifying new business opportunities.

Businesses must monitor and control different aspects of their operations in order to succeed. One of the most important areas that requires monitoring and control in any business is the finance function. The use of accounting information in this area is crucial to the continued success of the business and this type of information will be used by management to make decisions about the future of the business.

Financial information will often be computerised and many companies make use of financial monitoring software such as Sage, Pegasus and Quickbooks.

The provision of information is not enough. Management must have access to the correct type of information so that they can make informed decisions. Sometimes, decisions will be easy to make, based on the available information. The information used to make decisions may be financial (quantitative) or it may be in the form of a written report with recommendations (qualitative).

Businesses also use information to measure their performance. Business performance may be measured using different criteria:

- financial performance
- meeting output targets
- meeting targets for staff
- individual department targets.

Whatever criteria are adopted, all successful businesses will depend on a variety of information to measure their performance. It is useful for management to compare internal reports on their performance with reports produced by third parties. Any reports produced by third parties will usually take the form of qualitative reporting since it is unlikely that they would have access to sensitive quantitative data.

Business managers will also make use of information (usually available in the public domain) to identify new business opportunities. For example, by studying economic statistics, it is possible to identify potential areas of growth in the economy and then develop a business idea to meet the need in that area.

TOPIC SEVEN: Examples of information technology

Computers are used throughout business today and most businesses would not be able to operate without them. They are used to collect, store, process, retrieve and display data and information to be used in decision-making processes.

Information technology used in business today is changing rapidly; some current examples include:

- mainframe computers
- mini computers

- **laptop computers**
- **notebook/handheld computers**
- **networks:**
  - **Local Area Network (LAN)**
  - **Wide Area Network (WAN)**
- **Information Communication Technology (ICT)**
- **e-mail**
- **multimedia**
- **CD-ROMs**
- **the Internet.**

Let's take each of these in turn to explain more about them and how they are used in business.

MAINFRAME COMPUTERS

Mainframe computers are large computers which can deal with millions of operations at the same time; they are extremely powerful and expensive. Several decades ago, a mainframe computer would have occupied a large room in an office building and would have had to have been kept in a temperature-controlled environment. They were seen as the pinnacle of computer technology and only people who had been trained in their use and operation were allowed to use them. In fact, their use was strictly limited.

Nowadays, huge advances in computer technology mean that the computer that sits on your desk is likely to be as powerful, if not more powerful, than the mainframe computers of the 1970s. Mainframe computers are still used and are often referred to as supercomputers. Their use is restricted to very specialised tasks and they remain the most powerful, the fastest and the most expensive computers in the world. They are much smaller than their predecessors and are used mainly by government agencies and large companies for scientific and engineering purposes. One of the most prolific users of supercomputers in the world is the US military and NASA (the National Agency for Space Administration) of the USA.

IMAGE 3.
Mainframe computer

MINI COMPUTERS

'Mini computers' is the term given to a whole range of computers which are smaller in size than mainframe computers. Nowadays, we are most likely to use this term when describing a desktop machine but it can be extended to include portable machines, laptops, notebooks and handheld computers. We will consider some of these later.

The birth of the mini computer began back in the 1980s. The need for mini computers was borne out of the need for a variety of people within organisations to have access to computer facilities. Very few organisations actually had computers and those that did were restricted to the use of one mainframe. As more and more people within the organisation wanted to be able to use the computer facility, more pressure was put upon the time available on the mainframe. At the same time, IBM (International Business Machines) was developing the personal computer as it identified

a need in the market for a small computer that could be used in the workplace by the individual. Little did it realise that its invention of the personal computer in the 1980s would create such great wealth and success for the company. The success of the personal desktop computer went beyond all expectations and throughout the 1980s and 1990s it continued to develop, increasing in power and reducing in size while it continued its migration from the office and into the home. Nowadays, almost every home and office has a computer and the increase in power of the desktop machine means that there is no requirement for more powerful machines such as the mainframe computer.

LAPTOP COMPUTERS

Laptop computers are a product of the late 1980s and early 1990s and the Japanese obsession with miniaturisation. They differ from desktop computers mainly because they are smaller and are often referred to as portable computers. As well as laptop computers, the late 1990s saw the introduction of so-called notebooks and handheld computers. Notebooks differ from laptops in the respect that they will usually have a 'footprint' of no more than the size of a piece of A4 paper. Handheld computers are smaller again and are able to be held in the palm of your hand. Typically, these small computers are much less powerful and have limited functions when compared to their larger family members.

Laptop computers have the following characteristics:

- **small size, making them portable**

- **hinged screen to allow closure for transport**

- **LCD (liquid crystal display) screen which is light and has low power consumption**

- **battery powered (typical battery endurance is 3–5 hours) although many powerful laptops are power-hungry**

- **trackpad or rollerball device to replace the mouse**

- **all the other features that you would expect to find on a desktop machine, including built-in modem, connections for USB and parallel ports, CD/DVD drive, CD burner, network capability.**

The most well-specified laptops have evolved in size and weight but this is at a cost. As size and weight have reduced while processor speed and screen size have increased, this has led to greater power consumption and more dependence on mains power. There is also the financial consideration to be made. A top-of-the-range laptop costs in the region of £3000 plus, whereas a similarly specified desktop machine can be purchased for half the price. How much do you value reduced size and style?

IMAGE 5.
Laptop computer

UNIT 1

NETWORKS

The use and development of computer network technology is a relatively recent development in the history of computing. Much of the technology in operation today is based on client-server technology. This is a relatively inexpensive and flexible way of harnessing the power of many computers connected together. A computer network is where several computers are connected together using special hardware and software.

The main advantage of the latest computer networks based on client-server technology is that they are all connected to a central computer or server. The server is just a normal computer that acts like a traffic warden on the network, directing information and messages across it. It operates and controls the network using special software. Each user connected to the network will have their own login name and password to access network facilities.

Computer networks can be 'wired' in two different ways. The traditional method of connection for machines on a computer network is by using cables or wires. This has the instant disadvantage of meaning that every computer that is connected to the network must have a cable connecting it to the server that operates the network. Imagine, for example, a computer network of 500 machines in an office building with 500 individual cables throughout the building, eventually terminating at the server. On a large network, cabled networks can get very messy.

The latest alternative to the traditional cabled network is the 'wireless' network. This type of network operates in the same way as a traditional network but instead of relying on cables to connect the computer, it uses radio communication technology. This removes the need for cables and the technology can operate easily within the confines of an office building up to a range of about 150 metres. However, there have recently been concerns raised about the security of wireless networks and the ease with which information can be stolen from them using relatively simple telecommunications equipment.

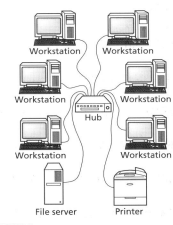

IMAGE 6.
Computer network

Local Area Networks (LANs)

Local Area Networks or LANs are a common feature in business today. They are most often used where several (a few or even several hundred) computers have to be connected over a small common area, e.g. an office or a building.

They possess the following characteristics:

● **computers are linked using cables or by radio communication (sometimes referred to as 'air port')**

● **network covers a small geographical area**

● **the main use of the network is to share information and peripheral devices**

● **there is a low error rate**

- it is easy to set up and maintain

- detailed technical knowledge is often not required

- relatively cheap

- secure

- peripheral devices can be shared

- Internet access can be shared across the network.

Wide Area Networks (WANs)

Wide Area Networks or WANs are networks that operate over a geographically dispersed area. They are unlike LANs because the computers that are connected to the network may be in a different town, city or country and are not in the same office or building. The method of connection used in a WAN is, therefore, not the same as that used in a LAN. It would be impractical to suggest that a computer operating in Glasgow could be connected on a network to a computer operating in Aberdeen via a cable such as that used in a LAN. The method of connection for a WAN utilises telephone lines, high-speed cable connections and even satellite links. Sometimes where a business operates a WAN, say between offices in different towns or cities in the same country, it will use a method of connection called a leased line. A leased line is a dedicated high-speed telephone line which is leased from a communications company for the sole use of the business. This means that no one else has access to the line and only the business can use it for communication purposes. The downside to this is that leased lines are usually very expensive.

The main characteristics of WANs are:

- computers linked via telephone lines or dedicated leased lines or even satellite link

- many different world locations can be attached to the network at any one time

- network coverage is over a wide geographical area and may even be global

- there is a higher risk of error when compared to LANs

- the main use of the network is communication

- many owners and organisations can be connected to the network

- more expensive to set up, maintain and operate, compared to a LAN

- more likely to require technical expertise to operate and maintain, compared to a LAN

- greater chance of data being intercepted by third parties

- the network may not be permanently 'live'.

WANs are usually used by global organisations such as IBM and Apple Computer.

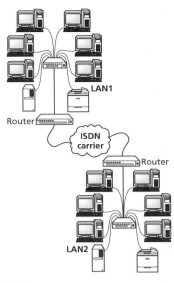

IMAGE 7.
WAN

QUESTION

Q4

(a) **List at least three examples of information technology in use today.**
(b) **What is a mainframe computer and why is its use in modern business less widespread than in the 1970s?**
(c) **What is a LAN? What is a WAN? How are they different?**
(d) **How might a modern business make use of different types of computers? Try to mention at least two different types.**

TOPIC EIGHT: Information Communication Technology (ICT)

Information Technology or **IT** is a phrase with which you should be familiar. It is the term used to describe the use of computers and computer technology.

Information Communication Technology (ICT) is the term used to describe all the different technologies that exist in the field of IT as well as the emerging technologies that involve both IT and communication technology. The Internet is at the forefront of communication technologies and is probably the most easily recognised piece of ICT.

Recent developments in telecommunications technology have utilised the telephone network, e.g. the Internet. The telecommunication companies have been eager to expand their networks and improve the services that they are able to offer. As the Internet has developed, it has started to outgrow the current telephone network which was never originally designed with its current use in mind. The existing telephone network in the UK is constantly being replaced and updated.

Internet access speeds can be improved dramatically through the use of digital telephone lines such as ISDN (Integrated Services Digital Network) and ADSL (Advanced Digital Services Line) which offer much faster communication when compared to the normal telephone network. Unfortunately, the cost to consumers is still high and the newest technologies continue to be used mainly by businesses which can afford to use them.

The telecommunications network spanning the UK and beyond is used for a wide variety of different purposes. The most common are as follows:

- the Internet
- e-mail
- Telnet
- Prestel

CHAPTER:TWO

TOPIC EIGHT

- **FTP**
- **JANET** (Joint Academic NETwork)
- **on-line and Internet banking.**

We will consider each of these applications in turn.

THE INTERNET

The Internet is a good example of a Wide Area Network (WAN) and it is an easy way of sharing information cheaply across the world. The most commonly used part of the Internet is the World Wide Web (WWW).

Many people think that the World Wide Web **is** the Internet but it is, in fact, only a small part of it. The Internet comprises three main areas: e-mail, newsgroups and sharing information (i.e. the World Wide Web). The pie charts opposite demonstrate how use of the Internet has altered over the past 30–40 years.

The Internet is, therefore, made up of three distinct but connected areas: e-mail, newsgroups and an area to share information.

E-mail is the communication tool of the Internet. We will consider it later in this chapter.

Newsgroups are sometimes referred to as discussion groups or bulletin boards and provide forums for people to post messages and respond to messages from other people.

The final part of the Internet is where **information** is **shared**, **stored** and **retrieved**. The fastest-growing part of the Internet for sharing, storing and retrieving information is the World Wide Web. As well as the World Wide Web, information can be shared using a facility called File Transfer Protocol (FTP). This is basically a set of computer rules for sending and receiving information. Before the advent and development of the World Wide Web in the mid-1990s, FTP was the main method for sharing information on the Internet.

The Internet has actually been in existence since 1969 but it was only in the mid-1990s that it truly became available to the wider public. Within a very short space of time, the Internet has been recognised and developed as a major tool for communication and a valuable source of information which can be used by both individuals and businesses alike.

The Internet makes use of existing telephone lines and other faster means of communication to connect computers throughout the world. The main reason for connecting computers is so that they can share information and communicate with each other.

Internet availability and use have mushroomed in the past few years as the cost of computers has fallen and it has become easier to get connected to the Internet. The main prerequisites for connection to the Internet are:

- **fast, modern computer**
- **up-to-date Internet browser software**
- **56kps modem**

Internet use (circa 1970)

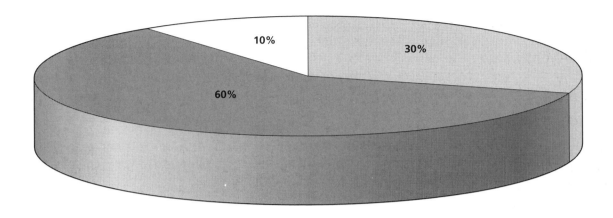

30%

10%

60%

Internet use (circa 2000)

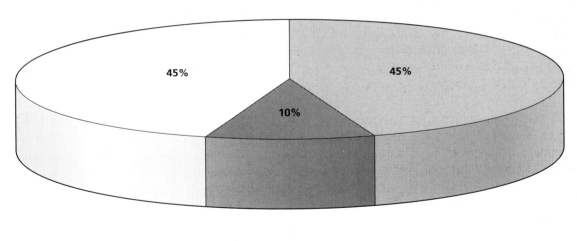

45%

45%

10%

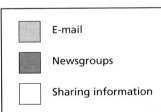

E-mail

Newsgroups

Sharing information

IMAGE 8.
Changes in Internet use

- **telephone line**
- **subscription to an Internet Service Provider (ISP).**

The Internet Service Provider (ISP) provides individuals and businesses with a connection routed through its powerful network of computers which are connected direct to the Internet. There is now a wide variety of deals available from many different ISPs. Some offer 24-hour access seven days a week for as little as £15 per month with no other charges. Other deals available often depend on connecting to a local call rate number which means that the cost is directly linked to the amount of time spent on-line.

The importance of the Internet to business cannot be underestimated in the current economic climate. Most businesses now have an Internet presence and often offer their products and services for sale via their websites. The Internet has become as important a tool for business as it has for the person using it for leisure or personal interest.

The scope and content of this course cannot significantly address the changing phenomenon that is the Internet. If you are interested in learning more about the Internet, a good source of reference is *The Rough Guide to the Internet* by Angus J Kennedy, published by Penguin. The book is updated every year.

E-MAIL

E-mail is the electronic worldwide postal service supported by the Internet. It is a very fast and efficient way of communicating and does not depend on time zones. Information can be communicated across the world in a matter of seconds.

In order to send e-mail, you require a connection to the Internet and a valid e-mail address. There is little restriction on the type of information that can be communicated via e-mail. Different files can also be attached, e.g. pictures and spreadsheets.

The **advantages** of using e-mail include:

- **fast and efficient communication**
- **cheap compared to normal post**
- **messages can be easily filed and tracked**
- **messages can be sent at any time of the day or night.**

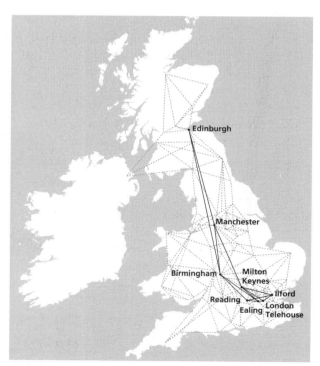

IMAGE 9.
Basic topology of the Internet in the UK

The **disadvantages** of using e-mail are:

● **it is only useful if people know how to use it properly**

● **people's reactions and responses are different when communicating via e-mail so there is a need for the rules of 'netiquette' to be followed**

● **receipt and successful delivery of e-mail require the person receiving the e-mail to check their account**

● **immediate communication on your part does not always guarantee an immediate response**

● **junk mail (spam) can become a problem and means that more important messages get lost amongst the junk.**

TELNET

Telnet is one of the original uses of the Internet. It allows remote access by one computer network to another, via a standard telephone line connection.

For example, many libraries operate a Telnet facility to allow users to access basic functions at the remote site, e.g. search the library catalogue.

PRESTEL

Prestel is a method of providing information via a computer which is connected to a remote network. A typical use of Prestel is in travel agencies where the computers connect to a central network which gives information on holiday and flight availability and allows the user to make bookings.

Some banks still use Prestel to allow their customers on-line access to their accounts. This is being superseded by the introduction of Internet banking.

FTP

File Transfer Protocol is a set of computer rules which allows the transfer of files between computers via a network, e.g. the Internet.

Using an FTP program, the user is able to send information from his computer to the host computer (upload) and copy information from the host computer to his own computer (download).

JANET

The **J**oint **A**cademic **NET**work is a computer network covering the UK which links all of the universities and colleges of further and higher education.

ON-LINE AND INTERNET BANKING

Increased competition within the banking sector has meant that the high street banks have had to think of new ways to attract new customers and retain their existing customers. The ability to access account details and carry out account maintenance and transactions on-line increases the usefulness to customers who have a computer and access to the Internet.

Most banks now offer an on-line service for their customers. This has two distinct advantages: as far as the bank is concerned, it stops people from going to the branch, thereby reducing congestion and, as far as the customer is concerned, it is much more convenient to carry out bank business at any hour of the day or night and not be restricted by the normal opening hours of the bank.

 **Minola Smoked Products, Abergavenny**

Hugh and Jane Forestier-Waker, partners.

As one of the most progressive traditional smokers of oak smoked Scottish salmon, fish game poultry and cheeses in the UK, we supply many of the best hotels, restaurants and Gourmets worldwide via the Internet.

Internet Banking from Bank of Scotland offers us a free means to manage our funds.

Payments are available instantly, and account reconciliation is much tidier now, the problem of unpresented cheques becomes a thing of the past, as we no longer handle them due to enhanced safety of online transactions.

Our cash management has also been made easier due to the consistency provided by regular scheduled payments. Suppliers also respond positively to our use of Internet Banking – telling them that we make payments by BACs inspires confidence, and they see it as a more proactive and business-like service.

(*www.bankofscotland.co.uk/business/internetbanking/ibcasestudies.html*)

 **QUESTION Q5**

(a) **List two ways in which using Internet banking services has benefitted Minola Smoked Products.**
(b) **How does the use of Internet banking facilities make Minola Smoked Products able to operate in a global market?**

OTHER INFORMATION TECHNOLOGY USED IN BUSINESS
Multimedia systems

Multimedia systems utilise a variety of different media primarily for the purpose of presentation. Typically, this involves the use of:

- text
- text and sound

- text, sound and pictures
- text, sound and video
- video and sound
- interactive elements:
  - voice
  - mouse
  - keyboard
  - touch screen
  - live participation.

Common uses of multimedia include:

- **interactive training videos**
- **video conferencing**
- **CD-ROMs**
- **DVDs.**

Interactive videos are used for training staff as they can easily demonstrate simulations of the workplace environment. Employees can then be tested on their reactions to these and learn from the scenarios.

Video conferencing is a multimedia facility which was developed many years ago but it has never really been developed or utilised to its full potential except by, perhaps, big business. The use of video and audio links enables a 'virtual' meeting to take place where the participants are in different locations, sometimes in different countries. There is obviously a cost- and time-saving aspect to be made, compared to the situation where people have to travel a great distance at great cost in order to meet in a common place. More recent advances using Internet technology mean that video conferencing technology has been superseded to some extent; the use of a cheap webcam and an Internet connection can achieve very similar results. Another reason for the lack of success of video conferencing can be attributed to the fact that humans like face-to-face contact in person; something that video conferencing could never achieve.

CD-ROMs are a convenient way of storing, sharing and recording electronic information. They can be used to store both computer data and music files. 'ROM' means 'read only memory' and means that the media can only be read from and not written to, i.e. nothing can be saved on the CD. It is, however, also possible to buy CDs which can be recorded. These are called CD-Rs and permit only one recording to be made. CD-RWs are CDs which allow multiple writes to be made but these tend to be more expensive.

DVDs are the new standard in video technology. 'DVD' stands for 'Digital Versatile Disc' and a DVD looks just like a CD-ROM. The difference is that an entire movie can be stored on a single DVD and then played back on either a DVD player or a computer equipped with a DVD drive. Most new computers come with a DVD drive which will also read CD-ROMs. DVD-R discs are also available which allow the user to 'burn' their own movies on to disc. There is a great improvement in quality when watching and listening to a movie from a DVD compared to a video cassette.

Facsimile (FAX)

The fax machine was one of the great inventions of the 20th century. It allows documents to be sent from one fax machine to another, using the normal telephone network. Nowadays, they are cheap to buy and offer relatively fast transmission times. The main form of competition comes from the use of e-mail.

Telex

Telex is a relatively old means of communication which has now been virtually replaced with the advent of e-mail. It uses the telephone network to transmit information which is read and converted to text by the receiving machine.

EPOS and EFTPOS

Electronic Point of Sale (EPOS) and **Electronic Funds Transfer at Point of Sale (EFTPOS)** are two systems which are in common use in the retail industry.

These systems allow an electronic record to be kept of all purchases and returns and assist in the control of stock and ordering. In the case of EFTPOS, this system also encompasses payment in the form of a debit card such as Switch or Delta.

These systems are attractive to both the retailer and the customer for different reasons. The retailer usually receives payment more quickly than payment by cheque and the customer does not have to carry cash or a cheque book in order to carry out transactions.

QUESTION Q6

(a) What do the letters 'ICT' stand for and what does ICT mean?
(b) Give at least three examples of modern use of the telecommunications network.
(c) Briefly explain how each of the examples that you have identified in the previous question works.
(d) Give at least one advantage and one disadvantage of e-mail.
(e) How might a business make use of developments in IT and ICT to expand its operations? You may wish to focus on an example of a modern business that uses these developments to its advantage.
As a guide, your answer should be in the region of 150–200 words.

TOPIC SUMMARY

- Computers that are in common use today may be one of the following types:
  - mainframe
  - mini
  - laptop
  - notebook
  - handheld.

- The use of networks has transformed the way in which we use computers in modern business and society.

- A LAN is a local area network typically used in an office.

- A WAN is a wide area network, e.g. the Internet.

- Information Communication Technology (ICT) has transformed the way we use computers to communicate and makes extensive use of the telephone network.

- E-mail is the preferred form of business communication; it is fast and cheap to use.

- The Internet has revolutionised business and the way in which businesses communicate.

- Use of the Internet continues to expand and new Internet technologies and uses are being developed.

- Other examples of IT include multimedia, CD-ROMs and DVDs.

TOPIC NINE: IT in business

 IT and ICT in business are both powerful tools which can provide management with the ability to handle large amounts of data and information. The effective control, management and processing of this information means that management is able to make more informed decisions.

The decision-making process is aided by the provision of more high-quality, relevant and up-to-date information from a wider variety of sources, thereby allowing good decisions to be taken in a shorter space of time.

The use of the Internet as a main source of business communication has removed time delays and the restrictions of time zones so that business can operate 24 hours a day around the world if the need arises.

Developments in the use of IT have also led to great benefits in the production processes for manufacturing business. A good example of an area where the use of new technology has had a very positive impact is the car industry. Great reliance is placed on the use of computer-aided design (CAD). Product research, development, design, production and testing are all integrated and computerised so that the time taken from design to availability to the consumer has been greatly reduced. This has also led to huge cost savings.

Many manufacturing processes are highly automated and computers are used to control armies of robots all carrying out different tasks. The use of computers and robots can often achieve better results than the use of human labour.

Innovative use of the Internet

Scotland is first to see interactive online recruitment advertising.

www.ScottishAppointments.com, Scotland's market leader in online recruitment, is the first UK service to offer interactive job adverts online.

This pioneering application of interactive advertising takes online recruitment advertising to new heights, at a time when recruitment giants Stepstone and TopJobs are pulling out of Scotland, leaving the niche market to specialist companies like ScottishAppointments.com.

ScottishAppointments.com users are the first to benefit fully from the potential of new Internet technology. The software behind the adverts has been created in-house, here at Scotland On Line, enabling companies to advertise cost-effectively with sound, video and still images.

Johanna Cordery, Editor of *Online Recruitment* magazine, confirms Scotland On Line's claim of an industry first:

'*Online Recruitment* magazine concurs with Scotland On Line's statement that it is the first online recruitment site in the UK to use this kind of advertising.'

ScottishAppointments.com is a recruitment website devoted exclusively to Scotland and has already built up a substantial audience since its launch in April 2001, doubling visits to the site and exceeding its traffic targets.

Since launch the site has had 160,000 unique users visiting 1.5 million pages. Even more staggering is the 31.4% level of repeat visits, each lasting an average of seven minutes. Users from as far afield as the USA, Australia and Europe have registered with the service, finding it a valuable method of looking for a job in Scotland.

(*www.insider.co.uk*)

The computer games industry in Scotland

The Scottish computer games industry has grown from a couple of companies three years ago to over a dozen international players employing between 400 and 500 people. It is predicted that 1200 will be employed in the industry by 2002.

VIS Interactive plc was established in 1995 as a result of a management buy-out from Balgray Communications group.

Scottish Business and Industry Minister Lord Macdonald today praised the success and fresh ideas of the Scottish computer games industry in competing in the international market.

Speaking after a visit to Dunfermline based computer games developer VIS Interactive plc, Lord Macdonald said:

'Games companies are an important example of the knowledge economy. They show that economic value is to be found in intangible things, such as new ideas. The Scottish games sector is overflowing with fresh ideas which are attracting worldwide interest.

It is encouraging to visit an ambitious company like VIS at a time when the Scottish computer games industry is a real success story. The industry is growing all the time in Scotland and I am delighted to see that VIS is participating in this sector in such an innovative way.

Our games companies have the talent, drive and determination to build on their fast-growing international reputation. Massive opportunities are available and VIS has shown that Scottish firms can compete successfully with the best in the world to create exciting and innovative products for a global market.'

News Release: 2045/98
9 October 1998
(***www.insider.co.uk***)

Burns Express Freight Ltd

Burns Express Freight Ltd was formed in 1993 by Carolyn and Derek Burns after having been employed for several years in the Transport and Distribution Industry. The company is based in Paisley and initially started with 3 vehicles and attained a turnover of £267,000 in its first year. From then, it has attained an average 20% per year growth and now has a turnover of £1.3 million and a fleet of 15 vehicles.

Three years ago, the company introduced a computer network to the business and computerised many of their previously manual jobs. At the same time, they installed satellite tracking into all their vehicles. This was a customer-led decision as customers were increasingly asking if this service was available, particularly when dealing with customers in the hi-tech computer sector. Although this was a big financial investment, it soon became clear that the benefits to be gained would more than pay for the system in its first two years.

It is now possible to track a vehicle and its driver from start to finish so there is no room for error on timesheets. An exact route can also be planned for a driver going abroad to assist him and the customer can be told exactly where a driver is and how long it will be before he gets to his delivery point. In the past, the driver would have to have been contacted on his mobile phone; now there is active use of the satellite system and it is more cost effective.

Carolyn and Derek firmly believe that as technology becomes more and more sophisticated, they will have to make as much use of it as possible or face being left behind. Companies in competition with them in the distribution industry will become less competitive if they do not use the latest technology.

The Internet and e-mail are also a central part of every day business and the latest use of technology allows their customers to access the company's website and make a booking online. These jobs are then automatically logged into the booking system and when the delivery has been made it can be checked immediately via fax, e-mail or on the Internet.

www.burnsexpress.co.uk
(with thanks to Carolyn and Derek Burns)

New communication technology

KDA-PR

Westhill, Aberdeenshire; April 2002: Invsat Limited, the Aberdeenshire headquartered maritime telecommunications systems integrator, has launched its new £1million C and Ku Band Teleport facilities, providing two principal services — end-to-end broadband satellite communication services and terrestrial connections to fibre optic and microwave circuits for voice, data traffic, multimedia and video conferencing.

Michael Salmon, General Manager of Invsat Limited, said that the new Teleport would strengthen Invsat's communications capabilities and broaden the range of options for its customers to access the increasing array of communications services on offer. 'Broadband satellite delivery is a rapidly expanding service and it is characterised by a very high demand for communications and entertainment services.'

About Invsat

Invsat Limited is a wholly owned subsidiary of Inmarsat Ventures plc. The company project manages and delivers VSAT solutions, satellite and broadband networks and VPNs to a global client base, incorporating the maritime, oil and gas, government and emergency services sectors. Further information is available from the Invsat website at www.invsat.com.

(***www.insider.co.uk***)

TOPIC TEN: Costs and benefits of IT and ICT

The use of IT and ICT gives rise to a series of trade-offs. Generally speaking, businesses will be happy to spend money on IT and ICT where it can be demonstrated that the overall benefits to be gained from implementation outweigh the associated costs.

The main costs and benefits of business information systems are shown below.

Costs of using IT:

● initial and recurring costs of hardware and equipment

● ongoing costs of replacing and upgrading obsolete systems

● installation costs, e.g. the costs of installing a network infrastructure can be high

● new furniture to house equipment

● staff training – this will inevitably lead to a loss of working time

● losses in efficiency as even staff who have been trained to use the new system will be unfamiliar with it for a period of time and more likely to make mistakes

● teething problems will also contribute to inefficiencies

● possibility of losing information

● computer viruses

● increased risk of commercial espionage and hacking

● health and safety issues for staff, e.g. repetitive strain injury, backache

● the continued use of IT leads to a dependency culture which becomes more and more difficult to escape.

Benefits of using IT:

● increased efficiency

● increase in the amount of data and information that can be handled

● increased customer satisfaction

● competitive edge – at least until rivals catch up

● possibility of reduced staffing costs

● creation of home workers

● access to new markets and customers.

TOPIC ELEVEN: Business software

Business software for computers encompasses a huge global market which has evolved over a short space of time.

In the field of applications for the personal computer, one company has grown quickly to dominate the market. That company is Microsoft. The most well-known products from Microsoft are the Windows operating system (now in 'XP' edition) and its Office Suite of programs.

The most commonly used business software covers the following areas:

- **word processing**
- **spreadsheets**
- **database**
- **presentation**
- **desk top publishing**
- **decision-making packages.**

WORD PROCESSING

The term 'word processing', when used to describe a piece of modern word processing software, is somewhat misleading. Over a period of less than 20 years, the humble typewriter has been transformed into a huge computer program which can perform many different tasks besides the production of typed text.

In fact, word processing software has become so sophisticated that it is able to replace many other pieces of software for even complex tasks.

The market leader is, without a doubt, Microsoft's Word application. Now in '2000' format, this application has grown to be the industry standard. It is a very comprehensive piece of software and, arguably, the most respected piece of software that Microsoft has developed. Cynics have dubbed it 'bloatware' due to the sheer size of the program and the huge number of tasks that it is able to perform.

Other word processing applications that you may have heard of include WordPerfect, Lotus, AmiPro, StarOffice and ClarisWorks.

Microsoft's Word application forms part of a suite of programs designed to fulfil the computing needs of most businesses or offices. These programs are often referred to as a 'family' of

UNIT 1

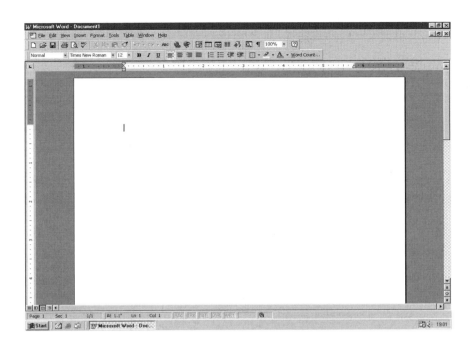

programs owing to their close relationship and the fact that they are sold as a package. The cost of a copy of Microsoft's Office Suite is currently in the region of £300–£500, depending on the particular edition. Other manufacturers offer similar suites of programs and some are even available free of charge, e.g. Sun Microsystem's StarOffice which is available to download free from the Internet and manages to mimic Microsoft's Office Suite.

Returning to word processing software, we are able to identify some features that are common to all examples:

- text entry – **enter text into a document**

- text delete – **remove text from a document by character, word, block or page**

- moving and copying text – **text can be moved or copied within a document or to another document**

- text enhancement – **characters, words, blocks or entire documents can have text size or appearance changed, e.g. bold, italic, underlined, colour**

- fonts – **a variety of different typefaces is available**

- grammar tools – **grammar can be checked as you type or in blocks of text or the entire text**

- spellchecker – **spelling can be checked as you type or in blocks of text or the entire text. The built-in dictionary can be customised for your own particular use**

- thesaurus – **allows the replacement of words with one of several alternatives offered**

CHAPTER:TWO

TOPIC
ELEVEN

- undo – **allows the last, or more, action(s) to be reversed (always a useful feature!)**

- page setup – **allows the page size, margins, orientation, etc. to be altered**

- word count – **a useful feature which saves you having to count the number of words for those important essays**

- saving – **the ability to save files using your own filenames and in your chosen location**

- printing – **allows you to print a hard copy and with most programs what you see on the screen is exactly what will be printed**

- file import and export – **the ability to open files previously saved in different formats and to save files to other formats so that they can be opened in other programs**

- clipart – **allows the inclusion of pictures or photographs in a document.**

This is not an exhaustive list but serves to demonstrate the main features of a piece of modern word processing software.

SPREADSHEETS

Spreadsheets are primarily used as a tool for calculations and manipulating numbers. They are often used by managers to manipulate data and aid the decision-making process. They are particularly useful for displaying complex information and are often used in the human resources department to help with calculations of staff wages and salaries.

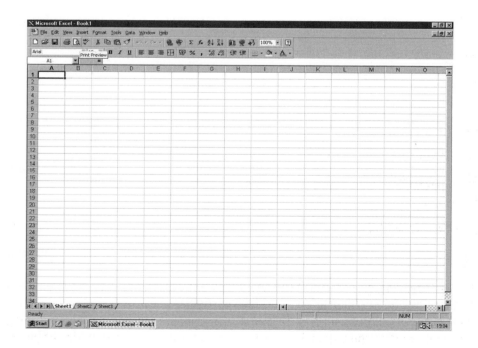

IMAGE 11.
Microsoft Excel

BUSINESS ENTERPRISE

The market leader for spreadsheets when the application first became available was Lotus. Microsoft is now the market leader and Lotus is a name from the past; a result of Microsoft vigorously developing its product to meet the market demand and stretch the usefulness and ability of spreadsheet software. Its product, Excel (currently Excel 2000), is a very powerful piece of software and forms part of the Microsoft Office Suite.

There is a list of terminology associated with spreadsheets, just as we have already looked at the terminology of modern word processing. One of the great strengths of Excel is its similarity in appearance to its sister product, Word. This gives users a sense of ease when using it for the first time.

A spreadsheet file is usually referred to as a **workbook**. Each workbook contains several **worksheets** and each worksheet is made up of individual **cells**.

In addition to the features that we have already identified for word processing, a spreadsheet program would have the following features:

● calculation – **the ability to perform calculations based on information entered into cells in a worksheet**

● automatic recalculation – **this is where new data are entered into a worksheet and there is an automatic update of the outcome on the sheet**

● mathematical/statistical/financial functions – **the ability to utilise complex functions to solve problems**

● displays – **the ability to display information on a worksheet in different formats, e.g. graphs.**

Spreadsheets are typically used for a wide range of business applications, including:

● **accounting**
● **payroll**
● **cash flow forecasting**
● **interpretation**
● **preparation of plans**
● **project management**
● **decision-making**
● **management accounting.**

DATABASE

A database is like an electronic version of a filing cabinet.

The most commonly used commercial database package is Microsoft's Access (currently Access 2000) which forms part of the Office Suite. Other applications in use include Oracle and Filemaker Pro.

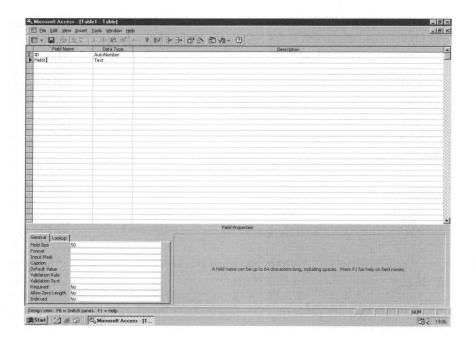

Databases also have their own terminology. Each database is made up of **tables** and each table holds a series of **records** which are made up of **fields**. Each field in a record holds a particular piece of information, e.g. postcode or telephone number, and each field is designed to hold a particular type of information, e.g. text, number, currency.

All database packages have the following features:

- sorting – **this allows the user to sort the information in the database table into any order that is required**

- querying – **this allows the user to question or search the database according to the criteria set, e.g. in a database of employees a search could be performed to find all employees aged 25 and over**

- calculating – **calculations and functions can be performed in a database**

- reports – **a database can produce different styles of reports based on the information contained in the database or queries that have been saved.**

PRESENTATION

The area of presentation software is a growing market as more and more business people realise the potential for creating their own presentations, especially when so many of them have access to a computer or have one of their own as part of their job. Presentation software is no longer limited to use by teachers and lecturers and people who carry out staff training.

Computer programs such as Microsoft PowerPoint (currently PowerPoint 2000) make it easy to create professional layouts and presentations that can be produced on paper or overhead transparency or displayed on screen or projected onto screens.

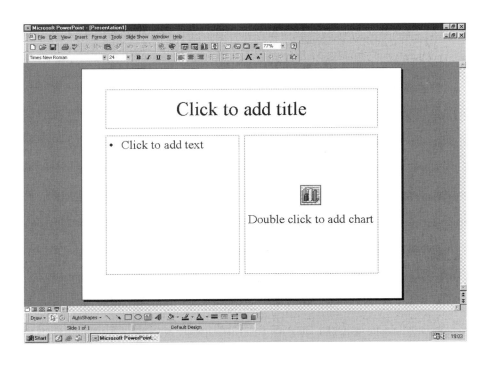

IMAGE 13.
Microsoft
PowerPoint

There is even the ability to make presentations run like movies and insert files or objects from other files created using other Microsoft products, e.g. Word and Excel.

DESK TOP PUBLISHING (DTP)

Desk top publishing software allows the user to create materials with a professional appearance. Professional results are easily achievable even by people who are not particularly skilled in the use of computers.

The results that can be achieved using a desk top publishing package could only have been achieved in the past through the use of a professional printer.

Some features that are encompassed in desk top publishing can also be found in other programs such as word processing and presentations.

The main facilities that are available on a desk top publishing package are:

- **text manipulation – the ability to manipulate text into many different appearances and formats**

- **graphics – the ability to import and manipulate graphic images**

- **drawing – the ability to create original graphics**

- **import – the ability to use files or graphics previously created in another application**

- **typeset – the ability to adjust the spacing of text characters.**

DECISION-MAKING PACKAGES

Decision-making software allows analysis of business data and presentation in ways which are useful to users who have to make business decisions.

Information can be gathered and processed and displayed as:

- comparisons
- projections
- a list of consequences when different actions are considered.

These software programs are used by the military and agencies such as NASA. They will often be custom-designed to take account of particular needs.

COSTS AND BENEFITS OF SOFTWARE

TASK THREE HIGHER

'My business manages just fine without ICT. Why should I spend money on something that I don't need or understand?'

Discuss the above quote with particular reference to the likely costs and benefits of employing ICT in a business today. Your answer should be in the region of 250 words and may include relevant examples from business today.

The costs and benefits to business of using different pieces of business software may be summarised as follows.

Costs associated with business software:

- initial purchase price

- costs of future product upgrades

- staff training

- loss of staff time as staff have to be released for training

- compatibility problems with existing pieces of software

- possible loss of data during transfer to new systems

- risk of losing competitive advantage if you do not upgrade software while others do

- replacement costs of hardware as software evolves and requires more powerful hardware

- increased dependency on IT carries an increased risk of future problems if there are no other systems in place and the IT fails.

Benefits associated with business software:

- increased productivity
- increased speed of data handling and processing
- increased efficiency
- improved decision-making as a result of access to better-quality information
- increased flexibility
- reduced staff costs due to greater reliance on IT.

TASK FOUR HIGHER

Can you think of any further costs and benefits associated with the use of business software?

QUESTION Q7

(a) List at least four different types of business software.
(b) Identify at least three facilities provided by a word processing program.
(c) Identify at least three facilities provided by a spreadsheet program.
(d) Identify at least three facilities provided by a database program.
(e) Identify at least three facilities provided by a desk top publishing program.
(f) What kind of organisation might make use of a decision-making package?

TOPIC SUMMARY

- Be aware of the different uses of information technology in business.

- Be aware of the different costs and benefits of using IT.

- The main pieces of business software are:
  - word processing
  - spreadsheet
  - database
  - presentation
  - desk top publishing
  - decision-making packages.

- Be aware of the different characteristics and features of the different pieces of software.

- Be aware of the costs and benefits associated with business software packages.

TOPIC TWELVE: Data protection legislation

The increased use of computers as a medium for the electronic storage of information has brought many advantages to business, however it also carries additional risks. For example, there may be instances where the information held by a business about an individual is incorrect or the use of the information held on the individual may be questionable.

The Data Protection Act 1998 aims to protect the rights of the individual by providing legislation to govern the collection, storage and use of information that is held in electronic or paper file systems.

The Data Protection Registrar holds a list of businesses that are registered under the Data Protection Act and it is the responsibility of the individual business to register its interest with the Registrar. This means that if you are running a business and you hold information on third parties, it is your responsibility to register your business under the Act and follow the rules of the law.

There are eight basic Data Protection Principles which organisations must follow:

- **Obtain and process data fairly and lawfully.**

- **Register the purpose for which the information is held.**

- **Not to disclose the information in any way that is different from those purposes.**

- **Only hold information that is adequate, relevant and not excessive for the purposes they require.**

- **Only hold accurate information and keep it up to date where necessary.**

- **Not to hold the information any longer than necessary.**

- **Take appropriate security measures to keep the information safe.**

- **Give individuals copies of the information held about themselves if they request it and, where appropriate, correct or erase the information.**

The Data Protection Principles apply to organisations in both the public and private sectors and also to information held about children.

The main job of the Data Protection Registrar is to oversee the enforcement and application of the rules of the Act. The Registrar also has the power to have inaccurate records corrected or erased, and deals with complaints by members of the public. A complaint may be raised by an individual where there is a failure to allow access to records or where there has been a breach of one of the Data Protection Principles.

In cases where there has been a serious breach, the individual concerned may be entitled to compensation if it can be successfully proven that they have suffered loss or damage as a direct result of incorrect information being held by the organisation.

The Data Protection Register is a list of all companies who are registered with the Data Protection Registrar. It is a public record and can be viewed on the Internet at ***www.dataprotectionregister. gov.uk***

BUSINESS ENTERPRISE

The information that appears on the register includes:

- **the name of the organisation**

- **the type of information it holds**

- **the type of individuals that the organisation holds information about**

- **what the information is used for**

- **where the information was obtained from**

- **any other party to whom the information has been disclosed**

- **the name and address of the person to whom that individual should write if they wish to obtain information.**

There are certain circumstances in which the individual does not have a right to access information. Specific examples are where the information is held for the purpose of:

- **preventing or detecting a crime**

- **catching or prosecuting offenders**

- **accessing or collecting taxes or duty**

- **restrictions relating to information held by the government departments of Health and Social Work.**

The rules of the Data Protection Act also state that where an individual writes to an organisation and requests a copy of the information held about them, the organisation must reply within 28 days and provide the information to the individual. Some organisations may charge a minimal administration fee for this service but it is an offence under the terms of the Act not to reply within the 28-day period.

In summary, the Data Protection Act 1998 is a piece of legislation that aims to protect the rights of the individual with regard to the storage of their personal information by third parties. The burden of responsibility is placed with the organisations holding the information and penalises them where the information held is incorrect or causes damage or loss.

QUESTION

Q8

(a) What is the scope of the Data Protection Act 1998?
(b) List at least five Data Protection Principles.
(c) What is the maximum time limit that an organisation has to respond to a request for information?
(d) List at least two circumstances where an individual could be refused access to information held about themselves.

CHAPTER SUMMARY

At the end of this chapter you should be able to:

● **Accurately analyse and describe different sources of information in terms of their reliability and value for a particular business.**

● **Accurately analyse the main types of information technology used in modern business.**

● **Discuss the main costs and benefits of information technology to business.**

● **Identify the main features of different types of business software in common use today.**

● **Discuss the main costs and benefits to business of using different software packages.**

● **Discuss the main principles of the Data Protection Act 1998.**

PREPARATION FOR ASSESSMENT

HIGHER ASSESSMENT

Assess the value of information and the application of information technology to business enterprise

There are 3 PCs (Performance Criteria) for this unit. What you will need to know will be much the same for all the assessments, however, what will be required may vary slightly from one assessment to another.

PC (a) – Assessment of different sources of information is accurate in terms of their reliability and value for particular business enterprises

In the first part of this assessment you will be asked to identify information from **primary**, **secondary**, **internal** and **external** sources, and justify or explain why this is an example for each of the sources. You should use different examples for each of the sources of information.

An example for primary information could be information from customers. This is first hand information collected by the organisation and used for a particular purpose.

You can justify your choice by further explanation of this information being accurate and up to date.

The second part of this PC will ask you to assess the reliability and value of information derived from that source. Using the example above you could say that it is obtained direct from the source, so you know how accurate it is, and you can go back to the original source and ask other questions. It will be appropriate to the needs of the organisation as they gathered it themselves for a particular purpose.

PC (b) – Assessment of main types of information technology is accurate with respect to their uses and their costs and benefits to business enterprise

Here you will be asked to identify a number of different types of technology and then describe the benefits of using this technology and the costs (not just money costs). You must show you understand why what you have said is a benefit will actually benefit the organisation.

An example you could use is e-mail. Here you could write about how e-mail provides almost instant written communication with anywhere in the world protected by a password, this will reduce costs for telephone etc. and remove the delays caused by using letter mail services. A cost may be the loss of personal contact, either through meeting face to face or talking on the phone, which reduces the chance of good working relationships and increases the possibility of misunderstanding.

There are no marks available for simply identifying the type of IT so you need to know the costs and benefits.

PC (c) – Assessments of the uses of business software is accurate in terms of its potential applications to business activity and its costs and benefits to business enterprises

Here again you must identify a number of pieces of software and describe the costs and benefits of using them. Again there are no marks available for the identification of the software, but you still need to know them. It is better if you can identify the type of software rather than a brand name, for example database rather than 'Access'.

If you use the example of a database you could describe the benefits of keeping records electronically such as space saved, the ability to sort records into any order, and to filter them to show specific groups of records. This would allow managers to make better decisions by obtaining accurate up to date information quickly and easily.

An example of a cost could be the cost of the system crashing and the information being lost or even becoming unavailable for a period of time. Loss of data would be very serious as it would mean essential information for decision making is lost.

 INTERMEDIATE 2 ASSESSMENT

The assessment for this level is more complicated and comes in different parts of the course. The first assessment covers only information.

1 Explain the nature and importance of business information

PC (a) – Different types of information are accurately described and each is evaluated with reference to a particular aspect of business activity

Here you will be asked to identify different types of information and describe the value each one of these might have for the organisation. One mark will be given for each type, for example, written, oral, pictorial, etc. You will then be asked to explain why and where each would be valuable.

For example, if you identified graphical information you could say that it is good as charts and graphs show information clearly in ways people can understand easily.

PC (b) – Explanation of the importance of business information is accurately related to the uses of information in business

Here you are being asked to identify the uses of information, for example, monitoring and controlling, decision making, measuring performance, etc. You will also be asked to give an example of each. If you chose decision making then you could say that information obtained from customers from market research.

PC (c) – Sources of information are accurately explained in terms of their potential costs and benefits for a particular business purpose

Here you will be asked to explain different types of sources of information (primary, secondary, internal, external), and then describe one cost and benefit for each.

You could say that primary information is information gathered first hand by the organisation for its own purpose, and that it is expensive to collect both in terms of time and money, however, you know how accurate it is and it is up to date.

The second assessment appears in Unit 2 of the course under the heading Information Technology.

2 Explain the uses and importance of Information Technology to the operation of organisations

PC (a) – The uses of information technology are accurately explained with reference to a range of organisational activities

Here you will be asked to identify different types of technology, for example personal computers, and then describe ways in which they could be used. For PCs you could say that they can run spreadsheets to help with financial record keeping and decision making.

PC (b) – The benefits and costs of information technology are accurately explained in terms of their effects on organisations

Here you are being asked how IT helps make organisations more efficient or effective, and what costs are involved. An example may be a website which may obtain sales from around the world and give the organisation more publicity. The costs could include the cost of constantly upgrading and maintaining the website, and training staff how to use it.

PC (c) – The effects of information technology are accurately explained with respect to employees and the structure of the organisation

Here you will be asked to describe how IT will affect the employees and how the business is organised. You should identify a type of technology such as databases and say that employees will need to be trained how to use it, and that fewer employees may be needed to maintain a large filing system with records centralised, allowing for an increased span of control.

3

The third assessment for this topic is a practical one involving the manipulation of spreadsheets and databases, and is linked to the finance assessment and the one above. You should be experienced in using spreadsheets and databases before attempting this assessment. It is not possible to give further advice in this textbook.

CHAPTER THREE

UNIT:1 BUSINESS ENTERPRISE

DECISION-MAKING IN BUSINESS

At *Intermediate level 2* there are two areas that this chapter covers that are required for internal and external assessment:

INTERMEDIATE LEVEL 2

- The different **types** of decisions:
  - strategic
  - tactical
  - operations.

- The decision-making **process**, including:
  - the role of managers in decision-making
  - the need for decisions to fit with the organisation's objectives
  - the influence of stakeholders on decisions
  - ways in which stakeholders can influence decisions.

At *Higher* level there are four main areas of study in this chapter:

HIGHER LEVEL

The first is *decision-making* where we will look at:
- The **nature** of decisions.
- **Types** of decisions: strategic, tactical and operational.
- The role of **managers**.

Secondly, we will look at the decision-making *model*:
- Identify the problem.
- Identify the objectives.
- Gather information.
- Analyse information.
- Devise alternative solutions.
- Select from alternatives.
- Communicate the decision.
- Implement the decision.

- Evaluate the effectiveness of the decision.
- The influence of ICT on decision-making.

The third part of this chapter deals with *SWOT analysis*:
- Development of a SWOT analysis.
- Drawing conclusions from a SWOT analysis.
- Justification of the conclusions.

The fourth part of the chapter deals with the *problems* of using a structured decision-making model:
- Time.
- Ability to collect all relevant information.
- The problems involved in generating alternative solutions.
- Lack of creativity.

Guidance and information on the internal assessments are given at the end of the chapter.

TOPIC ONE: The nature of decisions

One of the main functions of management is decision-making. You could say that management is about making decisions, where a decision is the process of making the choice between different options to achieve an aim or goal. Good information leads to good decisions being made. In order to make those good decisions there is a process that managers should go through to make sure that they are making the best decision for their organisation at that time.

Some decisions are very easy to make. For example, we all make decisions every day about what to eat, what to wear, what music to listen to, etc. These are routine decisions that we normally don't have to spend a long time thinking about, and are usually easy to make.

Some decisions take a little longer to make. For example, if one of your long term aims was to go on holiday next year, you then have to decide how you are going to pay for it. This will involve some budgeting decisions; how much you can spend on clothes, entertainment etc, will be influenced by your aim to go on holiday.

Other decisions involve what we want to do in the future, our life goals, such as what career we want. These decisions may take some time to make, and we don't make them very often.

It is the same in business. Managers have to make routine decisions that are easy to make, but can still be very important, for example whether or not to recruit more staff. If they do, it will cost the business money, but if they don't, then they could end up not being able to supply their customers, and so lose business.

They also have to make decisions that affect the long term prospects of the business. For example: should they develop a new product? They have to decide whether the cost of development will be too high, or whether they should risk losing customers in the long run, by not developing a new product.

Decisions involve making a choice from a number of different options. Effective decisions are those decisions which achieve the desired goal or aim of the organisation.

There are three main **types** of decisions:

- strategic
- tactical
- operational.

STRATEGIC DECISIONS

- These are the 'long term' decisions about where the organisation wants to be in the future.

- They are often made by the most senior managers and the owners of the organisation.

- They don't go into great detail about how these decisions will be achieved.

- Major policy statements represent strategic decisions.

- There are a large number of variables to consider about the future of the organisation, and as such these are non-routine decisions.

Examples:

- **what products the business will produce**
- **what sections of the market the business will aim for**
- **to increase market share by 10% within five years**
- **to maximise sales**
- **to have 100% customer satisfaction.**

Strategic decisions define the aims or objectives of the organisation. All businesses have objectives, and the managers of the organisation will be judged on their effectiveness by how they set and how well they achieve these objectives.

Businesses have to define their objectives in order to give direction to the organisation. They capture the essence of the company, usually through a mission statement which will tie employers and employees to a single set of goals or values, which will then motivate the business. It is also a legal requirement for many organisations.

Strategic decisions influence the direction of the organisation. An example could be 'providing 100% customer satisfaction'. This statement will then influence all other decisions made within the organisation. No real thought has gone into how this statement will be achieved, nor does it say what the customer satisfaction level is at the moment, simply that this is one of the main objectives of the business.

To plan a long term strategy for the organisation you will have to consider:

- **Where are we now?**
- **Where do we want to be in 5, 10, 20 years' time?**
- **What resources will we need to achieve this?**
- **What changes do we have to make in order to achieve our new goals?**
- **How can we do better than the competition?**

Tesco's senior management decided they wanted to become the number one supermarket chain in the UK. At that time they were number two to Sainsbury's. In order to achieve their aim they decided to increase the quality of their products to match Sainsbury's, introduce new services (such as their financial services and Internet shopping, and open Tesco Extra stores) which would make Tesco more attractive than Sainsbury's to the consumer.

In order to achieve the objective of their strategic decision they had to make **tactical** decisions.

TACTICAL DECISIONS

- **These are the 'short term' decisions about how the strategic decisions are going to be achieved.**

- **They are often made by middle managers within the organisation, in finance, operations, human resources and marketing.**

- They are based on achieving the goals or the aims of the organisation.

- They go into detail about what resources will be needed and how they will be used to achieve the aims.

- They will be subject to change as political, economic, socio–cultural, competitive and technological factors change.

Examples:

- to increase the number of staff employed

- to re-name the business (Royal Mail to Consignia and back to Royal Mail)

- to issue more shares on the stock market in order to fund a new factory.

Tesco opened more stores and recruited more staff to man tills and help with bag packing. They sought new suppliers who could provide better quality at a price that would compete with Sainsbury's. They opened 24 hours. They invested heavily in resources for Internet shopping. Although middle management would be involved in a lot of this decision-making, senior managers would have to agree to the huge amount of resources put into these changes.

OPERATIONAL DECISIONS

- These are the 'day-to-day' routine decisions.

- They can be made by all levels of management, but mostly by lower-level managers and supervisors.

- They are made in response to relatively minor but sometimes important problems that arise each day or week, so they are routine and repetitive.

Examples:

- arranging work rotas
- dealing with customer complaints
- ordering materials from suppliers.

An example for Tesco could be staff being switched from shelf-stacking to bag-packing when the shop is busy or additional staff brought in to cover for staff who are off ill.

Visit Tesco at
www.Tesco.com

An important part of decision-making is evaluating how well your decision worked. Were the objectives of the decision met? What happened that was not expected? If things did not go to plan

UNIT 1

then some changes may be needed. Decisions may not be successful for a number of reasons. It could be due to internal factors such as poor employee relations, or external factors such as changes in the economy. It is important that managers evaluate their decisions and make adjustments if necessary. Quality decision-making depends on checking at all stages, so that any necessary changes can be made and the organisation can best meet its objectives.

WHO NEEDS TO KNOW ABOUT THE DECISIONS AN ORGANISATION MAKES?

Everyone who is affected by a decision has to be informed about the aims and objectives of the organisation. As we have seen, all the stakeholders have an interest in what decisions have been made.

Employees

Employees should all see where the business is heading, and what it is working towards, otherwise they may see no point in changes that have been made and may become suspicious. This leads to resistance to change and in some cases sabotage may occur. It is very important that the changes are explained clearly to employees and that any fears they may have are properly addressed. The organisation depends heavily on its workforce, especially during times of change.

Investors

Investors are important because the business relies on their investment to finance the decisions that it takes. They may, for example, become worried that the business has no overall direction and look for other places to put their money. They may not see the benefit of decisions, particularly long term ones which could affect the amount of dividend they receive. If they are very unhappy they could seek to replace the managing director, chairperson, or even members of the Board of Directors. This would leave the business weakened and prone to take-over.

One way to avoid these problems is to issue a **mission statement**. This could be included in the business's annual report to shareholders.

The mission statement summarises the strategic aims of the business. It can be released to the press to help market the business and its products, and issued to all employees and other stakeholders. It will show that the business has plans for the future, and how those plans will affect the stakeholders.

The mission statement may contain information on how the business will treat shareholders, the environment and most importantly consumers.

QUESTION

Q1 Explain why it is important for managers to communicate their decisions to stakeholders.

TOPIC TWO: Constraints on decision-making

It is one thing to decide that your company should be the market leader in five years' time, however the senior managers have to be realistic about what they can actually achieve. There will be a number of constraints that businesses face, and these can be split into two categories:

INTERNAL CONSTRAINTS

Finance available

Just as we never have quite enough money to do all that we want to do, so it is with businesses. They have to work with the finance that they have available in the form of retained profits, available borrowing or investment from shareholders. Becoming a market leader could involve a huge amount of investment, and if the business cannot get hold of the funds needed, then the target will never be achieved.

Company policy

The push for growth that is necessary for the business to become a market leader may lead to conflict with the company's own policy.

For example, Dyson announced that it was relocating all vacuum cleaner production to the Far East to take advantage of cheaper production costs. This would allow it to achieve its strategic aims of growth and heavy investment in new technology and allow it to launch new products faster.

Visit Dyson at
www.dyson.com/news

For some businesses this would run contrary to their stated policy of keeping production in the UK.

The employees' abilities/attitudes

How the employees react to the proposed decisions, and how able they are to react, will have a great influence on whether or not these decisions are successful. Are they motivated for the changes? Are they capable of the tasks that will be expected of them?

EXTERNAL CONSTRAINTS

Government and EU legislation

Whatever actions the business may wish to take, they will have to be legal. For example, any actions which are deemed to be anti-competitive will be subject to investigation and possible prosecution by the Department of Trade and Industry and the Competition Commission. Anti-competitive actions could be any actions which prevent other businesses from entering the market, which would not be in the best interests of consumers. It could involve price-fixing, where prices are kept artificially low for a time to keep other businesses out of the market.

To find out more visit
www.dti.gov.uk

BUSINESS ENTERPRISE

Competitors' behaviour

No matter what decisions the business makes, others will be making other decisions which will affect how effective the decision is. More than one business in the market may have the same objective, and so cancel out much of each other's work done to achieve this aim.

Lack of new technology

As we have seen from the example above, Dyson relies heavily on the development of new technology for its success. Where that technology is not available, it will be difficult to enter or develop new markets.

Economic environment

During boom periods when the economy is growing quickly it is much easier to increase sales and market share, as the market itself is usually growing. However, in times of recession, growth in the economy slows, meaning that markets will shrink, making it much more difficult to achieve any increase. Some businesses may benefit from a recession as they are more able to weather the bad times so when the market recovers they will survive while others have gone out of business, giving them a larger share of the growing market.

QUESTION

Q2 Identify the main constraints that are placed on managers when making decisions.

TOPIC THREE: The outcome of decisions

Along with the responsibility for making decisions, managers also have responsibility for monitoring and investigating the outcome of these decisions. During the process of implementing the decisions they have to check that they are working as planned.

They must constantly:

- **review – what was actually achieved?**
- **evaluate – was this what was expected?**
- **alter – are changes required?**

Something that is of great benefit during times of change is flexibility. The more flexible the organisation is, the more easily it can react to changes as its environment changes.

Strategic decisions are mainly those to do with the long term goals of the organisation. They are not concerned with details, but with setting objectives for managers to work towards.

CASE STUDY — Clarion Printers

Clarion Printers was a new company set up from scratch 10 years ago to meet the demand for headed note paper and other stationery that could be used in modern laser printers. It is located in good-sized premises in a small industrial estate on the outskirts of Aberdeen. Its early success saw it grow from a company employing two office staff, five print workers and three sales people with an annual turnover of £345,000 in the first year, to a company employing five office staff, 15 print workers and five sales people with a turnover of £12,450,000.

Now its products are in such demand that it has to sub-contract most of its non-specialist work to other local printers. By using its Aberdeen connections it has managed to secure contracts with some of the biggest oil companies.

The directors of the company are suitably proud of their success, and particularly of the fact that of the many companies that tried to enter this market locally, Clarion is the only one that has succeeded. This is mainly due to the fact that at the very beginning they decided to purchase the most up-to-date machinery that they could afford. They took the view that it would be money well spent despite the cost, in order that their products would be superior to the competition, and that they could develop a reputation for quality and good delivery service. It was a big gamble, and it paid off for them.

The directors had set themselves a target of trading at a profit within the first three years, and had succeeded within two. From the start they employed the best sales people. They saw this as a necessary step to ensure their survival, and had committed funds to ensure that their sales people received the very best training in sales techniques and the products that they could produce.

Strategic decisions

QUESTION Q3

(a) Identify the strategic decisions that were made by the directors when setting up Clarion Printers.

(b) What were the reasons for making these decisions about the company?

(c) Identify two other strategic decisions that could have been made at the time of setting up the company which are not mentioned above and which would have contributed to the company's success.

The success of Clarion Printers has not gone unnoticed, and in particular the high profits that it has made in its first years of trading. A recent newspaper article has stated that two large printing companies are hoping to bring up to 150 new jobs to the Aberdeen area when they open new premises in or around the city.

One of the companies is a large multinational which has access to technology far superior to that which Clarion currently owns. Both have existing contracts with all but one of the large oil companies that Clarion deals with in Aberdeen.

BUSINESS ENTERPRISE

Oil companies have recently been looking at their suppliers for all different types of purchases, and arranging deals with only one company for each. The Clarion directors suspect that the same may happen for stationery.

QUESTION

Q4
(a) Outline the various strategic options open to Clarion Printers.
(b) Pick the one that you would recommend to the directors of Clarion Printers as a corporate target and explain why you have made that choice as opposed to the others.

Tactical decisions

Once you have made your strategic decisions, you then have to make decisions about how you are actually going to achieve those targets. These decisions are called tactical decisions, and refer to the how resources within the organisation are to be used in order to achieve the targets, and also whether additional resources are to be acquired.

QUESTION

Q5
Using your corporate target as your main objective, describe how you would then go about making sure that the company achieves its objective.

Operational decisions

Operational decisions are those decisions which are made in response to changes in the environment in which an organisation works. They are usually short term in nature, and tend to be concerned with unforeseen circumstances.

QUESTION

Q6
Below is a list of new pieces of information now available to the directors of Clarion Printers. For each, describe what actions you would take, if any.

(a) One of the printers Clarion uses for sub-contracting work is considering early retirement. He has put the business up for sale, but the directors consider the price a little too high, particularly as most of the work he gets is from them. However, they will need to use his business in future unless another printer can be found.
(b) One of the large printing firms has decided not to proceed with the opening of new works premises in Aberdeen. However, it is opening a small sales office in the city.
(c) The multinational company is finding it difficult to locate suitable land to build its new factory, or to find suitably experienced staff. Its Chief Executive has been trying to contact the Managing Director of Clarion for the past two days.

(d) Clarion's workforce have become very uneasy about all the changes that are going on. They have heard some rumours about the company being in trouble or being taken over.

(e) Two of the best sales people are rumoured to be on the point of handing in their resignations. Their sales figures are somewhat lower than expected for the past two months.

TOPIC FOUR: The role of management

 Sir John Harvey-Jones in his television series 'Troubleshooter', where he went in to organisations to help them overcome problems, described management as an art. He said that there is not one solution that will solve the problems in all businesses; rather that it is the manager's role to identify those bits of management theory that fit best with that organisation's problems. The aim must be to encourage constant change at a speed that the organisation can best cope with.

Management theorists describe the role of managers in different ways:

● 'A manager is one who is responsible for getting things done through people instead of doing the job himself' – W F Coventry.

● 'The quality and performance of the managers determine the success of a business, indeed they determine survival' – Peter F Drucker.

These two statements summarise the theoretical role management plays within an organisation. They are a unifying resource, bringing together the people, materials, machines and money in order to solve problems, make decisions and make sure that the business gets the best possible return from its resources.

In 1973 Henry Mintzberg published his book *The Nature of Managerial Work* with findings of his study of what managers actually do, as opposed to what they ought to do. He found that managers perform a wide variety of roles which can be grouped into three broad areas:

● interpersonal role – the relationships a manager has with others

● informational role – the collecting and passing on of information

● decisional role – the making of different kinds of decisions.

Henri Fayol, who in the early part of the last century spent some time researching what managers do, identified what he called the five functions of management:

● Plan – **looking ahead, seeing potential opportunities or problems and devising solutions, setting targets, and setting aims and strategies.**

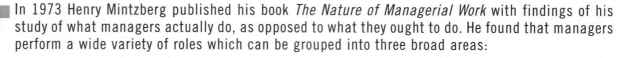

UNIT 1

● Organise – **arranging the resources of the organisation to be there when people need them and acquiring additional resources if required.**

● Command – **this involves the issuing of instructions, motivating staff and displaying leadership.**

● Co-ordinate – **making sure everyone is working towards the same goals, that all the work being done fits together, and people are not duplicating work or working against each other.**

● Control – **looks at what is being done, checks it against what was expected, and makes any necessary adjustments. This is the monitoring and evaluating role of management.**

Modern managers are likely to include:

● Delegate – **give subordinates the authority to carry out tasks. This helps with motivation and reduces the manager's workload. The overall responsibility will still lie with the manager who delegated the authority.**

● Motivate – **rather than simply telling workers to work harder, which is not likely to be successful, a manager encourages them by helping them to enjoy their tasks through team-working and participation in decision-making, and by giving them some power.**

Decisions are often made by groups of managers in teams. This allows for a wider variety of ideas and experience to be used when making the decision. The number of people within the group and the different roles they play are important in effective decision-making.

Professor Simon Garrod's study

A recent study by Professor Simon Garrod of Glasgow University suggests that group size is vital for decision-making, with one or two dominant speakers swaying the discussion in larger groups of 10 or more making it a poor size for gaining a true consensus. Smaller groups of up to seven people are much more successful in coming to an agreement among the group members.

Professor Garrod suggests that companies seeking an innovative, creative solution to a business problem should limit group sizes to up to seven people.

QUESTION

Q7
(a) Identify Mintzberg's three main roles of management.
(b) Describe Fayol's five functions of manangement and identify two other functions modern managers would employ.

TOPIC FIVE: Organisational objectives

Whether the decisions are strategic, operational, or tactical, they must fit with the organisation's objectives. For example, if social responsibility is an objective of the organisation then its decision-makers at the various levels of management must ensure that they do not make decisions which clash with this objective, such as giving up recycling materials to reduce costs, or buying from countries which have a poor human rights record. In doing so they could face criticism from pressure groups such as Amnesty International, who work to reduce human rights abuse around the world.

Each stakeholder in the organisation will have some influence on the decisions made. For example, shareholders can vote at the AGM (Annual General Meeting) to change decisions, or force different courses of action on the managers of the organisation.

The objectives of the organisation, the stakeholders and the ways that they can influence the organisation are dealt with in Chapter 1. You should refer to them at this stage to see how each will influence the types of decisions made.

> **QUESTION**
> **Q8**
> (a) Identify five possible objectives for an organisation.
> (b) Identify three stakeholders and describe at least two ways they could influence decision-making within an organisation.

TOPIC SIX: A structured decision-making model

Effective decisions can be made on the spur of the moment by managers using their experience or 'gut feeling'. However, success is not easily guaranteed, and many other good options could be ignored or missed. In practice, managers should go through a proven process in order to give the best possible chance of success.

Whatever the decision that has to be made, it is always best to follow nine simple steps. This way you have the best opportunity of making the right decision.

STEP 1 – IDENTIFY THE PROBLEM

Set the aims.

- **Where do we want to go?**
- **What do we want to achieve?**
- **What do we need to do to be the best?**
- **What exactly is wrong?**

It is not always obvious what the actual problem is. For example, when a famous brand shampoo found that its sales were falling it tried various promotions and advertising to try to boost sales, with little effect. It wasn't until it carried out market research that it found that the problem was that it had not increased its prices in line with its competitors and so it had become one of the cheaper well-known brands. Consumers viewed this low price as an indication of poor quality. The solution was very simple and effective; it increased the price and quickly regained market share.

STEP 2 – IDENTIFY THE OBJECTIVES

- **What is it we want to achieve?**

Managers have to decide on exactly what it is they want to achieve. In most cases business organisations will not use the structured model when they are looking for a simple quick fix. If the organisation is going to go through the process of implementing major changes then there will be a variety of objectives that can be achieved at the same time.

STEP 3 – GATHER INFORMATION

Good information leads to good decision-making. The more information that can be gathered, the better the chance of success the decision has. Extensive use of internal and external information is required.

STEP 4 – ANALYSE INFORMATION

- **What can you do, and what can't you do?**
- **What will help, and what won't?**

Study the information you have collected. Much of the information gathered will not be of direct use in the decision-making; this will have to be sorted, and then a decision made as to what information is relevant and what is not.

STEP 5 – DEVISE ALTERNATIVE SOLUTIONS

Using the information you have collected, decide on a number of different courses of action you can take that will meet the aims. Having a range of options will make the process much more flexible should you have to alter things later on due to changes in the business environment.

STEP 6 – SELECT FROM ALTERNATIVE SOLUTIONS

From the alternative courses of action that you have devised, select the one you think will be mostly likely to meet the aims of the organisation under present circumstances.

STEP 7 – COMMUNICATE THE DECISION

This is a very important stage. All those involved must know exactly what is going to happen, what effects these changes will have, and why you have decided on this course of action. Failing to inform all those concerned properly will result in a less effective implementation. If everybody knows what they are doing and why, they will be far more motivated to succeed.

STEP 8 – IMPLEMENT THE DECISION

Arrange for the resources to be put into place. Changes will need to be resourced adequately if they are to be successful. Issue appropriate instructions, and ask for feedback on how things progress.

STEP 9 — EVALUATE

Compare the information you are collecting on how the process is going to what was expected to happen. This will ensure that everything is on target and will allow you to make further changes as necessary to ensure that the final goal will be achieved in the most effective manner.

Find out how good you are at decision-making at
www2.kpmgcareers.co.uk/career99/apply/challenge

QUESTION

Q9

Describe the nine steps involved in the structured decision-making model.

TOPIC SEVEN: Using ICT in decision-making

As we have already seen, continued developments in computer hardware and software have allowed them to become more and more sophisticated. What we currently use in the home and in most offices is still a number of stages behind what organisations such as the government and the military are using. As these become available, this will allow the decision-making process to be completed more quickly and efficiently, as the information available can then be analysed more quickly and efficiently.

Records held on database can be accessed, sorted and processed into a structure that helps decision-making. Spreadsheets can run 'what if?' analyses to compare the outcomes of different courses of action. Management decision-making software can also help identify the best solution from a number of alternatives. The Internet can provide huge amounts of up-to-date information on any number of topics, including market information such as trends and competitors' products.

All this means that decisions can be made more accurately than before, with increased speed. The only major drawback, apart from the costs involved, is information overload, with many managers finding that there is too much information being received, and time will have to be spent selecting the information that is relevant.

This is a particular problem with e-mail in that it is just as easy to send an e-mail to one person as it is to send it to everyone on your mailing list. In fact, it takes longer to select a few recipients, so there is a tendency to send an e-mail to anyone who might be interested within the organisation rather than only those who need the information.

TOPIC EIGHT: SWOT analysis

One other tool that management can use to help with decision-making is SWOT analysis. It is used to evaluate where the organisation is now and where it should be in the future. It helps with planning, deciding the way forward for the organisation, and looking at strategies which could be used.

UNIT 1

SWOT analysis looks at all internal and external factors. Internal factors are the resources within the organisation. External factors are those things within the organisation's environment that are happening now or are likely to happen in the future.

- **S**trengths
- **W**eaknesses
- **O**pportunities
- **T**hreats

SWOT analysis is a tool that can be effectively used for any decision-making, however it is often used when making **strategic** decisions and in **marketing** decisions.

Strengths and weaknesses are **internal factors**. Opportunities and threats are **external influences**.

SWOT analysis can be used to cover the first four steps in the structured decision-making process and at the end to help decide if the decisions made were successful. SWOT analysis should not be seen as a one-off exercise. It should be part of the continuing process of evaluating how the organisation is doing now and what it should be doing in the future.

Not all organisations would find it useful to carry out SWOT analysis, for example the owner of a small corner shop would keep much of this information in his head, and would be well aware of all internal and most external factors.

INTERNAL FACTORS – STRENGTHS AND WEAKNESSES

Internal factors are the things that the organisation has control over and refer to the resources of the organisation, or the factors of production. The skills of the workforce and management, including its entrepreneurial skills, will be included in the study. How well the capital is being used to provide efficient production and distribution will be looked at, as will financial performance and the range of products. These can be compared to the market leader to analyse how successful the organisation is in these areas.

The strengths and weaknesses will reflect the current position of the organisation. These strengths and weaknesses are often obvious, but may be rarely considered. It is only when management decides to spend time looking at them that they will be dealt with appropriately. The organisation can build on its strengths, using them to its best advantage, and work to reduce or get rid of its weaknesses.

When making strategic decisions the organisation will look at all aspects of the organisation, including:

- Human resources – **the workforce, including all levels of management, represents an investment by the organisation, and also a resource which will have strengths or weaknesses in the quality of the management team, the level of entrepreneurial skills, and the numbers and skills of the workers.**

- Capital – **a major strength of an organisation will be its financial performance. A profitable business will have money available to carry out some changes it needs to make to respond to changes in the market, and will also have the ability to attract investment from shareholders or lending from the bank for major changes.**

Assets represent investment in the organisation by the owners. The higher the level of this investment, the more attractive it is to potential investors and banks.

- Marketing
  - **product range**
  - **marketing mix**
  - **distribution network**
  - **production process.**

The organisation will decide which it does well and which it could improve upon in order to gain an edge over the competition.

QUESTION

Q10 Identify the main internal influences (strengths and weaknesses) in an organisation.

EXTERNAL INFLUENCES – OPPORTUNITIES AND THREATS

The organisation cannot control external factors directly. However, it will be able to take advantage of any opportunities that come along, and try to avoid or take steps to overcome threats.

The external influences will come from the business environment in which the organisation operates. Evaluation of these opportunities and threats is critical to the success or failure of the business.

Sony

For example, Sony managed to get its PlayStation 2 on to the market in November 2000, well in advance of Microsoft's X-Box (March 2002) and Nintendo's GameCube (May 2002). In doing so it was able to capture a large section of the games market with sales to date (March 2002) of 18 million worldwide. Even if its competitors' products are technically superior, it is unlikely that they will be as successful as PS2 for some time, as those likely to buy the new games consoles will already have invested heavily in games. It is reckoned that around 30% of households in the UK currently have a video games console and that this figure could double within the next three years. With the X-Box retailing at £299 and the GameCube selling for £150, the market will eventually be decided by what games are available on which formats.

The external influences can be grouped under the headings:

- **political**
- **economic**
- **socio–cultural**
- **technological**
- **competitive.**

BUSINESS ENTERPRISE

Looking at these areas is also known as **PEST analysis** which organisations often carry out in conjunction with the SWOT analysis, as it allows for a better view of the business environment.

Using these headings, the organisation can look more closely at the various areas.

Political

The major source of potential threats or opportunities politically is when the government decides to introduce new laws or to alter taxation rates. For example, increases in the taxation on petrol are a threat to car sales, so manufacturers produce cars with more fuel-efficient engines. The introduction of the minimum wage was seen as a major threat to many small businesses, however this did not result in the large scale unemployment that was predicted.

The other major area is in government initiatives. For example, the present government's desire to use PPP (Private Public Partnership Finance Initiative) to fund the building of new schools, hospitals, etc. has created opportunities for building companies and finance companies to generate new markets within the public sector.

 *Find out more about PPP at*
www.scotland.gov.uk

Economic

How the economy is performing has a major influence on the level of success of a business. Those organisations which are very dependent on borrowing will find their costs rising and falling with the interest rate, and so therefore will their profits. This makes businesses less likely to borrow money for major projects when rates are high.

Interest rates also affect consumer spending. When rates are low consumers are much more likely to borrow and spend money; this in turn creates more sales for business. However, it is also true that when rates are high consumers will borrow and spend less, decreasing the level of sales.

The exchange rate affects the prices of imported and exported goods. When the pound is valued highly against other currencies the price of our imports becomes cheaper, however our exports then become much dearer for other countries, making them less attractive and reducing sales levels.

 **Report by food policy charity Sustain**

According to a report by the food policy charity Sustain, supermarket chains such as Tesco, Sainsbury's and Asda import up to a quarter of their groceries. Once, proud-to-be British companies like Marks and Spencer, Reebok and Kangol boasted that their clothing lines were UK-made; now they buy from cheaper foreign suppliers. Today tens of thousands of jobs have gone in the clothing and textiles industry as production shifts overseas in order to cut costs.

Also, during a recession people have less money to spend on luxury goods, so manufacturers will produce cheaper alternatives until the economy comes out of recession.

Socio—cultural

Organisations have to take account of changes in the tastes, lifestyles, and attitudes of consumers. Tastes in fashions change from season to season and from year to year, so clothing manufacturers have to ensure that their latest products meet the consumers' tastes. More women are working than ever before, and this has had two effects.

First, women themselves have a far greater influence on what is bought within the household. This was something that was identified early on by car manufactures who realised that marketing cars just to men was a mistake. So they adjusted their advertising and their products to suit women's tastes rather then just men's.

Second, as women were working their lifestyles changed, meaning less time to spend on shopping and preparing food, looking after children and daily household chores. This led to growth in a wide variety of family convenience foods and fast food outlets; growth in childcare facilities and nurseries; and growth in small house-cleaning companies and ironing services.

Consumers are far more aware of social issues such as Third World poverty, health issues and environmental concerns. Organisations have adapted their products, their image and their processes to take account of consumers' concerns. For example, most supermarkets will carry a range of organic produce and a range of 'fair trade' goods, label the contents of their products, and offer recycling facilities.

Technological

The introduction of new technologies forces change on organisations. Mass production techniques allow capital intensive automated processes which are more efficient than labour intensive production. Producing 'high-tech' consumer goods such as computers uses very sophisticated robotics. As new developments in computer components are introduced, this requires new automated machinery. Firms have to keep up-to-date in order to survive.

As these new computers are introduced to some businesses, other businesses will then need to update their systems in order to keep up-to-date.

The Internet is seen by many as the new market place for buying and selling goods, with many traditional high street shops and supermarkets setting up sites to allow shopping on the Internet. There is a great deal of competition for customers with each business trying to produce faster, more user-friendly sites. The cost of updating hardware and software to keep up with the competition is very high.

Competitive

Probably the biggest concern for most businesses is (rightly or wrongly) the actions of their competitors. Businesses look at how their product competes in terms of what it can do, what it looks like, what price it is or what offers are being made, and what after-sales service is available.

CASE STUDY

Text messaging

The hottest new way to market a company, brand or product is to use text messaging. Although these unsolicited messages are irritating, a recent survey suggests that 55% of the companies surveyed planned to use text messaging as a marketing tool in 2003.

SMS marketing company Flytxt argues that text messaging campaigns have a very high success rate if they are carefully designed, with a 10% response rate for a relatively low cost. They were responsible for Cadbury's campaign where customers learned if they had won a prize by sending a text message to a number on the chocolate bar wrapper. The campaign allowed Cadbury to collect information about the times when customers ate certain bars and which other bars they liked. Flytxt is also responsible for running 'Smash Hits' text club.

Lastminute.com sent the text message 'If you were a chicken, you'd be impeccable ... Get loved up at lastminute.com/valentines' as an unsolicited text message.

Visit flytxt at
Flytxt.com

QUESTION

11

Briefly describe the main external influences on an organisation.

SWOT analysis is most often laid out in a grid form as below:

Strengths	**W**eakness
Opportunities	**T**hreats

In each box, under the appropriate heading, a list is made, and this provides a snapshot of where the organisation is at this time and what the possibilities are for the future. Having to go through the physical process of writing it down allows for a greater degree of thought to go into the process. Discussion will lead to items previously unthought of.

It is common for a number of people to work on the SWOT analysis, with others adding to it during the process. It is probable that different managers will have different views on what each of the elements is.

For example, what one sees as an opportunity another may see as a threat. The wide variety of opinions on whether or not the UK should adopt the Euro and what benefits and problems it will bring if we do, or if we don't, shows that different people who are thought of as experts (such as managers) will view factors in different ways.

It is also possible that some threats may also be opportunities, depending on how the organisation reacts to them.

 **OnDigital**

The introduction of OnDigital (later ITV Digital) created a direct national competitor for Sky. Sky reacted by giving away decoders and introducing low-priced installation. OnDigital replied by giving away its equipment and spending a fortune in buying football rights. The original threat became an opportunity for Sky as it greatly increased its customer base and ITV Digital was forced into administration due to its inability to make money and the expense from televising live football.

Strengths may become weaknesses very quickly and vice versa.

TOPIC NINE: Drawing conclusions from a SWOT analysis

The purpose of SWOT analysis is to help make decisions, mainly about what needs to be done now and what is likely to happen in the future. The conclusions will be the basis for the future of the organisation so it is important that the SWOT is interpreted correctly.

The **strengths** will identify areas where the business is doing well at the present time, and where possibilities for the future exist. For example, having new products in the development stages ready for launch will provide a very good platform for the business to progress.

The **weaknesses** will highlight the areas where attention needs to be paid now in order to ensure survival. For example, having a high level of borrowing will make the business vulnerable to changes in the economy, and as part of the strategic plan steps should be taken to reduce borrowing.

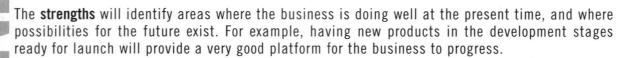

Opportunities have to be carefully measured to make sure that the business makes the best of them. These opportunities could come about from any of the factors mentioned in the PEST analysis. To take advantage of these opportunities the business must include them in its strategic planning.

For example, when the government sold off the licences for mobile phone bands, many rushed in and paid what is now seen as far too much to make them profitable in the medium term. With the mobile phone market now saturated, these companies will only start to see a reasonable financial return through the development of additional services such as Internet connection which consumers are slow to pick up due to the high cost.

As with opportunities, **threats** come from the political, economic, socio–cultural, technological and competitive forces. It is necessary for the business to take action to deal with these threats to ensure survival.

For example, the problems with British meat and the cost of dealing with the legislation put in place to deal with it have brought huge problems for farmers across Scotland. Some have sold up or been forced out of business. Others prepared themselves for the rapid reduction in demand by switching production or diversifying into other areas of farming such as the growth in demand for organic produce. Their forward planning allowed them to survive the threat.

The SWOT analysis should not be thought of as a one-off process. Evaluation of the conclusions drawn should take place to ensure that decisions were accurate. Carrying out another SWOT analysis will allow the business to see if its conclusions were correct.

TOPIC TEN: Problems of the structured model

TIME

The structured model does not go for the 'quick fix'. If a solution is needed in a hurry then the structured model will add too much time to the process, and so the response may come too late to solve the problem. It takes time to go through all the steps involved, and in taking that time more thought will go into coming up with the best solution. Some decisions are easier to make than others. The greater the amount or detail of the information, and the greater the options therefore available, the longer it will take to decide the correct course of action.

THE ABILITY TO COLLECT ALL THE INFORMATION NEEDED

It is not always possible to get hold of all the good information required to make the best decisions. Some information will be hard to get hold of. On the other hand, you may get large amounts of information but have to search to find the parts that are relevant.

PROBLEMS OF GENERATING ALTERNATIVE SOLUTIONS

It may be difficult to come up with alternatives. People can be reluctant to make hard decisions, and may not favour solutions which will affect them badly even though that solution is the best for the organisation. It is almost impossible to realise all the consequences of different decisions.

LACK OF CREATIVITY

Some good managers will feel they already know what to do, based on experience. The process will put them off making decisions which are riskier but could be more beneficial. Managers may not be able to come up with imaginative alternatives, and stick with what they know best.

QUESTION Q12 Identify the main problems in using a structured decision-making model.

THE BENEFITS OF USING A STRUCTURED PROCESS OF DECISION-MAKING

The time taken

Because the process of going through each of the steps takes some considerable time, decisions will not be rushed. Managers will have had sufficient time to put thought into the process. They will have had time to see what needs to be done and how best to do it, and to evaluate all possible outcomes from the various alternatives.

The quality and quantity of information used

Care is taken in gathering, checking and analysing information. Using the best information available gives the best chance of the decision being successful.

Alternative solutions

Generating alternatives will allow for some creativity to be included in the decision. It also allows for 'fall back' plans should the original preferred solution turn out to be wrong. Time will be available to assess the consequences of each possible alternative.

QUESTION Q13 What are the main benefits of using a structured decision-making model?

TOPIC ELEVEN: Aids to decision-making

There are a number of tried and trusted ways of helping managers to generate new ideas, to co-operate, and finally to arrive at what is hoped to be the best decisions.

BRAINSTORMING

The step-by-step process of the decision-making model may make it difficult to be creative in finding alternative solutions. Brainstorming is when a group meet to try to come up with as many alternative solutions as possible. Each member of the group comes up with as many ideas as they can, no matter how 'daft' they might appear, and all the ideas are written down as they are suggested.

Once everyone has finished, the group works its way through each of the ideas in turn, discussing the possibilities contained in each. This way, it can often come up with the most creative ideas because it encourages everyone to participate in an informal setting without the members of the group feeling that they are in some way being judged.

BENCHMARKING

This involves comparing what you do with what the very best organisations do. You could, for example, look at what the market leader does and then try to copy it. In this case the market leader is the 'benchmark' or ideal standard that you want to achieve. Benchmarking is used widely in operations to ensure quality, however it is equally valid as a method to aid decision-making in any of the organisation's functional areas.

CHAPTER SUMMARY

By the end of this chapter you should be able to:

- Assess the influence stakeholders will have on decision-making.

- Identify and describe the three main types of decision – *strategic*, *tactical*, and *operational*.

- Describe and analyse the role of managers in the decision-making process.

- Identify and describe how the organisation's objectives will influence the managers decision-making.

- Describe and effectively use a structured decision-making model.

- Describe and effectively use a SWOT analysis.

- Identifying the costs/drawbacks of using a decision-making model or SWOT analysis.

PREPARATION FOR ASSESSMENT

HIGHER ASSESSMENT

There are four PCs (Performance Criteria) that must be covered in this chapter. You will be expected to analyse the process of decision-making in a business enterprise. To do this you will be given a detailed case study which you will have to read carefully. It is always a good idea to read this once, then read the questions, and then go through the case study again with a highlighter to note the pieces of text which you will need to answer the questions.

PC (a) – Analysis of different types of decision is accurate and related to the objectives of the organisation

There are two parts here. The first is to identify the objectives of the organisation. This will be a business enterprise so maximising profits will be an obvious choice. It is not an organisation in the public sector so providing a public service would not be a good choice. Other answers you could give may include increasing market share, growth, social responsibility, etc. However, you should remember that you will have to relate these to the business in the case study.

The second part will be to identify and analyse at least one each of strategic, tactical, and operational decisions. This will depend very much on what is in the case study, but the marks will be for the analysis as well as for identification. For example: why would the business want to maximise profits? You could say that it wants to make as much profit as possible so that it can invest in new technology, or to give the shareholders a greater return on their investment, or so that it can repay borrowing quickly, however it will have to be related to one of the objectives identified in the first part of the PC.

PC (b) – Analysis includes an accurate explanation of the role of managers in decision-making in an organisation

Much of your answer here should relate to the structured decision-making model. How you answer the question again depends very much on the case study and the actual question you are asked. For example, you may be asked to identify one of the managers in the case study and describe the role he or she played in the decision-making process for the organisation. You could identify some of the steps in the model from the text or you may simply have to list the steps, explaining each briefly. However, you should start your answer by explaining that managers play an important role in decision-making because it is through their decisions that the business is actually able to meet its aims.

PC (c) – Analysis includes the development and evaluation of a suitable SWOT analysis for a business enterprise

This PC is usually awarded the most marks, and it is relatively easy to achieve full marks here. Where candidates fail this PC it is usually because they have simply made a list in each box of their SWOT without any indication of why each factor is a strength, weakness, opportunity or threat. To achieve full marks, you cannot leave any of the boxes in the SWOT blank, and must identify at least one of each.

PC (d) – Analysis includes reasoned justification for conclusion drawn from the SWOT analysis

'Analyse', 'justify' and 'conclusions', are all words which cause problems for students in the internal and external exam. What exactly do they mean? Now would be a very good time to use a dictionary, or to go and speak to an English teacher.

You may have identified that there was a problem with the suppliers for the business in your SWOT. This would be part of your **analysis** of the case study. It would be a **conclusion** that something should be done to rectify this. **Justification** for your conclusion would be that problems with suppliers could affect production and therefore sales.

Try carrying out a SWOT analysis of Clarion Printers as practice.

INTERMEDIATE 2 ASSESSMENT

This internal assessment has three PCs (Performance Criteria). In order to answer the questions in the assessment you will be given a case study. The purpose of the assessment is to allow you to show that you can explain decision-making in a business enterprise.

PC (a) – Distinction between strategic, tactical and operation decisions is accurate

Here you will have to explain and describe each of these types of decision. There may be examples in the case study, or you may be asked to suggest some. Either way, the first part is to describe each in turn. For example, strategic decisions are long term decisions, usually made by senior managers about where they see the business going in the future. They do not go into great detail about how they will be achieved. Examples could include what products the business will produce, to aim for a particular section of the market, or to maximise sales.

You would then have to do the same for tactical and operational decisions.

PC (b) – Explanation of the role of managers in decision-making is accurate and related to organisation objectives

There are two parts to the question here. The first is to explain the role of managers. You should explain that managers take responsibility for running the business, using all of the information available so that they can make good decisions, and to make sure that all staff they are responsible for are made aware of decisions and are kept informed of any changes.

The second part relates the role of managers to the organisation's objectives. You should explain that good decision-making is essential to allow the business to meet its objectives and that managers must make the right decisions if the business is to achieve its goals. In order to make the right decisions, managers should use the decision-making model.

PC (c) – Explanation of the ways in which stakeholders other than managers can influence business decisions is accurate

Here you are being asked to explain how stakeholders can influence the decisions managers make. You may be given examples in the text, or you may be asked to refer to stakeholders mentioned in the case study. Either way, you should be able to draw from the information given in the previous chapter of the book regarding stakeholders' influence. You should be aware of at least two ways in which each stakeholder can influence the business.

For example, employees can influence the business's decisions through their trade unions negotiating changes in the way the employees work. Also, the quality of their work can affect how customers view the business's products, and whether or not they come back to buy more.

CHAPTER (FOUR)

UNIT:2 BUSINESS DECISION AREAS
INTERNAL ORGANISATION

This chapter deals with the following:

INTERMEDIATE LEVEL 2

- Functional activities or organisations – marketing, human resources, finance, operations, research and development.

- Forms of organisational structure – hierarchical, flat, formal and informal structures.
- Factors affecting organisational structure – size, technology, market, product.

HIGHER LEVEL

- Grouping of activities – function, product/service, customers, place/territory, technology, line/staff.
- Functional activities of organisations – marketing, human resources, finance, operations, research and development.

- Forms of organisational structure – hierarchical, flat, formal and informal structures and matrix, entrepreneurial, centralised and decentralised.
- Aspects of organisational structure – organisation charts, span of control, formal and informal structures, organisational culture, changes in structure, the role and responsibilities of management.

INTERNAL ASSESSMENT:

- This topic is assessed internally at Higher but not at Intermediate level 2.

- However, it can still appear in the final examination, and is included in the course at both levels.

- For Higher pupils there are two PCs to worry about.

- The first PC is on the grouping of activities: functional, place/territory, customer, technology, and product/service. Here you should be able to give a description of the characteristics of each, an example of each with an explanation of why you think it is a good example.

- The second PC is about structures: tall/hierarchical, flat, matrix, entrepreneurial, centralised and de-centralised. Again, you should be able to describe the characteristics of each with examples.

- Details of the characteristics and appropriate examples are contained on the following pages.

- How many marks are allocated to each PC, and how many questions are asked, will depend on which assessment or **NAB** your teacher/lecturer uses.

WHAT IS AN ORGANISATION?

In Chapter 1 we looked at the different types of business organisation. There were profit-making and non-profit-making, public and private, each made up of a group or groups of people working towards a set of goals or objectives. What defines an individual organisation is the unique ownership or control from where the organisation gets its leadership and decision-making power.

Any business would have been set up by an entrepreneur who organised the resources (human, man-made and natural). The relationships between the people in the organisation form the structure of the organisation. Each organisation has a name to give it a corporate identity which its customers can recognise.

So when looking at the internal organisation of a business, what we are looking at is how these resources are organised to achieve the business's objectives.

WHY IS STRUCTURE IMPORTANT?

The structure defines how the organisation operates. It defines the role(s) of individuals within the organisation, and what authority they have. It defines the relationships between groups and between individuals. It channels the activities within the organisation towards its goals. It helps make best use of scarce resources.

It is relatively easy for one person to make all the decisions in a small business, but impossible in large businesses. We have already seen the importance of making good decisions, so it would make sense to put people in charge of areas of the business who are experts in that area. For example, the business could employ an accountant to look after all the organisation's finance.

Questions which will need to asked could be:

'Who can make decisions, and what can they make decisions about?' and 'Who is responsible for what?'.

QUESTION

Q1

(a) Schools have Principal Teachers in charge of departments. Explain why schools need Principal Teachers to be in charge of individual departments.

(b) What decisions can they make for their departments?

TOPIC ONE: Groupings of activities

Organisations will have to decide how they should be organised. There is not one single way which suits all businesses. In fact, as every business is different, so is the way they are organised, however there are some basic ways in which they group their activities. Most businesses will use one, or more likely a mix, of these groupings. This mix is called a hybrid structure.

FUNCTIONAL GROUPING

This is a very traditional way of organising the business, and was the main structure used up until 30 or so years ago when it was seen that UK businesses were falling behind other countries in the production of goods and services.

The organisation is split into departments which represent the main functions of the business. These would typically be:

- **Human Resources (Personnel)**
- **Marketing**
- **Finance (Accounts)**
- **Operations (Production, Purchasing and Distribution)**
- **Research and Development**
- **Administration.**

Businesses may have different departments from those above, depending on the type of business they are in.

QUESTION

Q2 Your local supermarket will have very different departments in store from those mentioned above. What will its departments be?

How big the departments are will depend on how important they are for the organisation. For example, if the business had only one or two big customers then the Marketing department may not be very big; if the business does not employ a large workforce then the Human Resources department would not be very big. However, it would not be uncommon for departments in a big business to have a large number of staff working within them.

QUESTION

Q3 Identify one organisation which would have a large Human Resources department, and justify your choice.

When the business is organised into departments based on these functional activities it means that all the people within the department will have similar skills or expertise in that area, and that they will use similar resources. This can have many advantages for the organisation.

ADVANTAGES OF FUNCTIONAL DEPARTMENTS

The resources of the organisation will be better used

If all Human Resources work is carried out in one department it will mean that there is no need to keep duplicate records relating to the staff, and the staff within the Human Resources department can talk face-to-face without having to travel or use costly ICT.

Staff will become experts in their own field

Staff working in Human Resources will share their knowledge and experiences and so learn from each other.

Career paths are created within the departments

Because there are likely to be one or more levels of management within the department, there will be opportunities for staff to move up the 'promotion ladder'.

For example, a Human Resources department may have a manager; an assistant manager; and supervisors for training, staff welfare and recruitment. A new employee can see a possible career progression to supervisor, then assistant manager and then manager as jobs for the future.

Communication and co-operation within the department are excellent

Because the staff in the Human Resources department see each other every day, they will get to know each other well and become comfortable working with each other. They will be able to talk freely and discuss problems.

Team-working improves

Working together means that they have a feeling of 'all being in it together' and they are motivated to work harder for each other and for the department. This also improves their abilities to solve problems.

Decision-making is better

The Human Resources manager makes the decisions for the department, and is the expert that senior managers from other departments can ask for advice in that area. Because each department has its own manager, decisions for the business can be made centrally, with these few departmental managers being able to speak for all their workers under their control. This centralises decision-making; allowing decisions to be made quickly for the whole organisation by just a few senior managers.

DISADVANTAGES OF FUNCTIONAL DEPARTMENTS

With all these advantages why change? There are some disadvantages that can arise from organising into departments, and management should be aware of these.

Staff loyalty to the department

Forming part of a team of workers can leave staff feeling that their first loyalty is to the department rather than the business. They can see other departments as being competitors, either for business or for the resources of the organisation. Money spent on one department may leave other departments feeling resentful and less co-operative towards other departments.

CASE STUDY

Network of PCs

This is not uncommon in schools where the functional departments are created around the different subjects. For example, most Business Education departments need a network of PCs which will cost tens of thousands of pounds. Other departments may think that they could use that money better in their own departments.

Communication barriers between departments

Although there is excellent communication within the department, it is often only the managers of the departments who have formal contact with each other.

This means that communication between departments can be slow; this can lead to decision-making for the whole organisation becoming less effective and more time-consuming than it should be.

Slow response to changes in the business environment

This was probably the biggest driving force for moving away from the functional structure. The modern business world changes much faster than it did in the past. If the business cannot move quickly to meet the new challenges then the business will fail, as many have done.

Many of the major manufacturing industries in the UK have disappeared because foreign competitors could react much more quickly to changes in what the consumers wanted, and could produce their products more cheaply as they were able to take advantage of changes as they took place.

Some decisions take a long time to make

There will be some decisions that the senior mangers cannot make without consulting their departments. Because of the structure of departments, with many employees at many levels in each, consultation will take a long time.

Some problems cannot be solved by one department

Many day-to-day problems will need the attention of more than one department. Again, delays will happen. It may be difficult to identify who has overall responsibility.

QUESTION

Q4

(a) Describe what you understand by 'functional grouping'.
(b) What are the main advantages and disadvantages of a functional grouping?

Visit the Student Loan Company Ltd at **www.slc.co.uk/noframe/corpinfo/orgchart.html**
to see an example of functional grouping.

TOPIC TWO: The functional activities

Although functional activities are covered in detail elsewhere in the book, it is helpful at this stage to understand the specialist knowledge and skills that are shared within these departments, and know what the key tasks are.

MARKETING

Marketing is a key function of **all** businesses. They must sell their goods or services in order to survive. How they go about this will depend on the type of business, but there are some main tasks which all marketing departments will carry out.

Marketing is the communication between the business and its customer. The needs of the customer are those with which the marketing department will be most concerned.

The staff will first of all find out what consumers want, both now and in the future. For example, it can take up to five years to develop a new model of car, so they must have some idea of what the customer will want in the future. They will then decide how to satisfy those wants, bearing in mind that they must make profits at the end of the day. Market research will be the tool used to get this information.

They then decide upon the correct **marketing mix** for the organisation. The marketing mix is made up of the four Ps:

- **product**
- **price**
- **place**
- **promotion.**

The **product** will be designed to do what the consumers think it should do, in terms of both performance and overall quality.

The **price** has to be one that consumers are willing to pay, and still allows the business to make acceptable profits.

The **place** is concerned with getting the product to the market in the right place at the right time, in the right quantities.

The **promotion** will communicate with consumers to tell them all about the product.

HUMAN RESOURCES

Staff are major stakeholders in an organisation. They are resources, which on one hand should be exploited for their full potential like all the other resources, but, unlike the others, they are people, individuals who respond in different ways to their treatment and environment.

The Human Resources department manages the staffing of the business. It will organise recruitment, staff training, staff appraisal, keep employee records, and be concerned with staff welfare. It will deal with the employees as individuals, helping them develop, and as a whole in dealing with areas such as negotiations on pay and conditions.

The staff will have to be experts in employment law, making sure that the business meets all the legal requirements it has for its employees.

FINANCE

This is also a function of all businesses. The finance department will be responsible for the keeping of all the financial records of the business; control of money flowing in and out of the organisation; and making sure that the business can pay its debts in order to keep on trading. It will find the best sources of borrowing, when required, and on the best conditions for the business.

The staff will provide senior management with the information needed to make decisions, by forecasting the financial outcome of different courses of action, and preparing budgets. They will also be responsible for drawing up the reports and accounts of how the business has done over the financial period.

OPERATIONS

Operations is concerned with the production of the goods or services, although this forms only one part of the Operations main tasks. It is also responsible for selecting the best suppliers of materials needed for the business, and will be involved in what is done with the finished product in terms of storage, delivery and distribution to the customer.

This is easily seen in a manufacturing business such as an ice-cream producer, but more difficult in a service industry such as banking. In banking, Operations would be organising the resources such as bank branches, ATMs, cheque books and cards, and keeping the accounts accurate and up-to-date, providing the services that the customer wants.

Whether it is goods or services that are provided, the same model applies:

IMAGE 14.
Input>process>output model

ADMINISTRATION

Administration is responsible for how the information that the business uses flows around, and in and out of the business. The Administration department provides all the office support and information systems for the business. With the increase in use of electronic communication such as e-mail, fax, video conferencing and the Internet, this area of the business has seen its role become more and more important.

UNIT: 2

BUSINESS DECISION AREAS

It is also concerned with Health and Safety issues, and the layout and design of the business.

RESEARCH AND DEVELOPMENT

The size of this department really depends on the type of business. Research and Development will have to work closely with marketing to ensure that customers will have the products they want in the future. The staff are constantly looking for ways to produce new products or improve existing products.

Medical companies such as Wellcome, and electronic companies such as Sony, will spend huge amounts of money on Research and Development in trying to bring new products to the market. On the other hand, a national car dealer such as Arnold Clark will expect the car manufacturers and finance companies to provide new products for their consumers.

QUESTION

Q5

(a) **Identify the main functional activities of organisations, and briefly describe what they do.**

(b) **Explain how each of the functional departments interacts with, and is dependent on, each other.**

TOPIC THREE: Other groupings

We have seen that all businesses need certain core functions such as marketing, finance, operations, etc. Within other groupings these functions will still exist, but they may not be individual departments operating within the organisation, for example there may be no Human Resources department. Rather, these departments/functions will be split amongst other groupings around which the business is organised and operates.

PRODUCT/SERVICE GROUPING

Here the organisation's activities are grouped around the different products or services that are provided by it. Each product or service requires specialist knowledge and expertise so it makes sense to gather all staff with this knowledge and skill in one grouping.

A business may produce many different types of products. For example Unilever makes products such as ice-cream and washing powder, amongst many others. It is a large multinational company and it makes more sense for it to organise itself around the different products it makes.

It has set up divisions, with each division making a different product or group of products. Each division is like a company on its own. Often these divisions will have a separate company name, for example, Van den Bergh which makes margarine such as 'Flora'. These companies are called **subsidiary** companies and are wholly owned by the **parent** company, in this case Unilever.

Advantages of product/service grouping

- **Each division will be a self-contained unit.**

- **Each member of staff in that division will have knowledge about that specific product.**

- It is easier to see which part(s) of the organisation is/are doing well and which is/are having problems.

- This grouping allows for a quicker response to external changes such as changes in customer requirements.

Disadvantages of product/service grouping

- Because each division requires its own support staff (Administration, Finance, Human Resources departments, etc.) there is bound to be duplication of resources, tasks and personnel.

- It is difficult to share research and development or equipment.

The divisions will be able to make most of their own decisions, with the organisation decentralised. They will all have their own functional staff, and these may well be formed into smaller departments.

QUESTION

Q6

The Virgin group provides a wide variety of goods and services. Identify as many of their products as you can, and then describe what advantages and disadvantages Virgin have in grouping this way.

Visit Balfour Beatty at
www.bbpd.co.uk/contacts.htm

CUSTOMER GROUPING

Some businesses have seen the need to put the customer first. Where the individual needs of different customers are important, then businesses will set themselves up in such a way that they have close contact with their customer. A car manufacturer can make a limited range of cars that will suit most consumers, rather than make individual cars to individual customers needs, however many service industries such as insurance and other financial services find that each customer has their own set of needs.

The Clydesdale Bank, for example, has Personal Bankers who keep in contact with their customers and provide a service for each individual customer's needs. They will carry out a yearly appraisal to see if the customer is getting the best products to suit their needs.

Suppliers such as those to the oil companies in the North Sea will have a few big customers. It makes sense for them to create teams which work for these oil companies. Often the suppliers will be based in the oil company's office and on their platforms. Each team or group will work closely with one customer on a daily basis and can respond quickly to changes in the customer's needs, and with their close contact can anticipate what the customer will want in the future.

Advantages of customer groupings

● Because the customer's needs are identified as a priority, customer loyalty can be built up.

● The customer gets the feeling of receiving a personal service, even when dealing with large firms.

● The organisation can respond much quicker to the customer's needs.

Disadvantages of customer groupings

● Administration of such a grouping can be time-consuming as individual customer needs take time and effort to meet.

● If staff changes occur then the feeling of personal service can be lost.

● Again, there will be duplication of personnel and resources.

QUESTION

Q7

Insurance companies will group their organisation around the different categories of customers they have, such as life assurance, motor insurance, house insurance, etc.

Describe why insurance companies will do this, and what the drawbacks of such a grouping would be.

Visit William Nimmo and Partners at **www.wnp.co.uk/documents/org.htm** *to see an organisation chart for customer groupings.*

PLACE/TERRITORY GROUPING

Businesses whose customers are spread over a wide area of a country, or over many countries, often find it better to organise themselves around the place where their products are delivered.

CASE STUDY　　　**Frozen foods**

Within Unilever's product/service or divisional structure for ice-cream and frozen foods, it has separate companies operating in most countries in Europe.

Bird's Eye Walls make frozen foods and ice-cream in this country. In other countries around Europe, different companies make and sell Unilever's frozen foods and ice-cream. This allows it to adapt its products and marketing for local tastes and cultures. Even naming products can be difficult as a well-known product name in one country can have very different meanings in other countries.

The other main reason for organising in this way would be because of where the business's raw materials are located. The oil extraction industry exists where oil exists, so the oil companies and their suppliers will organise themselves in these areas such as the North Sea, Brazil, the Middle East, etc.

In the UK many national companies would organise themselves around the different parts of the country, with regional offices for Scotland, the South-East, etc. This allows them to appoint regional managers who can then better control the activities in their area, and take account of different market conditions in different areas in the country.

 **CASE STUDY** | **Housing market**

The housing market is often very different in areas of the country. Edinburgh is going through a housing boom, with a shortage of houses on the market, and prices are being paid well over the asking price or valuation. This will allow builders to maximise their profits from sales without having to offer any incentives to buyers, such as free legal fees, or free carpeting.

In other parts of the country it is a very different story, with houses being much harder to sell. Here, regional sales managers will have to allow their sales teams to offer incentives. Without this local decision-making the builder may offer unnecessary incentives in Edinburgh or fail to sell houses in other areas.

Advantages of place/territory grouping

- Local offices with local knowledge can cater for local clients' needs.

- Local offices can overcome problems caused by different countries having language and cultural differences.

- Because the local office is accountable for that area, it can be held accountable for success/failure in that area.

- Customer loyalty can be built up through a local personal service.

- The local office is more responsive to changes in customer needs.

Disadvantages of place/territory groupings

- Administration can be time-consuming.

- If staff change then continuity of personal contact is lost.

- Duplication of personnel and resources.

UNIT 2

QUESTION

Q8

Shell exploration and production has facilities all around the world. Explain why it would group geographically, describing the benefits and drawbacks of such a grouping.

Visit First Choice at *www2.diagonal.co.uk/firstchoice/orgChart.shtml* to see an example of place/territory grouping.

TECHNOLOGY GROUPING

Here, activities are grouped around the technological requirements of the product, mostly in its manufacture or in its delivery to the customer.

In the manufacturing industry there are often distinct processes or stages which a product has to pass through on its way to completion. Each of these stages requires different technical inputs, and it may make sense for the manufacturer to organise its business around each of these technical processes.

For example, in car production there are separate processes that a car has to pass through to get to the end of the production line. Modern cars have many layers of paint and protection from rust. The technologies involved are very different from those involved in installing the braking system. Both are very important and complicated in terms of the technology.

It makes sense that the car manufacturer should group around these processes as there are a number of benefits in doing so. Workers in the paint area will become highly skilled and will be able to make sure that defects in the finish or quality are kept to a minimum. There is no need for them to be involved in learning other processes, and so the work that they do can be kept as simple as possible, making easier to train new staff and adapt to changes.

Advantages of technology grouping

- Using this grouping, you can increase the degree of specialisation in the production process.

- Problems with the technology can be identified easily.

Disadvantages of technology grouping

- A high degree of specialised training of the staff is required.

- These industries tend to be very capital-intensive, which is expensive.

QUESTION

Q9

W H Smith organises its activities around three areas: wholesale operations; retail operations; and Internet sales. Explain why W H Smith could be described as grouping around different technologies used in different processes.

LINE/STAFF GROUPING

The activities of the business can be separated into two types: **core** activities and **support** activities. Core activities are those that are the main purpose of the business. For example, a car manufacturer such as Ford would see car production and sales as a core activities. These are the activities that bring in money to the business and so allow it to earn profits.

Support activities are those activities that are needed to make sure that the businesses operates properly. For example, each Ford factory would have a Human Resources department. The department itself contributes nothing to the revenue the firm makes from sales, but without it there would be problems in the recruitment and training of staff, and problems in maintaining good industrial relations.

The core activities are carried out by what we call **line** departments. They are directly involved in the production of the goods or services that the organisation provides. These would be operations departments, involved in the processes that lead to manufacture of the final product.

The support activities such as Human Resources, Finance, Research and Development, etc, are what we call **staff** departments. They provide specialist support and advice to the line departments, to help them with their operations. They will typically be much smaller than the line departments, with a few highly specialist staff providing support and advice to the whole organisation. For example, the Human Resources department would be responsible for advising on employment legislation. This is a complicated and highly specialised area and it would be unreasonable to expect line managers to have a great deal of knowledge of current legislation.

How these departments work with each other will be looked at in greater detail later in this chapter, however it is important at this stage to understand that using this grouping means that there has to be formal relationships between departments. Who is in charge of what decisions?

The Finance department will have a lot of influence on what the operational departments can do. For example, it may ask that a Production department change its supplier of raw materials to reduce the cost of production. This would be described as **staff authority**; the relationship here is that the Finance department has direct authority over that Production department. At other times the Finance department will simply advise and inform the Production department and this would be described as a staff relationship.

Line relationships describe the relationship between a superior and his or her subordinates. The superior is in charge of the subordinates and has responsibility for ensuring that their work is satisfactory. This line relationship or authority is spread throughout the organisation. At the top of the organisation there will typically be a Board of Directors who have responsibility and authority over the whole organisation. The line of authority will then work its way down through the organisation from the top to the bottom, from senior managers who will be in charge of middle managers, who will then be in charge of junior managers, etc.

UNIT 2

QUESTION

10 Within your school/college, identify those activities which could be described as core, and those which could be described as support.

TOPIC FOUR: Forms of organisational structure

HIERARCHICAL STRUCTURE

The line relationships that have been described form what we call a hierarchy within the organisation. When studying an organisation's structure we can first look at who is in charge of who and what. Obviously, the higher up the structure you are, then the more authority and responsibility you will have, and the higher or better the pay and conditions (you would hope).

A senior manager will have a lot of responsibility and will make a lot of important decisions, but he or she cannot make all the decisions for the part of the business under their control. So middle managers may be appointed and given the authority to take charge of some of the areas of the senior manager's responsibility. Middle managers will then have junior managers who may have the authority to make some of the decisions in the area controlled by that middle manager. Junior managers may then have supervisors appointed to make some decisions.

Each of these levels of management represents a layer of authority. The further up the organisation, the fewer the number of staff at that layer; the further down the organisation, the higher the number of staff at that layer. If we look at the structure on a chart we can see that it forms a pyramid shape. This is what we call a **hierarchical** or **pyramid structure**.

Within this type of structure there is a great deal of control. The important decisions will be made at the top of the organisation and then passed down through the various levels, along with the instructions for what is to be done. Each level of management will have certain decision-making powers which it can then pass down the structure to its subordinates. The information that is needed to make those decisions will flow back up the chain of command through the hierarchical structure.

```
        Top
   management
    personnel
Managing Director
General Manager
Senior Executives
Company Secretary
─────────────────────
Middle management
   personnel
Subordinate managers e.g.
Personnel, Marketing, Financial
and Production Managers.
Foremen and Supervisors
─────────────────────
     Employees
```

IMAGE 15.
Hierarchical or pyramid structure

Because of the way this structure operates, with clearly defined line relationships, it is possible to give each person within the structure clearly defined roles and tasks to be performed, and also clearly defined procedures for carrying out those tasks. Each member of staff will have someone who will supervise their work, and so a great deal of control can be exercised over the whole organisation.

The tasks each member performs will often be highly specialised. That is to say, they will only be expected to carry out a limited number of tasks, and so should become expert in the performance of those tasks. Because they are specialists in a particular function or area of the business, this allows the organisation to be grouped around the main functions of the organisation, and so a hierarchical organisation will structure itself around the functional departments.

For example, one member of staff may prepare invoices for a number of the business's customers. It makes sense for them to be placed with other staff who prepare invoices, as they will all use the same information and resources of the organisation (for example, price lists, discounts, VAT details). Their supervisor(s) will probably report to the finance manager, and so they will be grouped with other workers who report to the finance manager. It then makes sense for these other finance workers to be in the same place or area as the finance manager, and so a Finance department is created. As they will all be using similar resources, and are now all working together, the business can save money by having only one set of resources for these workers to use, rather than having them duplicated throughout the organisation where finance staff are working. These savings are called economies of scale. By having one big Finance department, it may save money.

The main problem with the hierarchical structure is that it is designed for close control of the organisation or business, rather than what the business needs to do. Although some decisions can be made quickly by senior managers, decisions which require information from the various levels can take a long time. Communication can also be slow, as the information makes a stop at each level on the way up and the way down the hierarchy.

Most businesses nowadays need to be much more customer-orientated. The set roles and procedures within the this structure do not allow it to adapt or change very quickly. If a customer wants something even slightly different from the organisation, then the business can often find it difficult to respond to the customer's request, and so it loses business.

This inability to change quickly also makes the business vulnerable to changes in the market in which it operates. Nowadays, change is constant, most markets do not stay the same from year to year. This is because of changes in competitors' actions, changes in legislation, changes in socio–cultural trends, changes in the economy, and changes in technology.

All organisations will to a greater or lesser extent have some hierarchy within them. Someone has to be the boss. Someone has to make decisions. The bigger the organisation, the more people you will need to make decisions, and they all have to know what they can make decisions about. However, most businesses in the profit-making private sector have moved away from the pyramid structure to one that best suits the market they operate in.

In other sectors the hierarchical structure is still very common, particularly in areas where close control of the whole organisation or individuals within it is seen to be very important. Government-run or government-funded organisations have to be seen to be taking great care in how the taxpayers' money is spent, so the pyramid structure, with its close control, makes sure that everything is accounted for, and it is quick and easy to spot problems. Large organisations like the Civil Service departments, the local Health Trusts and Education Departments will have many layers of authority.

QUESTION

Q11
(a) Describe what you understand by a hierarchical structure.
(b) Identify the advantages and disadvantages of this type of structure.

BUSINESS DECISION AREAS

FLAT STRUCTURE

In response to the fast-changing markets in which they operated, and their lack of ability to change quickly, many businesses started to look at ways of trying to be more responsive to their consumers and the competition in their markets. One way was to abandon the pyramid structure and re-organise into either one (or more likely a combination) of the groupings previously mentioned. Another was to reduce the levels of management within their organisations. This process is called **de-layering**.

De-layering means stripping out levels of management and thereby flattening the organisation. This has a number of effects. First, the number of layers that information has to pass through is reduced, making it much quicker for information to flow up and down the organisation. Secondly, because there are fewer layers, gathering information and consulting staff takes less time, and so some decisions can be made more quickly. The removal of management or supervision levels means that there is less control throughout the organisation.

The span of control – the number of workers one manager has responsibility for is increased. Work is checked less often, so the workers must be reliable. In order for it to be successful, workers must be given more power to make decisions, and trusted to make the right decisions. This is called **empowerment**.

In flat structures there are few levels of management. Smaller organisations tend to have few levels. With a flat structure you do not get the same problems with communication, decision-making and slow reaction to changes in the market.

This sort of structure helps make the whole business a more effective team. There is less likelihood to be any rivalry between departments, and this teamwork will allow the business to respond to changes in the market more quickly, and so the business will have a much better chance of surviving and being profitable.

QUESTION

12
(a) Describe what you understand by a flat structure.
(b) Identify the advantages and disadvantages of this type of structure.
(c) Explain the meaning of the terms empowerment, and delayering.

MATRIX STRUCTURES

These structures tend to be used when the business is involved in a number of large projects such as a construction firm who may build bridges, new schools, hospitals etc, or where the business has a few large customers such as suppliers to the oil industry. They both have reasonably long-term contracts with their customers to produce goods or services. Teams are formed with staff from all, or most, of the functional departments. Each member of the team will have their own specialist skills, and will be responsible for their own particular expertise. For example, the accountant for the team will deal with all the financing for the project, and staff from the engineering department will provide all the technical support. However, because they are attached to the team rather than a department there will be an opportunity to become involved in areas outwith their normal expertise. This is called **multi-skilling**, where employees get the opportunity to develop skills and expertise in other areas, while still being highly skilled in their functional area.

The matrix structure allows for the possibility for individuals to have more freedom to use their talents effectively. There may be a team leader, but generally the team will have no hierarchy, with each member having the same level of authority and responsiblity.

Staff may be moved during or at the end of the contract to another team. This means that they will work on a variety of projects over time. In some businesses staff may be involved in two or more projects at the same time, and all this allows for staff development, increased job satisfaction and motivation.

The problem with this is that it is an expensive way of organising, with each team needing to have its own support services and staff. They will often work away from the organisation.

For example, oil suppliers can usually be found working in the oil company's building. They will need their own computers and administration staff. This leads to duplication of resources across the business, and so they lose the economies of scale that are available in the pyramid structure.

QUESTION

Q13
(a) **Describe what you understand by a matrix structure.**
(b) **Identify the advantages and disadvantages of this type of structure.**
(c) **Explain the meaning of the term** multi-skilling.

ENTREPRENEURIAL STRUCTURE

Small businesses tend to have only one or two main decision-makers, usually the owner(s). Other staff may be consulted, but will often have little input into the decision-making process. For example, a shop with an owner/manager and six members of staff will rely wholly on the owner's expertise. If one of the staff members has a great deal of experience, then they may be involved in some decision-making, and be given some authority and responsibility. All decisions will be made centrally by these key workers.

Some larger businesses also adopt this structure. The editors of daily newspapers have to make decisions very quickly and rely very much on their own expertise on what should appear in that day's edition. The may discuss this with one or two assistants, but again all decisions are made centrally. It is also common in areas of the banking industry where large amounts of money are moved between different markets throughout the day.

The problem with this type of structure is that it relies very heavily on these key decision-makers. If they are unavailable, then the decisions can't be made. Also, it places a very heavy workload on these few individuals. The stresses involved often mean that the decision-makers can only work effectively for a relatively short period of time with that workload.

As small businesses grow it is likely that they will change their structure, employing more key staff so that the workload can be shared, and the stresses reduced.

BUSINESS DECISION AREAS

Q14
(a) Describe what you understand by an entrepreneurial structure.
(b) Identify the advantages and disadvantages of this type of structure.

CENTRALISED STRUCTURES

Like the entrepreneurial structure, centralised structures rely heavily on a number of key individuals who make most of the decisions within the organisation. There may be more of them, but all control of the organisation is held by these key members of the organisation. Usually they will be the senior managers or directors of the business, but they could also be the owners.

Hierarchical structures are often highly centralised in terms of decision-making, and they share many of the same advantages. Economies of scale are available through centralised purchasing.

 **CASE STUDY** **McDonald's**

McDonald's restaurants throughout the UK and much of Europe are supplied by a small number of suppliers. McCain's supply all their fries, and so purchasing from one supplier allows the contracts to be so large that they can negotiate lower prices and good credit terms. Also, McCain's have to make their fries to an exact specification, using a specified type of potato. This means that all the fries take exactly the same time to cook in McDonald's fryers, and will taste exactly the same no matter where you are. The advantage of this is that there is very little waste, and few customer complaints.

Although McDonald's has created divisions to cater for different parts of the world, leadership at the top of the organisation, and at the top of the divisions, is very strong, with senior managers having control over all aspects of the business, even the franchises. These decisions are made for the whole organisation or division rather than for individual restaurants. These senior mangers will be very experienced and so the decisions made should be sound.

McDonald's has a world-wide corporate image that it can maintain through its centralised structure. All restaurants have similar or identical decor, staff wear the same uniform, products have the same name, and the service should be identical throughout the world or the division. The double arches are recognisable world-wide and, no matter what country you are in, you will already know and trust what the products will look like and taste like.

 QUESTION

Q15
(a) Describe what you understand by a centralised structure.
(b) Identify the advantages and disadvantages of this type of structure.

CHAPTER:Four

TOPIC
FOUR

DECENTRALISED STRUCTURES

Most businesses now try to find customers wherever they can, and in any part of the world. The Internet and the World Wide Web have opened up foreign markets for many Scottish businesses as they can now market their products world-wide. In addition, the removal of trade barriers and the movement towards global free trade have removed many of the restrictions which would have previously prevented them trading in many of the world's countries. Whilst this has created many new opportunities, it has also created many new threats in that foreign businesses now find it much easier to sell their products in Scotland.

This process is called 'globalisation', and it has meant that in order to survive Scottish companies must be able to quickly change what they do, and how they do it. This level of flexibility is not available with highly centralised formal structures, and so there has been a move towards decentralised structures.

These decentralised structures offer many of the benefits of flat structures, while still retaining a good level of overall management control. More of the decision-making is left to middle and lower management levels. In particular most of the operational decisions and some of the tactical decisions can be delegated by senior managers, allowing them to concentrate on more important decision-making. Obviously, this means that lower management levels have more power, however the overall responsibility still lies with senior management.

There are distinct advantages to decentralisation:

● As has been pointed out, it allows the organisation to be more responsive to changes in the market or environment in which it operates. This is because decision-making can be quicker as there is no need to refer matters up the chain of command.

● Secondly, the people now making the decision are much closer to their customers and have a far better knowledge of their customers' needs, and will also have a better knowledge of what is possible within their departments. The quality of decisions should therefore improve.

● Delegation and empowerment of staff allows them to develop their professional skills and gives them greater opportunity to display their own abilities. Being trusted to make decisions can make the staff feel more wanted and appreciated, which in turn increases their motivation, making them harder-working.

● Having the power to make decisions means that staff who are aware of their customers and market can prepare for possible changes in advance. This reduces the amount of negative impact on the organisation. Part of this process would include building in flexible practices such as multi-skilling where workers can take on a number of roles within the organisation.

QUESTION

Q16
(a) Describe what you understand by a decentralised structure.
(b) Identify the advantages and disadvantages of this type of structure.

TOPIC FIVE: Factors affecting the internal structure of an organisation

SIZE

As a business grows it becomes harder to control all the staff within the organisation. In order to keep control, managers will be appointed to look after groups of workers. As these groups grow, departments will be formed and the number of levels of management will increase.

The bigger the organisation, the more organised it will have to be. So large businesses will tend to have tall organisational structures. Small businesses will need less organisation and so will tend to have flat structures.

TECHNOLOGY

The introduction of new technology can change the structure of a business. For example a new information technology system could reduce the need for a large Administration department.

There are now more employees working from home than ever before. This is because modern communications technology allows the worker to keep in touch with the office throughout the day, and information can be transferred easily over telephone lines by downloading completed work. The departments that they previously worked for will virtually disappear.

Greater use of the Internet may change how the Sales department is organised.

PRODUCT

Having a small number of large customers for your product means that a flat structure using teams may be more appropriate.

For example, a building firm will have only a few large jobs on at any one time, so the staff will be split between each of these jobs.

MARKET

If the market is small and local then the organisation will be small. For example, a hairdressing business market will usually be the local community, so a flat structure with few employees will be all that is needed.

If the market is big and widespread then the organisation may well be large and organised around the geographical areas it covers. For example, a national double-glazing company will have a head office and a number of regional sales teams for different parts of the country.

QUESTION

Q17 Look at the following examples and then decide what type of structure would best suit them and describe the factors that made this the best choice.

(a) A national supermarket chain.
(b) A supplier of drilling equipment to a single oil company in Aberdeen.
(c) A small graphic design business.

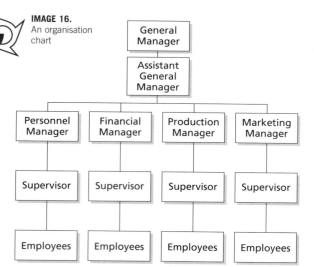

IMAGE 16.
An organisation chart

Chart boxes: General Manager → Assistant General Manager → Personnel Manager, Financial Manager, Production Manager, Marketing Manager → Supervisor, Supervisor, Supervisor, Supervisor → Employees, Employees, Employees, Employees

ASPECTS OF ORGANISATIONAL STRUCTURE
Organisation charts

Where there are a large number of employees within an organisation it is often useful to show the staff employed in a diagram, indicating where they work, what position they hold in the organisation, who they are responsible to and who they are responsible for.

They are particularly useful for new employees, customers, suppliers, and senior management. However, in very large organisations they would be useful to all employees as they could see who to contact about specific matters.

They are useful because

● **New members of staff can immediately see who they are responsible to, and identify other members of their department.**

● **Each member of staff is included, showing which department they work in, their job title, and who they are responsible to and for. It could also include telephone or room numbers and in some cases photographs may be used to identify key individuals.**

● **Customers or suppliers can easily identify the various functional departments, and identify who to contact in that department.**

● **Senior managers can have an overview of the whole organisation, identifying where problems with communications may occur either up and down the hierarchy or between departments. They will also be able to see the number of employees each manger has immediate responsibility for** (span of control). **This will allow them to identify possible problems with control, and appoint assistants if necessary.**

Organisation charts can only give a very general overview of the organisation. In practice other lines of communication between individuals and between departments may have been established. For example, teams made up of members of different departments could not be shown on the chart along with the functional structure.

Span of control

The span of control is the number of people any manager or supervisor has working directly for him or her. In the example below we can see that the production line supervisor has a span of control of three. There are three production assistants who report directly to the production line supervisor.

The size of the span of control is important because the bigger the span, the less supervision or control that can take place. Flat organisations tend to have a wide span of control for managers. Highly centralised organisations might tend to have small spans of control. The correct size

BUSINESS DECISION AREAS

UNIT 2

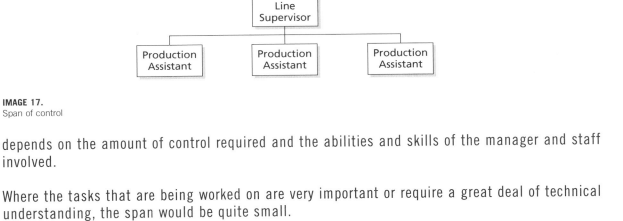

IMAGE 17.
Span of control

depends on the amount of control required and the abilities and skills of the manager and staff involved.

Where the tasks that are being worked on are very important or require a great deal of technical understanding, the span would be quite small.

 CASE STUDY **Hospitals**

In a hospital operating theatre the span would be very small because of the importance of the task and technical skills involved. Even in the wards, many hospitals adopt a system of double checking. For example, when a patient is being weighed, two nurses are required in case one misreads the measurement on the scale. It is very important because the amount of drugs given to the patient depends on their body weight. If the weight reading is wrong, then the dosage will be wrong, which in some cases could prove fatal. So although weighing a patient is a minor routine task, it is also very important, and one nurse has to supervise another.

In schools some departments can have one teacher while others may have seven. The size of the department or the amount of work they have to do determines the span of control. A Principal Teacher of English may have a span of control of six or seven whereas a Principal Teacher of RME may have a span of control of one.

The individual manager or supervisor will have their own level of inter-personal and leadership skills. Where these are high, the span of control can be high as staff will be highly motivated to work without supervision. Where the level of skill of the manager is low, the span of control should be low.

The span is also dependent on the skills and abilities of staff. Where staff are skilled and highly motivated they need less supervision, so the span of control can be high. Where there is a lack of skilled motivated workers, supervision will need to be a lot higher, so the span of control will be lower.

 **QUESTION** **Q18**
(a) Explain why organisation charts can be useful.
(b) Explain what you understand by the term span of control.

Visit **www.case-jc.demon.co.uk/orgn.htm** to see an alternative to organisation charts.

TOPIC SIX: Formal relationships

LINE RELATIONSHIPS

Where a member of staff is in charge of another member of staff then this is what we call a line relationship. In the organisation chart you can see a line drawn between a manager and the staff for whom he is directly responsible. This line represents the relationship the manager has with the member or members of staff. It is a vertical line which shows who is responsible for whom, and who reports to whom.

For example, one of the Assistant Head Teachers in a school would have responsibility for the English Department. The Principal Teacher of the English Department would have a line relationship with that Assistant Head Teacher.

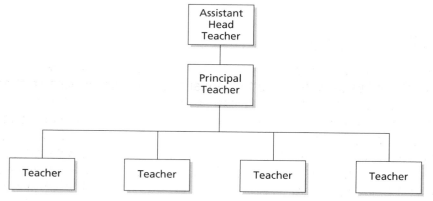

IMAGE 18.
Line and functional relationships

FUNCTIONAL RELATIONSHIPS

The relationship between members of staff on the same level of responsibility is called a functional relationship. The managers of the various departments within an organisation would have a functional relationship. On an organisation chart they would appear as a horizontal line.

For example, in a college the Head of the Computing Department would have a functional relationship with the Head of the Engineering Department. Each is responsible for what happens within their department, however some courses would require that students spend time in both departments. The two Heads of Department have to work together to organise these courses for the students and this would be part of their functional relationship.

STAFF RELATIONSHIPS

In many organisations there are individuals, or in some cases groups of individuals, who do not fit neatly into an organisation chart because of what they do for the business. They are specialists in a particular field and provide a level of expertise and advice that support the organisation as a whole rather than individual departments. These individuals would be described as having a staff relationship within the organisation. Company lawyers or ICT specialists would be examples of individuals who would have a staff relationship within the organisation. They do not have formal line or functional relationship with the business.

QUESTION Q19

Look at the list of organisational relationships below and then explain whether they are 'line', 'functional' or 'staff'. (NB: some of the examples may be of more than one type.)

(a) Personnel department of a large oil company.
(b) An expert on the European Union appointed to a company trading with France for the first time.
(c) A lawyer working full-time for a national newspaper.
(d) A foreman mechanic working in a local garage.
(e) Sales Manager for a double-glazing company.
(f) The Marketing department of a supermarket chain.

TOPIC SEVEN: Informal structures

Although not all organisations actually draw up an organisation chart, the chart describes the formal structure of the business. It shows the formal relationships between staff and the formal lines of communication within the organisation. However, organisations are made up of individuals who will establish friendships and good working relationships outwith these formal lines. This could be for a number of different reasons. For example, an assistant within the Accounts department may play badminton with the manager of the Sales department. There is no direct line or staff relationship between them, however, as they know each other well they may discuss business matters outside work, or even contact each other directly in the workplace to discuss customers' accounts, as this would be quicker than using the formal structure.

Some management theorists argue that organisation charts are a mistake because they do not reflect what a business actually does and are therefore misleading.

It could be that the formal structure is not good enough and staff create informal structures simply to get the job done. For example, if there are bottlenecks in the flow of information, where unacceptable delays take place, then staff will go around the bottleneck. If, as in the previous example, the Sales Manager needs urgent information for a customer, he may contact an appropriate member of the Accounts department that he or she knows direct, rather than use a written request to the Accounts Manager, in order to keep the customer happy.

These informal communication structures within the organisation should be of concern to the senior management. The individuals involved may form close relationships and share some information only between themselves, excluding others. For those involved there is an added feeling of belonging and an additional layer of support for them as individuals. For those not involved there is a feeling of isolation and dislike of what they see as a clique. They may form other informal groups to avoid what they see as a potential threat to their position within the organisation. This can lead to hostility between members of staff and the destruction of teamwork. It can also lead to the informal groups working against the decisions, and the aims and objectives of the organisation. Senior management need to be aware of these informal groups and work to ensure that as far as possible they remain only social groups, and maintain good working relationships and effective teamwork.

These informal lines of communication are often described as 'the grapevine'. The information that flows through the grapevine is often outwith the management's control and can be incorrect or misleading. Senior management must ensure that staff are kept informed of developments within the organisation to counteract any possible misinformation flowing through the grapevine. They may also use the grapevine in addition to the formal lines of communication to pass information quickly throughout the organisation.

ORGANISATIONAL (CORPORATE) CULTURE

All social groups of people form their own culture. For example, a group of friends, whether they are aware of it or not, will behave towards each other in particular ways. They may have acceptable forms of dress; they will talk to each other in a way that assumes a set of beliefs about each other and their environment which can make it difficult for an outsider to join in their conversations; they will socialise in their own particular favourite places.

Organisations are made up of individuals who will form their own culture, given enough time. Management can influence this culture for the benefit of the organisation in its dealing with customers, and for the establishment of good practice and teamwork within the organisation.

To do this, managers must understand what will influence the culture within the organisation. As with the group of friends above, it will be about behaviour, attitudes, values and their environment.

All new members of staff will want to 'fit in' as quickly as possible. To do this they will take their lead about how to act or behave in the workplace from those around them. If management put in place appropriate policies, for example about how to deal with customers, then this will influence the behaviour of all staff.

The attitude of staff can be influenced by the actions and motivation of management. A positive leadership style should quickly lead to a positive attitude taken by staff. On the other hand, any negative signals from management will also be quickly picked up by staff.

The values of the organisation as a whole are dictated by the actions and communications of the management. For example, the business's mission statement will set out what the business expects to achieve, what its goals are in terms of the goods and services it provides. A mission statement which states that the organisation wants to achieve 100% customer satisfaction should lead the staff to value their customers more, and see their satisfaction as a measure of how successful they are in their career.

The physical environment in which staff work will affect how they act. For example, an open-plan office where staff are visible to each other and movement is unrestricted should lead to an openness between staff with few barriers in terms of communication, social or work interaction. Having an individual office, on the other hand, will create physical barriers between that member of staff and others which will in turn make them appear less approachable for both social and work interaction.

Managers who adopt an 'open door' policy towards staff can overcome these barriers through simply leaving the door open, and letting staff know that they should feel free to come and see them. This overcomes the problem of work interaction, but also keeps unnecessary social interaction to a minimum.

Other environmental factors that could influence the organisation's culture could be dress code or the use of a staff uniform which identifies individuals as belonging to that organisation, satisfying their emotional need to belong or 'fit in'. Many shops use uniforms to give all the employees an identity belonging to the organisation. When they put that uniform on they are mentally 'now at work'. It also promotes a single corporate identity to customers who see a member of that organisation rather than just another individual.

The type of corporate culture the organisation creates is dependent on the organisational structure. If the organisation is centralised and hierarchical in nature, then the culture will be much more formal, whereas in a decentralised flat structure staff will tend to be less formal. In either case, a management-inspired organisational culture can be a very positive force for motivation and for accepting the organisation's goals and objectives as personal for each member of staff.

QUESTION Q20

All organisations develop a corporate culture, whether it is intended by management or not. Your school or college has its own corporate culture, part of which is decided by the management of the school/college, and part of it by the students.

(a) Describe the corporate culture of your school/college as you see it, and identify those areas which are decided by the management and those decided upon by the students.

(b) The role of the school/college is to provide a caring atmosphere in which students can learn. Which parts of the corporate culture work towards this aim and which parts work against it?

(c) Describe action which the management of the school/college could take to improve the corporate culture.

(d) Using the answers to the previous questions as a guide, explain why the management of a new medium-sized electronics company may wish to introduce its own corporate culture as soon as possible.

TOPIC EIGHT: Changing structures

We have already seen why organisations have been forced to move away from traditional hierarchical single structures. The increasing rate of change in the business environment has forced organisations to re-organise so that they can be much more responsive to these changes.

In addition to the speed of change, the past 30 years or so have seen Scotland's manufacturing industries go through a period of decline. Much of this has been seen as a natural development for a mature economy as it goes through the process of what is called de-industrialisation. During this time service industries such as banking and insurance, which are very successful in Scotland, have seen an increase in output.

Many foreign multinational companies have opened centres in Scotland. Their management structures and organisational operations are very different to the traditional hierarchical structures. In order to do business with these multinationals, Scottish organisations have been forced to change their operations to match those of their new customers.

Traditional structures:

● **have direct lines of responsibility**

● **employ people to do as they are told**

● **pay people for the position they hold**

● **all decisions are made by management and management must be allowed to manage.**

Our production needs to be revolutionised, just becoming more efficient will not be enough. To gain a competitive advantage we must be innovative and imaginative in our approach to management.

Industries in Western economies have tried a number of approaches to make their businesses more competitive. One of the first approaches used was Total Quality Management (TQM). However, TQM brought problems of its own:

● **A number of organisations were unable to introduce TQM successfully, for a number of reasons.**

● **Others found that in order to achieve TQM they had to change their operations significantly.**

● **Many organisations found the cost too high despite the available long-run benefits.**

● **For others there was simply not the will amongst management and staff to achieve TQM successfully.**

Some of these organisations had to either change significantly or cease to exist. For others, TQM was only the first step on a long, hard road to achieve a competitive advantage, and so remain in world markets.

Modern management issues centre around change, quality, cost, and most importantly survival. Some of the more successful management strategies for survival are:

● **business corporate re-engineering**
● **empowerment**
● **outsourcing**
● **downsizing**
● **de-layering.**

RE-ENGINEERING

This is the most radical step management can take. It involves a complete change in the way the firm operates in order to be the best it can possibly be. The whole organisation is changed. Departments may disappear completely, to be replaced by project or customer teams.

EMPOWERMENT

This is more than just the delegation of some decision-making powers to employees. It also involves a fundamental change in management attitude to employees at all levels if it is to be successful.

OUTSOURCING

This may follow on from an exercise in downsizing where part of the operations of the organisation is passed to a specialist who will be able to do the job better than the organisation itself. For example, many firms used to have their own 'in-house' ICT specialists. The cost involved in recruiting and keeping these staff was high due to skills shortages, which meant that there were always better opportunities for the best employees elsewhere. A solution is to employ a specialist ICT consultancy which then carries out the work for a fee and deals with the problems involved in training and retaining ICT personnel.

QUESTION

Q21
(a) **Explain why organisations may feel they have to change.**
(b) **Describe what you understand by the term 'outsourcing'.**

DOWNSIZING

Downsizing involves reducing the operating costs of the organisation by looking for what it does not need to spend money on. This could include:

- **reducing the scale of operations to meet actual market demand**

- **removing excess capacity within the organisation**

- **consolidating complementary operations under one function**

- **reducing the resources of the organisation following increases in productivity**

- **focusing only on core operations.**

Following recessions, organisations need to look very closely at ways of reducing costs in order to survive. Many find that their productive capacity exceeds the actual or planned demand for their product. Even after coming out of recession, the demand for their products may continue to be less than it was before.

For some organisations downsizing means the closure of factories or productive units. For others, it means the merging of two or more separate operations, originally under separate management, being brought under the one management umbrella. And for some it simply means the scaling-down of their productive capacity.

Duplication occurs not only in production and management, but also in areas such as sales, research and administration. For example, having two separate sales forces for different product ranges is an expensive luxury which may have been sustainable, and even profitable in the past, however, with ever-increasing competition many organisations find that the additional cost makes them uncompetitive.

Outsourcing allows firms to reduce their direct obligations to payment for resources and passes the burden to other companies. The cost of employing staff is far greater than simply their wage or salary. The firm also has to pay to equip the worker and provide accommodation. If these costs are being paid for by someone else then there the organisation simply pays for what it needs when it needs it, and can more readily increase the demands on outside contractors than it could on its own employees.

Downsizing inevitably leads to unemployment, however the level of unemployment is much lower than if the company itself had failed.

QUESTION

Q22

Why would trade unions work against attempts to downsize an engineering business?

DE-LAYERING

Changing from a tall structure to a flat structure would involve the removal of layers of management from the hierarchy. De-layering is the removal of levels of management or supervision from the organisation.

Some management levels in the organisation exist just to supervise the work of other staff. The cost of employing these managers or supervisors has to be weighed against the cost of any mistakes that they make in their work. If the cost involved is higher then continuing to employ these managers does not make economic sense. In addition, organisations have to weigh the cost of their employment against the costs of additional or continuing training for these members of staff to ensure errors are at their minimum. Again, if the cost is higher then their continued employment does not make economic sense.

When fully trained, the staff will be more aware than any supervisor or manager of what operational, or in some cases tactical, decisions should be made. If the staff are then empowered to make these decisions, then there is no longer a necessity to employ the manager/supervisor.

As we have already seen, additional levels of management slow down the communication process and consequently the ability to change quickly in response to changes in their market.

Many middle managers lost their jobs in the 1990s because of the process of de-layering. Whether this process was successful for the individual organisation depended on whether it was simply trying to cut staffing costs or whether it was genuinely trying to re-organise itself to meet its customer needs better. In the majority of cases they went too far and then found themselves having to re-employ managers.

All of these approaches can be used in an attempt to make the organisation more responsive to change and therefore more competitive. However, the main function of the structure of the organisation is to best meet its strategic aims and it is management's responsibility to make sure that this is the case.

One of the main problems with changing the structure is the resistance to change among the staff employed by the organisation. Any change has to be managed properly. This would include planning within a realistic time-scale; keeping staff informed and updated about the changes, including reasons for them; and monitoring the impact of changes as they take place, with adjustments as necessary.

If management fails to convince staff of the benefits of change then the outcome will be worse than if the change did not take place at all.

QUESTION

Q23 Look at the proposed structure for a new secondary school at Oldmeldrum in Aberdeenshire. Taking into consideration how schools are usually organised, how could this be described as an attempt to de-layer the management of the school?

CHAPTER SUMMARY

By the end of this chapter you should be able to:

● Identify and analyse the factors that will influence the internal structure of an organisation.

● Identify and describe the main functional activities of an organisation including Marketing, Human Resources Management, Finance, Operations, and Research and Development.

● Describe the main forms of organisational structure such as: Hierarchical, Flat, Formal and Informal, Matrix, Entrepreneurial, Centralised and De-centralised.

● Describe with examples the different grouping of activities including Functional, Product/Service, Customer, Place/Territory, Technology, and Line/Staff.

● Identify and describe various aspects of organisational structure including the use of Organisation Charts, and Span of Control.

● Show awareness and understanding of Organisational Culture, Changes in Structure including Downsizing and Delayering, and the role and responsibility of management.

PREPARATION FOR ASSESSMENT

 HIGHER ASSESSMENT

The assessment for this chapter will focus on two PCs (Performance Criteria).

PC (a)

This is concerned with organisational groupings: functional, product/service, customer, place/territory (geographical) and technological. It is unlikely that there would be any marks available for naming these in the assessment, but it is possible that marks will be available in the final exam, so you should always be able to identify them.

There are at least five different questions (NABs) you could be asked, and the marks available will vary, however each question will allow you to show that you can explain what each grouping is and can identify an appropriate example, detailing the advantages and disadvantages of some or all of the groupings.

Using an example is probably the best way to show that you know **and** understand what you are writing about. Good examples will always give you a better chance of achieving full marks, and you may even be given some examples in the text.

For example, when talking about functional groupings, identify an organisation that has, or is likely to have, all or most of the functional departments. This will show that you know what the functional areas are, and that your example is organised into departments around these functions. The next part is to show that you know why they decided to organise in this way.

So, for the example of functional groupings, you would have to describe the advantages of organising this way. You should also be able to list the disadvantages of each grouping.

PC (b)

This is concerned with the different types of structure an organisation may adopt. You should be able to identify at least four: tall (pyramid), flat, entrepreneurial and matrix. Again, much depends on the question that you are asked, however you should be able to describe the advantages and disadvantages of each type of structure, and explain when each would be an appropriate structure for an organisation.

For example, an entrepreneurial structure would be most suitable for a small business, as it can be run by one or two key workers, allowing it to respond quickly to its customers' demands, etc.

Again, using examples will give you the best opportunity to show that you know **and** understand about business structures.

The following questions are very similar to ones that you might be given as part of an assessment. Use them as practice, and then check your answers against the solution.

The actual assessment may involve a case study or some stimulus material which you should read first.

1. (a) **B Land Ltd groups its activities around** customers **and** function. **Explain what each of these terms means.** (2 marks)

    (b) **For both of the groupings above, explain why B Land Ltd might have decided this as the best method for grouping their activities.** (2 marks)

    (c) **For** each **of the other groupings listed below, explain what each is:**
    *   place
    *   technology
    *   product/service. (3 marks)

    (d) **Using appropriate examples, explain why an organisation may decide to use** each **of these groupings.** (3 marks)

    (e) **Describe one disadvantage for** each **of the five groupings that they may bring to the organisation.** (10 marks)

2. (a) **B Land Ltd's organisational structure could be described as a flat structure. Analyse the** advantages and disadvantages **of this form of structure.** (4 marks)

    (b) **Identify and describe an alternative structure that B Land Ltd could adopt, and explain when this structure would be most suitable for an organisation.** (4 marks)

1. (a) Grouping around customers means that each of its customers or groups of customers has different needs, so they are organised to best meet these individual needs.
    Grouping around function means that the business has a departmental structure, with those working in the same functional areas such as operations, will all belong to the same department.

    (b) Grouping around customers allows the organisation to provide an individual service for its customers, and so customer loyalty can be built up.
    Grouping around function means that those working in the department can develop expertise in that area, and share similar resources, so reducing costs.

    (c) Place – grouping by geographical area.
    Technology – grouping by the different technological processes involved in production or distribution.
    Product/service – grouping by the different products or services offered by the organisation.

    (d) Place – Asda would group by place as it will have stores across the UK, so management of its stores can be split into geographical areas, with regional or area managers.

CHAPTER:Four

Technology — **WH Smith uses different technologies for its retail, wholesale and Internet sales. Each requires different expertise, so this can be developed and based where it is most needed.**

Product/service — **The Virgin group provides a wide range of very different products, from air travel to financial services. Each requires very different expertise, so this expertise is based where it is needed most.**

(e) Place — **Asda can vary its product range to cater for local tastes. However, there will be duplication of resources as each area manager will need administrative support.**

Technology — **increased specialisation can be developed in the production or distribution process. However, there is high cost in terms of purchasing capital equipment and the specialist training required.**

Product/service — **Products can be developed to best meet the needs of the market for each product. However, it is difficult to share research and development or equipment.**

2. (a) **A flat structure has fewer layers of authority or management. Communications are passed more quickly from one layer to another. This makes quicker decision-making possible. There is greater responsibility for employees with less supervision, which helps motivation. A flat structure can respond more quickly to changes in the business environment. Improved working relationships are possible as it is easier for employees and managers to get to know each other.**

(b) **An alternative structure would be a matrix structure where people with specialist skills are grouped into project teams to complete tasks. There is no hierarchy, with everyone on the same level of responsibility. It is good for staff development as staff can work on a variety of projects over time. It allows for multi-skilling. It allows for close contact with individual clients so the business can respond quickly to their needs. It needs expensive support systems such as administrative support.**

CHAPTER FIVE

UNIT:2 BUSINESS DECISION AREAS

MARKETING

This chapter covers the marketing function of the organisation for Intermediate 2 and Higher levels. At *Intermediate level 2* there are three areas are to be covered in the course:

INTERMEDIATE LEVEL 2

The marketing concept:
- The role of marketing in different organisations.
- Market share.
- Market growth.

The marketing mix:
- Product.
- Price.
- Place.
- Promotion.

Market research:
- Assessing customer requirements, including surveys and samples.

At *Higher* level there are four main areas covered:

HIGHER LEVEL

The marketing concept:
- Marketing as a strategic activity of the organisation.
- The marketing of goods and services.

The marketing mix:
- Place, including channels of distribution.
- Pricing strategies, including long and short term strategies.
- The product/service.
- The various promotional activities available to the organisation.

Targets markets:
- Market segmentation.
- Methods of segmenting markets.
- Niche marketing.
- Market share and market growth.

Market research:
- Market research techniques, including surveys, questionnaires, interviews, test marketing.
- The assessment of customer requirements.

Internal assessment is at both levels and guidance and advice can be found at the end of this chapter.

Marketing is one of the main functional areas of an organisation. It is an important part of any business, whether in the private or public sector. What marketing means to a business depends very much on its size and type. It is one of the main strategic areas of the business, and how successful the marketing is directly influences how successful the business is.

To understand what marketing is, we first have to understand what a market is. A market is a place where buyers and sellers meet to exchange goods and services for money. The simplest form of market is the local market where local producers bring their produce to sell. Your city or town may have a weekly or monthly market, like the farmers' market in Perth where farmers can bring their produce to sell directly to the public.

At this market the farmers can quickly find out what sells best, and by talking to customers they can find out what else their customers like, and what else they would like to buy at the market. Here the buyers and sellers are meeting face to face, talking about products. The information the farmers get can be used by them to better meet the needs of their consumers.

Large manufacturers rarely get the chance to meet their customers face to face, or to discuss what products they would like to see, or what changes they would like to see from their products. This problem led to the introduction of marketing as a function of modern business.

Marketing is communication between the producers and the consumers who under normal circumstances would never meet face to face. Modern marketing has been described by the Chartered Institute of Marketing as the process involved in identifying, anticipating and satisfying consumer requirements profitably.

IDENTIFYING

What does the consumer want from a good or service in terms of price, features, quality, colours, delivery, packaging, image, after-sales service, etc? This involves communicating with the consumer in order to best meet their needs. If the company gets it right, a sale will take place; if it gets it wrong, there will be no sale.

ANTICIPATING

Products can take a number of years to develop, so meeting the customer's needs now is no guarantee of success in the future. Business have to try to anticipate what consumers will want in one, two, three, four or five years' time, depending on how long it takes to develop the new product. A new model of a car can take five years and billions of pounds to develop, so it is essential that the car is one that will meet customers' needs. Again, this involves communicating with the consumer.

However, sometimes the consumer is totally unaware of what they will be buying in the future. Who could have guessed that teenagers would see a mobile phone as an essential survival item five years ago? The marketing departments of the mobile phone manufacturers and network operators did.

SATISFYING

The business must produce the right product, at the right price, at the right time, otherwise the customer will simply buy a competitor's product. There are always alternatives that the customer can buy if your product is not available, or at the wrong price. So if you get it wrong, you lose sales.

QUESTION

Q1 Why is marketing important to organisations?

BUSINESS DECISION AREAS

Strategic decisions usually involve marketing, so it can be described as a strategic activity of the organisation. For example, to increase market share you have to get customers to buy more of your product, and to buy less of your competitors' product. Marketing is the tool that will be used to achieve this.

CASE STUDY   The tea industry

Tea Board India, the state agency that represents the tea industry in India, has just launched a global marketing push with the strategic aim of boosting exports by about 50% within five years. Exports of tea from India have fallen to an all-time low, and India's traditional dominance of the world tea market has been eroded. The UK has increasingly turned to cheaper sources of supply such as Indonesia and Vietnam which are lower-cost producers.

Market research shows that tea consumption has fallen from 46 grammes per person in 1989 to 32 grammes in 2002, although it is still the UK's most popular drink, with 40% of the market. However, tea consumers tend to be older people, who will not be replaced by younger drinkers.

The tea industry has decided not to spend a lot of money on advertising but to concentrate on special promotions to create a strong image for its tea. It has recognised that it cannot compete on price so instead is concentrating on dominating the top-quality segment of the market. To do this it has signed co-operation deals with retailers including Harrods, Fortnum and Mason and Selfridges, using Indian-themed events. It plans to open a dedicated Indian tea bar at the Savoy Hotel in London. The hope is that by using these upmarket venues, the product will acquire a glamour status that will eventually lead to increased sales in supermarkets.

The industry hopes to position tea in the market as a soothingly natural product, with advertising shifting to emphasise tea's health-giving properties. It has no calories, is rich in heart-boosting oxidants, and is even supposed to be good for your teeth.

The success of the campaign will be decided by how well it overcomes the problem of being an ageing market, with most people now in too much of a hurry to bother making tea properly, with consumers much more focused on convenience and instant gratification. Britons see tea as just another hot drink, although the recent resurgence of coffee, through the national chains of coffee shops, may make this campaign successful as consumers look for a successor to the now-declining coffee shop culture.

The industry has now started to produce a wider range of tea products with flavoured teas, decaffinated tea and even single-estate teas.

QUESTION
2

Describe how the information on the tea industry highlights the main functional areas of marketing:

- market research
- product development
- pricing
- distribution
- promotion and advertising.

TOPIC ONE: The objectives of marketing

Using marketing, organisations hope to achieve a number of objectives which are essential for success.

TO INCREASE SALES REVENUE AND PROFITABILITY

Sales revenue is the money that the business receives from the sales that it makes. Using marketing to increase sales can increase the profitability of the business, provided that the additional money more than covers the increase in marketing and production costs.

TO INCREASE OR MAINTAIN MARKET SHARE

Your competitors will use marketing, so if you fail to do so then they will increase their market share at the expense of yours. Successful marketing will not only increase or maintain your market share but may also increase the size of the market, attracting new customers, rather than just taking existing buyers from your competitors. So market share and market growth must both be considered.

TO MAINTAIN OR IMPROVE THE IMAGE OF THE BUSINESS, ITS BRAND OR ITS PRODUCT

Marketing can be used to convince consumers of the quality of a product.

 **Volkswagen**

When Volkswagen bought Skoda it had to deal with the very poor image that Skoda had. It used the very successful Volkswagen image successfully to change the public's perception of Skoda. Even now, the previously poor image of Skoda is used in its advertising, with the person taking the test drive jumping out of the car and running away as soon as they realised they could be seen in a Skoda.

 You can see the adverts and get the history of Skoda at
www.Skoda.co.uk

TO TARGET A NEW MARKET OR A NEW SEGMENT OF THE MARKET

Marketing can be used to enter new markets with their products, or to enter new segments of the market. Mobile phones were originally designed for business use, however, as they became cheaper to make and use, marketing was switched towards young people, with a great deal of success.

TO DEVELOP NEW AND IMPROVED PRODUCTS

Production of new and better products is one of the functions of marketing. This is vital for the success of many businesses. Pencil makers may not need to spend a huge amount of time and effort in product development, however businesses like Sony put a great deal of emphasis on developing new ideas and products.

Describe the main objectives of marketing.

TOPIC TWO: Types of markets

There are two main types of market – **consumer** markets, which we are in and are very familiar with, and **industrial** markets, where other organisations purchase goods and services in order to produce other goods and services.

Consumer markets are made up of individuals who buy goods or services for their own personal or domestic use. The products that they buy can be classified into three major types.

- **Convenience goods, or non-durable goods, are products that we normally use only once, and then have to replace on a regular basis, such as newspapers and magazines, foodstuffs and toiletries.**

- **Shopping goods, or durable goods, are longer-lasting and need to be replaced only after a number of years. Cars, washing machines and televisions are examples of durable goods.**

- **Speciality goods are things like cosmetics, fashion items and speciality cars.**

The goods and services bought on the **industrial** market can be similar to those in the consumer markets. For example, consumers use banking services and so do businesses, however industrial goods will also include plant and machinery, raw materials, consumable supplies and business services.

TOPIC THREE: Product orientation

A product-orientated business is one that concentrates on the production process and the product itself, rather than trying to establish what it is that the consumer wants. For example, it may focus on trying to improve the efficiency of its production or to produce goods which are far more advanced in terms of their technology.

It is the basic idea or novelty value of the product that would sell it. When home computer systems were first produced in the UK it was the technical wonder of the product that sold them. There were few companies to compete against each other, and there was a growing domestic market. There were also few overseas competitors. The product sold itself.

Some industries are still product-orientated. A firm operating at the edge of innovation, such as bio-technology, pharmaceuticals or electronics, must innovate to survive. Although businesses may have a final product in mind in anticipation of consumer demand, the research is often 'pure' research – the researcher does not have a specific end product in mind. The research is being done to find out what is possible. Many of the most modern products on the market today are the result of research carried out for the US space programme.

Concorde is a good example of a product-orientated product. The development of the aircraft was carried out between the UK and France to see if it was technically possible and for political co-operation between the two countries. Although Concorde achieved its aim of being the first and only successful large civilian passenger plane capable of supersonic flight, it did not sell. Only British Airways and Air France, both of which were government owned at the time, bought them, so it never recovered the development costs. The same could be said for the Channel Tunnel which is unlikely ever to pay off its development and construction costs.

TOPIC FOUR: Market orientation

 A market-orientated business continually identifies, reviews and analyses consumers' needs. Consumers are central to the firm's decision-making. They are also sometimes known as customer-orientated businesses. Products are developed in response to changing consumer needs.

 **Sony Walkman**

The Sony Walkman was conceived after market research revealed that people wanted music they could listen to as they travelled, without disturbing anyone else. The engineers at Sony were then given an empty box the size of the Walkman and told to come up with something that played music and could be used with earphones that would not be too obvious. Nothing like this existed beforehand, and new technologies had to be developed in order to come up with the product.

 **QUESTION Q4**

Explain why it is likely that product-orientated organisations are likely to be less successful in modern markets.

TOPIC FIVE: The role of marketing

Individual organisations will have different marketing needs. Organisations in the private sector will use marketing to make profits on what they sell; on the other hand, organisations in the public sector, such as your local council, will use marketing in order to try to provide the best services they can to the local community.

They may use market research to find out what the community needs are; they will advertise their services through their own publications and at their various offices and sometimes local post offices. They will develop new services if market research shows that the community wants them. The council will be driven by the councillors' need to satisfy their voters and the need to meet the legal requirements of national government.

Small businesses' marketing needs are very different from those of big businesses. For example, the local corner shop would not need to worry too much about marketing because it continually meets its customers face to face, and so has direct communication with them. It may offer promotions or discounts from time to time in order to keep customers, or it may advertise its opening times in the local paper, but generally its marketing will be very limited.

Big businesses are unlikely to meet their customers, so they will rely heavily on marketing to keep communicating with their customers.

It will also depend on how many customers a business has. For example, an organisation operating in the industrial markets may have only a few big customers, so they will keep in close contact with them.

PRODUCTS

There are two main types of product that an organisation can produce – **goods** and **services**.

Goods

These are products that we can see and touch. They may be durable (like mobile phones, televisions and motor cars), i.e. things that we can use again and again, or they may be non-durable (such as burgers, stamps or a newspaper).

Services

These are things that are done for us. We cannot see them but we should feel some benefit for having used them. Banking and finance, tourism, insurance and education are some of Scotland's biggest employers, and these are all services.

Some goods come with services. Using the examples from the goods above, mobile phones need the services of a network operator to be of any use; Sky provides satellite and digital services so that we can be entertained; burgers are produced using the services of a fast food outlet, and Royal Mail will deliver your letters.

QUESTION

Q5 Describe the difference between goods and services, giving examples of each.

 MARKET SHARE

A market is made up of all the consumers and producers, buying and selling a product. For example the market for mobile phones includes all the manufacturers such as Nokia and Motorola, all the network operators such as Vodafone and Orange, and all the consumers who buy and use mobile phones.

For the manufacturers, their share of the market will be the percentage of all users with one of their phones; for the networks, their market share will be the percentage of users connected to their network.

The businesses involved in the market will be continually trying to keep or increase their market share. For the networks, this means that they will have more customers, and so will make more sales which should make them more profitable.

CASE STUDY — Nokia

In the mobile phone market Finland's mobile phone group Nokia is the market leader, with 35% of the market in 2001 compared with 30.6% of the market from a year earlier. The nearest rival is US manufacturer Motorola, with 14.8%, up just 0.2% from the previous year.

For an alternative view on market share visit
www.bbc.co.uk/dna/h2g2/alabster/A668630

MARKET GROWTH

In increasing its market share a business will increase its sales at the expense of those of one of its competitors, however firms can also increase their sales if the whole market grows. Market growth takes place when the number of people buying or using the product increases.

CASE STUDY — Mobile phone market

The mobile phone market enjoyed an average growth rate of 60% every year between 1996 and 2000. However, in 2001 the total world sales of mobile phones fell for the first time, to just under 400 million, down 3.2% compared with the previous year. One of the main reasons was that the European markets had become saturated. Other factors included the removal of subsidies by phone makers which used to sell handsets at marked-down prices.

QUESTION Q6

Explain what you understand by the terms market share **and** market growth.

TOPIC SIX: Influence of the government on marketing

Like most areas of business, marketing is subject to government legislation, and this has to be taken into consideration when making marketing decisions. You would be unhappy if you spent money on a product that didn't work, or didn't do what it was supposed to do, or was unsafe. You would also be unhappy if you felt you were 'conned' by the advertising that made you buy the product in the first place.

THE TRADE DESCRIPTIONS ACT

The goods or services which consumers buy must do what the advertising claims they can do. For example, cosmetics and medicines must be clinically proven to achieve what is claimed of them.

MONOPOLIES AND MERGERS ACT

A monopoly is in theory a market where only one firm exists to serve the whole market. This would give the firm tremendous market power to charge what it liked and provide only what services it would like.

For example, until the market was opened to competition, BT was the only national telephone company in this country. It had complete monopoly power. The government put legislation in place to make sure that BT was controlled in terms of pricing and services, until such times as national competitors arrived.

Although there are no real monopolies left, some businesses are so big that they dominate the market and so have some monopoly powers in terms of pricing, and in terms of what is sold on the market. The Act works to limit the power of these businesses for the benefit of consumers.

FAIR TRADING AND COMPETITION ACTS

Fair trading and competition Acts try to ensure that no businesses work to prevent competition in the market. Competition is thought of as being healthy for the market and for consumers, driving down prices and giving consumers a wider choice.

CONSUMER PROTECTION LAWS

Consumer protection Acts work to ensure that the products that we buy are safe. They set minimum standards of safety for things like car tyres and furniture. They also ensure that a business is liable for any damage which its defective goods may cause to a consumer.

To find out more about fair trading and consumer protection, visit
www.dti.gov.uk/for_consumers.html

CODE OF ADVERTISING PRACTICE

Any business undertaking advertising must conform to the British Code of Advertising Practice. This states that adverts must be legal, honest and truthful and not cause offence. The ITC (the Independent Television Commission) controls advertising on television and radio.

CASE STUDY — ITC

In 2000 the ITC received complaints from 49 viewers about IKEA's television adverts. The complaints were about the fact that IKEA used infidelity, marriage break-up and the start of a gay affair in the campaign. The ITC rejected the complaints, saying that, although it acknowledged that the adverts may have upset or distressed a number of viewers, they would be considered generally acceptable by many others.

To get more information on the work that the ITC does, visit
www.itc.org.uk

The Advertising Standards Authority is a voluntary body set up by advertisers and marketing companies to monitor advertising in the UK.

QUESTION

Q7

Describe the governmental constraints placed on marketing.

TOPIC SEVEN: The marketing environment

The government is one of the external factors which affect marketing. The marketing environment is made up of the following:

- the government
- competition
- technology
- the economy
- consumer trends and behaviour.

These factors must be taken into account and considered when making any marketing decisions.

COMPETITION

All markets are subject to some competition, either directly or indirectly, from what we call close substitutes. Consumers can substitute one good or service for another.

For example, ScotRail has the franchise for rail travel in Scotland, however it is in competition with the bus companies for many of the same routes.

Some markets have only a few big producers, such as the soft drinks market, where the biggest producers are Coca Cola, Pepsi, Cadbury Schweppes and Barr's. There are a lot of local producers of soft drinks, but they generally have a very limited and local market share. Other markets have many producers, such as the market for electrical goods, where there is a huge choice of different manufacturers.

The number of manufacturers does not always decide how competitive the market is. For example, the market for televisions was very un-competitive during the 1980s and 1990s as the manufacturers managed to keep prices high through anti-competitive practises such as only supplying shops which would guarantee not to reduce prices.

In order to sell in competitive markets the manufacturer's product must have something that makes the customer decide to buy their product rather than that of one of their competitors. This is called a **unique selling proposition** (USP). To do this, the manufacturer must be continually offering new and improved products at prices the consumer is willing to pay.

Some modern marketing experts believe that a USP is difficult to obtain and maintain with so much competition in the market. No sooner is it achieved than it is lost. They believe that much more important is the **emotional selling proposition** (ESP) – 'Do I like you?' Here, it is believed that consumers will respond emotionally to product and brands, sticking with what they like and trust, making it difficult to get them to switch brands.

QUESTION

Q8

What do **the terms** unique selling proposition **and** emotional selling proposition mean?

TECHNOLOGY

The continuing development of technology means that in order to at least keep up with the competition or to gain some competitive advantage, organisations have to use the very latest technology available.

In the home computer market, advances are being made at such a fast rate that new models can be issued within a few months of the previous model being launched on the market. It is now likely that new computers will come with a specification far in excess of what will be needed for home use for the foreseeable future. However, manufacturers see this as the only way to keep ahead of the competition.

The introduction of more and more sophisticated production methods will allow for higher quality, faster and cheaper production. New technology has allowed far better communications and made more information available to consumers.

Market research

Market research has become far more sophisticated, with the introduction of new information and communications technology. Microelectronics in Scotland is an organisation (set up in June 1999) to double the size of the microelectronics and semi-conductor industry in the country within five years. It has not been successful but it does provide links to market research partners who use the most up-to-date ICT market research, analysis and decision-making.

Visit them at
www.microelectronics.org.uk

The Internet and the saturation usage of mobile phones allow businesses new ways to tap into new markets for their products.

ECONOMIC FORCES

The economy has a major influence on consumer behaviour and on organisational behaviour. During times of economic growth and high confidence, consumers will be willing to spend more money and will feel more confident about their job security. Organisations will spend more on developing and marketing new products. During recession, consumers will spend less and organisations will tend to concentrate on reducing production costs and prices.

CHAPTER:Five

TOPIC SEVEN

When interest rates are high, borrowing becomes more expensive so consumers are less likely to buy the high-value, high-cost products, while organisations will attempt to reduce borrowing and make offers like interest-free credit in order to attract sales.

Exchange rates will affect imports and exports, as when the value of the pound is high foreign goods and services will become cheaper for consumers, and Scottish manufacturers will find their products more difficult to export. When the pound's value is low then UK goods become more attractive in terms of price.

CONSUMERS

Demographics

Demographics is the study of the structure of the population, in terms of age, gender, household income, buying patterns and lifestyle. It is very important for marketing because it gives the manufacturers a great deal of information about their customers, and their potential customers.

A vast range of information on demographics is available. Market research companies and the government constantly update their statistics, some of which is free, however the most up-to-date and most detailed information usually has to be paid for.

 You can access free statistics for students from **www.areadata.co.uk/freedata.htm**

The following table shows some of the information taken from the available data:

AREA	AGE	NUMBER	FEMALE (%)	% OF TOTAL POPULATION
Grampian	0–4	33,919	48.9	6.3
	5–9	34,122	49.2	6.4
	10–14	34,180	48.6	6.4
Central Clydeside	0–4	94,551	48.7	6.2
	5–9	102,237	48.7	6.4
	10–14	102,776	49.1	6.4

(Source: BMRB International 1999)

Age

What we can see from the table is that the number of children being born is reducing in both areas. The fall in Central Clydeside is very high for 0–4-year-olds. So what does this mean for marketing? First, the size of the market for goods and services for children is shrinking. Market growth will be difficult without introducing new or improved products. There will be less demand for education and health services, children's clothes, toys, etc.

Other data show that there is an increase in the number of people aged 65 and over. Demand for services in this area is increasing, particularly in health, leisure activities, holidays and financial services.

UNIT 2

Gender

The data above also show that more males then females are being born (good news for the girls!). As males and females have different buying patterns, this will be of concern for marketing professionals as it indicates that goods and services for males will form a bigger market than for females.

Household income

The make-up of households has changed dramatically in recent years. Far more people are living on their own, leading to a growth in the market for convenience goods for single-person households. There are many more one-parent families, and combined families where couples who are divorced set up home with the children from both previous marriages. Each of these factors leads to different or new demands for goods and services.

At the same time, the disposable income (income left after tax) of families has greatly increased. This has led to a big increase in demand for clothes, holidays, DIY, cars, leisure and furnishings.

Another major change in households is the increasing number of women who are working, many of whom would previously have been classified as housewives. They obviously have less time to spend on household chores and so this has led to growth in demand for convenience foods, child-care services, labour-saving devices and more flexible shopping hours, such as supermarkets opening 24 hours a day.

It is becoming more common for men to stay at home and become 'house-husbands', and this has led to changes such as TV companies taking this into account when drawing up the schedules for day-time television.

Location

Consumers living in different parts of the country will have different needs and spending patterns. For example, those living in the rural areas of Scotland will have to spend much more on travel, and will have to spend more of their disposable income on food, as supermarkets in rural areas tend to be more expensive. Different parts of Scotland have different weather patterns which will lead to different house types, clothing, diet, etc.

Social class

Although marketing professionals categorise consumers by their disposable income, they also split the population into six general classifications, as this tends to reflect their spending more accurately. The reason for this is that people tend to have similar interests and tastes within these broad classifications.

The classifications are:

Classification	General description and examples
A	Upper or upper middle – Senior Managerial/Professional – Company Director, Surgeon, Professor.
B	Middle – Intermediate Managerial/Professional – Bank Manager, Head Teacher, Accountant, Lawyer.
C1	Lower Middle – Supervisory – Shop Manager, Bank Clerk, Sales Representative, Nurse.

C2	Skilled Working – Electrician, Heating Engineer, Mechanic.
D	Working – Semi-skilled – Machine Operator, Slater, Driver, Call-Centre Worker.
E	Lowest Subsistence Level – Unskilled, Low Paid – Cleaner, Porter.

So although an electrician can earn a lot more than a bank clerk in some cases, their spending patterns will be more likely to match those within their social classification than those on the same income level.

Lifestyle, taste and fashion

Consumers' lifestyle affects what products they buy. For example, those who are interested in a healthy lifestyle will be much more conscious of what they eat and drink, and of exercise. They are far more likely to buy organic produce; eat less fast food, sweets, and high sugar-content drinks; they will be far more likely to buy bikes, sports equipment and clothes.

Those who are concerned with environmental issues will opt for products that suit their beliefs. They will only buy dolphin-friendly tuna; they are far more likely to use bikes and public transport; and use only ozone-friendly aerosols. They will try to use energy-saving products like solar energy or wind turbines.

Those who are concerned with their own self-image will be very interested in fashions. They will look for the most up-to-date clothing, house decoration, mobile phones, etc.

Personality

Consumers' personality will dictate what products they will be interested in buying. Extroverts are more concerned about getting themselves noticed and will opt for products that make them stand out from the crowd, such as unusual clothing. Introverted consumers are much more concerned with fitting in and will tend to buy well-known brands in an attempt to be more socially acceptable. All consumers have one of these traits to a greater or lesser extent and so marketing based on personality types can be successful.

Political

Many consumers have strong political views and this will influence their purchases. Newspapers support different political parties, so consumers will buy a newspaper that most agrees with their own politics.

QUESTION

Q9 What are the main factors that affect the buying decisions of consumers?

BUSINESS DECISION AREAS

TOPIC EIGHT: Target markets

Marketing is a major cost for many businesses, so it is important that it is effective in communicating with the consumers who may buy their product.

UNDIFFERENTIATED (MASS) MARKETING

Some products appeal to the majority of consumers and so marketing is directed at all consumers, the whole market. An example could be milk, which appeals to consumers of all ages, gender, income groups, etc. It is seen by many as an essential item, so the Scottish Milk Marketing Board does not need to spend too much on advertising.

Another example is the Mars Bar. Although young people tend to buy more sweets, older people also enjoy them, and with Scotland having a very high consumption rate of sugar and fat-based foods, advertising tends to be based on beating the competition rather than trying to convince people they will enjoy them.

Undifferentiated marketing is where one product is sold to the entire market. There tend to be very high-volume sales, so the manufacturers involved tend to benefit from economies of scale. There tends to be a lot of competition in the market, with Mars competing with Cadbury and Nestlé for the same snack-sized chocolate bar.

DIFFERENTIATED MARKETING

This is when businesses offer different products to different groups within the total market. This is done by altering products to suit the different needs of different consumers.

 **ScotRail**

ScotRail offers train services across Scotland, however it charges different prices for the same journey for different people. Cheaper fares are available off-peak which will appeal to older and younger people who may have no need to travel at peak times. First and Second Class compartments are available on some journeys so that those who want to travel in more comfort can do so.

MARKET SEGMENTATION

Businesses are able to use differentiated marketing by using market segmentation. This is when the whole market is split into different groups who will have similar wants and needs and so a business can produce goods and services specifically for that group. In doing so it can more closely meet the needs of those customers, and so is more likely to make a sale. The marketing can be targeted at those who are most likely to want to pay for the product and so costs can be reduced. Businesses can dominate specialist parts of the market for their product, which should lead to higher sales, and so increase the businesses' profitability.

How a business can identify these segments of the market depends very much on the product it has for sale. It may be based on the tastes or preferences of consumers. For example, Scottish country dancing appeals mostly to females, but of various age ranges. This does not mean that it will appeal to all females, however, producers of dancing shoes are more likely to advertise in publications which women read, or more specifically in any publication available for Scottish country dancing, or concerned with Scottish country pursuits.

Using the example of targeted publications, we can look at the other ways the market can be segmented, for example by age – *Smash Hits*; by gender – *Heat*; by socio–economic group – *The Daily Record*; by education level – *The Scotsman*; by income – *Ski Monthly*. Other ways it can be split is by the structure of the household, by geographical location, or by religion.

NICHE MARKETING

Niche marketing involves a business aiming a product at a particular, often very small, segment of the market, where the consumers' needs and wants can be clearly identified. It can be a local market or a small national market.

CASE STUDY — **Niche marketing**

An example could be Auld's of Greenock who manufacture bakery products, and are well known for their Scotch pies; however, they attempt to meet the demands of a local market in the west central belt of Scotland. Another is Mackie's ice-cream which manufactures a variety of high-quality ice-creams in Aberdeenshire. Its products sell very well in the local national supermarket chains even though they come with a much higher price than well-known UK brands.

Visit Mackie's at
www.mackies.co.uk

The advantages involved in niche marketing are that you can take advantage of small markets that will have been overlooked or ignored by other firms, and so you are able to avoid competition in the short term. You can focus on the needs of consumers in these segments which will give you an advantage over businesses which target the wider market. In the case of Mackie's it has been producing its quality ice-cream in volume since before Haagen Dazs or Ben and Jerry's entered the Scottish market.

The disadvantages of niche marketing are that if the business is successful it may attract competition. Niche markets are often too small to accommodate two or more firms in competition. Large national firms deciding to enter the niche market can often force other businesses out. Secondly, as niche markets contain small numbers of consumers, they tend to be faced by bigger and more frequent swings in consumer spending than larger markets.

QUESTION
Q10 Describe how differentiated marketing can be more effective than undifferentiated marketing.

TOPIC NINE: The marketing mix

In order to market or sell its product successfully, a business must develop a strategy based on four key elements – **product**, **price**, **place** and **promotion**. Together, these elements are called the four Ps. How these elements are combined in the marketing strategy is called the **marketing mix**.

PRODUCT

The good or service which the business is trying to sell must be one that the customers want, and are willing and able to buy. The product tends to be the most important element of the marketing mix as it determines what the price will be, how it is promoted and where it is sold.

For example, a top fashion designer will not sell their garments for a low price, they will not advertise in the *Sunday Post*, nor will they allow their products to be sold in Poundstretcher. The garments will have a very high price, promotion will be through the major fashion shows, and they will sell them themselves, directly to clients.

Each product will have to satisfy a basic need of the consumer if it is to be sold. For example, the basic function of clothing is to keep you warm. Any clothing that satisfies this need is called the **core product**. However, if all we wanted from clothing was something to keep us warm we would simply buy the cheapest and most effective clothing that serves this basic need.

Very few consumers purchase clothes in this way. What we actually buy meets a whole range of needs – to make us feel good, to be comfortable, to look good, to fit in or to make a statement, and to suit the various social or work activities. This is what we call the **product concept**.

Most product markets tend to be very competitive, so businesses continually try to add new features to the product or its packaging in order to make their product more attractive to the customer. The product with the additional features is called the **augmented product**.

Washing powder manufacturers

There are only two major washing powder manufacturers: Unilever and Procter and Gamble, however they are very competitive. Initially, they competed by having a wide range of powders under different brand names, but eventually they competed by augmenting their products to make them more attractive to their customers. They brought out liquid detergent, then concentrated liquid detergent, then liquid combined with fabric softener, then tablets, then tablets with a bag, then stain digesters, etc. Each change to the product either added a new feature or tried to be more convenient to use for the consumer.

What decides whether or not the consumer thinks the product is desirable will be how well it meets their needs in terms of its basic function, plus the features which make it attractive, which may include reliability, value for money, design, image, status and quality. The quality of the product will reflect the quality the consumer expects from the product. A Rolex watch will have a very different level of quality from a Swatch watch, however both may be successful in meeting their own customers' requirements.

Other features which can influence the consumer to buy your product include credit/finance facilities, after-sales service, manuals and guarantees.

QUESTION
Q11
Describe the difference between the core and augmented product.

The product line

Most businesses produce a range of products which have similar uses and have similar characteristics.

Cadbury produces a huge range of chocolate-based products, most of which are very well known, from the basic product of 'Dairy Milk Chocolate' to all the other sweets that have been developed for different tastes and occasions, e.g. Cadbury's Creme Egg.

See Cadbury's full range at
www.cadburyschweppes.com

The **benefits** involved in having a product line are:

● It spreads the risks. If the market for one product fails, then the organisation has many other products to fall back on.

● It gives the consumers the impression that the organisation is a specialist producer in that particular line of products.

● It allows new products to be launched with existing customers at least willing to try them.

There are a number of possible **disadvantages** to having a product line:

● Bad publicity for one product could affect the sales of other products.

● Operations within the business can become very complicated, with lots of different machinery and processes needed for each of the different products.

Most businesses will see their product lines grow over time. For example, Mackie's ice-cream now comes with a wide variety of added ingredients including whisky, and more recently it has added organic ice-cream to the range. Firms tend to add new lines in order to make more profits, or if their product line is too long, profitability may be increased by dropping products.

The product range (mix)

The product range is the combination of the different **types** of product that a business manufactures and sells.

CASE STUDY — Nestlé

Nestlé's product range includes beverages (Nescafé, Perrier); chocolate and confectionery (Kit Kat, Fruit Pastilles); milk products and ice-cream (Carnation, Petits Pots, Maxibon); prepared dishes (Findus, Buitoni); cat and dog food (Friskies); and pharmaceutical products (Opti-clean).

As with the product line, having a wide range of products spreads the risk for the business, but here the company is operating a number of different industries, so is not relying on one industry.

QUESTION

Q12 Describe the benefits for a business of having a range of products.

The product life cycle

It is said that a product has a natural 'lifespan' through which it passes until it is withdrawn from the market. For some goods or services it is easy to see, for example the Sega Dreamcast is now being withdrawn from the market as competitors' products are seen as much better. For others, it does not seem to be true. Barr's 'Irn Bru' is still very popular after more than 50 years on the market.

It may be that some products have a much longer lifespan than others or that the manufacturer has been very successful in using **extension strategies** to prolong the life of the product. However, all products do go through a number of distinct phases:

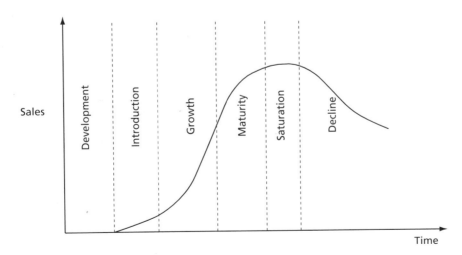

IMAGE 19.
Product life cycle

The **development** stage is when the product will start its life. A large number of products will never progress past this stage, perhaps as much as 80%. There are a number of reasons for this. It may be found that it is impossible to make at a cost which will allow sufficient profit from the price consumers would be willing to pay, or management may decide that the risk in entering the market is too great.

Development is essential for most businesses in order to bring out new or improved products, however the costs involved can be very high. The Ford Mondeo took six years and $6 billion for research and development, market research, and start-up costs such as setting up plants with new machinery.

If the business decides to go ahead at this stage then, as there have been no sales, the product will initially make a loss for the organisation.

Before launching the product on to the whole market, the business may decide to **test-market** the product. This is part of the organisation's market research. The product is launched to a small segment of the market to see how it reacts. The organisation will quite often use one television area, such as Grampian TV, as the launch can be backed up with appropriate advertising on television and the local press.

Modifications can be made to the product as a result of consumers' reaction to it, prior to the launch on the whole market. Choosing the correct market for testing is very important, for example Yorkshire TV area has very similar characteristics in the proportion of age, gender, class, etc, to the whole of the UK, so it is often used for test marketing.

At the beginning of the **introduction** stage the product is launched onto the market. Heavy advertising spending is necessary at this stage as consumers are generally unaware of the product and will have loyalty to other products or brands. Sales are slow and the selling price at this stage does not cover the development and start-up costs so losses are usually made on sales. How long this stage last varies between products. A new chocolate bar will have a fairly short introduction stage, however a new technical product will take some time before consumers feel confident that the product works and is superior to the others on the market. Such was the case with the Dyson vacuum cleaner. Although it is now the market leader, consumers took some time to decide that such an expensive machine was worth the additional cost.

During the **growth** stage consumers become more aware of the product and sales start to grow rapidly. It is during this stage that the product begins to become profitable.

As the product reaches the **maturity** stage its sales reach their peak. This is the highest level of sales that the product will achieve without the business taking some action. Spending on advertising will be much less as the product is fully established on the market, and any advertising will be aimed at maintaining sales levels rather than making consumers aware of the product.

At this stage all the development costs should have been repaid, and the product will be at its most profitable. These profits can then be used in part to fund development of new products. The business will work to keep the product in this stage for as long as possible. This can be done by using extension strategies.

Eventually, all products will reach the **decline** stage. Sales and profits will start to fall, and the business's new replacement products should be in the growth stage. Life cycles are becoming shorter, especially in industries that are based on new technology. For example, new computer models tend to last for no more than six months to a year, by which time new specifications from competitors have led to a rapid reduction in sales.

As we have already seen, sales of mobile phones have already started to decline slightly. Although this is still a highly profitable business, if the mobile phone companies wish to remain in business they will have to create a new demand for mobile phones.

QUESTION

Q13 Describe the Product Life Cycle referring to Costs, Sales, and Profits at each stage.

Extension strategies

These are the methods employed by businesses to prolong the life of their products and stop them going into the decline stage. The most successful extension strategies will actually lead to periods of sales growth.

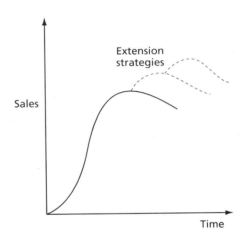

IMAGE 20.
Extension strategies

PROMOTING MORE FREQUENT USE OF THE PRODUCT

Perhaps the most obvious way of achieving this would be by reducing the price. For mobile phones, this could mean reducing the costs of making phone calls or receiving e-mail and text messages. This would be risky, however the success of low cost airlines such as Easyjet, Ryan Air, Buzz, etc. has been based on the fact that they can offer much lower air fares. Air travel was suffering from slow growth for many years prior to the introduction of these services.

DEVELOPING NEW MARKETS FOR EXISTING PRODUCTS

Mobile phones and computers were both originally manufactured for the business market. However, they both managed to achieve huge growth in sales by selling to the home market.

FINDING NEW USES FOR EXISTING PRODUCTS

A classic example here is in the market for fire-lighters. As consumers switched to gas and electric heating, demand for the product fell. A new market was found in the growth of the use of barbecues. Manufacturers were able to switch their attention to this new market.

DEVELOP A WIDER RANGE OF PRODUCTS

Introducing new versions of the same product can develop new interest from consumers, and can also generate new interest in the original product.

The traditional 'Irn Bru' bottle has been added to with a range of can and bottle sizes and fruit chews, and has even entered the 'alco-pop' market.

By simply introducing a slightly different product, manufacturers can stimulate new sales growth.

Football clubs in Scotland generate much-needed income by introducing new strips each season which they can then sell to their fans.

A successful advertising campaign can stimulate a short-term extension to the product's life, however it will be much more effective to combine the advertising with one of the above.

QUESTION Q14
Identify the life cycle extension strategies available to an organisation.

IMAGE 21.
Product portfolio

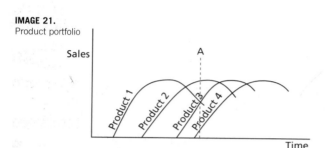

At point A:
Product 1 - decline phase	• Profit levels remain steady
Product 2 - maturity phase	• Risk spread across product range
Product 3 - growth phase	• Profitable product support
Product 4 - introduction phase	• Launch of new product

Product portfolio

It does not make sense for a business to wait until its product goes into decline before launching a replacement. Sales and profits would be lost, so businesses plan the introduction of new products to replace existing ones before they become unprofitable. The range of products that a business produces is known as its product portfolio.

Each of the products in the portfolio will be at a different stage in its life cycle. This allows the business to spread its investment across a range of products, thereby reducing the level of risk.

By having a portfolio of products at different stages in the life cycle, profit levels can be relatively stable making the business easier to manage, and the most profitable products can support the development and launch of new products.

Sony has a huge product range including televisions, VCRs, DVD players, cassette players, CD players, digi-tape, Mini-disc players, digital cameras, cam-corders, etc. Its televisions are constantly being replaced with new and improved models with extra features.

IMAGE 22.
Well known brands

Branding

Branding can be a very successful marketing tool, and is widely used by businesses to create USPs (unique selling propositions) and ESPs (emotional selling propositions). The business chooses a word or symbol, or both, then registers them so that they can only be used on its products. It then designs a marketing strategy to distinguish its products from all other similar products by using this brand. Baxter's, Oxo, Cadbury's and Heinz are all well-known brand names. Using branding you can create a form of **product differentiation**.

UNIT 2

BENEFITS OF BRANDING

A well-known brand allows for instant recognition of the product by the customer. The colours used by Cadbury make their products easy to identify, even from a distance. This makes it easier for the buyer to choose that brand from amongst a range of very similar products.

Because the consumer knows, trusts and likes that brand, they will have brand loyalty which will lead them to buy that product again and again – repeat purchases. This leads to a stable level of demand for the product, which is good for the manufacturer and the retailer. For the manufacturer, it allows for better production planning.

Because of the level of trust the consumer has, it is very difficult to get them to change brands, or experiment with new brands. We do not like to spend money on things we may not like. Consumers believe that the product will be better than its competitors, and so the manufacturer can charge premium (higher) prices.

DRAWBACKS OF BRANDING

It takes a great deal of time to establish a brand. During this time, promotion costs will be high, and even after it is established it is necessary to keep promoting to maintain brand visibility.

Whilst the business can quickly launch new products successfully under the brand name, a single bad event, with bad publicity, can affect the whole range of same-brand products.

You have to be able to protect your brand name world-wide, and this can often be difficult with huge markets producing 'fake' products. These imitators are very difficult to stop and legal actions against the imitators can be time-consuming and costly.

Manufacturers such as Burberry, Rolex and Calvin Klein who can charge premium prices for their products suffer most at the hands of the forgers. They find it almost impossible to prevent the production of 'fake' items, particularly in the Far East. Trading Standards and organisations such as FACT (Federation Against Copyright Theft) spend a lot of time working to prevent the sale of counterfeit goods in Scotland.

Check out how to establish a healthy brand image at
www.bcentral.co.uk/marketing/basics

OWN BRANDS

Most of the major supermarket chains, and many large retailer chains such as Boots, offer a wide range of products under their own brand names. Asda, for example, uses the Smart Price label to sell its own brand of groceries.

Any product that sells in high volume would be considered for own-brand labelling. These retailers have a good reputation for value and/or quality, and their own-brand goods, sitting next to premier brands such as Heinz (who may also make the supermarket's own brand), offer an additional choice to their customers.

Asda does not make any of its own-brand goods; it asks various manufacturers to do it. The advantages for the manufacturer are that they have a guaranteed sales contract with Asda, and they are protected from direct damage should any of the brand products attract bad publicity as it is Asda's name on the label.

Asda has the goods made to its own specification and at its own price. The often cheaper own-brand products attract more customers and more sales within the store. However, they may be seen by consumers as being of lower quality than established brand names ('You get what you pay for'). Some of these own-brand products look very like the real thing. Own-brand colas tend to look very like Coca-Cola in their packaging.

QUESTION Q15

What are the advantages to an organisation of creating a successful brand?

PRICE

Price is important for a number of reasons. First, consumers will only pay what they can afford, and what they think is a reasonable price for the product. Secondly, consumers use price as a measure of quality. A high price would infer high quality, and vice versa, although this is not always the case.

When setting price there are a number of factors which a business should consider. The price of the product will have to cover the costs of production and allow the business to make a reasonable profit in the long run. New products can often sell for a higher price due to their novelty value. For example, VCRs were originally very expensive for what was, compared to now, a very basic model. Today you can buy one for less than £80 which is about a tenth of the price charged when they were introduced, in real terms.

The market price, or the price charged by competitors, must be taken into account, as is how price can be used to increase sales.

Finally, some markets are regulated by the government in terms of price, for example the government wants unleaded petrol to be cheaper then leaded.

Long term pricing strategies

Businesses can adopt a number of different pricing strategies for different markets and different market conditions.

LOW PRICE

A business may decide to charge a price lower than those of competitors where there is price elasticity of demand. This means that consumers respond positively to changes in price, and lower prices will result in much higher sales. It is most appropriate where there is little brand loyalty and competition in the market is high. Supermarkets attract high volume sales of DVDs, CDs and computer games by charging lower than market prices.

MARKET PRICE

Setting your price at the market rate means that your prices are broadly in line with those of competitors. It is usual in markets where price competition does not benefit any of the businesses, such as in the petrol market where there are a few large companies, with very little difference between the competitors' products. Petrol price wars in the past have simply led to one firm cutting the price, just for another to match it, or even better it, the next day. This was good for the consumers but resulted in a loss of profits for the petrol companies and no real change in demand. They tend to compete on things other than price, such as offering air miles.

HIGH PRICE

High price is adopted in the long term by businesses offering high-quality, premium goods and services where image is important, such as in perfumes.

In the short term it can be used for innovative products when they are first introduced to the market, such as recording DVD machines.

Short term pricing strategies

SKIMMING

This involves using a high price initially, usually for a new product where there is little competition. Consumers are willing to pay a high price for the novelty value of the product, however, as more competition enters the market, the price will be lowered.

PENETRATION PRICING

This is usually used in order to introduce a product to an established market, and allows the business to achieve sales and gain market share very quickly. It involves setting a low price, sometimes at a loss, to attract customers to the product in an established market with strong competition. As the product becomes established in the market, the business can increase price.

DESTROYER PRICING

Again, this involves setting a price below those of competitors, but this time at an artificially low price in order to destroy competition. The business will probably be running at a loss in terms of its sales, however as soon as the competition is eliminated the price will return to market price or above. It is often used by established companies to prevent new companies entering the market, however it may be considered anti-competitive by the government and could result in legal action.

PROMOTIONAL PRICING

This is used to boost sales in the short term by lowering the price of the product. It can also be used to create interest in a new product. Supermarkets use promotional pricing for some of their sales lines, as loss leaders. They will advertise the low price for these products, attracting customers into the store in the hope that they will buy a whole range of other goods at the same time.

DEMAND-ORIENTATED PRICING

Here, price varies along with the demand for the product. It is usual in crop markets such as the market for coffee. When the harvest has been poor, successful producers can charge a higher price due to the number of manufacturers chasing a limited supply.

QUESTION

Q16 Describe the various pricing strategies that a business could use.

PLACE

This refers to how the product is taken from the production line and made available to consumers. There are two parts: first the channel of distribution, and second the type of retailer or outlet that will sell your product to the consumer.

The channel of distribution

This is how the product gets to the market. There are a variety of methods that are available to manufacturers. These can involve wholesalers, retailers, agents and importers/exporters, and which, if any, are used depends on the product itself.

WHOLESALER

The wholesaler provides a link between the producer and the retailer and in doing so can provide a good source of market research, marketing information and services for the retailer which will attract sales.

The wholesaler buys in bulk from the retailer and breaks the product down into smaller quantities for the retailer.

For example, it is far cheaper for Cadbury to deliver large quantities of its products to the wholesaler, who will then break up the pallets into smaller boxes which the corner shop will then buy. This leaves Cadbury free to concentrate on production rather than distribution to thousands of small outlets across the whole of the Scotland. Also, it can arrange for delivery of finished products straight to the wholesaler and avoid the cost of storage.

Some wholesalers will finish off the product in terms of packaging and pricing, again reducing the cost to the producer. It should be remembered, however, that the wholesaler will have to make a profit on their activities, which will then add a further cost to the consumer.

The wholesaler has to play their part in the marketing strategy, if they do not promote the product in the way the business wants, they could destroy the business's marketing mix.

RETAILER

The retailer is the local outlet for the business's products, where the consumer can physically buy the goods or services. They offer a variety of goods and services form a variety of producers. They store the goods on their premises, prepare them for sale and display them for sale.

They provide information for consumers through advertising, displays and trained staff. They also offer related services such as credit facilities, hire purchase, after-sales service, guarantees and delivery for large items.

AGENT

Agents attract the customer by carrying out promotional activities, and then sell the product to the consumer. For doing this they take a commission (a percentage of the sales price). Examples are estate agents, travel agents, insurance brokers, etc.

Many smaller car manufacturers use agents to sell their cars in foreign countries. This is because the agent will have a good knowledge of the local market, including any local customs or legal requirements that have to be met.

Importers and exporters play an important role in identifying new or potential markets for products around the world. Their role is similar to that of the agent in that they will have a good knowledge of local markets around the world, and that they can generate sales through their own promotional activities. In many cases they act as retailer as well.

DIRECT SELLING

Of course, the manufacturer can also sell directly to the public. This is common when the manufacturer is a small local business like a baker, who will have their own shop(s) to sell to the public. It is also widely used where products have to be made individually to a customer's specific requirements, as in double glazing; and where the product is highly technical, such as machines which are made for another manufacturer. Direct selling is common in the industrial markets.

Choice of distribution channel

How the product gets to the consumer will be decided by a number of factors:

- **the product**
- **the market**
- **legal requirements**
- **buying habits**
- **the business.**

THE PRODUCT

This is probably the most important factor to consider. If the product is perishable, with a limited shelf-life, then a direct channel is best. For example, McDonald's cannot cook and then distribute its products through other outlets; it has to sell them direct from the restaurant.

However, many perishable products like fish, fruit and vegetables, sometimes go through specialist wholesalers who buy from a large number of small producers in order to make up the bulk needed for many retailers.

New products are often treated differently by manufacturers. They will select which wholesalers or retailers to use in order to keep control over the marketing of the product. Highly technical products will usually go direct to the buyer, however convenience goods such as tinned food will be distributed in bulk, either directly to the major supermarkets' warehouses, or to the wholesaler who will break down the bulk for individual retail outlets.

High-quality, premium brands will only be sold through very selective outlets. Calvin Klein and Levi's have fought Tesco to prevent them selling their products in store.

THE MARKET

Where the market is large and spread throughout the country, the use of wholesalers and retailers is much more efficient. Mars, for example, would find it very expensive and time-consuming to deliver the small quantities of Mars Bars to every shop and outlet in the country.

Where the market is small and local, direct selling is more likely to be appropriate where the producer sells directly to the consumer. Where your customers are also influences the choice of

CHAPTER:five

TOPIC
NINE

MARKETING

channel. For example, products aimed at the tourist market will be sold at the major tourist destinations in Scotland.

LEGAL REQUIREMENTS

Some goods and services can only be sold through licensed premises or authorised outlets. For example, chemists are the only shops that are allowed to dispense certain drugs, and the Post Office can offer services that are not available at other outlets. And, of course, alcohol can only be sold through licensed premises.

BUYING HABITS

Consumers often decide how products will be distributed. Remember that one of the main functions of **place** is to get the products to the consumer and in a place where the consumer would expect to find them. The increase in car ownership has led to the growth in out-of-town shopping centres, so consumers expect to find supermarkets, carpet stores, furniture stores, DIY and gardening outlets in these places.

THE BUSINESS

Some companies have their own distribution networks with their own warehouses and transport. This was common with the larger businesses, however many have now outsourced these functions.

QUESTION

Q17 Identify the factors that will affect a business's choice of channel of distribution.

Types of retailers

There are a number of different types of retailer, and which one or ones are used depends on the product being sold. The most common type is the independent retailer, usually with just one shop such as your local corner shop. However, they do sometimes join forces in order to buy in bulk and offer some competition to the larger chains, e.g. Mace.

Multiple chain stores have a number of outlets spread across the country. They are usually well known, such as Marks and Spencer. Supermarkets offer a wide range of groceries, and now more commonly clothing, and household and electrical goods. Department stores, such as House of Fraser, offer a range of goods in the different departments within the store. They tend to specialise in higher-priced premium brands. Franchises, which were dealt with earlier in this book, offer new businesses the opportunity to trade using an established name such as McDonald's.

Other types of outlets available are mail order such as Freeman's catalogue, where rather than having the expense of a chain of shops, they issue catalogues to consumers who can choose products in the comfort of their own home and at their own pace. They are successful because of the credit facilities that they offer.

Other companies such as Avon offer a door-to-door selling service with a catalogue. With the growth in the popularity of cable and satellite TV there has been a growth in the use of TV shopping channels, which again allows consumers to buy from the comfort of their own home.

PROMOTION

Marketing is about communicating with consumers, and promotion is the method used to pass information to the consumer. It is an essential way of keeping existing customers and getting new ones. There are a number of different methods of promotion:

- **advertising**
- **sales promotions**
- **public relations**
- **exhibitions and trade fairs**
- **merchandising**
- **direct mail**
- **personal selling.**

Advertising

Advertising is the method that most of us would consider first when talking about promotion. However, it can be very expensive and is not always successful. There are four main types of advertising:

INFORMATIVE ADVERTISING

This is used to pass information to the consumer about new or improved products, or to give information about a technical product. The government uses informative advertising in the press, on television, and in its own publications.

For example, the Health Education Board for Scotland regularly runs adverts on TV about the dangers involved in smoking, taking drugs and alcohol abuse. The anti-smoking advert actually became very popular, possibly for the wrong reasons.

PERSUASIVE ADVERTISING

This is an attempt by the manufacturers to get us to buy their product. It is usually used in very competitive consumer markets, where consumers see little difference between one product and another. They use powerful images and language to imply good things about you if you buy this product. They are an attempt to build an emotional reaction in the consumer and use qualitative statements (opinions) rather than fact. An example is: 'Probably the world's favourite lager'.

CORPORATE ADVERTISING

This is more concerned with promoting the whole company rather than individual products. The advertisements will often put forward their image as being responsible and caring. For example, BP adverts do not tend to try to get you to buy their petrol, but to convey a 'green', socially responsible image.

There is often a growing pressure for the company name to become a brand in its own right, and businesses will use slogans or catchlines to help this become established: 'The world's favourite airline' (British Airways).

GENERIC ADVERTISING

The beef industry in Scotland has used generic advertising to promote and give reassurance about the quality and safety of the product following the BSE and Foot and Mouth scares. Generic advertising is where a number of advertisers or the whole industry come together to promote the industry rather than individual products.

Choice of advertising media

How and where an organisation carries out its advertising will depend very much on how it can best reach its existing and potential customers. Targeted advertising can be much more successful and effective. For example, if you are targeting a younger audience, then using magazines aimed at the youth market, or advertising during TV programmes popular with young people, like 'Hollyoaks', will be more effective. However, if you are targeting older people then advertising in the Sunday newspapers and during daytime TV will be best.

Products that are aimed at the whole market are usually advertised best during very popular TV programmes like 'Coronation Street'.

There are three main types of advertising media:

- print **media, such as newspapers and magazines**
- broadcast **media, such as television and radio and the Internet**
- outdoor **media, such as billboards, around football grounds and on buses.**

Which is used will depend on the following factors:

COST

Television advertising can be the most expensive, particularly during the most popular programmes such as 'Coronation Street', however it does reach a huge audience either nationally or in the local television area such as STV or Grampian. It is best used for mass marketing.

TARGET AUDIENCE

National newspapers can also be expensive, however they can be read again and again, although the adverts here are less entertaining than TV adverts. The newspapers tend to be designed for different socio–economic groups, so the advertising will be more targeted. If the market is local, then a local newspaper would be most appropriate.

COMPETITORS' ADVERTISING

In order to compete effectively it may be necessary to match your competitors' choice of media. Most banks and building societies use newspaper adverts extensively as it allows the reader to spend time going through the sometimes complicated offers. In order for the consumer to make comparisons, the competing products will appear in the same types of media.

IMPACT REQUIRED

If you are launching a new product then it is likely that you would use a wide variety of different media to get as much attention and interest in the product as you can, as quickly as possible.

There are legal restrictions on what advertising can take place where, and also advertising guidelines which have to be followed. There are restrictions on tobacco and alcohol advertising and also restrictions on adverts which may be unsuitable for young children.

QUESTION
Q18 Identify the factors that will affect the business's choice of advertising media.

Sales promotions

As part of the overall marketing strategy sales promotions are short term inducements used to encourage customers to react quickly and make a purchase. Sales promotions can be given to the wholesaler/retailer or to the consumer.

PROMOTIONS INTO THE PIPELINE
These are designed to encourage the wholesaler or retailer to take more stock than they would otherwise and they include:

● **Dealer loaders** where, for example, the retailer is given six boxes for the price of five.

● **Point-of-sale displays**, posters or video cassettes. Video hire shops are given display material to encourage hires of new videos. Some stores run videos of new products for customers to watch.

● **Dealer competitions** where they can win prizes that would appeal to them.

● **Staff training** for the shops' staff in order for them to deal more effectively with customer enquiries.

● **Sale or return**, which is offered by most newspapers, where if businesses do not sell all their newspapers they can simply return them without charge.

● **Extended credit** – where the shop does not have to pay for the products for some months, allowing it to take stock and receive payment for sales before it actually has to pay for them.

PROMOTIONS OUT OF THE PIPELINE
These are promotions which give a direct benefit to the consumer in order to encourage them to make the purchase. They include:

● **Free samples** or trial packs which are given away in store or with other products. Magazines are a common way of distributing free samples.

● **Bonus packs** where, for example, 50% is given free. These are common with many convenience goods such as coffee or washing powder.

● **Price reductions**, which are short term pricing strategies to encourage sales. For example, a pack may carry '50p off' on its packaging.

CHAPTER:Five

TOPIC
NINE

- **Premium offers** where one product is given free when you buy another.

- **In-store demonstrations or tastings.** Tastings are common in supermarkets where customers are allowed to taste and try new products.

- **Merchandising.**

The benefits that are gained from sales promotions tend to be short term, and must be combined with the other elements of the marketing mix if they are to be successful in the longer term.

QUESTION

Q19 Identify the different types of promotions into and out of the pipeline.

Public relations

Public relations is the way the organisation communicates at a corporate level with the rest of the community. This would include the public, the press, the government and shareholders. These are planned communications by the company in order to enhance the image of the organisation.

The role of the Public Relations department is an important one and may involve issuing press statements, making charitable donations, sponsoring events and arranging for product endorsement by well-known personalities. In some organisations the Customer Care or Services department will be involved in public relations.

Publicity

Publicity arises either within the organisation by the company itself through press releases or public announcements, or outwith the organisation through news reports or through consumer programmes or publications. It is not usually paid for by the organisation, but can become advertising for the business if it is good publicity.

QUESTION

Q20 Describe the differences between Public Relations and Publicity.

Packaging

Sometimes referred to as the fifth P, packaging is a very important element of the marketing strategy. Good packaging can increase sales of the product, whereas poor packaging can result in a loss of sales.

There are a number of factors to consider:

SHAPE AND WEIGHT
These can affect how easy the product is to distribute and handle, which can lead to higher costs.

PROTECTION

The packaging must be robust enough to ensure that the product and its packaging are not damaged in transit or storage. The packaging must also protect the product from possible damage from light, heat and dust.

CONVENIENCE

It is important that the packaging is easy for the consumer to handle; awkward shapes and sizes will put the customer off buying.

DESIGN

The design should be eye-catching to allow it to be distinguished easily from competitors' brands. Colour may be important as, for example, some foodstuffs and colours do not mix. As with Cadbury's, the colour of the packaging may be used to promote the brand image.

INFORMATION

Food products are subject to legal requirements about their ingredients appearing on the packaging, and some technical products, such as light shades, must show the maximum wattage of bulbs that can be used.

ENVIRONMENTAL FACTORS

There has been a great deal of public concern regarding recyclable materials being used on packaging, coupled with a pressure to reduce the amount of unnecessary packaging.

Merchandising

Merchandising is an attempt to encourage the customer to buy at the point of sale in shops, petrol stations, etc. Display material such as window displays, in-store posters, etc. will attract attention from customers.

The actual layout of products can encourage customers to follow particular routes around stores, with popular items at the back or sides of the store in order that customers have to pass other products. Stores will keep related items together, such as all washing detergents in the same lane. The position of a product on the shelves is also important, with those at eye level being in the best position to achieve sales.

The shelves should always be well stocked otherwise sales will be lost, and the creation of the right atmosphere within the store will affect customers' buying, for example using bright lighting close to fresh food items to give an image of cleanliness, and bread or coffee smells to make the customer hungrier.

QUESTION

Q21 Explain why packaging is important in marketing.

CHAPTER:Five

TOPIC NINE

TOPIC TEN: Market research

If promotion is the communication from the business to the consumer, then market research is the communication from the consumer to the business. It is very important because it is the method that businesses use to identify and anticipate consumers' needs and wants, and so will decide how profitable or successful the business is.

It includes research on:

- **What types of consumers buy the product now.**
- **What the consumers think of the product.**
- **What prices consumers are prepared to pay for the product.**
- **What competition exists in the market and what potential competition there is.**
- **What types of packaging and promotion are most appropriate.**
- **How best to distribute the product and where to sell it.**
- **Whether any legal restrictions or regulations apply to the product.**

Good information in sufficient quantities is essential for good decision-making. Failing to carry out market research will lead to lower sales and sales revenue than would otherwise be available.

There are two main types of market research: **field/primary** and **desk/secondary**. These have been dealt with extensively earlier in the book and you should refer to them at this stage.

FIELD RESEARCH TECHNIQUES

The main **advantages** of field research are that the information is up-to-date; it is collected for the exact purpose required; and that it is not available to competitors, giving the organisation a competitive advantage over its rivals. Primary information is usually gathered through a survey.

Population

How do you carry out market research? You could survey every possible consumer in the market, however this would be very expensive and time-consuming. The information would probably be out of date by the time you had collected and analysed it.

The 'population' for a survey refers to all the persons or companies to which you would like to direct questions. Rather than use the entire population, it is more appropriate to take a **sample** of that population. The sample should be representative of the population as a whole.

Sampling

There are three decisions to be taken when planning a sample to research. The first is '**Who is to be surveyed?**'. This will be the population that you plan to target in your research. Once this has been established you then develop a **sampling frame** – this is a way to make sure that everyone in the population you are targeting has a chance of being included in the sample.

The second question is '**How many people/companies should be surveyed?**'. The larger the sample, the more accurate your survey will be, however it will also be more expensive. It has been shown

UNIT 2

that samples of less than 1% of a population can provide sufficiently reliable information if the sampling frame is correctly developed.

The final question is **'How do we choose those to be included in the survey?'**. There are two main methods – **random** sampling and **quota** sampling.

RANDOM SAMPLING

Random sampling involves producing a random list of individuals to survey. Those picked for inclusion in the sample could be generated randomly, using a computer and the telephone directory or the electoral register. Many market research companies hold huge amounts of information on all different types of consumer, and have access to government information from which they can generate random lists.

The main **advantage** of this method is that there is no chance of bias being introduced when selecting individuals for the sample, and it is simple to do.

The main **disadvantages** are is that it may not be focused on any particular market segment; it assumes that all members of the group are the same, which is not always the case; and finally the random sample must be maintained – if someone is chosen for the sample then they must be interviewed.

QUOTA SAMPLING

This type of survey is preferred when carrying out research. Here, those chosen to be surveyed are selected in proportion to the whole population by social status, gender, age, etc. Once they have reached the quota for, say, males aged between 15 and 21, then no more are surveyed.

The **advantages** of this method are that it is cheaper to operate than random sampling; statistics are available showing the proportions of different groups within the population are readily available; and interviewers can substitute someone else if the interviewee is not at home at the time of the visit or phone call.

The main **disadvantage** is that the results from quota sampling can be less representative than using the random sampling method.

QUESTION
Q22 Describe the differences between random and quota sampling.

Questionnaires

Once you have decided how you will sample and who will be included, you then have to decide how you are going to obtain their responses. The two most common methods are **interview** and **questionnaire**.

The **interview** will involve a researcher asking a series of set questions, usually based on a questionnaire, whereas the questionnaire will be filled in by the person who has been chosen to be included in the sample. So the good practice involved in questionnaire design is also applicable in interviewing.

The purpose of the **questionnaire** is to gain information from the respondent on a wide variety of different issues, including what they own, what they would like to own, what they plan to buy, and about their values, attitudes and beliefs.

In order to be successful the questionnaire must be one that the respondent is willing to complete. The purpose of the questionnaire should be clear, with an explanation of why they would benefit if they take the time to fill it in.

The questions should be clear and easy to understand, and not too heavily based on the respondent's memory, as the information given may be guessed at. In order to get them started, the opening questions should be easy. The more complicated questions can be kept for nearer the end to avoid putting them off. The closing 'filter' questions should categorise the respondent by age, income group, etc. However, you should use banded questions, e.g. (age 30–39).

The questions should follow a logical order, with questions on the same topic grouped together. The questions should use terms that mean the same to all or most people, for example, the term 'often' can mean once a day to one person, and once a month to someone else. You should vary the question types to maintain the respondent's interest.

It is always worthwhile testing the questionnaire before you use it. What seems obvious to you may not be for someone else.

Interview

Where the questions have to be more detailed, using a trained interviewer has a number of advantages. First, because of the two-way communication, the interviewer can explain questions, encourage answers, and ask follow-up questions where appropriate. It also allows for more detailed responses than the questionnaire where answers will usually be no more than one or two word answers.

These are time-consuming and expensive, and poor interviewers may influence the answers given. However, they can give much more detailed information.

The interview can take place in a number of ways. They can be personal interviews, face-to-face in the street, in an office or at home, and they can be carried out over the phone provided that the respondent is willing to answer the questions.

QUESTION

Q23 Describe how interviews can be used to gather market research information.

Other methods

There are a number of other ways to gather primary data: **test marketing**, which was discussed earlier; **consumer panels**, where small groups of consumers are brought together to get their views on a number of different new and existing products, detailed questions can be asked, and feedback on changes can be obtained; and the **hall test** where a larger number of consumers are asked to comment on a range of products.

Most major cinema releases are shown first to a test audience who will then be asked to discuss what they thought of the film. Changes can be then made, or scenes re-shot, even changing the ending is common. Once the test audience's changes are made, the film will be put into general release.

SECONDARY DATA/DESK RESEARCH

Although this is much cheaper and easier to obtain than primary data, much of the information is historic, collected for another purpose, and available to competitors. The most useful in terms of marketing advantage is your own sales force's estimates of future demand, however, like all market research, it may not be accurate.

Businesses now use a variety of methods to keep up-to-date research on their customers. For example, loyalty cards contain information on the customer, and every time they use it it records what that customer purchased. This allows the business to track customer spending patterns. Also, the use of bar codes and electronic check-outs keeps track of what is being purchased in different parts of the country in different stores. Both of these methods are examples of how modern technology is being used in marketing.

Of course the other obvious way is through the Internet.

Check it out yourself at
www3.gartner.com/Init

CHAPTER SUMMARY

By the end of this chapter you should be able to:

● **Identify and describe the role of marketing in relation to different types of organisations in the public and private sectors.**

● **Differentiate between goods and services.**

● **Describe and analyse Market Growth and Market Share.**

● **Describe the Marketing Mix, and correctly identify each of its components – Price, Place, Product, and Promotion.**

● **Describe the role of Market Research, and identify how it is used to assess consumer needs.**

● **Identify and describe the use of Research Techniques such as:**
Surveys and Sampling,
Questionnaires, Interviews, and Test Marketing.

● **Identify and describe the strategies used in Pricing and Promotion.**

● **Describe how organisations are able to identify Target Markets using Market Segmentation and their methods for segmenting markets, and the use of Niche Marketing.**

CHAPTER:Five

TOPIC

TEN

PREPARATION FOR ASSESSMENT

HIGHER ASSESSMENT
Analyse marketing decisions

There are four PCs (Performance Criteria) for this assessment. As usual, the questions you will actually be asked, and how the marks are allocated, will depend on which assessment your teacher or lecturer gives you. However, the marketing assessments do tend to have more marks allocated to them than the others.

PC (a) – Evaluation of the role and importance of marketing to business is accurate and makes reference to product and market orientation

There are potentially four different parts to this PC. The first is the role of marketing: what is it for? Your answer should discuss marketing as being the only method of communication between a large producer and the consumers. It allows them to understand what customers want, and to give information to consumers on their products.

The second is the importance of marketing, and your answer should include making sure that consumers are aware of the products offered; identifying, anticipating and satisfying customers' needs, and how essential marketing is to the success of the organisation. Marketing will allow the business to meet its objectives in terms of making profits, sales, etc.

The third part is the description of the product and market orientation. Your answer should include the fact that product orientation is the concentration on the product and/or the production process, whereas market orientation is where the business constantly reviews the customers' needs.

The fourth part could be some analysis of either market or product orientation. For example, product orientation is only successful for a product which is so technically advanced, or has a sufficiently high novelty value, that the product will sell itself. The company may not provide what the consumers actually want, and so it will lose sales, and not keep up with new developments in the market.

PC (b) – Analysis of the marketing decisions of an organisation is accurate with respect to its marketing mix and target markets

There are two parts to this PC. The first is the analysis of the marketing mix. There will be no marks for identifying the four Ps. To gain full marks, you will have to identify at least two examples of each element from the text given. The examples are fairly obvious so you should not have too much difficulty in identifying them. If there is time you could try to identify more than two of each in order to make sure that you get all the marks you can.

The second part of this PC refers to target markets. The assessment will ask you to discuss:

- undifferentiated marketing
- differentiated marketing
- market segmentation
- niche marketing.

To gain full marks here you will have to be able to describe each of these and relate them to the text. The description itself will not gain marks. Relating it to the text will be fairly simple. For example, you could simply say that Company X appears to carry out undifferentiated marketing because its products are aimed at all or most sections of the market.

PC (c) – Evaluation of the product mix of an organisation is accurate and makes reference to new product development and ways of prolonging the life of existing products

Again, there are two parts to this PC. The first relates to the product mix, and how the business's product portfolio should include products at different stages in their life cycles, so that as one goes into decline, new products are going through the growth and introduction stages. You could also mention that new product development can be funded from products that are at the profitable stage of the growth phase or in maturity phase.

The second part relates to prolonging the product life cycle. Here you should describe how businesses can extend the product life cycle. The main methods are contained in this chapter and you should make yourself aware of them.

One of the case studies used in assessment is about a garden centre, and students are often tempted to talk about the life cycle of the plants, and how they can be kept longer by feeding, being kept in greenhouses etc. This will attract **no marks**.

PC (d) – Analysis of reasons for market research is accurate and makes reference to market research techniques

Once again, there are two parts here. The first relates to the importance of market research. In your answer you should discuss how market research gets information about the current situation: who their customers are, how much they will pay, what they buy, etc; to find out what types of new products customers would buy; and to test out new product development.

The second part relates to market research techniques. The assessment will ask you to explain different types of research and you should discuss those available such as surveys, interviews, test marketing, desk research, etc. If the question is related to the text in the case study, you may be asked to justify your choice – why is this a suitable method for Company X?

INTERMEDIATE 2 ASSESSMENT
Explanation of the marketing function in an organisation

This assessment will be based on a case study which your teacher/lecturer will give you before the assessment. Some case studies are quite long, and the best way to deal with them is to read through them, highlighting those pieces that relate to marketing. You should also get the PCs in advance, so that you will have some idea of what you will be asked.

There are three PCs (Performance Criteria) in this assessment.

PC (a) – Explanation of the importance of marketing to organisations is accurate and related to the type of organisation

There are two parts to this PC. The first is about the importance of marketing; the second is about why or how it is important to different types of organisations such as manufacturers, private service providers such as building societies, public service providers such as a local council, or a charity.

The answer for each type of organisation is basically the same. They all want to communicate with their customers, finding out what they want and what they will pay for, or in the case of charities what they will donate. For each, this will help them achieve their objectives such as profit maximisation or helping good causes for the charity.

PC (b) – Explanation of the elements of the marketing mix is accurately related to a specific business situation

There are no marks here for naming the four Ps. You need to explain each of them in turn:

● Product – **the good or service that is actually sold to the customer.**

● Price – **what the consumer will pay in order to purchase the good or service.**

● Place – **the channel of distribution and point of sale.**

● Promotion – **making consumers aware of the product and why they should buy it, through advertising, sales promotions, etc.**

You will then need to identify examples of each of these from the case study. The difficult point may be finding something to say about the product – here, you should describe what is on sale in the text, giving as much information as you can.

PC (c) – Explanation of market research is accurate and its importance related to the type of organisation

There are three parts here. The first part asks you to explain what market research is. Your answer should include how market research helps businesses to find out what customers want now and in the future, what is happening in their market, etc.

The second part is about the importance of market research, and you could use your answer to the first part to help you answer this. For example, it is important to find out what consumers want in order to help you plan new products, so that you can stay ahead of the competition.

The last part is relating market research to the type of organisation. You will be expected to know about the different methods of market research such as interviews, questionnaires, test marketing and desk research. You should be able to describe each, and then show why it might help the organisation in the case study, which should be the same for almost any type of organisation.

CHAPTER SIX

UNIT:2 BUSINESS DECISION AREAS

FINANCIAL MANAGEMENT

The purpose of this chapter is to cover Financial Management at *both* Intermediate 2 and Higher levels.

Each of the two levels will be covered in turn as they each deal with different issues of financial management.

The topics covered are as follows:

INTERMEDIATE LEVEL 2

- The role of the finance function:
  - payment of wages and salaries
  - payment of accounts
  - maintenance of financial records.
- Financial information:
  - purpose of the profit and loss account, balance sheet, cash flow and accounting ratios.
- Use of financial information:
  - controlling costs and expenditure
  - monitoring performance
  - manipulation of data using a spreadsheet to inform decision-making.
- Users of financial information:
  - management
  - owners
  - creditors
  - employees
  - citizens.

HIGHER LEVEL

- Cash flow:
  - use
  - purpose
  - interpretation.
- Financial reporting:
  - description of components and interpretation of profit and loss account and balance sheet.
- Ratio analysis:
  - analysis using the following accounting ratios:
    - gross profit/sales
    - gross profit/cost of sales
    - net profit/sales
    - current ratio
    - acid test ratio
    - return on capital employed.
- Budgets:
  - uses of budgets.

TOPIC ONE: The role of the Finance function

 The Finance function of any modern business plays a vital role in its overall success or failure. It exists to carry out such functions as the maintenance of financial records, the payment of bills and expenses, the collection of accounts due, monitoring of business funds, payment of wages and salaries and reporting to management. The main role of the Finance function is to provide information to managers and decision-makers within the business.

PAYMENT OF WAGES AND SALARIES

The staff, or human resources, of any business are its life-blood. Without staff to carry out the daily duties of the business, it will not survive. Therefore, one of the most important tasks performed by the Finance function is the payment of wages and salaries to the organisation's staff.

The Finance function will work in close proximity with the Human Resources department when calculating and paying staff wages and salaries. The Human Resources function holds personal information for all the staff employed by the business. Certain personal information is required by the Finance function in order to calculate and pay staff wages and salaries. For example, names, addresses, wage or salary amounts, bank account details and any sickness days all have to be reported before payment of wages and salaries can take place.

Depending on the nature and type of business an organisation carries out, staff may be paid either a wage or a salary. Typically, the difference is that a wage is paid weekly (i.e. once every week) and a salary is paid monthly (i.e. once every month or sometimes once every four weeks).

Wages and salaries are not usually paid to staff in cash although some businesses do still operate on this basis. Developments in electronic banking, many years ago now, mean that most businesses will use a system called Bankers' Automated Clearing System (BACS) to transfer wages and salaries electronically, directly to employees' bank accounts. There are several advantages in using this service:

- no need for large sums of money to be kept on the business premises

- no need for large sums of money to be transported to the business premises

- cheaper for the business.

 TASK ONE INTERMEDIATE

Find out from two different people how they are paid by their employer.

PAYMENT OF ACCOUNTS

Depending on the size and nature of the business, there may or may not be a distinct section or department dealing with the business accounts that must be paid.

Accounts that are payable by the business will fall into two different categories:

- **cash**
- **credit.**

Accounts which are payable in **cash** will usually be to companies or individuals that the business does not normally deal with regularly. These bills would usually be settled using the petty cash system in operation within the business. The petty cash system will usually be administered by an individual employee and be audited by a more senior member of staff in order to maintain its security. Petty cash works by setting aside a sum of money called the imprest. This amount will be decided by the business and may be several hundred pounds or more. The purpose of petty cash is to meet the daily cash expenses of the business. At the end of each week (or month), depending on the frequency of use, the petty cash will be audited and the imprest amount restored to the original amount with money taken from the business bank account. Each amount of money that is paid out from petty cash must be authorised and a receipt offered in exchange, to be entered in the petty cash record of account.

For larger amounts of expenditure, it is usual for a business to have a line of **credit** with other business organisations with which it deals. This means that the business is able to receive the benefit of goods and services from another business and make payment for them at a later date; usually one month later. The amount of credit and the timescale for payment will be decided by the organisation providing the credit. It will be dependent on the 'credit history' of the business and its reputation, as well as any reference taken up from other providers of credit to the business, e.g. a bank.

Credit must be managed carefully and it is usual for most businesses to employ someone who is responsible for the control and payment of credit invoices. Too much credit can over-commit the business and lead to financial difficulties. It is the responsibility of the employee in charge of credit control to provide information to management on the control and payment of credit within the business. It is usual for most credit agreements to require payment within one month of the business taking delivery of goods or using services that have been provided on credit.

Some companies will offer a discount for early settlement of accounts, to encourage fast payment.

All businesses must be careful not to abuse the provision of credit facilities because they are a valuable source of free credit which aids the smooth running of their businesses. Companies which are regularly late in paying their invoices will quickly build a reputation as slow payers and may eventually have the provision of free credit removed, meaning that they will have to pay in cash immediately for all goods and services that they require. Conversely, businesses should not make payment too soon as by doing so they fail to utilise fully the provision of free credit.

TASK TWO INTERMEDIATE

List some of the factors that will be taken into account when one business is deciding whether or not to provide a line of credit to another.

MAINTENANCE OF FINANCIAL RECORDS

All companies must maintain financial records. Financial records are an essential part of every business as they are basically a history of all the business's activities and provide the basis for internal control, internal reporting and external reporting to agencies such as the Inland Revenue.

The Inland Revenue requires that businesses retain financial records and related documents for a period of six years in case of possible investigation. It is an offence if this is not done.

Furthermore, limited companies fall under the scope of the Companies Acts of 1985 and 1989 which state that it is an offence not to maintain proper financial records.

Financial records form the basis of many business decisions and, without proper financial records, the business would not be able to operate effectively or efficiently.

Financial records can take several forms:

- daily record-keeping
- manual record-keeping
- electronic record-keeping
- information presented for internal decision-making
- information presented for internal reporting
- information presented for external reporting
- information presented as a requirement of statute (law).

In Topic two we will consider some the financial documents that are of most importance to the business.

TASK THREE INTERMEDIATE

If you have access to the Internet, find out about some of the software that is available for financial record-keeping. You could start by visiting *www.sage.com*

TOPIC TWO: Financial information

Financial information may be presented by a business in different formats. For example, the business will have different formats for information that is used internally and information that is presented externally.

There are three main financial statements that all businesses use:

- profit and loss account
- balance sheet
- cash flow statement.

In addition to these statements, which will usually be produced for both internal and external use, most businesses will also find it useful to calculate accounting ratios based on their financial records. The three main financial statements are usually used as the basis for the calculation of the accounting ratios.

THE PROFIT AND LOSS ACCOUNT

The profit and loss account is used by businesses as a statement for both internal and external reporting. The form that it takes will differ according to its use but nonetheless it will still provide the same basic information. For example, the profit and loss account used for internal reporting may be produced on a monthly basis and go into great detail, whereas that produced as a statutory requirement at the end of the financial year will take a much reduced form and will contain much less detail in the information it provides.

What does the profit and loss account show? It details the business's **income** and **expenditure** over the course of the financial year. The business expenditure is matched to the business income and where the business income is greater than the expenditure, a profit is recorded. Conversely, where the business expenditure is greater than the income, a loss is recorded.

It is an important feature of the profit and loss account, and a requirement of accounting conventions, that the business properly matches its income and expenditure for the period for which the profit and loss account is drawn up. This ensures that the profit (or loss) calculated is not overstated and that a true reflection of the business's trading activities is shown.

The profit and loss account is a continuation of the business's trading account. The trading account records the difference between how much money the business generates from selling and how much the goods it is selling actually cost, i.e. cost of sales.

The trading account then shows the **gross profit** of the business. The gross profit is the profit before any of the business's expenses are taken into account; it gives an indication of the business's trading performance.

| TURNOVER |
| COSTS |
| PROFIT |

| TURNOVER |
| COSTS |
| LOSS |

A simple trading account might look something like this:

General Traders

Trading Account for the year ending 31 March 2002

	£	£
Turnover		180,000
Cost of sales		
Opening stock of goods	40,000	
Purchases	95,000	
	135,000	
Less: Closing stock of goods	(45,000)	90,000
GROSS PROFIT		90,000

The profit and loss account follows on from the trading account and a simple version would look something like this:

General Traders

Profit and Loss Account for the year ending 31 March 2002

	£	£
Gross profit		90,000
Other operating income		
Rent received	10,000	
Interest received	1,000	11,000
		101,000
Expenses		
Rent and rates	25,000	
Heating and lighting	8,000	
Telephone	900	
Advertising	250	
Postage	400	
Wages and salaries	45,000	
Insurance	2,000	81,550
NET PROFIT		19,450

A more complicated format of the profit and loss account is used for limited companies. Such companies fall under the jurisdiction of the Companies Act 1985 and they must produce their year-end accounts in accordance with the formats prescribed by the law. All other types of business will produce a similar type of profit and loss account but it will usually be less detailed than that required from the limited company.

BUSINESS DECISION AREAS

An example of a profit and loss account for a limited company is shown below:

Proudfoot Prefabrication Ltd

Trading, Profit and Loss Account for the year ending 30 June 2002

	£	£
TURNOVER		5,200,000
Cost of goods sold		2,100,000
GROSS PROFIT		3,100,000
Operating expenses	120,000	
Other operating income	100,000	
Net operating expenses		20,000
OPERATING PROFIT		3,080,000
Investment income		320,000
NET PROFIT BEFORE INTEREST PAYABLE		3,400,000
Interest payable		260,000
PROFIT ON ORDINARY ACTIVITES BEFORE TAX		3,140,000
Corporation tax		740,000
PROFIT ON ORDINARY ACTIVITIES AFTER TAX		2,400,000
Preference dividend		350,000
PROFIT ATTRIBUTABLE TO ORDINARY SHAREHOLDERS		2,050,000
Ordinary dividend	150,000	
Transfer to reserves	700,000	850,000
UNAPPROPRIATED PROFIT FOR THIS YEAR		1,200,000
Balance brought forward		2,700,000
Balance carried forward		**3,900,000**

 *If you have access to the Internet, you can look at a huge variety of company reports at the site of Company Annual Reports On Line: www.carol.co.uk*

Once you have registered, you can choose which accounts you would like to access – this is a free service.

The type of profit and loss account that is produced will depend on the type of business, e.g. sole trader, partnership, private limited company or public limited company.

Partnerships and limited companies produce an extra and final section in their profit and loss accounts, called the **appropriation account**. This simply shows how the business's profit or loss is to be shared. Profits may be distributed in a number of different ways:

Group Profit and Loss Account for the year ended 31 March 2002	Scottish and Southern Energy PLC		Total 2002 £m	Total 2001 restated £m
Turnover				
Group and share of joint ventures			4,056.5	3,706.7
Less: share of joint ventures			50.9	121.1
Group Turnover		3	4,005.6	3,585.6
Cost of sales			(2,989.2)	(2,611.1)
Gross profit			1,016.4	974.5
Distribution costs			(225.8)	(223.8)
Admistrative costs			(188.6)	(184.5)
Operating profit		4		
Group			602.0	566.2
Share of joint ventures			28.8	25.4
Share of associates			35.7	37.5
Total operating profit		3	666.5	629.1
Income from fixed asset investments			1.6	2.1
Net interest payable and similar charges		7		
Group			(74.2)	(67.7)
Joint ventures			(13.2)	(11.8)
Associates			(19.3)	(22.3)
Other financial income		8	24.3	21.0
Profit on ordinary activities before taxation			585.7	550.4
Taxation		9	(154.6)	(143.8)
Profit on ordinary activities after taxation			431.6	406.6
Equity minority interests in subsidiary undertaking		24	0.5	0.4
Profit attributable to ordinary shareholders			431.6	407.0
Dividends		10	(278.5)	(257.0)
Retained profit for the financial year		23	153.1	150.0
Earnings per share (p)		11		
—basic			50.3	47.6
—adjusted basic			54.7	50.9
—diluted			50.2	47.4

The above results are derived from continuing activities and there were no acquisitions during the year.

The accompanying notes are an integral part of these accounts

Profit and loss account terminology

Trading account	Provides a summary of the business's trading activity during the financial year.
Sales	Monies that the business has received from selling goods and/or services.
Turnover/Net sales	The value of the business's sales less the value of any returns.
Cost of sales	The cost of the sales to the business, i.e. before a sales or profit margin is added.
Opening stock	The value of the stock of goods at the start of the financial period.
Purchases	The cost of goods that the business has bought for resale to its customers.
Carriage inwards	The cost of transporting or delivering goods purchased by the business for re-sale.
Purchase returns	The value of goods purchased but returned to the supplier, e.g. wrong colour, faulty.
Closing stock	The value of unsold stock at the end of the financial period.
Gross profit loss	The profit (or loss) recorded as the difference between the business's sales and purchases.
Expenses	Any expenses incurred by the business in the course of its normal operation.
Net profit/loss	The profit (or loss) recorded after all business expenses have been deducted.
Corporation tax	A tax on business profits payable to the government.
Dividend	Proportion of the business profit paid to shareholders and dependent on the number of shares they own.
Unappropriated profit	Profit retained in the business, i.e. not distributed to either owners or shareholders.

UNIT 2

- **payment of corporation tax**
- **payment of a dividend to shareholders**
- **appropriated amongst the business partners**
- **retained in the business.**

THE BALANCE SHEET

The profit and loss account records the history of the business activity **throughout** the financial year, whereas the balance sheet shows a snapshot at a **particular** date in time; usually the last day of the financial year.

Whereas the profit and loss account details **trading activity**, the balance sheet records the **financial worth** and the financial position of the business at a particular point in time. For this reason alone, the balance sheet of any company is out of date by the time it is published. It forms part of the historic accounting records of the business.

Historic accounting is so called because it uses information from the past to compile statements and reports that are of use to other businesses and individuals.

What does the balance sheet show? The balance sheet basically shows three different things:

- **assets**
- **liabilities**
- **capital.**

We can combine each of these three categories of items in the accounting equation:

$$CAPITAL = ASSETS - LIABILITIES$$

Balance sheet terminology	
Fixed asset	Something the business owns and depends on to operate on a daily basis. Usually has a degree of permanence.
Current asset	Assets that are likely to be changed into cash in the short term. They frequently change in value.
Current liability	Something that the business owes money for in the short term, i.e. a debt. It must usually be paid with a period of 12 months.
Long term liability	Debts of the business that are not due to be repaid for more than 12 months.
Capital	A special kind of liability. The money invested by the owner(s) of the business to set it up. This money is owed back to the owner(s) by the business.
Net current assets	This is the difference in value between the total current assets and the total current liabilities. The total of the current assets should usually be more than the total of the current liabilities.
Reserves	Money and profits that are retained in the business, perhaps to buy new assets or to safeguard against future losses.
Net assets/Net worth	The financial value or worth of the business.

The balance sheet is presented in two parts; the top half and the bottom half (when displayed in the usual vertical format). The top half of the balance sheet displays the assets and liabilities of the business. **Assets** are things that the business owns and these are categorised as either fixed or current. **Liabilities** are the opposite of assets and are things that the business owes money for. They can be either current or long term.

Fixed assets are the productive assets of the business. Without these assets, the business would not be able to function on a day-to-day basis. These are things like buildings, machinery and other equipment. They are usually listed in descending order of permanence, i.e. the one that is expected to last the longest will be listed first.

Current assets are assets that change on a daily basis and can be turned into cash easily. They are listed in descending order of liquidity, i.e. how easily they can be turned into cash. The most illiquid (or most difficult to turn into cash) is usually listed last. Examples of current assets are money in the bank, stocks of goods and debtors.

Current liabilities (sometimes called creditors falling due within one year) are also listed on the top half of the balance sheet and are shown as a deduction from current assets. This is because the business will (eventually) turn all of its current assets into cash and subsequently use this cash to pay its current liabilities. These liabilities are known as current because they will normally have to be repaid within a period of 12 months. The most common example of a current liability is creditors, i.e. people or other businesses to whom the business owes money for goods or services supplied on credit.

The difference between the total current assets and the total current liabilities is highlighted on the balance sheet. This is known as **net current assets**. This figure is extremely important because it highlights the business's ability to meet its short term debts. This figure should usually always be positive, i.e. the total of current assets should always be more than the total of current liabilities. Where the total current liabilities are greater than the total current assets of the business, this shows that the company is in potential financial difficulty as it may be unable to meet its most immediately payable debts. In extreme cases, where the company does not have sufficient current assets to pay its short term debts, it may have to resort to selling off some of its fixed assets to survive. This is, however, a dangerous practice as without its fixed (productive) assets, the company will not be able to function properly and may ultimately fail.

Long-term liabilities (sometimes called creditors falling due after more than one year) are listed on the top half of the balance sheet, after net current assets. These represent liabilities that the business must repay after more than one year. Examples include debentures and other longer-term loans which may or may not be secured on assets belonging to the business.

The total of fixed assets plus the net current assets minus long term liabilities is known as the business's **net worth**. This means the 'value' of the business in monetary terms on the particular date specified on the balance sheet. The relative usefulness of the balance sheet is limited, however, as it only provides a snapshot of the business and, like other accounting records, is based on transactions from the business history.

The bottom half of the balance sheet represents the 'capital' side of the accounting equation. Depending on the type of business, this half of the balance sheet may comprise owner's or owners' funds or share capital contributed by the shareholders of the company.

As the balance sheet is comprised of two halves that represent the accounting equation, the total of the top half of the balance sheet must equal the total of the bottom half of the balance sheet, i.e. the accounting equation must be satisfied.

An example of a balance sheet follows:

Arsen Animations Ltd

Balance Sheet as at 30 April 2002

	£000	£000	£000
Fixed assets			
Premises		1,500	
Computer equipment		800	
Motor vehicles		200	
			2,500
Current assets			
Stocks	600		
Debtors	400		
Cash at bank	200	1,200	
Creditors due in < 1 year			
Trade creditors	500		
Taxation	150		
Dividends	100	750	
Net current assets			450
Total assets less current liabilities			2,950
Creditors due in > 1 year			
Bank loan		200	
Debenture loan		1,000	1,200
Net assets			1,750
	£000	£000	£000
Capital and reserves			
Ordinary share capital		1,000	
Retained profits		750	
Net worth			1,750

TASK **FOUR** HIGHER AND INTERMEDIATE

Go to *www.carol.co.uk* and compare the final accounts of two different companies.

CASH FLOW

Cash and cash management are the most important aspects of business. Without cash, the business will fail. In a recent online survey of the top 65 reasons for business failures, poor cash management was the second most popular reason.

The role of cash in any business at any time (whether business is good or bad) cannot be underestimated. The cash flow cycle demonstrates the role of cash in business. Take a minute to study the following diagram.

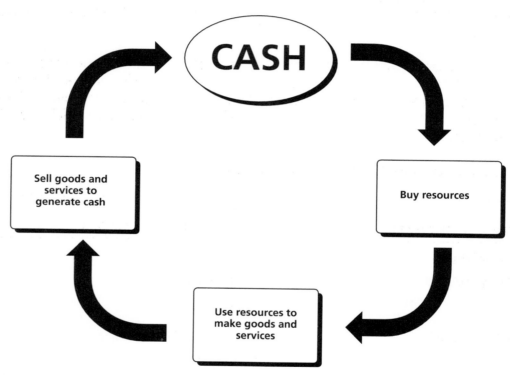

IMAGE 24.
Cash flow cycle

As the diagram suggests, the movement of cash (or cash flow) in and out of the business is central to the success and efficient operation of the business. We have already looked at the component parts of the balance sheet and identified the need for the business to maintain sufficient liquid assets to meet its ongoing debts. The concept of cash flow is centred around liquidity, that is the provision of or the ability to have access to cash or near-cash assets to meet the everyday commitments of the business.

UNIT: 2

The terminology of cash flow is concerned with the movement of money in and out of the business. In this context, the following terms are used:

- **cash inflow** – a movement of cash into the business, e.g. cash sales

- **cash outflow** – a movement of cash out of the business, e.g. cash purchases.

A **cash flow statement** is produced as part of the year-end accounts of a limited company and also as a useful financial statement by many other businesses. It shows the movements of cash in and out of the business over the course of the financial year. The term 'cash' has a special meaning in the context of a cash flow statement and can mean cash, money in the bank and other cash equivalent assets, i.e. assets that can be converted to cash quickly.

The cash flow statement itself is constructed from the information contained in the profit and loss account and the balance sheet. When a cash flow statement is produced at times other than the financial year-end, the business will have to collate information from its accounting records in order to produce it.

The Accounting Standards Board, which governs the accounting profession, encourages all businesses, no matter how large or small, to produce cash flow statements on a regular basis. As we have already mentioned, most businesses fail because they run out of cash and not because they lack success or profits. A cash flow statement provides an easy means by which to track the movements of cash.

Here are some common examples of inflows and outflows of cash:

INFLOW Cash coming into the business	OUTFLOW Cash going out of the business
Decrease in debtors	Decrease in creditors
Increase in creditors	Dividend payment
Loan received	Drawings
New capital investment	Increase in debtors
Profits	Loan repaid
Sale of a fixed asset	Losses
Sale of stock	Purchase of a fixed asset
	Purchase of stock

Think about each of the following situations and whether or not a cash flow statement would help to identify problems:

- The local newsagent (a sole trader) makes £45,000 profit this year but has £55,000 in drawings.
- Karen and Kevin buy some business premises and plan to open a new gym. The building is very run down and needs a lot of work done on it before they will be able to open for business. The building works will cost in the region of £60,000. This money is needed before they can open for business and offer memberships to the public.
- A new supermarket has opened less than 100 metres from Jim's local convenience store. He is finding that much of his business has been lost to the supermarket and his takings are down. He decides to offer all his customers credit on all purchases over £25. Business soon picks up again but he finds that many of his customers take more than a month to settle their accounts while he has to settle the business credit accounts in just 14 days. He is worried that if he withdraws his credit facility he will lose customers again but, at the same time, he is finding it increasingly difficult to meet all of the business expenses and bills on time.

Example of a cash flow statement:

Consolidated Cash Flow Statement

	Note	28 weeks ended 11 November 2000 £million	28 weeks ended 13 November 1999 £million	52 weeks ended 29 April 2000 £million
Net cash (outflow)/inflow from operating activities	11	(33.0)	140.9	422.5
Return on investments and servicing of finance				
Interest received		39.7	24.4	53.2
Interest paid		(41.1)	(1.8)	(31.7)
Preference dividends paid		-	(2.2)	(4.4)
		(1.4)	20.4	17.1
Taxation paid		(9.7)	(1.0)	(24.5)
Capital expenditure and financial investment				
Purchase of fixed asset investments		(9.1)	(13.0)	(28.5)
Purchase of tangible assets		(109.07)	(64.6)	(200.5)
Sale of tangible assets		0.1	10.1	25.5
Loans to related untertakings		-	-	(0.2)
		(118.7)	(67.5)	(203.7)
Acquisitions and disposals				
Cash consideration for acquisitions		(1.9)	(2.2)	(467.0)
Net cash aquired with subsidiaries		-	0.1	1.5
Cash consideration for partial sales of subsidiaries	3	7.6	242.2	251.7
Cash consideration for acquisition of associates		0.2	-	(9.5)
		5.9	240.1	(223.3)
Equity dividends paid		(67.8)	(53.4)	(107.7)
Net cash (outflow)/inflow before management of liquid resources and financing		(224.7)	279.5	(119.6)
Management of liquid resources				
Decrease/(increase) in current asset investments		117.6	(117.7)	(44.5)
Financing				
Issue of ordinary share capital		7.9	11.1	15.2
Return of capital to shareholders		-	-	(121.1)
(Decrease)/increase in debt due within one year		(42.9)	(1.8)	28.9
Increase/(decrease)in debt due after more than one year		28.4	(3.3)	337.8
		(6.6)	6.0	260.8
(Decrease)/increase in cash in the period	12	(113.7)	167.8	96.7

(Source: www.carol.co.uk)

INTERPRETATION OF PROFIT AND LOSS ACCOUNT, BALANCE SHEET AND CASH FLOW STATEMENT

The final accounts of a business are made up of:

- **profit and loss account – to calculate the profit earned by the business over the last year**

- **balance sheet – to show the assets and liabilities of the business**

- **cash flow statement – to show all the money that has flowed into and out of the business over the course of the last year.**

These financial statements are of limited use if we simply just look at the figures as they are presented. Careful interpretation of the final accounts can give much more information. One tool which can be used is ratio analysis which is considered later in this chapter. Another useful source of information is statements issued by the company themselves. Consider the statement on the business performance of Thus plc, a division of Scottish Power that follows.

Thus plc 31-Jan-01

Summary results and trading update

Quarter ending 31 December 2000

Highlights

*Third quarter sales growth accelerates, with overall turnover up 12% to £59.9 million on quarter two and up 11% year on year. Business service sales grow 26% on quarter two to £43.4 million and 42% year on year.

*Growth driven by increased sales across Internet, data and telecoms and contact centre services.

*Internet sales under the Demon brand up 13% to £20.3 million on quarter two and up 6% year on year. Internet Magazine awards on 'Best ISP on the Planet'

*National connectivity in place. Completion of Southern network ring and service launched in Birmingham, Bristol, Gloucester and Milton Keynes during current period.

Commenting on the results, William Allan, Chief Executive said:

'These results demonstrate a strong improvement in both our sales growth and in the management of our operating costs.

Our transition to a national, business focused telecommunications services company is now largely complete. We are beginning to see the scale effects from corporate contracts for data and telecoms, Internet and contact centre services announced earlier this year. Business customers are attracted by our comprehensive national network, advanced data and service strategy and leading quality of service. Going forward, our aim is to increase both the share and the value of the sales that we achieve in this faster growing, higher value market segment.

The acceleration in sales growth achieved in the third quarter gives us further confidence that the Company will deliver enhanced revenue growth throughout the second half of the current financial year.'

(Source: *www.carol.co.uk*)

Interpretation of the **profit and loss account** may include answering questions such as:

- How did this year's trading compare with last year's?
- How did this year's trading compare with that of our rivals?
- Has the net profit improved when compared to last year?
- Are we making efficient use of our stock?

Interpretation of a **balance sheet** may include answering questions such as:

- Do we have sufficient liquid assets to meet our short term debts?
- Are we making enough use of free credit facilities available to us?
- Is our level of debt comparable to that of our competitors?

Interpretation of a **cash flow statement** may include answering questions such as:

- Has the net debt position of the business changed dramatically over the last year? If so, why?
- Have we kept proper control of cash flow throughout the year?
- How does our liquidity compare to that of our rivals?

TOPIC THREE: Using financial information

Financial information can be gathered about a business from its financial statements. The main areas that it is likely to cover are profitability, liquidity, efficiency and capital structure.

Managers and other people who have an interest in the operation of the business will use this information to:

- review past performance and compare it with the most recent performance
- assist with planning for the future of the business.

Comparisons should also be made:

- with the same company over a different time period
- with competitors in the same line of business over the same periods of time.

Comparisons are important in order that a true picture of the business performance can be drawn up. This also means that management can make informed decisions about the future of the business, based on reliable information.

Analysis of financial data may also lead to a focus being made on a particular area of the business. For example, spiralling costs may lead to particular focus on one area of expenditure and investigation as to the reasons behind the increase.

Useful financial information has certain characteristics:

- it should be relevant to the group intending to use it;
- the information should be reliable and traceable to its source;
- free from bias and personal opinion;
- clear and understandable;
- it should allow comparisons to be made easily;
- it should be realistic and give a true and fair view;
- consistency;
- presented in a reasonable time scale;
- irrelevant information should not be included;
- all information should be disclosed to give a rounded view, even where some of the information is 'not good'.

TOPIC FOUR: Users of financial information

The users of financial information are varied and the range of people who have an interest in the activities of business organisations continues to grow:

- shareholders
- potential shareholders
- short term creditors
- long term creditors
- government and local authorities
- competitors
- employees
- analysts
- management
- customers
- general public.

Shareholders have an interest in the financial information provided by a company so that they can assess the performance of the Board and so make further decisions about investment or disinvestment.

Potential shareholders use financial information to assess whether or not the company will be a worthwhile investment or whether the risk attached is too great to bear.

Short term creditors have an interest as they must decide whether or not credit should be granted in the first instance and then to assess whether or not future debts will be paid.

Long term creditors must decide whether or not to lend money. They will also be keen to assess whether they consider interest payments can be made and if the amount of the loan will be able to be repaid when it falls due.

The **government** and **local authorities** will look beyond the financial statements and to the future plans of the business which are often laid out in the directors' report. They may be interested to see if the company has future plans that will affect the local area. The government (Inland Revenue) will use the accounts to assess the amount of tax that is payable.

Competitors will look to see how the company has performed and if it has increased its market share. They will also be interested in any future plans that the company discloses, to see whether or not it conflicts with their own plans.

Employees are increasingly taking an interest in the activities of the companies that employ them. Their interest is often linked to the company's ability to pay for wage claims although they may also be interested in the future viability of the business.

Analysts, such as economists, use the financial information as a basis for research and to compile statistical records.

Management require financial information to evaluate their past performance. The results of this evaluation are plans and predictions for future performance. Linked to this is the attempt to control the future performance of the business through past experiences.

Customers and the **general public** may look to the financial statements of a business to assess whether or not it is likely to continue to operate in the foreseeable future. There is also a general interest in business activities, e.g. what effect is Company X having on the environment?

TASK SIX   INTERMEDIATE

Using a copy of published accounts (paper copy or online), make a list of information that would be of interest to each of the groups listed above.

QUESTION Q1

(a) What four main areas does financial information cover?
(b) For what purpose might a manager use financial information?
(c) List at least four characteristics of useful financial information.
(d) List at least five users of financial information.
(e) Taking the list of users of financial information that you have just made, suggest a reason for each of them to be using the information.

BUSINESS DECISION AREAS

UNIT: 2

TOPIC FIVE: Accounting ratios

Accounting ratios are used as a tool in the decision-making process and as an aid to financial interpretation and planning. They may be used by managers within the business as well as outsiders who are interested in the performance of the business or who have an interest in the business.

Ratios can be categorised according to the function that they perform:

- **profitability**
- **liquidity**
- **efficiency.**

Several different ratios can be calculated under each of the headings. This can then allow comparisons between different years for the same business, comparisons with other businesses in the same sector or comparison with averages for a particular business sector. This process is often referred to as ratio analysis.

Ratio analysis may also be used for more sinister purposes, e.g. by another business or individual planning a take-over. It may also prove to be a useful tool in the forecasting or budgeting process.

It is worth noting, however, that accounting ratios have their limitations:

- **The accounting information used to calculate the ratios is historic, i.e. it is based on information that is out of date.**

- **When comparisons are made with other businesses then the comparison is only valid where the business is of the same type and size.**

- **Comparisons with other businesses can be difficult as many businesses publish only very limited financial information.**

- **Comparisons must be made using the same ratio calculations – many businesses 'tweak' the ratio formulas to suit their own needs.**

- **When comparisons are made over a series of years, either for the same business or in the same business sector, the external effects of the general economy are not reflected in the ratio calculations and this must be taken into account.**

- **Comparisons of ratios with different businesses in the same sector may be meaningless if the ratios are not calculated on the same basis, i.e. using the same formulae.**

- **Ratios are of little use on their own. They must be used as an aid to interpretation and in the context of the business sector to which they apply. It is, therefore, essential that the user is also able to understand both how the particular business operates and how it reports its financial results.**

- **Other sources of information should also be utilised when interpreting the accounts, such as the Directors' Report, Auditors' Report, Notes to the Accounts and accounting policies of the business.**

- The users of financial ratios must beware of 'window dressing'. This is where a company temporarily improves its working capital (net current assets) in order to improve its ratios. This effect can be achieved through increasing stock levels or taking out a short term loan.

The users of financial information can include stakeholders in the business, investors, creditors, customers and employees. They will want to know the answers to questions such as:

- Is the business profitable?

- Can the business pay its debts on time?

- How is the business financed?

- What percentage of the full business worth is financed?

- How does this year's performance compare with last year's?

- How does the performance of the business compare to other businesses in the same sector?

Ratio analysis can provide easy answers to all of these questions without the need to go through pages and pages of accounts. If you have had the opportunity to access company accounts online at *www.carol.co.uk* or been able to look at a set of published company accounts then you will appreciate that it can be difficult to interpret the huge amount of information provided.

The most common ratios that are calculated are:

- Profitability
  - gross profit as a percentage of sales
  - gross profit as a percentage of cost of goods sold
  - net profit as a percentage of sales.

- Liquidity
  - current ratio
  - acid test ratio.

- Efficiency
  - return on capital employed.

TOPIC SIX: Ratio analysis – Calculation of ratios

For each of the ratios that we will analyse, we will make use of the summarised financial statements of Gill's Gym Equipment Ltd which follow:

Profit and loss accounts for the years ending 30 June	Year 1 £000s	Year 2 £000s
Turnover	850	900
Gross profit	90	110
Interest payable	(15)	(15)
Taxation	(50)	(60)
Net profit	25	35
Dividends	(15)	(20)
Retained profits	10	15
Note to the accounts:		
Cost of goods sold	600	700

Balance sheets as at 30 June	Year 1 £000s	Year 2 £000s
Fixed assets	600	700
Current assets		
Stock	300	350
Debtors	200	100
Cash	50	250
	550	700
Less: current liabilities	(250)	(350)
Net current assets	300	350
Net assets	**900**	**1050**
Financed by:		
Shareholders' funds		
Ordinary shares	700	800
Share premium	60	135
Retained profits	10	15
	780	**950**
15% debentures	120	100
Capital Employed	**900**	**1050**

PROFITABILITY RATIOS

Gross profit as a percentage of sales

This ratio is used to calculate the gross profit as a percentage of sales turnover. Where the percentage is high, it may indicate that the business has a prudent buying policy. Changes in the ratio can be caused by an increase or a decrease in the selling price (usually a deliberate company policy) or an increase or a decrease in the cost of goods sold (usually outwith the company's control).

The formula used is:

(Gross Profit ÷ Sales) × 100%

Gross profit as a percentage of cost of goods sold

This ratio is used to calculate the gross profit as a percentage of cost of goods sold. Where the percentage is high, it may indicate that the business has a prudent buying policy. Changes in the ratio can be caused by an increase or a decrease in the cost of goods sold (usually outwith the company's control).

The formula used is:

(Gross Profit ÷ Cost of Goods Sold) × 100%

Net profit as a percentage of sales

This ratio is used to calculate the return on sales when compared to the total costs of the business. Where a low figure is calculated, this shows that the company's expenses may be high and should be further investigated. This ratio is often used to highlight efficiency and control of costs.

The formula used is:

(Net Profit ÷ Sales) × 100%

LIQUIDITY RATIOS

Current ratio

The current ratio is used to indicate the business's ability to meet its short term debts without having to borrow money. There is no ideal figure for this ratio, although it should normally fall within the region of 1:1 and 3:1. Where the ratio is very low, this indicates that the business may have problems in meeting its short term debts. Conversely, where the ratio is high, although this indicates that there is more than enough money to cover short term business debts, it can also indicate that there is too much cash in the business not being utilised to best advantage. Spare cash can be invested, even in the short term, and earn additional income for the business.

The formula used is:

Current Assets : Current Liabilities

UNIT 2

Acid test ratio

The acid test ratio is similar to the current ratio although it takes into account the fact that stocks of raw materials and goods for re-sale may take some time to be turned into cash. The business's ability to pay its short term debts is therefore assessed without the inclusion of the value of stocks. The average figure of 1:1 should be used as a guideline, although anything less than this would indicate that the business would not be able to meet its short term debts without selling stock or borrowing money. It is worth noting that some businesses can operate with an acid test ratio of less than 1:1 and the typical ratio will depend on the type of business.

The formula used is:

Current Assets — Stock : Current Liabilities

EFFICIENCY RATIOS

Return on capital employed

This ratio measures how well, or how badly, a business has utilised the capital that has been invested in it. This gives a more useful interpretation of performance than merely looking at the profit figure.

For example, imagine that Company X reports a profit of £1m and Company Y reports a profit of £500,000. Company X would appear to be the more successful company, based on the information provided, but a quick calculation, taking into account the capital invested in these companies, shows that Company X earned £1m profit from capital invested of £10m while Company Y earned profit of £500,000 from just £4m capital invested. Company Y has made better use of its capital as Company X used more than twice the amount of capital to produce just double the profit of Company Y.

The formula used to calculate return on capital employed:

(Net Profit ÷ Capital Employed) × 100%

The table below shows the ratios for Gill's Gym Equipment Ltd. Check that you are able to apply the formulae to give the correct results.

Gill's Gym, Equipment Ltd – Financial Ratios	Year 1	Year 2
Gross profit as a percentage of sales	10.6%	12.2%
Gross profit as a percentage of cost of goods sold	15%	15.7%
Net profit as a percentage of sales	2.9%	3.9%
Current ratio	2.2:1	2.0:1
Acid test ratio	1:1	1:1
Return on capital employed	2.8%	3.3%

If you have access to the Internet, find the accounts for the year ended 31 March 2001 for Scottish Power. These can be accessed through the website *www.carol.co.uk* or at *www.scottishpower.co.uk*

Calculate the ratios that appear in the following table and see if your answers match.

Scottish Power – Financial Ratios	31 March 2001
Gross profit as a percentage of sales	30.6%
Gross profit as a percentage of cost of goods sold	44.1%
Net profit as a percentage of sales	6.0%
Current ratio	0.6:1
Acid test ratio	0.57:1
Return on capital employed	6.2%

By comparison, the accounting ratios of Scottish and Southern Energy plc (a company operating in the same business sector as Scottish Power) has the following accounting ratios:

Scottish and Southern Engergy plc – Financial Ratios	31 March 2001
Gross profit as a percentage of sales	27.5%
Gross profit as a percentage of cost of goods sold	37.9%
Net profit as a percentage of sales	12.0%
Current ratio	0.47:1
Acid test ratio	0.45:1
Return on capital employed	23.4%

Let us consider each of these ratios in turn.

GROSS PROFIT AS A PERCENTAGE OF SALES
Scottish Power has a ratio of 30.6% and Scottish and Southern Energy plc has a ratio of 27.5%. This means that for every £100 of sales, Scottish Power made £30.60 in profit before expenses and Scottish and Southern Energy plc made £27.50 in profit before expenses. Before expenses are taken into account, Scottish Power is the more profitable company. A closer look at the accounts for each business reveals that

Scottish and Southern Energy plc had a boost to its turnover due to acquisitions during 2001. Despite this apparent advantage, it has still not managed to outperform Scottish Power.

GROSS PROFIT AS A PERCENTAGE OF COST OF GOODS SOLD
Scottish Power has a ratio of 44.1% and Scottish and Southern Energy plc has a ratio of 37.9%. This means that for every £100 spent on the cost of sales, Scottish Power made a profit before expenses of £44.10 but Scottish and Southern Energy plc made a profit of just £37.90.

NET PROFIT AS A PERCENTAGE OF SALES
Scottish Power has a net profit percentage of 6% but Scottish and Southern Energy plc has a net profit percentage of 12%, exactly double that of Scottish Power. This demonstrates that Scottish Power may not be exerting full control over its business expenses. The difference between the gross profit percentage and the net profit percentage is greater for Scottish Power and this suggests that the company has too many expenses. A return on net profit in the region of 10% would be more acceptable.

CURRENT RATIO AND ACID TEST RATIO
Both companies have very low current and acid test ratios. In fact, they are so low that neither of them would be able to meet their short term debts if they became immediately payable. However, close inspection of the accounts reveals that neither the current assets nor the current liabilities of either business are particularly substantial. Two conclusions can be drawn from this: any spare cash in the business is invested for maximum gain in the short term and it is symptomatic of this business sector that these ratios are low.

RETURN ON CAPITAL EMPLOYED
The return on capital employed for Scottish Power is a disappointingly low 6.2% when compared to the figure of 23.4% achieved by Scottish and Southern Energy plc. Scottish and Southern Energy plc has approximately one third of the capital of Scottish Power and yet Scottish Power managed to achieve a return of only £382m while Scottish and Southern Energy plc achieved a return of £430m.

Further investigation of the reasons behind Scottish Power's poor performance is required. One explanation could be that Scottish and Southern Energy plc has had a particularly good year, thereby making an unfair comparison within the sector.

CONCLUSION
Care must be taken when using and interpreting accounting ratios. It must be remembered that they are of limited use in isolation and their usefulness is increased only marginally when used in conjunction with other sources of information. They do, however, remain a popular and useful tool for quickly displaying financial statistics about a company's performance.

TASK EIGHT HIGHER

Access accounts for the following companies from their Internet sites (or from *www.carol.co.uk*):

- ASDA
- Tesco
- Sainsbury's
- Safeway.

Draw up a table and compare the ratios that you have calculated. Each of these businesses operates in the same sector and in direct competition with each other. Are their accounting ratios similar? Can you explain why there are similarities or differences?

TOPIC SEVEN: Budgets

A budget is simply a statement of anticipated future expenditure. It will usually cover a specific time period, e.g. a month or a year. Budgets are usually financial in nature although they can be expressed in other units.

The main uses of budgets are:

- **Monitoring and control** – setting a budget and then comparing it to actual performance means that comparisons can be made on a regular basis and changes adopted quickly to remedy problems.

- **To gain information** – budgets allow managers to see how well the business is performing.

- **To set targets** – this gives managers and employees limits to reach.

- **To delegate authority** – the use of budgets means that managers can give responsibility to employees.

Cash budgets are a common type of budget that are used by most businesses to monitor, control, obtain and present information.

They can be used to monitor the cash position of a particular department, section or project or the business as a whole. They can also be used as a management decision-making tool to assess the validity of a particular project or scenario. A cash projection may be used as part of a submission to a lender to secure finance.

Budgets are often produced using accounting software or a generic spreadsheet package. This means that changes can be made to the budget very easily and the effects of these changes will be automatically updated in the rest of the budget.

An example of a cash budget is shown opposite:

UNIT 2

Airwave Ltd.
Budgets for the 6 month - January 2002 to June 2002

Cash Receipts Budget:

	Apr (£)	May (£)	Jun (£)	Jul (£)	Aug (£)	Sep (£)	Total (£)
Receipts from debtors	5,000	5,000	6,000	7,000	4,000	6,000	33,000
Total Cash Inflows	5,000	5,000	6,000	7,000	4,000	6,000	33,000

Cash Payments Budget:

	Apr (£)	May (£)	Jun (£)	Jul (£)	Aug (£)	Sep (£)	Total (£)
Payments to creditors	2,000	3,000	4,000	4,000	3,000	2,000	18,000
Direct labour	2,000	2,000	2,500	2,500	1,100	1,100	11,200
Variable overheads	300	400	300	200	400	500	2,100
Maintenance contracts	100	200	300	400	400	400	1,800
Total Cash Outflows	4,400	5,600	7,100	7,100	4,900	4,000	33,100

Cash Payments Budget:

	Apr (£)	May (£)	Jun (£)	Jul (£)	Aug (£)	Sep (£)	Total (£)
Opening Cash/Bank Balance	1,000	1,600	1,000	(100)	(200)	(1,100)	1,000
Cash Inflows	5,000	5,000	6,000	7,000	4,000	6,000	33,000
Cash Outflows	4,400	5,600	7,100	7,100	4,900	4,000	33,100
Closing Cash/Bank Balance	1,600	1,000	(100)	(200)	(1,100)	900	900

The cash budget is just one example of the use of a budget. It is usual for other budgets to 'feed into' the cash budget. These other budgets are usually referred to as **functional budgets**.

Examples of functional budgets are shown below:

The Central Company Ltd.

Budgets for the 3 month period - April 2002 to June 2002

Raw Materials Usage Budget (units):	kg				
	Per	Apr	May	Jun	Total
	Unit	(kg)	(kg)	(kg)	(kg)
Opening Stock		15,000	21,290	25,085	15,000
Purchases		5,000	2,500	3,000	10,500
Materials available for production	5.00	20,000	23,790	28,085	71,875
Used for Budgeted Production		(1,290)	(1,295)	(1,290)	(3,785)
Closing Stock		21,290	25,085	29,375	29,375

The Central Company Ltd.

Budgets for the 3 month period - April 2002 to June 2002

Direct Labour Hours Budget	Hours				
	Per	Apr	May	Jun	Total
	Unit	(hr)	(hr)	(hr)	(hr)
Budgeted Hours for planned production	5.00	1,806	1,813	1,806	5,425
Direct Labour Hours Budget	Rate				
	Per	Apr	May	Jun	Total
	Hour	(£)	(£)	(£)	(£)
Budgeted Labour Cost of planned production	£4.00	7,224	7,252	7,224	21,700

The main benefits to management of using cash budgets can be summarised as:

● Planning – management can look ahead to set aims and strategies. This allows problem-solving to be planned rather than having to react to situations as they happen.

● Organisation – allows the right resources to be in the right place at the right time.

● Command – when management are able to make informed decisions, this enables them to instruct their subordinates. The management will have access to all the budgets for each department which will be fed into the master budget, e.g. the cash budget.

● Co-ordinate – management can give instructions to those in charge of departmental budgets and keep a clear overview of the business as a whole.

● Control – evaluation and review of budgets allow management to exert control over the organisation as a whole.

● Delegation – management should make subordinates responsible for a suitable range of tasks and give them the authority to carry them out.

● Motivation – management have a responsibility to motivate their staff. This can be done through setting realistic targets in the budgets and introducing concepts and practices such as teamwork, empowerment and incentives for meeting targets or operating within the budget.

TASK NINE   HIGHER

Prepare a simple cash budget of your own, detailing your income and expenditure over the course of a four-week period. Do you have enough money to operate?

CASE STUDY

Burns Express Freight Ltd
Financial management Case study

Burns Express Freight Ltd was formed in 1993 by Carolyn and Derek Burns after having been employed for several years in the Transport and Distribution Industry. The company is based in Paisley and initially started with three vehicles and attained a turnover of £267,000 in its first year. From then, it has attained an average 20% per year growth and now has a turnover of £1.3 million and a fleet of 15 vehicles.

To maintain company growth, the company have found an investment policy to be essential. Vehicles are renewed regularly and investment in staff and driver training is on an ongoing basis. After initially renting premises, the company bought its own premises in Paisley and has gradually upgraded over the past five years. Image is also very important and the company has spent money on vehicle livery, uniforms and advertising in an attempt to project the right image to its customers.

As the company has grown in size, it has become necessary to move with the times and embrace the computer age. In the past, everything from invoicing to entries in the job book were done by hand. This was a very laborious and time-consuming job and as the business grew, even the typing of invoices tied up one member of staff for two full days every week.

Three years ago, the company invested in a computer network and software to take care of dispatch management and the finance function. Carolyn and Derek firmly believed that money spent on computers would save them money in the longer term. Since the computer system was implemented, they believe that they have become more organised and professional.

Invoices can be produced at the touch of a button and it is easy to manage customers' accounts and keep track of sales history, prices and repeat jobs. These tasks would have been too time-consuming in the past.

(*www.burnsexpress.co.uk*)
(With thanks to Carolyn and Derek Burns.)

CHAPTER SUMMARY

At the end of this chapter you should make sure that you are aware of the following:

- **The main** profitability **ratios are:**
  - **gross profit as a percentage of sales**
  - **gross profit as a percentage of cost of goods sold**
  - **net profit as a percentage of sales.**

- **The main** liquidity **ratios are:**
  - **current ratio**
  - **acid test ratio.**

- **The main** efficiency **ratio is:**
  - **return on capital employed.**

- **Calculation of ratios is not enough;** analysis **must also take place.**

- **Analysis of ratios may include comparisons over a number of years or comparisons with other businesses in the same sector.**

- **Accounting ratios can be calculated for any business that produces financial reports.**

- **Ratios are usually calculated to highlight the areas of profitability, liquidity and efficiency.**

- **The use of accounting ratios has limitations of which you should be aware.**

- Useful financial information should cover the areas of profitability, liquidity, efficiency and capital structure.

- Financial information becomes more useful when it is used as a comparator.

- Useful financial information has certain characteristics.

- The users of financial information are a varied group.

- You should be aware of the reasons for users of financial information showing an interest in a company's financial statements.

- Budgets are statements showing future expenditure and are used as a management tool.

- Budgets are useful for monitoring and controlling business operations. They are also useful for gaining information, setting targets and delegating authority.

- A cash budget is a good example of a budget.

- Budgets are most easily used when created using a piece of appropriate computer software.

- The role of the finance function in an organisation includes:
  - payment of wages
  - payment of accounts
  - maintenance of financial records.

- The purpose and use of:
  - profit and loss account
  - balance sheet
  - cash flow statement.

PREPARATION FOR ASSESSMENT

HIGHER ASSESSMENT

There are three PC's (Performance Criterion) for this assessment. Here you will be asked to interpret financial information used in business. The assessment will normally be based on a case study which you should read carefully before attempting to answer the questions.

PC (a) – Interpretation of cash flow information is accurate and related to possible cash flow problems

If you have studied Accounting and Finance this may be a little confusing because what you are normally given is a cash budget rather than a cash flow statement from which you have to identify possible problems for the organisation involved, and then explain the implications of what this will mean for the organisation.

The most obvious indication of problems will appear in the closing cash balances if they become negative, or reduce over a period of months, this will highlight where the problems exist. The first thing to look for is falling sales receipts. This could be due to seasonal factors or poor sales techniques. In either case if they are not matched by a fall in payments then there will be a problem. Look out for big items of capital expenditure such as new machines.

The implications may be that the organisation will have to reduce some of their payments. You will have to say which, and explain why. If there is a large item of capital expenditure, then perhaps the organisation should have considered getting a loan and paying it off over a period of time, or perhaps they should now consider sale and leaseback in order to solve their cash flow problems.

PC (b) – Appropriate financial ratios are used correctly to interpret the performance and liquidity of an organisation

The ratios will already have been calculated for you, what you have to do is decide which are profitability ratios, and which are liquidity ratios. The easy way to remember is that profitability ratios will mention gross or net profit, whilst liquidity ratios will be concerned with current assets and current liabilities.

You will be expected to compare the ratios of two companies, or two different years for the same company, and state which is better or worse and why. There are plenty of examples in this chapter for you to look at.

PC (c) – Explanation of budgets is accurate and refers to their role in monitoring and controlling business activities

It is important to remember that we are talking about budgets here, **not just** cash budgets. Your answer should include details of how budgets allow managers to plan for the future: they help set targets for managers, making them accountable for their decisions; they can be used to compare actual performance to the budgeted performance and take appropriate action where necessary; and they allow managers to see how they are progressing towards their objectives.

 INTERMEDIATE 2 ASSESSMENT

Here there are two PC's (Performance Criterion) to be concerned with. You will be asked to read a case study and then answer a number of questions. The number of marks and questions will depend on the assessment used. Remember to read the case study carefully as it will provide many of your answers.

PC (a) – Explanation of the uses of financial information in business is accurate

Here you will be asked to identify what the main uses of financial information in business are, and what it is used for. Your answer should include: controlling costs so that the business stays profitable, and pays its bills on time; to forecast trends in costs such as wages, raw materials, etc.; to monitor performance to compare with previous years; and to prepare budgets in order to plan for the future.

PC (b) – Explanation includes accurate descriptions of the potential users of financial information and the value of such information

Here you will be asked who uses financial information and why they use it. There are a large number of different groups who will use the information and most of them will be stakeholders in the organisation. For example, the employees would be interested to see how profitable the business was so that they can see how secure their jobs are, and how much they should ask for as a pay rise. You could include management from the previous PC to controlling the business or preparing future plans.

CHAPTER SEVEN

UNIT:2 BUSINESS DECISION AREAS

HUMAN RESOURCES MANAGEMENT

This topic is covered at *both* Higher and Intermediate level 2. The content for both courses is very similar and *both* are assessed internally, with the contents of the assessment being very similar. The depth of answers required will be different at either level, however Intermediate 2 and Higher students should read the whole of the chapter to increase their understanding of the topic.

The chapter covers:

INTERMEDIATE LEVEL 2

- The elements of human resource management:
  - recruitment
  - selection
  - training and development
  - maintenance of personnel records
  - terms and conditions of employment
  - awareness of employment laws.
- Employee relations:
  - local and national agreements
  - trade unions
  - works councils.

HIGHER LEVEL

- Changing patterns of employment within organisations, including trends towards the greater use of part-time and casual staff and the role of the core labour force within the organisation.
- Recruitment and selection techniques, including job analysis, job description, person specification; internal and external sources for recruitment; selection methods including application forms, interviews, and testing.

- Training and staff development, including the reasons for training and development and the techniques and processes available to organisations.
- Employee relations, looking at the main institutions for employee relations; the processes involed in employee relations; and the management of employee relations.
- The various laws that affect employment including discrimination law, employment law, and health and safety.

Guidance and advice on the internal assessments can be found at the end of the chapter.

The people who work for an organisation represent a big investment for their employers, in terms of time and money. Each and every employee makes a contribution towards the organisation achieving its objectives, through the jobs that they do. Employees are resources of the organisation, and so human resource management aims to make the most efficient use of these resources, as, the better they are at their job, and the harder they work, the more successful the organisation will be.

TOPIC ONE: Objectives of human resources management

The objectives of human resources management will vary between organisations, however the main ones are:

- to promote a policy of continuous learning and staff development

- to recruit, develop and retain people with the appropriate skills and attitudes required for present and future jobs

- to manage employee relations, both on a one-to-one basis and on a collective basis, and to maintain the commitment of the workforce

- to design, implement and manage remuneration, reward and appraisal schemes, which motivate people towards achieving the organisation's objectives

- to maintain and improve the physical and mental well-being of the workforce by providing appropriate working conditions and health and safety conditions

- to take account of all government legislation relevant to human resources management.

QUESTION

Q1 What are the main objectives of HRM?

Human resources management (HRM) is still sometimes called personnel management, and it is one of the main functional areas of an organisation.

The size of the HRM department will depend on the number of people the organisation employs, however even a small organisation with just one employee has to manage that employee in terms of getting the best out of him/her. In addition, there is whole range of legal responsibilities that an employer has, and so even a 'one-employee business' has to perform the HRM function.

The department is responsible for drawing up policies and strategies for the management of staff, and making sure they are implemented, and for ensuring that the organisation meets all its legal requirements as far as the employees are concerned.

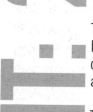

THE MANAGEMENT OF PEOPLE

It is important for the HRM department to understand what motivates its workforce in order that it can use that motivation to increase its productivity. In 1954 an American researcher called Abraham Maslow put forward a theory on workers' needs based on his research. He suggested that people's needs are complex, but can be classified into five main types. Workers will be motivated by trying to satisfy these needs.

The first is their **physiological** needs for things such as food, clothing, shelter and warmth. These needs are satisfied by wages and various financial bonuses high enough to meet weekly bills.

The second is their **safety** needs which can be satisfied through job security, their contract of employment, membership of a trade union, and protection of the various employment laws.

The third is their **emotional** needs for love and belonging. These can be satisfied through teamworking, job rotation and social clubs.

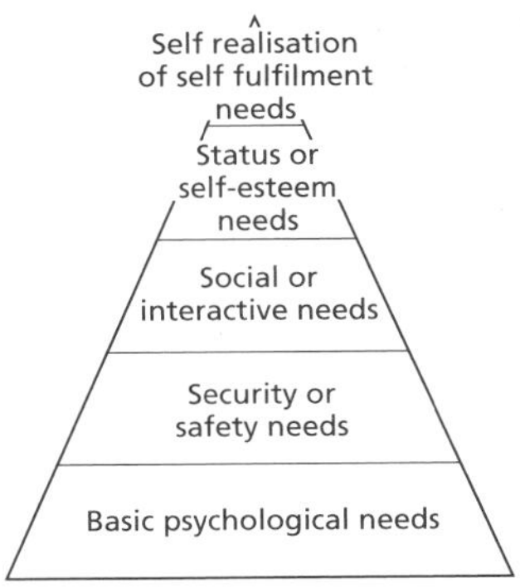

Esteem needs are the need for self-respect and the esteem of others. This can be done by recognition, promotion, merit awards, job title, even the size of office or desk that you are given.

Finally, **self-actualisation** needs are filled through self-fulfillment. They can be satisfied by promotion, more responsibility, ownership of company shares or self-employment.

There are two main management schools on what motivates people. They can be described as Theory X and Theory Y.

Theory X managers believe that workers are only motivated by money, and that they are lazy and dislike work. They are selfish, ignore the needs of the organisation, avoid responsibility and lack ambition. In order to get the best out of them, they need to be controlled and directed by management.

Theory Y managers believe that workers have many different needs which motivate them, and that they can enjoy their work. If motivated, the workers can organise themselves and take responsibility. They believe that managers should create a situation where workers can show creativity and apply their job knowledge.

IMAGE 25.
Maslow's Hierarchy of Needs

Self realisation of self fulfilment needs
Status or self-esteem needs
Social or interactive needs
Security or safety needs
Basic psychological needs

QUESTION

Q2 Describe Maslow's classification of needs and describe how they are satisfied through employment.

INCREASING MOTIVATION

There are a number of strategies that an organisation can employ to increase motivation in the workforce.

Quality circles are groups of between four and 10 workers who work for the same supervisor. They meet regularly to identify, analyse and attempt to solve work-related problems. They increase the motivation of the workers by involving them in the decision-making around their own jobs, thus increasing efficiency and raising profitability.

Job enlargement increases the number of tasks a worker will perform, making their jobs less repetitive and boring. It works best where the employees are organised into groups, where all the workers are trained in all jobs the group carries out. They use **job rotation** to allow workers to change the tasks they perform on a regular basis. It also allows for **multi-skilling**.

CHAPTER:Seven

TOPIC ONE

HUMAN RESOURCES MANAGEMENT

Job enrichment involves giving workers some opportunities to choose how to complete a particular task, again usually working as a team.

QUESTION

Q3 Describe three strategies that could be employed to increase employee motivation.

TOPIC TWO: The changing pattern of employment within organisations

The Human Resources department has responsibility for making the best use of the staff that it employs. The cost of employing staff is a major expense for the business so part of the HR role is to keep those costs to a minimum. Amongst the most popular methods that businesses have employed is to change the structure of their workforce.

In previous years, businesses would recruit staff on a full-time basis to perform set tasks, as and when they were needed. This often led to a large, inflexible workforce, which could become a burden to the organisation when demand for their goods or services fell. Redundancy payments can be expensive, and the workforce can become less co-operative.

Royal Mail

As part of Royal Mail's restructuring to get into profit, three Parcelforce depots in Scotland were to close – Glasgow West (where 500 people are employed); Dundee; and Irvine. The Union of Communications Workers said any job losses would be a disaster for the industry and would have a significant impact on the services provided. Union spokesman John Meechan said 'Our union has a proud tradition of looking after all our members. As soon as they make one compulsory redundancy there will be a national dispute within the whole of the post office industry.'

We have already seen that in order to be successful, organisations must be able to adapt quickly to changes in their markets. As a major part of the organisation, the workforce must be flexible too. This flexibility can be achieved by employing more part-time and casual staff, and the greater use of outside contractors to provide 'non-core' support services such as cleaning, accountancy services, ICT support, etc. This means that the people you actually employ are only concerned with the **core activities** of the organisation. The core activities are those that directly achieve the organisation's objectives.

For example, oil companies' main business in Scotland is to find and extract oil from the North Sea. The majority of employees in the North Sea work for contractors who supply a wide rage of services to the oil companies.

UNIT 2

The costs involved in employment not only include the wage or salary, but also other employment costs such as accommodation, National Insurance, paid holidays, sick pay, training and development, etc. Having someone else carry these costs often makes it cheaper to employ outside contractors.

PART-TIME WORKERS

Until recently, part-time workers did not have the same employment rights as full-time workers, and so the cost of hiring, employing, and releasing was much less. The 'Prevention of less favourable treatment' Regulations introduced in 1999–2000 meant that part-time employees had to receive the same benefits as their full-time colleagues.

Banks and building societies

One perk available to employees of banks and building societies is low-rate borrowing. Full-time staff can borrow money, for example to buy a house, at much better rates of interest than the public. This perk was not available to part-time workers until changes in the European Union employment laws gave part-time workers the same rights as full-time employees.

Around 3500 members of staff at the banking giant HSBC will receive around £25 million in backdated pension contributions following the bank's decision to recompense its part-time workers.

Find out more about part-time workers rights at
www.tuc.org.uk

One major benefit of still employing part-time workers is that you can often pay them less. In addition, they tend to be more flexible in their working hours, and some workers, particularly women, can only work part-time because of other commitments such as looking after young children.

Part-time workers have been found to have increased productivity levels, mainly due to a lower rate of absenteeism and also research indicates that part-time managers are more committed and motivated.

Find out more at
www.dti.gov.uk/work-lifebalance

CASUAL STAFF

Casual workers tend to be hired and released as and when they are needed. They do not have the same employment rights as full- or part-time workers at present.

Shops such as Marks and Spencer will employ casual staff around busy times of the year such as Christmas. They will be employed for a number of weeks. They will not enjoy the same pay and conditions as the permanent members of staff, and will be released once the busy time has passed.

CONTRACTUAL STAFF

Another common alternative to employing full-time permanent members of staff is to employ staff on a fixed-term contract of one or two years, or use agency staff. At the end of the contract the employee will either be released or will be offered a new contract. This brings benefits to the organisation as the contracted worker will not have the same employment rights or protection, and there is no need for the organisation to offer such things as membership of a pension scheme. In effect, the employee is self-employed. Agency staff are not employed directly by the organisation, and so can be hired or released as needed.

IMAGE 26.
An employment agency

 **Temporary workers**

The EU Fixed-Term Contracts Directive 1999, which the government plans to implement in July 2003, will give many temporary workers similar rights to permanent staff. The TUC fear that they may not be entitled to the same terms of pay and pensions, and wants new laws to cover the increasing number of agency workers.

Currently, 1.7 million people in the UK are on temporary contracts, 'casuals' or agency workers (7% of the total workforce). 16% of temporary workers are now agency workers, compared with just 7% eight years ago. 25% of temporary workers do not get paid sick leave, 14% do not get holiday pay, 47% of temporary workers get paid less, and 70% do not get access to company pension schemes.

 Find out more about temporary workers at
www.tuc.org.uk/theme/index.cfm?theme=temps

 **QUESTION 4**

Describe how the structure of the workforce has changed in recent years.

WOMEN AT WORK

There is a continuing rise in the number of women who are working. Although the highest growth rates in recent years are in full-time employment, there has been an increasing number of women in part-time employment. Across the UK there are an estimated 12.5 million women in work, 843,000 more than 10 years ago. This raises a number of issues which the HRM department has to address.

CASE STUDY

Women at work

In February 2002 a total of 1,115,000 women worked in the Scottish economy. Full-time workers accounted for 645,000 and part-time 470,000 of this total. This compares with, in February 1999, a female total of 1,072,000, with 622,000 full-time and 450,000 part-time.

Meredith Belbin, in his latest book *Managing Without Power*, says that the technological revolution, with its premium of communication skills, has allowed women to regain their economic status and influence, yet this has brought with it some problems. He says men tend to focus on long term goals at the expense of everything else, while women look more closely at knock-on effects, contingency factors and immediacy. Both these elements are necessary in successful teams.

Find out more at
www.peoplemanagement.co.uk

The main problem for HRM departments still lies with equality at work for women.

It is a legal responsibility of employers to ensure that men and women are treated the same in terms of pay and conditions for doing similar jobs. Failure to do so could result in fines and bad publicity for the organisation.

QUESTION

Q5

Describe the growing importance of women at work, and identify the issues that HRM are having to face.

TOPIC THREE: Other changes in the workplace

There have been a number of other methods employed by organisations to reduce the costs of employment, and make the workforce more productive. **Flexi-time** has been around for a number of years now, and involves workers having to be at their workplace only at certain core times of the day. They make up the rest of their daily or weekly hours at times that suit them best. This has the advantages of allowing staff to miss the rush hour and so reducing their time spent travelling, fitting in appointments, picking up children from school, etc. For the employer it means less time off work and a happier and more motivated workforce.

Hot desks are areas of the workplace set aside for staff who do not need office space all the time, for example salespeople. They have all the equipment they need at the hot desk, and so the organisation does not need to create office space for them individually.

Working from home/tele-working — with modern communications equipment, many jobs can now be carried out at home. Why spend hours a week travelling to work at a computer, when you could have the computer at home? This saves on accommodation costs for the organisation, and again can increase the productivity of the workers. The main drawback here is the employee's feeling of isolation.

DRAWBACKS OF THE FLEXIBLE WORKFORCE

Having fewer core staff leads to a number of problems for the organisation. First, the HRM department will spend much more time recruiting staff, and ensuring that there are enough staff available. The amount of training required will increase, much of which will be lost as the staff leave when they are no longer required. When dealing with customers, continuity of staff is important to ensure their repeat business. Finally, non-core staff are far less likely to be motivated towards achieving the organisation's goals and objectives.

QUESTION

Q6

What problems have been presented to firms who have reduced their core workforce?

TOPIC FOUR: Recruitment and selection

One of the major roles of the HRM department is to obtain the best staff possible to work for the organisation. The better the workforce, the more able the organisation is to meet its objectives. Even if the cost of employment was not a factor, it would still be difficult to make sure you had the best staff — but cost is a major factor and always has to be considered in recruitment.

At the heart of good HRM is human resource planning. This involves a range of factors that have to be looked at.

First, the current labour market trends. Fewer people are being born, which means we have an ageing working population. There will be fewer young people to recruit and train, so other areas of the labour market will have to be investigated. For example, more firms are turning to the over 50s to do jobs that were previously offered to young people. B & Q has a policy of employing the over 50s as they can offer their customers more experience when dealing with inquiries. The government has launched 'New Deal 50 Plus' to encourage employers and older employees by making it more financially attractive to employ older people.

To find out more on labour market trends visit
www.statistics.gov.uk or www.tuc.org.uk

Second, it involves forecasting any possible future staffing needs of the organisation, including likely staff turnover, promotion of existing staff, retirements and releasing surplus staff. This will

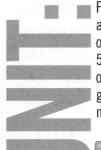

be a continuing process as staff needs will change with the organisation's environment (political, economic, socio–cultural, technological, and competitive). They will then compare this with the number of appropriately skilled workers who will be available.

Third, it involves looking at support for staff development in training and motivation. This will include the establishment of a corporate culture.

Fourth, it involves looking at any possible increase in workload, for example due to increased demand for the organisation's products, the development of new products, or the introduction of new technologies that will require new skills not available in the current workforce.

QUESTION

Q7 Describe the importance of good human resource planning.

TOPIC FIVE: The HRM function within the organisation

Most organisations will have an HRM department, however its importance and the role that it plays will vary between organisations. It will certainly be involved in all aspects of Human Resources work and planning, however a major aspect of the job is to provide advice and training to line managers so that they can be fully responsible for their staff.

Line managers may well be involved in drawing up job descriptions, selecting new staff, staff training, appraisals, looking at future staffing requirements, initially handling grievances, and implementing HRM policy in their departments.

HRM is a support function of the organisation and has a staff relationship with the other departments in the business. Within this function it will support the organisation through a number of roles:

● Facilitator – **this involves providing guidance and training to other managers within the organisation in all HRM policies and procedures and on practical aspects of their job such as interviewing for new staff and carrying out appraisals.**

● Auditor – **this involves monitoring and reporting on all the HRM policies within the organisation, ensuring that all staff follow procedures.**

● Consultancy – **here it provides managers with guidance and advice on specialist assistance to manage potentially difficult situations effectively, such as making staff redundant.**

● Executive – **HRM are the resident experts in all matters relating to HRM management.**

● Service – **providing useful, up-to-date information, for example on new employment legislation.**

Describe the five main roles that the HRM department plays within the organisation.

TOPIC SIX: Job analysis

This is the first step in the recruitment process. It initially involves establishing whether a vacancy actually exists. If a worker leaves, he or she may not need to be replaced if the work can be shared among existing staff. To do this you would have to look at what the job's main features are.

What are the main physical and mental elements of the job? What specific skills are required? What and who would the job holder be responsible for, and who would they be responsible to? Where will they work and what are the main health and safety considerations?

JOB DESCRIPTION/SPECIFICATION

Once the job analysis has been completed, and a vacancy identified, the next step is to draw up a description of the job that needs to be done. This will also be the basis for any advertisement of the vacancy. It will include:

- the job title
- the overall purpose of the job
- the main tasks and responsibilities
- what decision-making powers they have
- who they are responsible for and to, and who they will work with
- the skills, qualifications, and experienced required to do the job
- where the job will be based
- the resources required to do the job
- it can also include details of pay and conditions available to the post holder.

Business Analyst

A leader in information systems seeks an experienced Business Analyst to provide detailed financial support to brand teams and senior management across a product group. Having earned an accountancy qualification in the last two years, you will be looking for an opportunity which will challenge your financial skills and fully utilise your commercial knowledge.

This exciting role will suit a highly commercial & proactive individual with first class communication skills. You will work alongside the Financial Accountant setting up accounting systems, processes & procedures & provide commercially focused, value added financial information & analysis. Based in attractive offices in central Glasgow we offer a competitive salary and excellent benefits.

IMAGE 28.
A job advert

PERSON SPECIFICATION

The main purpose of the person specification is to identify the individual that you want to do the job. In addition to the details on skills, qualifications and experience, this will detail the qualities the ideal candidate will have. Common examples could be, 'Must be a good teamworker', 'Must be able to work on own initiative', 'Must be highly numerate', etc.

The HRM department should identify:

- what physical attributes the successful candidate should have in respect of personal appearance, etc.

- what skills, educational qualifications, training and experience the candidate should have

UNIT 2

- what level of intelligence is needed

- what kind of personality is preferred

- what special skills are required.

QUESTION

Q9

Identify the first three stages in the recruitment process.

Once these stages have been completed, the organisation must decide how they are going to recruit the member of staff. The first decision is whether to recruit internally or externally.

INTERNAL RECRUITMENT

A suitable candidate(s) may already work for the organisation, so someone within the organisation could simply be promoted. There are a number of advantages in recruiting internally.

● **The costs involved in promoting internally are lower than recruiting externally. Advertising the post in newspapers etc, selecting from a wide range of applicants, and the cost of induction training can be avoided.**

● **The person is already known to the organisation and so the risk of appointing the wrong person is reduced.**

● **The existing employee will have benefited from the organisation's own investment in training and so this will not be lost if the employee has to leave in order to get promotion.**

● **The prospect of internal promotion can be a strong motivator for employees, and helps in external recruitment where promotion possibilities are available.**

● **Large organisations will use internal recruitment as they have a large pool of workers that they can choose from.**

There are also a number of disadvantages in using only internal recruitment. First, it restricts the number of applicants for the post as the best person for the job, in the long run, may not yet work for the organisation. Secondly, new workers can bring new skills and ideas to the organisation, and thirdly, promotion will probably create another vacancy which will then have to be filled.

EXTERNAL RECRUITMENT

There is a wide variety of different methods of recruiting staff from outwith the organisation. What method(s) are used depends on the nature of the post involved. For example, if you wish to recruit unskilled or semi-skilled labour you could use the local Job Centre, or advertise in a local newspaper. If the post is a temporary one, you could use a local employment agency. For example, local health trusts use nursing agencies to fill short term shortages in ward staff. For management posts you could use national newspapers who will have set days each week for recruitment. This has the benefit of attracting the widest range of interested applicants with the right qualifications for the post. For specialist staff, such as software designers, there are trade magazines which are read by most of these specialists, or you could use a specialist 'head-hunting' agency who will have lists of specialists for a range of areas. The government has a range of 'New Deal' incentives for employers to get people back into work.

There is now a range of businesses specialising in Internet recruitment. They attract a range of applicants for either specific jobs or for jobs the applicants would like which may be available in the future. They match their database of applicants with jobs. Some sites cover a wide range of occupations, such as *www.gojobsite.co.uk*. Others specialise in certain occupations, such as *www.gaapweb.com* for accounting and finance jobs. There is even a site for students to get part-time jobs at *www.thestudentclub.net*.

Whether the organisation decides to recruit internally or externally, a successful process will achieve a suitable number of applicants from which the business can select a suitable candidate. This takes us to the next step — selection.

QUESTION

Q10 Describe the advantages and disadvantages for both internal and external recruitment.

SELECTION

When selecting the most suitable candidate, a number of steps should be involved. The first is to find out if the advertising process has been successful. Have you attracted the sort of candidates you were looking for? If not, then re-advertisement may be necessary.

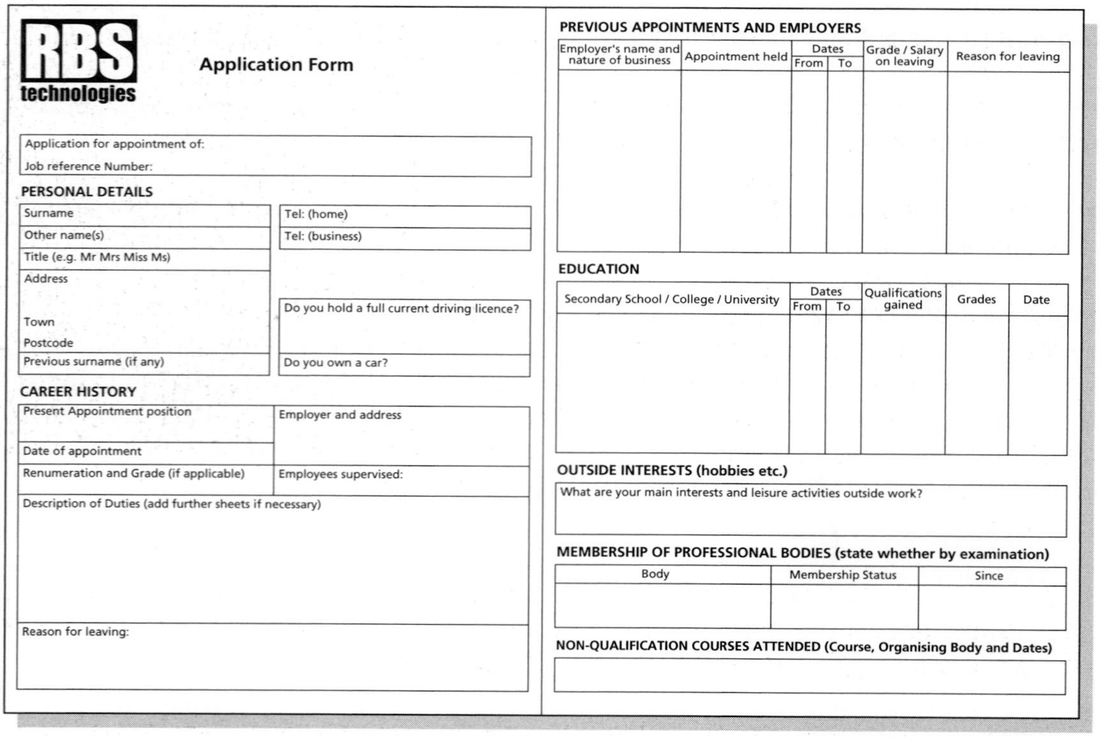

RBS technologies

Application Form

Application for appointment of:

Job reference Number:

PERSONAL DETAILS

Surname	Tel: (home)
Other name(s)	Tel: (business)
Title (e.g. Mr Mrs Miss Ms)	
Address	
Town	Do you hold a full current driving licence?
Postcode	
Previous surname (if any)	Do you own a car?

CAREER HISTORY

Present Appointment position	Employer and address
Date of appointment	
Renumeration and Grade (if applicable)	Employees supervised:

Description of Duties (add further sheets if necessary)

Reason for leaving:

PREVIOUS APPOINTMENTS AND EMPLOYERS

Employer's name and nature of business	Appointment held	Dates From	To	Grade / Salary on leaving	Reason for leaving

EDUCATION

Secondary School / College / University	Dates From	To	Qualifications gained	Grades	Date

OUTSIDE INTERESTS (hobbies etc.)

What are your main interests and leisure activities outside work?

MEMBERSHIP OF PROFESSIONAL BODIES (state whether by examination)

Body	Membership Status	Since

NON-QUALIFICATION COURSES ATTENDED (Course, Organising Body and Dates)

IMAGE 29.
Application form

BUSINESS DECISION AREAS

Application forms

The most common form of notification of interest in the position is the application form, however some organisations still prefer to have applicants submit a Curriculum Vitae (CV), whilst for some posts a simple telephone call may be all that is required.

Application forms are popular because they give applicants the same questions and opportunities to describe themselves. This makes it much easier to compare information from a large number of candidates.

The application forms will be compared to the person specification to see which appear to match. The HRM department will then look at all the applications and decide which applicants to reject at this stage. All rejected applicants should be sent a letter advising them that that they have been unsuccessful. However, the department may be able to identify candidates for whom there may be a position in the future and retain their details on file.

From the applications that appear to be suitable, a decision must be made as to how many should be invited for interview. The number to interview depends on the organisation, however interviews represent a cost to the business and this should be kept as low as possible. On the other hand, you will need to balance this with having a good selection of candidates to choose from. It may be that the organisation selects a long list of 10 or more candidates for a first interview, which will then be reduced to around five for a second interview, when a final decision will be made. Applicants under consideration should be invited for interview, and references sought from existing or previous employers or schools.

The interview

Interviews are the most common form of making a final decision on who the successful candidate should be, based on their match to the person specification. However, research shows that interviews are not a very successful way of finding how well a person will perform in a job. There are a number of reasons for this. First, in many instances it is not the HRM department which carries out the interviews; instead the line manager and possibly other senior managers will be involved. They are not suitably trained or experienced in the process of conducting an interview, and their decision will be very subjective, or in other words they will go with how they feel about the candidate. They are too easily persuaded by the appearance, personality and interview techniques of the applicant.

IMAGE 30.
An interview

It should also be remembered that the interview is a two-way process. It is an opportunity for the applicant to find out more about the job and the organisation. It may be that at the end of the interview process the applicant decides that the job is not for them.

Successful interviews will happen when the interviewer(s) have prepared fully for the interview, with set questions, and with full information on what is required. It may be helpful to prepare a checklist in advance. They also require training in interview techniques which will allow the interviewer to compare candidates more equally. For example, some candidates will find the interview situation less intimidating than others, however this does not make them the better person for the job.

Good interviewers will bring the best out of each candidate, by being open-minded and unbiased towards candidates, making them welcome and relaxed, controlling the interview, and ensuring that all relevant information is gained and given.

Interviews do help in the selection process in identifying the personality and characteristics of the applicant, and also give some indication of how they react in stressful situations, however some applicants may be highly experienced in interviews.

Because of the problems of interviews, other selection techniques have been devised to assist in the process.

Aptitude tests

These tests measure how good the applicant is at a particular skill such as mathematical skills, typing or shorthand speeds, driving ability, etc. These tests are objective in that each applicant's performance can be measured and compared. However, it should be remembered that people perform differently under test conditions than they would in their normal working day and this should be taken account of. This can be done through giving the candidate a number of opportunities to perform at their best.

CASE STUDY — Aptitude tests

Consideration is being given to using aptitude tests, similar to the SAT test used in the USA, for entry to English universities. It has been suggested that they give a better indication of ability than the pupil's school performance which could have been affected by a number of environmental factors.

Psychometric tests

These tests are designed to measure the personality, attitudes and character of the applicant. They are timed tests, usually multiple choice, taken under exam conditions and are designed to measure the intellectual capability of the applicant for thinking and reasoning, particularly logical/analytical reasoning abilities.

They are designed to be challenging but should not depend on having prior knowledge or experience of the post applied for.

Psychometric testing is most commonly used in management and graduate recruitment. However, doubts have been expressed as to how accurate and valid these tests are. If the questions are not prepared properly they will give an unfair advantage to certain types of applicant and should be checked for social, sex or racial bias.

Personality tests

These can give an indication as to whether the applicant is a team player or not, and what team role or roles they perform best. For example, Belbin's self-perception inventory is commonly used by organisations to establish how the applicant will fit into an existing team.

QUESTION

Q11 Explain what procedures are involved in the selection process.

Try some psychometric tests yourself at
www.2h.com

TOPIC SEVEN: Staff training and development

Training has always been important in business, however the concept of continuous training is seen as very important by all sectors of society. The Scottish Parliament has a Minister in charge of what it calls 'Life-Long Learning'. The concept is that modern society requires people to continue to learn after school, further, and higher education in order to be part of the country's economic activity.

Visit
lifelonglearning.co.uk/greenpaper

STAFF TRAINING

This is the process of teaching an employee how to do their job, how to do it better, or how to do a new job in which they have previously had no or little experience of. It should improve the efficiency of the employee, making them more productive and so they are more able to contribute to the organisation's objectives. Developing good skills can also motivate the employee.

There are a number of different types of training . All new employees should go through a process of **induction training**. This will make them more aware of what is expected of them in terms of the tasks they are expected to perform, and also allow them to quickly develop an awareness of the organisation's policy and practices, and become familiar with their surroundings. This will include simple things like where the toilets are, and much more complicated issues such as Health and Safety policy.

Depending on the job and the organisation, the induction training may take a day or a number of weeks to complete.

Established employees will also require training from time to time. This can be for a number of reasons, however there are two main types of training available to the organisation. **On-the-job training** takes place while the employee is actually doing the job. It can involve a more experienced employee showing another worker how to do a job ('sitting next to Nellie'); or the more experienced employee may watch and offer advice and instruction while the other worker completes the task (coaching); or the employee may work in different departments or areas of the organisation learning what each does — this is common for trainee managers so that they can 'learn the business'.

IMAGE 31.
This worker is being guided by a more experienced worker

Off-the-job training can take several different forms. The organisation may have its own training department where it organises its own courses, or it may invite in specialists to train staff. The employee may be sent on training courses organised by trade associations or employers associations, or to obtain qualifications from college or university.

QUESTION

Q12 Identify and describe the different methods of training available to the organisation.

STAFF DEVELOPMENT

Staff development is the process for helping employees to reach their full potential. It will certainly include training of some sort, but to achieve full development some of the training will not be specific to the employee's existing job, but will allow them to train in other areas and develop new skills.

One target for the organisation of staff development is to achieve a multi-skilled workforce. Where each member of the workforce can do a variety of jobs or tasks, the organisation can be much more flexible in responding to the changing needs of its customers.

Staff represent one of the most important resources of the organisation, so the introduction of a staff training and development programme will assist the organisation to get the best possible return from its investment in the workforce.

There are four major objectives in the introduction of staff training and development:

● **The first is to allow all workers to achieve the level of performance of the most experienced workers. For new workers this would be included in their induction training.**

● **The second is to make a wide pool of skills available to the organisation both for now and for the future.**

● **The third is to develop a knowledgeable and committed workforce which will be highly motivated.**

● **The fourth is to ensure that the organisation can deliver high-quality goods or services.**

THE COSTS INVOLVED IN TRAINING AND DEVELOPMENT

Sending people on courses will involve a number of costs including travel and subsistence, but it also means that the people involved will be away from their jobs, leaving the organisation with a choice of accepting lower output, or bringing in other staff to cover. If the organisation has its own training department, then staff here will add further employment costs to the business.

Research has shown that organisations in the UK fail to provide appropriate staff training and development. It tends to happen only when problems occur, for example when new technology forces it upon the organisation.

'Investors In People' campaign

In order to try to encourage organisations to be more pro-active in their approach to staff training and development, the government launched the 'Investors In People' campaign. Organisations can achieve IIP accredited status by developing a more strategic approach in terms of analysing their training and development needs, planning and implementing a programme for training and development, and finally carrying out an evaluation of the effectiveness of the programme.

Find out more about Investors in People at
www.iip.co.uk

The benefits from training are sometimes difficult to identify, and this is why many organisations fail to carry out proper staff training and development programmes. However, the costs of not training are; additional recruitment costs when new skills are required; untrained staff are less productive or motivated; accidents are more frequent. In addition, workers who are not in a process of training and development are far less likely to be aware of or work towards the organisation's objectives.

For case studies in successful training visit
www.greatplacetowork.gov.uk

STAFF APPRAISAL

One of the main methods used for establishing an individual employee's training and development needs is through appraisal. What else appraisals are used for varies between organisations, for example they may be linked to pay. They are meetings which take place on a one-to-one basis with the employee's line manager or a member of HRM department, to establish how the employee has performed in their job, usually over the past year. The process usually involves some preparation by both parties, and at the end an agreement on a set of goals for the employee. These goals will then form the basis of next year's appraisal.

The main objectives for the organisation are:

- **to identify future training needs**

- **to consider development needs for the individual's career**

HUMAN RESOURCES MANAGEMENT

- to improve the performance of the employee

- to provide feedback to the employee about their performance

- to identify individuals who have potential for future promotion within the organisation, or who have additional skills which could be useful now or in the future.

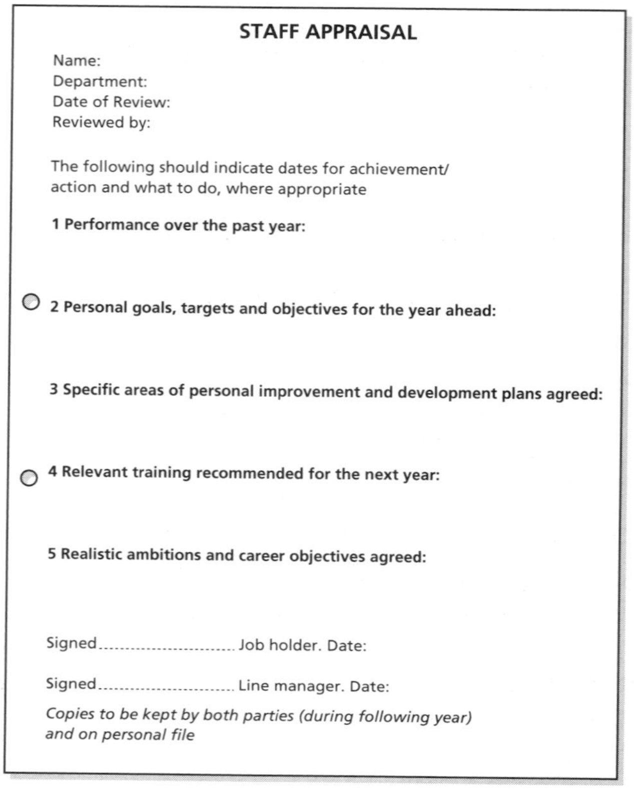

STAFF APPRAISAL

Name:
Department:
Date of Review:
Reviewed by:

The following should indicate dates for achievement/
action and what to do, where appropriate

1 Performance over the past year:

2 Personal goals, targets and objectives for the year ahead:

3 Specific areas of personal improvement and development plans agreed:

4 Relevant training recommended for the next year:

5 Realistic ambitions and career objectives agreed:

Signed........................... Job holder. Date:

Signed........................... Line manager. Date:

*Copies to be kept by both parties (during following year)
and on personal file*

IMAGE 32.
Staff appraisal form

QUESTION
Q13 Describe the benefits of a staff development policy.

TOPIC EIGHT: Employee relations

Employee relations is another major area of the HRM department's role within the organisation. It is how employers deal with and interact with their employees as individuals or as a group.

Good employee relations will help ensure that the organisation meets its objectives, as workers are usually much happier, and more motivated and committed to the goals of the business. They will be more accepting of change, will be more flexible in their response to requests, and will recognise the need for the organisation to achieve its objectives.

Poor employee relations will lead to less co-operation of the workforce, more industrial action, and a poor image of the organisation for its customers.

The HRM department has responsibility for drawing up and implementing the organisation's employee relations policies. What they cover will vary with the organisation but should include:

● **the terms and conditions of employment for staff**

● **procedures for dealing with staff complaints (grievances), the disciplining of staff, and redundancy including any agreed payments**

● **the involvement of staff in decision-making**

● **trade union recognition (some businesses do not recognise trade unions)**

● **collective bargaining i.e. discussions with trade unions on pay and conditions or changes to working practices for all employees.**

 **CASE STUDY** | **Scottish teaching unions**

The teaching unions in Scotland carry out collective bargaining on behalf of all their members with COSLA (Confederation of Scottish Local Authorities) which represents all the local councils (except Glasgow). All pay and conditions agreements are then applied nationally. The main benefit for the employers is that there is only one set of discussions, and so agreement can be reached more effectively. The teachers benefit by not having to individually negotiate on their own behalf with the management in each school.

 MAIN INSTITUTIONS FOR EMPLOYEE RELATIONS

Because of the importance of achieving good employee relations a number of institutions have been created to help ensure that disputes between employers and employees are kept to a minimum.

ACAS (Advisory, Conciliation and Arbitration Service)

Perhaps the best known of these is ACAS (the Advisory, Conciliation and Arbitration Service). They describe themselves as employee relations experts, helping people work together effectively. This ranges from setting up the right structures and systems for employee relations to finding a way to settle disputes. Nowadays they spend most time advising on how to avoid disputes through good practice and dealing with individual cases.

There are four main ways in which ACAS provides help:

● **Providing impartial information and help to anyone with a work problem, dealing with over 760,000 calls a year.**

● Preventing and resolving problems between employers and their workforces, helping to settle disputes. Their Advisory Service works with hundreds of companies every year to develop a joint approach to problem-solving.

● Settling complaints about employees' rights. Over 100,000 people a year complain to an employment tribunal. Before going to the hearing most cases are referred to ACAS to see if there is a less damaging and expensive way of sorting the problem out. For unfair dismissal cases they have started a new scheme giving people the choice of confidential arbitration instead of an employment tribunal.

● Encouraging people to work together effectively by running workshops and seminars on things like basic employment issues and the latest developments in legislation. Most events are targeted at small businesses with no HRM specialists.

Visit ACAS at
www.acas.org.uk
or try their quiz at
www.acas.org.uk/quiz/stage.swf

Employers' associations

Businesses in one sector of industry often form an association to look after the interests of all businesses in that particular industry. For example, businesses in the engineering sector may belong to the Engineering Employers' Association. They benefit from this association by having a single strong voice to lobby politicians, in their dealings with the engineering unions, and in dealing with the press and other media.

They can pressure and may influence government in areas such as providing support for research and development, taxation, consumer and employment laws. Market research can be gathered for the benefit of the members, many of whom may be small businesses, who would otherwise not be able to afford such research. The farmers' union represented the farmers during the recent Foot and Mouth epidemic, putting forward their views, and helped in re-establishing export and home markets.

CBI – Confederation of British Industry

This body tries to represent the employers from all the UK's industries. They are a much stronger voice in dealing with all of the above, but may voice their opinions on political matters that affect businesses, such as joining the single European Currency (Euro), although they are divided on what would be the best course of action.

Find out more about the CBI at
www.cbi.org.uk

TUC – Trade Union Congress

The TUC represents all trade unions in much the same way as the CBI represents the employers. As with the CBI, it provides information and advice to its members. Trade union membership has seen a rise in membership in recent years after decades of decline. The TUC is now more involved in research into employment and employment rights.

Trade unions

Trade unions were set up to protect employees from unscrupulous employers, and to provide a political voice for the working people of the country. The Labour Party was established by trade unions. However, with the success of their work in ensuring employment law, their role has changed.

IMAGE 33.
Scottish Trades Union Congress annual conference

They still represent workers in their dealings with employers, and still work to protect their rights and to improve their pay and conditions, and continue with their campaigns to introduce new laws that will protect and benefit working people. Individually, workers have little power in their dealings with employers and government, however by joining a trade union the worker has a much stronger voice and many more resources to make their point.

Trade unions are much more interested in working with employers and government for the benefit of their members, rather than confrontation and industrial action which could damage their members' jobs. To make their influence more effective, unions have merged to form 'super-unions' representing large numbers of employees.

For example, Unison is the largest union in the UK, representing workers in the public sector, in the voluntary sector, and in private businesses providing services to the public. It was formed by an amalgamation of a number of smaller unions.

Find out more about what Unison does at
www.unison.org.uk

There are a number of different unions in the UK representing different groups of workers. Some represent a wide variety of different occupations in a number of different industries, such as the Transport and General Workers' Union; others represent workers in a specific job or industry, such as the Education Institute of Scotland which represents primary and most secondary teachers, and some college and university lecturers.

Trade unions are organised locally and nationally, offering their members a wide variety of benefits, which could include discounts on purchases, insurance services, and free advice and support on all employment matters.

QUESTION
14 Identify the main institutions involved in employee relations.

TOPIC
EIGHT

TOPIC NINE: Employee relations processes

NEGOTIATION

The purpose of negotiation is to come to an agreement. Here employers and employees will meet to discuss issues that affect both parties to agree, plan and implement some changes in the workplace. What is negotiated will depend very much on the relations between the two parties, and what existing agreements are in place. Negotiation is often seen as the best method of achieving change in the workplace, as the co-operation and support of employees is essential to the successful implementation of change in order to meet the organisation's objectives. At the end of the day the success of the organisation should benefit the employee as much as the employers.

IMAGE 34.
Union and employer meeting

CONSULTATION

Consultation is enforced on employers under employment law for some changes within the organisation. However, what consultation actually means will vary from organisation to organisation. The definition of 'consultation' in the dictionary is 'to tell', and many organisations will simply tell employees or their trade unions what changes are planned and why, and then listen to their views. No agreement is necessary and the employer is under no obligation to take account of the views of the employees.

ARBITRATION

Where no agreement can be reached between the employer and employees, and a dispute resulting in some form of industrial action is possible, an independent arbitrator such as ACAS may be called in to try to resolve the problem. The arbitrator is unbiased and neutral to the dispute, will listen to both sides, gather other evidence as appropriate and offer a solution.

Binding arbitration is where both parties agree in advance to abide by the decision of the independent arbitrator. Where no agreement exists, both parties will then try to negotiate round the arbitrator's decision to come to some agreement.

CASE STUDY | The McCrone Report

The McCrone Report on Scottish Education was the result of a dispute between teachers and their employers (COSLA). At the end of the day, both parties decided to agree on the principles of the report and so the dispute was settled. However, negotiations are continuing as to how to implement the recommendations. This process is part of the collective bargaining between the employers and the teaching trade unions.

COLLECTIVE BARGAINING

It is unusual today for workers to try to negotiate new pay and conditions of employment with their employers. It is much more common for trade unions, staff associations, or professional associations to do this for them. Collective bargaining is the process where the trade union or other body negotiates with the employer on behalf of the employees, usually on pay or changes that are proposed in the workplace.

The process starts when either the employees' representatives or the employers propose some change to their existing agreement. For example, it could be that the employers offer a pay rise of 2% to their employees. The employees' representatives then ask their members whether or not this is acceptable. It usually isn't and so the employees make a counter-claim for a different pay rise, for example 5%.

It is generally understood that the employers will probably be willing to pay more than 2% and that the employees will accept less than 5%. Negotiations then take place to try to come to an agreement. With both sides keen to avoid any form of dispute, a compromise may be reached. It is common for a larger pay rise to be offered, say 3.5%, if the workers agree to some efficiency changes in the existing agreement on working practices. For example, overtime rates may be reduced, or more flexible working hours may be proposed.

Once both parties have an agreement, the employees' representatives will then take the offer back to their members, recommending that they accept. If all goes well, the new pay and conditions agreement will be implemented at an agreed date. To ensure a more settled workforce and better planning, it is now more likely that the agreement will be for a number of years, rather than just one. Within the agreement there will be percentage pay rises for the next few years.

CASE STUDY — The Scottish Police Federation

The Scottish Police Federation is a professional association not linked to the TUC, which represents police officers in Scotland. Following proposed changes in their pay and conditions of service by the Home Secretary, David Blunkett, they are now taking legal action to try to overcome the 1919 legal ban on police taking strike action.

A ballot of 15,000 officers across Scotland resulted in a 94.1% vote against the changes which offer a number of bonus payments and other performance-related special awards in return for reduced overtime pay and other amendments in conditions of service. A spokesman for the Police Federation said that while the rejection showed concerns about the pay deal, it also showed that officers were worried about the future of the police service.

The government says that changes are necessary to create a more flexible police service and that a 'no' vote would be a disaster for the police and the public, and that the rank and file officers should understand that it is a very good pay deal for all concerned. The government now plans to go through a process of arbitration and conciliation to settle the dispute.

Visit the Scottish Police Federation at
www.spf.org.uk

QUESTION

Q15 Describe the stages in the employee relations process.

INDUSTRIAL ACTION

Strike action is just one of the types of industrial action available to workers. In a strike all or most of the workers stop working – they withdraw their labour. This is usually only done as a last resort as stopping production of goods and services means a loss of sales and customers, which in turn will threaten the security of the workforce's employment. There is a legally binding set of procedures that a union must go through before it can call a strike. This will include balloting all its members in a secret ballot.

IMAGE 35.
Picket line

In extreme cases the employer may decide to sack the striking workers, however this is possible only where there is a good supply of other workers who can quickly be trained to do the jobs required. Or in the case of some big organisations they may decide to close the factory or move production elsewhere. This may lead to a **sit-in**, where workers occupy their workplace in an attempt to stop the employer closing the unit.

A **work-to-rule** is where employees work strictly to their terms and conditions of employment. The withdrawal of flexibility leads to a reduction in efficiency and output. An **overtime ban** also has the same effect; this is where workers refuse to do overtime. This would be extremely effective in the police dispute because overtime is essential to the efficient running of a police force. Officers could simply leave a crime scene when their shift is over.

Boycotts can be used when employers introduce new machinery or duties that the employees disagree with. They simply refuse to carry out the new duties or use the new machines.

QUESTION

Q16 Identify the main methods of industrial action.

TOPIC TEN: Management of employee relations

It is the responsibility of the HRM department to try to ensure that disputes and industrial action do not take place. There are a number of ways of that this can be achieved, however, whichever method is chosen, communication and inclusion of the workforce are essential. If the workers understand what it is that the employer is trying to achieve through the changes and why the changes are necessary then there is less likelihood of a dispute arising. This communication would have to be at each stage of the process. Even more successful is having representatives of the workforce involved in the initial decision-making process. The level of trust that can be built up when workers are included reduces the possibility of dispute to a minimum.

WORKS COUNCILS

This is a group of representatives from the workforce who have the legal right to access information from management and joint decision-making powers on most matters relating to employees. The European Works Councils legislation (2000) states that organisations with at least 1000 employees across the EU have to set up a Special Negotiating Body (SNB) to represent the workforce. The penalty in the UK for not doing so within three years is a fine of up to £75,000. If the organisation fails to do so then it will have an SNB imposed upon it.

There are some exceptions to the types of information that the SNB can access, but generally this will allow the employees to understand what is happening within the organisation, and allow them to become much more involved with the decision-making process.

Find out more about European Works Councils at
www.dti.gov.uk/er/europe/workscouncil.htm
or
www.tssa.org.uk/advice/leg/egewc.htm

SINGLE UNION AGREEMENTS

A single union agreement involves one union representing all workers at the workplace. There are a number of unions which represent different groups of workers:

● **general trade unions which represent any type of worker**

● **craft unions which represent skilled workers**

● **white-collar unions which represent office workers, nurses, teachers, etc.**

● **industrial unions which represent most workers in a single industry, e.g. NUM represents most coal miners.**

As a result, an employer may have to negotiate separately with a number of unions for changes in pay and conditions of service. Where a single union agreement exists, only one union will negotiate on behalf of the workers, to which all the workers belong. Because the employer only has to negotiate with one union there will be a reduction in the complexity of the negotiations, saving time and money and also reducing the possibility of conflict. It benefits the workforce as it then has one strong voice in negotiations which will bring a higher chance of success.

QUESTION
17 Identify two methods for the successful management of employee relations.

TOPIC
TEN

MAINTENANCE OF PERSONNEL INFORMATION AND RECORDS

 The HRM department is responsible for keeping records and personal information on the organisation's employees. In the workplace the organisation has a legal responsibility to look after its staff (**staff welfare**), and this information helps it to do that.

The information that it would hold will include:

- Personal information – **name, address, date of birth, qualifications, etc. Most of this will be taken from the application form when the employee applied for the job. It will also include details of any medical problems the employees may have.**

- Employment history – **as well as the terms and conditions of their employment, this will include details of sick days, or any other reasons for absenteeism, and lateness. If there has been any action under the organisation's discipline or grievance procedure it will also be recorded here.**

IMAGE 36.
Employee record file

- Appraisal records – **this will record what has been agreed during the appraisal process and any training that the employee has undertaken, or should undertake in the future.**

This information is highly confidential and the HRM department must ensure that no unauthorised people can get access to it. Files must be kept secure, with restricted access.

The terms and conditions of employment for employees are set out in their job contracts (contracts of employment). These will include:

- the job title
- the specific rules and duties relating to the job
- the pay scale and rate of pay
- how they will be paid, for example weekly or monthly
- the usual hours to be worked
- the availability of and rate of pay for overtime
- their holiday entitlement
- the arrangements in the event of illness
- any pension scheme arrangements
- the terms of notice required to be given by the employee and the employer
- details of the grievance procedure
- details of the disciplinary procedure.

The contract is a legally binding agreement made between the employer and the employee. It should be issued within 13 weeks of the employee starting work.

UNIT 2

Inter@ctive Systems

Dear Mr Mason

Further to the conversation that we have had thus far we are pleased to hereby confirm the conditions of your employment contract with Interactive Systems.

1. Commencement And Duration Of This Contract
This employment contract will commence on 1 September 2002 and will continue until either party gives to the other not less than one month's notice or statutory minimum notice whichever is the greater.

2. Nature Of Your Responsibilities
You will be employed as a Software Consultant. You will carry out activities to support the sale of products and software consultancy services that form part of the product line of Interactive Systems, as well as related activities in the broadest possible sense. As part of your activities you will offer technical support by email, fax, and telephone to the prospects and customers with whom Interactive Systems is conducting a dialogue, you will visit customers in order to advise and aid them in the design and implementation of software systems that make use of the technologies, technical standards and products offered by Interactive Systems, you will write technical articles for publication in trade magazines, give public presentations, and train prospects and customers in the technologies, technical standards and products offered by Interactive Systems. You will keep the account managers, product managers and functional managers who have end responsibility for the activities in which you are engaged informed of your progress on an ongoing basis.

3. Remuneration
You will be paid a salary at the rate of £18 500 per annum or such higher sum as may be agreed. In addition Interactive Systems will reward you for extraordinary efforts with a bonus payment that is based on 10 percent of the net revenues to Interactive Systems as a result of your efforts. The maximum size of this bonus will be 2 times your monthly salary.

4. Holiday Days
You have a right to 25 days of holiday a year, the dates of which you should decide together with Interactive Systems.

5. National Holidays
Apart from holidays as discussed under '4. Holiday Days' Interactive Systems will give you a free day on the following National Holiday days: New Year's Day, Good Friday, Easter Monday, May Day Holiday, Spring Bank Holiday, August Bank Holiday, Christmas Day and Boxing Day.

6. Working Hours
The working week consists of 40 hours. The working hours are from Monday up to and including Friday from 09:00 hours up to 17:00 hours, with a maximum of half an hour for lunch.

7. Overtime
Should this be in the interest of Interactive Systems, you are obliged to work overtime at reasonable times as determined by the management of Interactive Systems. You cannot legally claim remuneration or compensation for overtime as part of this contract.

8. Compensation For Expenses Incurred

IMAGE 37.
Contract of employment

QUESTION
18 What should a contract of employment include?

It is common for these to change each year, as the worker will expect some pay rise, but this may be linked to a change in their conditions, for example changing the hours of work.

QUESTION
19 What information should be contained in personnel records?

GRIEVANCE PROCEDURES

A grievance is a complaint by an employee against their employer. It may be because of the way they have been treated by another member of staff such as their manager. The employee must follow the agreed procedure which could include several stages involving the HRM department, local trade union representatives and management. If the employee is not satisfied by the response of the organisation, he or she can then approach ACAS or if that fails they can take their employer to an employment tribunal which has some legal powers to enforce their decisions.

DISCIPLINE PROCEDURES

Disciplinary procedures are actions taken against the employee by the employer, because the employee is thought to have done something wrong. This could range from persistent lateness to theft. If the action is very serious then the employee can be sacked on the spot (summary dismissal). However, it is more likely that they will be given a number of verbal and written warnings, and be given some support to try to overcome the problem first.

TOPIC ELEVEN: Legislative requirements

This section covers the legal responsibilities of the organisation. The laws that an employer has to take account of are varied and complex. They are continually being updated, and this requires specialist knowledge on the part of the organisation. It is normally one of the main functions of the HRM department to ensure that the organisation is fully aware of any legislation and to make sure it is implemented.

The basis for implementation will be the HRM policies of the organisation. The department must make sure that all the organisation's policies and procedures are in line with the current laws that affect two main areas: (1) employment and (2) health and safety.

This will also involve making sure that all managers within the organisation are aware of these laws and of any changes, and monitoring how the organisation is performing to make sure that they remain within the law.

EQUAL OPPORTUNITIES
Equal Pay Act 1970

This Act was introduced to make sure that men and women would receive the same pay and conditions for doing 'broadly similar' work. Up until then, employers could pay women less than men. The Act, which is now more than 30 years old, is monitored by the Equal Opportunities Commission who have found that employers still tend to pay women less.

Equal opportunities

A study by the Equal Opportunities Commission, published in March 2002, found that women graduates are earning 15% less than their male counterparts within five years of starting work. The pay gap facing older women is worse, with women graduates in their early 50s taking home 44% less than men of the same age.

On average women graduates get 37% less than men, exactly the same gap between male and female earnings when the Equal Pay Act was introduced in 1970.

In Scotland women's pay is so far behind men that it could take up to 45 years to close the gap according to a separate study by the Transport and General Workers Union.

The Equal Opportunities Commission has launched a joint campaign to encourage women to question potential employers about their pay policies, called 'Why are women going cheap?' It features posters of young women with '15% off' stickers on their foreheads.

The average pay gap between men and women in the UK is 18%, and to combat this the government has launched a fair pay award for employers.

IMAGE 38.
Equal Opportunities Commission campaign poster

To find out more visit the Equal Opportunities Commission at
www.eoc.org.uk

Sex Discrimination Act 1975

This Act was introduced to ensure that men and women are treated equally and fairly at work. Although most cases tend to be about discrimination against females, it applies equally to males. It covers a wide range of issues, however discrimination can be one of two types:

Direct discrimination is where an individual is discriminated against because of their sex.
Indirect discrimination is where the actions of an employer adversely affects a considerably larger proportion of males or females, and this covers three main areas of recruitment, treatment at work and dismissal.

In 2000, 186 successful cases were brought against employers under the Sex Discrimination Act with pay-outs by employers of almost £2 million.

Race Relations Act 1976

This Act deals with discrimination against employees because of their colour, race, nationality or ethnic origin. It is similar to the Sex Discrimination Act and covers the same areas of direct and indirect discrimination.

Disability Discrimination Act 1995

This Act deals with discrimination against an employee or potential employee because of their disability. Again, discrimination can be either direct or indirect.

All of these Acts cover a wide range of possible areas of discrimination, however for each there are exemptions. Discrimination is allowed in certain cases, such as advertising for a male attendant for a men's toilet; only employing Asian waiters at an Indian restaurant; or excluding a blind person from applying for a bus driver's job. However, employers must be very careful when preparing job adverts, introducing working practices, and even in their advertising to ensure they do not breach the current legislation. It is possible that the employer could be sued under the Human Rights Act 1998.

Discrimination danger areas

Job description – Call centre jobs excluding the visually impaired. There are grants available for converting phone systems to braille.

Job adverts – An advert for a waitress. The job can be done equally well by both men and women.

Selection – Asking a married female applicant if she plans to have any more children. This would be indirect discrimination.

Training – A management training course always held between Friday and Sunday. This indirectly discriminates against Jews and Muslims as these are their holy days.

Promotion – Senior posts only available to the over 35s with 10 years' service. This indirectly discriminates against women, who may well have had a break in service to have children.

Benefits – Shifts arranged so that out-of-school hours shifts are paid the highest. This may be discrimination against women.

Services – A company pension scheme allowing women to retire early.

Redundancy – Part-timers selected first for redundancy.

Dismissal – Religious 'holidays' counted towards a poor attendance record.

EMPLOYMENT PROTECTION

There is a wide range of range of legislation covering employment law. In most cases it protects the workers from what are seen to be undesirable practices by employers. Although employers would like to see a reduction in the amount of legislation, they do agree that most laws help to provide better working conditions for employees, and help with employee relations and output. Many employers will already exceed the minimum requirements of the legislation, and the laws are being continually updated by the government and the EU.

The main ones are:

- **Employment Act 1989**
- **Employment Relations Act 1999**
- **Employment Rights Act 1996**
- **National Minimum Wage Act 1998**
- **Working Time Regulations 1998.**

BUSINESS DECISION AREAS

The main areas covered by the employment Acts include the right for employees to a written contract of employment; a minimum period of notice before they can be made redundant; the right to redundancy payments; the right not to be unfairly dismissed; to have paid maternity leave and re-instatement afterwards; and the right to challenge unfair dismissal through an employment tribunal. At the time of writing, the government is about to introduce a new employment law which will give additional rights for matters such as paternity leave, and an extension of some existing rights.

The main problem HRM departments face is keeping up-to-date with the changes in legislation.

The Working Time Regulations place a limit of 48 hours a week on average which workers are required to work, although they can work more if they want to; a limit of an average of eight hours' work in 24 which nightworkers can be required to work; a right for night workers to receive free health assessments; a right to 11 hours' rest a day; a right to a day off each week; a right to an in-work rest break if the working day is longer than six hours; and the right to four weeks' paid leave per year.

The Youth Rate for 18–21 year olds under the minimum wage legislation will be £3.60 per hour, and the Adult Rate will be £4.20 from October 2002. It is set on the recommendations of the Low Pay Commission, an expert panel made up of business figures, trade union leaders and academics. Although now accepted by employers, it is against further rises, while the TUC is looking for a minimum wage of £5 in the near future.

CASE STUDY — TUC poll

According to a poll carried out by the TUC in 2002, just one in three young workers knows the rate of the adult minimum wage, while only one in six knows the Youth Rate. The poll of 500 employees aged between 16 and 21 has caused the TUC to express concerns that the lack of knowledge could lead to some employers taking advantage of younger workers.

EMPLOYMENT TRIBUNALS

When all other avenues between employers and their employees have not settled a dispute, and for cases of unfair dismissal, the employee has the right to take their employer or former employer to an employment tribunal. The tribunal is less formal than a court and aims to ensure that employers act legally in respect of the employment legislation.

IMAGE 39.
Inspector Fleming celebrates after being reinstated by Lincolnshire Police, following an employment tribunal claiming sex discrimination

HEALTH AND SAFETY

The main Act here is the Health and Safety at Work Act 1974, although many of the other pieces of legislation affect health and safety in the workplace. The aim of this Act is to continue to raise the standards of health and safety for all individuals at work and to protect the public whose safety may be put at risk by the activities of people at work. What the Act covers, and the duties of the employer are being constantly being updated. For example, when research shows that some practices pose a danger to health, then there is a duty on the employer to ensure the safety of their staff. Repetitive Strain Injury (RSI) — when an employee continually uses the same actions in the job (such as working at a keyboard) — is an example of how research overtook existing legislation.

Employers' duties

The employer must make sure that they take every reasonable step to ensure that all machinery is properly maintained; all hazardous substances are dealt with properly; all staff are trained and informed of potential dangers, and that the environment is safe and non-hazardous to the health of the employees. This will involve a 'risk assessment' of the building, operation of machinery, and of each task the employees are expected to carry out.

Employers have to appoint safety officers and committees which will carry out regular inspections of the workplace and assess the dangers involved in each job.

Employees' duties

The employees are expected to behave in a reasonable manner at work and must take some responsibility for their own actions. They must co-operate with their employers in ensuring that all health and safety requirements are met and follow all instructions and accept training where appropriate.

STRESS AT WORK

One current major concern that employers and employees have is how stress is affecting the workplace. The number of workers claiming damages from their employer for having too much stress placed on them, resulting in health problems, is increasing, and so is the amount being paid out to individual workers.

CASE STUDY

Survey of workers

The income protection insurance company Unum carried out a survey of 1200 workers in full- and part-time employment which showed that four out of five workers believe the workplace has become more stressful in the past five years. More than two-thirds said they felt either stressed or under pressure at work, and nearly three-quarters said that their performance was affected by stress. Mental and psychological claims received by Unum have risen by 88% over the past seven years, and those for chronic fatigue syndrome are up by 40%.

The survey suggests that a combination of long working hours and autocratic management styles are key sources of stress in the workplace. 'Managers should become more orientated towards a greater praise and reward culture, and should also adopt more flexible working arrangements to help strike a better balance between work and home', says workplace stress expert Professor Cary Cooper of the University of Manchester.

A survey by the Industrial Society in November 2000 found that three out of four employers said that stress was set to be their biggest health and safety issue over the next two years. The TUC claims that 90 million working days a year are lost through stress at work. Symptoms of stress include irritability, anti-social feelings, suppressed anger, concentration problems and sleeping difficulties.

A more recent survey found that the most stressed workers were in Scotland and London. Workload was cited as the biggest cause of stress, followed by staff cuts and change in the workplace. However, long hours, shift work, bullying and cramped conditions were also major factors.

Although many employers recognise the need to reduce stress in the workplace, their efforts to date have not been successful. Research has shown that reducing the workload on staff makes them more effective, reduces absenteeism and staff turnover, bringing significant savings to the organisation. However, the initial costs involved tend to put employers off.

Recent research has shown that stress management techniques introduced by business tend to be an extremely unfocused ragbag of ideas, doomed to failure because they were ill conceived and hastily implemented. Improvements in the working environment would be far more effective than any stress management course.

QUESTION

Q20 Identify the major pieces of legislation of concern to HRM departments.

Find out more from the Health and Safety Executive at
www.hse.gov.uk

CHAPTER SUMMARY

By the end of this chapter you should be aware of the following:

- The main elements of HRM are:
  - Recruitment and selection using internal and external sources.
  - Staff training and development.
  - Maintenance of personnel information and records.
  - Terms and conditions of employment.
  - Monitoring of HRM procedures throughout the organisation, including grievances and discipline.
  - The legal requirements of Health and Safety, Employment, and Equal Opportunities Legislation.

- That employee relations refers to the inter-relationship between employees and management, and that these relationships are managed through local and national agreements, trade unions and works councils.

- That there has been a change in the way employers use and employ staff with greater use of part-time and casual staff, and the establishment of a core workforce.

- That for successful recruitment and selection you should use:
  - Job analysis
  - Job description
  - Person specification
  - Interviews
  - Application forms
  - Aptitude tests
  - Psychometric tests.

- The importance of and reasons for staff training and development including the flexibility of the workforce, upgrading of skills.

- The different methods of training available such as induction, on-the-job, off-the-job, and staff development.

- The costs and benefits to the organisation of training and development.

- The main institutions involved in employee relations including ACAS, the various employer's associations, and trade unions.

- The process involved in employee relations of negotiation – consultation – and arbitration.

- The management of employee relations through instruments such as single union deals and works councils.

UNIT 2

PREPARATION FOR ASSESSMENT

HIGHER ASSESSMENT

PC (a)

There are two parts to this PC. The first concerns the initial stages in recruitment. What you will actually be asked will depend on the NAB that you are given by your teacher/lecturer, however it will cover the three stages of job analysis, job description and person specification. You may be asked to relate it to the case study you are given, however you should state that 'Job analysis is a study of what tasks are involved in the job, and what skills and level of performance are required. It will highlight whether or not a vacancy actually exists. Job description is a description of what tasks require to be completed within the job, and what level of experience, qualifications, and skills will be required. The job description may be used for preparing the job advert. Person specification is the profile of the person you actually want to do the job. It would look at the personality and other skills you would wish the job holder to have. It can then be compared with applications to find the best matches.'

The second part of this PC deals with internal and external sources of recruitment. Your answer should include: 'Internal sources are recruitment from within the organisation. These employees will already be known to the organisation and so there should be a grater chance of them being suitable for the job. Promotion prospects will increase motivation among staff, and will make it easier to recruit form outside the organisation. It is quicker and cheaper than external recruitment.' Your explanation of external recruitment should include: 'External sources give a much wider choice of candidates, and you can gain new skills currently not available within the existing workforce. It is useful when introducing new types of products or new technology to the organisation as it will reduce the cost of training existing staff. External recruitment also brings new ideas to the organisation.'

PC (b)

This PC will ask you about the effectiveness of selection and again is in two parts. The first is to identify methods of selecting applicants. Your answer should include: 'Application forms which allow all applicants to answer the same questions, are easier to compare than CVs. These can be matched to the person specification so that suitable candidates can be more easily identified. Interviews allow a meeting face-to-face with the candidates, where further questions can be asked of the applicants, and they also have the opportunity to ask questions. Interviewers should try to focus on the information rather than personal feeling about the applicant. The interviews should be fair to all applicants and give them the best opportunity to show why they should be given the job. References should be sought from previous employers/schools/etc. They are useful to check that the information contained in the application form is correct, and will give further information on the person's character. Testing will allow the organisation to find out more about the applicant's aptitude and personality, including their ability to problem solve and their most suitable role in teamwork etc.'

The second part asks why an effective recruitment process is so important. Your answer should include: 'An effective process will ensure that the correct applicant is selected. This will avoid the need to go through the process again, reduce staff turnover, and the need for additional training. It will give the applicant the opportunity to find out if they really want to work for the organisation.'

CHAPTER:Seven

PC (c)

This PC focuses on the importance of employee relations. Again, there are two parts. The first is on the importance of employee relations to the organisation. Your answer could cover the reasons for good employee relations, such as: 'Helping to increase cooperation of the workforce to enable the organisation to meet its objectives, helping to motivate the workforce and improve communication between staff and management, and to allow for the inclusion of employees in decision-making.'

The second part is on the forms of employee representation. Your answer could include: 'Works councils are regular meetings of representatives of employees and management to discuss issues that affect employees. The representatives have a statutory right to access information. Trade unions will have agreements in place with the employers and will meet to discuss issues of importance to the employees. Staff meetings could be arranged to discuss matters of concern to both employees and management, or to carry out consultation.'

 ## INTERMEDIATE 2 ASSESSMENT

There are at least five different assessments you could be given for this level. Your answers should be related to the case study you are given with the assessment.

PC (a) – elements of the human resources functions are accurately explained

Here you will be asked to explain what is involved in the main tasks undertaken in the Human Resources department. This could include recruitment, selection, training and development, personnel information and records, and grievance and discipline.

For **recruitment** your answer should include: 'How the organisation recruits staff. It includes finding out what staff are needed, preparing the job descriptions and specifications, and then advertising the job in an appropriate place.'

Selection should include: 'Using a suitable procedure for deciding which applicant to offer the post to, including drawing up a short list of the best applicants, interviewing them and possibly testing them, and then making a decision on who to offer the job.'

Training and **development** answers should include the different types of training: 'Induction training for new staff to make them aware of the organisation and its procedures. Training existing staff to do new jobs. Training can be on-the-job which is learning while actually doing the job, or off-the-job where employees can go on a course to learn or develop new skills such as a college course. Appraisal is where employees get the chance to say how they feel they have done, set new targets, etc.

Personnel information and records – your answer should include: 'This involves keeping records on staff on their personal details, employment history, and work record. These records need to be kept confidential and access should be restricted.'

Grievance and **discipline** answers should include: 'Grievance is where the employee makes a complaint about the employer, they can approach ACAS or their trade union for help. Discipline procedures should be fair and legal, there will be laid down agreed procedures.'

PC (b) – the management of employee relations is accurately explained with reference to the role of the human resources function

There are two parts to this PC. The first is about explaining what employee relations are, and the second is about the roles of the employer and employee, and an example of how formal relations are managed.

For the first part there are a wide variety of different answers to this question, however you should describe some different methods for managing employee relations. This could include: 'Employee relations are formal relations between the employees and employers, they will usually involve representatives of both parties. Works councils are an example of a formal group used to help employee relations. The government try to encourage good employee relations through ACAS and the work/life balance initiative.'

In the second part you should describe the roles of the employer and employee. Your answer should include: 'The employer should communicate with the employees to consult and negotiate with employees and their trade union or other representatives. Trade unions are appointed to represent the employees in their discussions with the employers. They will establish agreements through collective bargaining for pay and conditions of employment.' You could use works councils as an example of a formal structure for employee relations: 'They are made up of workers and management representatives to discuss matters that will affect the employees.'

PC (c) – description of the effect of legal requirements on the management of human resources is accurate and makes reference to current legislation

For this PC you should be able to describe some of the laws that are concerned with employment in this country. You could discuss the discrimination laws such as the Equal Pay Act 1974 or the Sex Discrimination Act 1975 or the Race Relations Act 1976 or the Health and Safety at Work Act 1974. All you have to do is say what they are about. For example, 'The Equal Pay Act exists to make sure that men and women get paid the same for doing broadly the same work.'

The second part of this PC is concerned with how these laws will affect the organisation in the case study. You could use any of the above examples and explain what the company will have to do in order to comply with the legislation. For example: 'Company X will have to make sure that they have a health and safety policy that meets all the requirements of the Act.'

CHAPTER  EIGHT

UNIT:2 BUSINESS DECISION AREAS

OPERATIONS MANAGEMENT

This unit is assessed internally at *both* Higher and Intermediate level 2. The course is very similar at both levels, so much of the text covers both Higher and Intermediate level 2.

At *Intermediate level 2* the course covers:

INTERMEDIATE LEVEL 2

- Purchasing (materials management), designing production systems, and how these systems operate.

- Job, batch and flow production, as with Higher (see below).
- Factors affecting quality, as with Higher (see below) but excluding TQM.

At *Higher* level the course covers:

HIGHER LEVEL

- The Operations process: input → process → output, including the types of production systems used in manufacturing, quality assurance, stock control (or inventory management), quality standards, purchasing, and payment systems (how employees are paid).
- Distribution and delivery, looking at warehousing and storage, transportation, scheduling (often called logistics).

- Some of the various methods of production including job production (producing one thing at a time), batch production (producing a batch at a time), and flow production (continuous production).
- Factors affecting quality, looking at methods or processes adopted by organisations to help achieve quality in their production systems, such as quality control, benchmarking, quality circles and TQM (Total Quality Management).

Guidance and advice for the internal assessments can be found at the end of the chapter.

 Operations management is concerned with the way organisations produce goods and services. It is a transforming process, turning inputs (resources) into outputs (goods and services).

| INPUT | → | PROCESS | → | OUTPUT |

It could be described as the core activity of the organisation, as it actually produces the goods or services for sale, however marketing could also claim to be the core activity as it achieves the sales that create revenue and profits for the organisation.

Ford Motor Company

In 2000, the then chief executive of the Ford Motor Company announced that it was considering outsourcing the production of its motor cars (getting someone else to make them) as the company's profits were created through sales, not production. That particular chief executive has since been replaced, and Ford continues to make the cars itself.

In the Higher Business Management course we will only be looking at production systems in **manufacturing**, where it is much easier to identify the inputs such as information (for example, sales forecasts) raw materials, labour, machinery, factories, etc. the process of making the goods, and the output of finished goods. However, in the service industries the operations process can be much more complicated. For example, for an airline such as 'Easyjet' the inputs would include the passengers who are transported (process) to their destination (output).

Although the diagram for operations management above is very simple, operations management itself is a very complicated function. We can split it into a number of key areas:

- planning
- production
- purchasing
- warehousing and storage – including stock control
- distribution/logistics.

Each of these will interact with the other functional areas of the organisation. For example, the planning of what to produce, how to produce it, and how much to produce will require input from Marketing, Finance, Human Resources, etc. Marketing will provide information on consumers' wants in terms of the product itself (features, quality, colour, etc.), how they wish to make their purchases (place), and how much they will buy. Finance will provide input on the costs of various suppliers, machinery and labour costs. Human Resources will provide information on the available workforce and their skills, and any legislative requirements (employment laws, health and safety, etc.).

Visit the Institute of Operations Management at
www.iomnet.org.uk

PRODUCTION PLANNING

Successful planning is essential to the success of operations management and for the organisation to achieve its objectives. Planning on how to produce will involve creating a production system that will most efficiently produce the goods for output.

Ideally, production should be at a constant level. The exact number of workers required, the materials to be used, and the number and type of machinery will be known in advance. The diagram below shows the ideal for production planning:

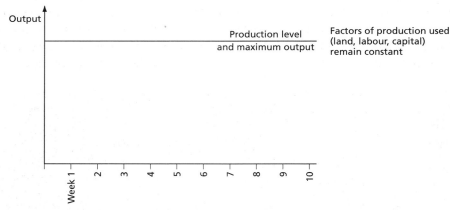

IMAGE 40.
Ideal production planning

It is more likely that production will vary over time, because of changes in consumer demand, staff shortages, machine breakdown and maintenance. So production will vary from day to day or week to week. The production curve will look more like this:

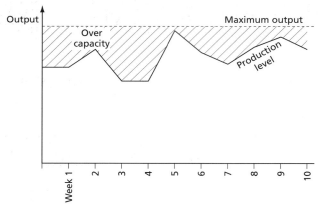

IMAGE 41.
Realistic production planning

In reality, it is rarely possible to have a continuous level of production, so the production system must be flexible.

 ## Glenmorangie Distillery

In May 2002 the Glenmorangie Distillery in Tain announced plans for a £500,000 investment to increase production by a third, due to increasing demand from across the world. The distillery will be extended to accommodate new fermentation vessels that will allow production levels to increase from 3 to 4 million per year. The distillery was first licensed in 1843 and many of the buildings at the Tain site date back to those days.

UNIT 2

TOPIC ONE: Production systems

The production system determines how the manufacturer will produce the goods for the consumer. The production system will be designed, starting with deciding the layout of the factory; then where each part of production will take place by which workers/machines, and how many workers/machines will be needed for each part of the production process. The splitting up of production into a number of different jobs is called the **division of labour**. A successful system will need a flow of stocks from one job to another to make sure that there are no delays due to **shortages** or **bottlenecks**.

IMAGE 42.
A production line in the Motorola factory, Scotland

A number of key factors will affect the decision on what type of production system to use:

The nature of the final product

Different products will be produced in different ways, for example the products in farming are tied up with the land that they are produced on; whereas producing a new bridge will require very different processes.

The market size

Where the firm is producing large numbers of standardised products (such as cans of Irn Bru), production can be simplified into a number of stages, whereas if you were producing customised software for individual clients, the processes would be more complicated and need a great deal of customer input.

The resources available

The production system will be restricted by the finance available, the number and skills of the workers, the size and capacity of the premises, and the machinery and tools available.

The stage of development of the business

When firms are first set up they will tend to produce small amounts, and their production system will be limited. As they grow they can increase their capacity and so the production system can grow and produce a greater variety of goods.

Labour-intensive versus capital-intensive production

Labour-intensive production is where the cost of labour is greater than the cost of capital. There are few industries in this country that would use labour-intensive production because of the high labour costs, which makes machines much more cost-effective. However in other parts of the world where labour is very cheap, labour-intensive production becomes more cost-effective.

There are still some parts of Scotland where the October school holidays are called the 'Tattie Holidays' as this was when school children would earn extra money for the family by picking potatoes on local farms.

Availability of technology – automation

The continuing developments in technologies such as **CAM** (Computer Aided Manufacture), **CAD** (Computer Aided Design) and **automation** (robotics to replace workers) allow firms to design, develop, and produce products quickly. They also allow firms to produce a much wider variety of similar products to appeal to different segments of the market.

Using robotics has the advantage of machines which can carry out very complicated tasks very quickly, and with a high degree of accuracy. Machines can perform in seconds jobs that may take even the most skilled workers hours or days to achieve; indeed, machines can do jobs which are impossible for human workers. There is far less waste when machines are used, and the quality is usually consistent.

The main problems with machines are that they are far more likely to break down than humans, and will only be able to carry out a very narrow range of tasks.

CASE STUDY

Sony Walkman

At present, Sony has at least 12 different versions of the Sony Walkman on the market. Each has the same basic features, all of which are made on the same production lines. Using technology in the design and production of the Walkmans can add different features to each model to appeal to different consumers, with prices ranging from £12 to £60.

This can sometimes be taken a step further, where mass manufacture can take place, with production being tailored to the individual customer's needs.

For case studies visit the biz/ed catalogue at
http://catalogue.bized.ac.uk/roads/opman.html

QUESTION

Q1

What factors will influence the type of production system that a manufacturer chooses?

TOPIC TWO: Purchasing — Materials management

 The materials that are included in the input stage will have a direct influence on both the process stage and the final product. Poor quality will increase waste during production and lead to poor quality output. It is essential that the correct suppliers are selected in order that the organisation can achieve what it wants in terms of the quality and cost of the output.

THE PURCHASING MIX

This refers to the main factors which have to be considered by the Purchasing team. The choice of which suppliers to use will depend on a number of factors:

Alternative suppliers

Are the suppliers dependable? Most manufacturers will run a series of checks on suppliers, including credit reference checks to make sure that they are able to supply as they have said. Should the business use a local or a national supplier? A local supplier will be able to supply at short notice if needed, but may not have the range of materials and may be more expensive than national suppliers. Will using local suppliers bring any other advantages?

Supermarkets have adopted a policy of using local suppliers for some of the produce they sell. This is part of their 'corporate responsibility' in encouraging local producers, which in turn provides good publicity for the supermarkets.

Are there additional costs? Some suppliers will make additional charges for delivery and insurance. Some will have already added this to the quoted price; others will add it on as an extra which will increase the overall price.

Delivery time

The time taken from placing an order to receiving the materials is called the **'lead time'**. How important this is depends on the needs of the organisation, for example it may operate a **'Just in Time'** system of stock control, where only enough stock to keep production going is held. If this is the case, then the supplier must be able to deliver the materials directly from its own stores. In other instances the supplier may not be able to supply straight from stock, in which case there would be a further delay in delivery. Delays can be acceptable, provided that they have been planned for, so that an order is placed far enough in advance for the materials to arrive when they are needed.

The suppliers will have to be reliable in their promised delivery times. If materials do not arrive when they are needed, this could mean that production has to stop. This will lose the organisation sales and customers, and will affect profitability.

Price

Ideally, the best price would be the lowest price, however prices are often open to negotiation. Discounts for bulk-buying may be available and these must be balanced against how much stock the organisation can buy and store at a time. Other discounts may be available if there is a guarantee that the organisation will place regular orders. The credit terms on offer will also be important. The longer these are, the longer it will be before the organisation has to pay for the materials it has received. This has to be balanced against any discounts that may be available for paying quickly.

Many organisations will enter into a contract with their suppliers which will set out the terms and conditions of supply and payment. Purchasing and Finance departments will work together to obtain the best price on the best terms.

 **CASE STUDY** **McDonald's**

McDonald's do not have contracts with any of their suppliers, which means that they can change suppliers without notice. Although this may seem hard on the suppliers, the size of McDonald's orders make it a very attractive proposition. The suppliers must meet McDonald's very strict quality standards.

Quality

What quality means is different for different organisations, however the quality that the supplier can bring to the organisation should be acceptable for the organisation's needs in terms of being suitable for the production process and for the customer's requirements. For consistent production, the quality of materials used should be consistent; if the quality is variable this will lead to increased wastage and poor quality of output on certain occasions. The supplier must be able to guarantee that the materials will be of a minimum standard.

Quantity

Although there may be discounts for buying in bulk, these have to be weighed against the cost of storage. It is thought that storage adds a further 15–30% to the cost of purchasing, so ideally the quantity bought should be as low as possible. The stocks may deteriorate over time, leading to them having to be scrapped. The organisation could also be left with unwanted stock as fashions change. These all mean further costs for the organisation, which should be avoided where possible.

Storage facilities

When making purchasing decisions the organisation must consider what facilities it has for storage. The capacity for storage should be more than the supplies held at any one time. The storage has to be suitable for the products being stored. They should be safe and secure to ensure that there is no loss through theft or poor control systems. Some materials need weather-proof storage; others can be left out in the open. Some need refrigeration; others need heated storage. The cost of insuring the stock also has to be considered.

 **QUESTION**

Q2 What are the main factors that will affect purchasing decisions?

TOPIC THREE: Stock control

Also known as inventory management when considered with purchasing, this is a very important part of operations management because inefficient stock control can lead to a large increase in cost to the business. Ideally, the organisation would operate with as little stock as possible, however this is not always possible. There has to be a balance between the cost of holding stock and the cost of lost production and sales. Efficient production needs a continuous supply of stock.

The decision of how much stock to carry at any one time will be decided at the planning stage. However, if the organisation wants to ensure continuous production it must calculate the economic stock level.

ECONOMIC STOCK LEVEL

This is the lowest level of stock that makes sure that production is not interrupted by shortages, but at the same time also makes sure that it is not carrying too much stock and keeps costs to a minimum.

The economic stock level will ensure that there is enough stock on hand for production to continue. This will be based on the following:

Minimum stock level

This is the level which ensures that there will always be stock for production, allowing for ordering and delivery times (lead time).

Re-order stock level

When stock falls to this level, then new stock must be ordered to make sure that the organisation does not run out. For example, if it takes a week for new stock to arrive, then the re-order level will be at the point where there is at least one week's stock left. In real life there will always be problems with delivery from time to time, so the organisation might re-order when there is 10 days' supply of stock left, just in case.

Re-order stock quantity

This is the amount of stock needed to bring the level back to the economic stock level.

QUESTION

Q3 What are the four main decisions to be made in minimising stock holding costs?

AUTOMATION IN STOCK CONTROL

It is common today to find that most organisations will use a computerised stock control system where, when the stock falls to the re-order stock level, the computer will automatically order more stock. There are a number of ways that such a system can be operated, but many use a bar-code system similar to the bar codes used by supermarkets. The principal is the same: as stock leaves the warehouse or stock room it is scanned by the bar-code reader which automatically adjusts the recorded stock level, and the same happens as new stock comes in and it date-records the when it has arrived to make sure that stock is issued in date order to avoid deterioration. This allows for an accurate check on the running balance of each stock item. Physical checks of the stock must be made from time to time to make sure that the recorded stock levels are accurate. There may be discrepancies due to theft, natural wastage or deterioration.

In supermarkets the bar-code system allows management to make decisions about what products are popular in what areas of the country, and so the stock levels can easily be adjusted to take account of local tastes.

CASE STUDY — Bar codes

Bar codes have now become the global language of business and are standardised and regulated so there is no danger that two companies will pick the same bar code for different products. Bar codes celebrated their 25th birthday in the UK in 2002. They are widely used by companies who trade electronically and make it very easy to describe the raw materials and products that are being bought and sold. In the future bar codes will be augmented with radio-frequency identity tags that can be scanned more quickly and have the information encoded on them updated.

'Without bar codes our operations would not work', said Robin Kidd, supply chain manager at Nestlé UK.

(*Source: BBC News*)

To find out more, visit
www.e-commerce.org.uk
who look after bar codes used in the UK.

QUESTION Q4
Why are bar codes important in modern business?

JUST IN TIME (JIT)

This is a popular method of operations for mass manufacturers as it limits the amount of stock held by the organisation to near zero. It works best where there is a very close relationship between the manufacturer and its suppliers.

In practice, it is very simple: the stock is held by the supplier and is only brought to the factory as and when it is needed. The whole production process has to be geared to working with the JIT system. The cost savings can be very high as there are none of the stock-holding costs such as the following:

- **Capital tied up in stock** – money can be used for other purposes or removed entirely from the manufacturer's expenditure.

- **Storage costs** – space, equipment, warehouse and stores staff, services, etc.

- **Stock losses/wastage** – theft, accidental damage, stock exceeding its shelf-life, stock obsolescence.

In a JIT system these costs are paid by the suppliers.

The whole production operation works on the JIT system in that nothing is produced unless there are customers to buy the products. The Marketing department will give figures on expected demand or actual orders, and only then will production take place. Supplies are ordered 'just in time' to become parts for the final product; these component parts are assembled 'just in time' to become finished products; 'just in time' to be sold to the customers.

 **CASE STUDY** — Just in Time (JIT)

Just in Time production was first developed in Japan by Toyota, the car manufacturer. In order to reduce the costs involved in holding stocks of materials and work-in-progress, Toyota devised a card ordering system known as Kanban. Toyota devised a policy that no components would be made, or supplies ordered, unless the instruction appeared on a **Kanban**. For example, if a worker fitted six steering wheels, a Kanban card would be sent to the production team to order another six steering wheels. These would arrive just in time before the worker ran out of steering wheels.

In order for this to be successful, Toyota had to ensure that its suppliers understood the system and were able to supply on demand. When it opened its UK plant it trained its suppliers in operations and quality procedures to make sure that they delivered the exact product at the right time. In some cases the suppliers had their factories next door to the Toyota plant to ensure that they could operate with the JIT production system. To secure long term contracts with Toyota, suppliers had to deliver, at short notice, small quantities of high-quality goods. The suppliers had to be completely reliable and would have to pay the costs of lost production if they could not deliver, or if they delivered faulty materials.

The advantages of using a successful Kanban system are that significant savings are made in the purchase and storage of materials and so production costs are lower; all stock purchased is used in production and so there is no waste; a close relationship is developed with suppliers which ensures that there are no production delays and the materials exactly match the organisation's needs. The main danger is the heavy reliance on suppliers who must be willing to co-operate fully with the organisation.

The Just In Time system does not suit all organisations, and so many still hold stock. In manufacturing this can often be because the organisation makes some or all of its own component materials. Where organisations decide that they must hold stock they have to manage the storage of the stock.

The first decision is whether the stock should be held in a centralised storage area or spread around different departments. Holding it centrally has several advantages:

- **Making the stock secure, with specialist staff to receive, check and issue it.**
- **Standard organisational procedures can be developed for ordering, receiving and issuing stock.**
- **Storage costs can be better controlled.**

The main costs would be the recruitment, training and salaries for the specialist staff and the cost of creating an area for storage. There would be time delays between ordering and receiving the stock.

Having a de-centralised stock system will allow for better decisions to be made about what stock to buy, how much to order, and for making sure that stock is always available for production.

QUESTION

Q5 Explain why JIT systems can reduce costs to business.

TOPIC FOUR: Payment systems

Workers must be paid for their work. Most production workers, but not all, will receive a basic weekly wage for a basic number of hours worked per week. However it is common for organisations to offer some additional incentives to encourage staff to work harder or better. How the workers are rewarded for their labour varies between organisations.

Overtime is paid when the employee works longer than their contractual hours, usually at a higher rate than the basic rate. This allows the employee to increase their earnings. In some jobs guaranteed overtime is available as part of the contract of employment, or it may be essential to ensure that the organisation runs efficiently. For example, the police and ScotRail depend on employees working overtime.

 **Overtime**

ScotRail depends on drivers working overtime to maintain services. During the overtime ban by the drivers in 2002, 180 trains had to be cancelled on the first day as drivers were not available to work on their rest days.

A report by the TUC in March 2002 said that the average employee works seven hours longer than contracted every week, worth about £5000 per employee per year. The number of employees putting in unpaid overtime has risen to over 5.5 million, with women in professional jobs more likely to work longer that their contracted hours. The TUC estimates that unpaid overtime is worth £28 billion each year to employers.

The CBI stated that tighter controls on the number of hours worked by employees was not the answer, and that people want to make their own decisions about working extra hours.

In small-scale manufacturing, **piecework** is commonly used. Here the worker is paid a certain amount (piece rate) for each good unit they produce. In some cases they will receive no basic wage. It allows for low levels of supervision, and staff will be motivated to work hard enough to earn a reasonable living. However, workers will not pay attention to the amount of waste they create, and will work hardest when they want the most money (e.g. before their summer holidays), and this may not be when demand for the product is highest.

Performance-related pay is an additional payment or **bonus** to staff who are seen to be working better than average, or who have met targets set by the organisation. On the face of it, this seems a good idea to encourage workers to work harder, however it is now recognised that it only encourages the individual, creating unhealthy rivalry between managers, and the destruction of teamwork.

A more modern approach which is becoming increasingly popular is **profit sharing**. Here, staff are given a share of the annual profits of the organisation. This can have a number of benefits. First, the staff see the success of the organisation in terms of profit-making as being directly good for them, putting them in the same position as the shareholders. Secondly, they will be encouraged to work more efficiently for the organisation without affecting teamwork. In some cases the share of profits is paid in the form of free shares which gives the employee part-ownership of the organisation.

Share save schemes and **share options** are other ways to create share ownership amongst employees. With share save schemes, employees save a regular amount each month for a set time period (usually five years), after which they can turn their savings into shares which they can either keep or sell at a substantial profit. This ensures the loyalty of key employees, and provides an incentive to keep profits up, which will in turn increase the value of shares. Share options are sometimes available for senior managers, where they are given the option to buy a certain number of shares at a discount at some point in the future. Again, this creates loyalty and motivation.

CASE STUDY

Share options

In August 2001 the former chairman of the food chain Iceland made a £3 million profit from the controversial sale of share options, and the former Chief Executive had made over £2.5 million despite spending just under five months in the job. Both the former senior members of Iceland sold their shares just before they announced a profits warning for the group, and just before they resigned.

CHAPTER:Eight

TOPIC FOUR

Fringe benefits are types of reward other than wages or salaries which the organisation offers to its employees. There is a wide range of fringe benefits, covering many different jobs. For managers these may include expense accounts, company cars, cheap loans, private medical insurance, etc. For other workers these could include free travel, subsidised canteen or crèche facilities, discounts on products, etc.

Many of these benefits are taxed as income by the government and so have become less popular then 15 years ago, however they are still widely used.

 To see case studies and up-to-date information on pay levels and other benefits, visit **www.irseclips.co.uk**

QUESTION

Q6 Describe the main types of payment to ordinary workers and those available to senior managers.

TOPIC FIVE: Distribution and delivery

 Distribution and delivery are an important part of business operations. The successful manufacture of goods is only one part of the overall business and safe and efficient distribution to wholesalers or delivery to the customer are essential.

Companies will often make use of warehousing facilities to bulk store their goods in bulk. Warehouse space may be owned by the company or leased or rented. The warehouse may be a centralised function of the business or it may be de-centralised and located at a distance from the main operations.

The main reason for utilising warehouse space is that most businesses will be unable exactly to match their output to the demand for their products. Stocks of finished goods will be stored in the warehouse in order to meet demand quickly.

It is important that the warehouse space is of suitable quality and offers security for the protection of stock. It should also offer the correct environment for the storage of stock, for example dry, temperature maintained.

The main aspects of warehousing are:

Design and layout

The design and layout of the warehouse are essential to the smooth operation of the business. Ideally, warehouses should be on ground level only as storage and retrieval of stock from additional floors above ground level will increase handling times. A system of stock rotation should be in operation to avoid deterioration of stock quality.

UNIT 2

Mechanical handling

Some businesses may decide to utilise specialist stock-handling equipment that can be incorporated into the design of a new building. This may be costly but there are substantial benefits to be gained in terms of the space used and time required to move stock.

Pallets are often used in warehouses and they are a relatively cheap method of organising stock. They can be easily moved using a forklift truck and enable stock to be stored off the floor. They can also be re-used.

Transportation

Businesses have a choice in the transportation that they use; their own, hired or public transport. The decision on which type of transport to use will be based on the needs of the particular business and the costs involved.

The advantages and disadvantages of each are summarised below:

TYPE OF TRANSPORT	ADVANTAGES	DISADVANTAGES
Own	Complete control	High initial investment and continuing running costs
Hired	No capital investment, ability to change requirements quickly	Less control
Public	No capital investment, cheaper	Unreliable, poor value for money, little control

TRANSPORT AND DELIVERY OF GOODS IN THE UK

During the last decade, the UK has become a nation that has become more and more dependent on the roads network for transport and delivery of goods and services.

The use of the railways has decreased and the road system is under constant pressure. Nowadays, over 80% of goods are delivered by road. The pie chart overleaf shows the most common methods of transport used in the UK today.

Over 60% of goods are transported by road in the UK. There has been a steady decline in the use of the rail network as a bulk carrier of freight, with more and more goods being delivered via the road network instead.

The UK government has consistently opposed the increasing use of the road network by imposing greater taxes on road users, e.g. fuel duty and road tax, and also by freezing expenditure on the upgrading of existing roads and building of new roads.

Ultimately, the choice of transport will be determined by assessment of the costs and benefits of each type of transport that is available and also taking into account the timescale involved for delivery.

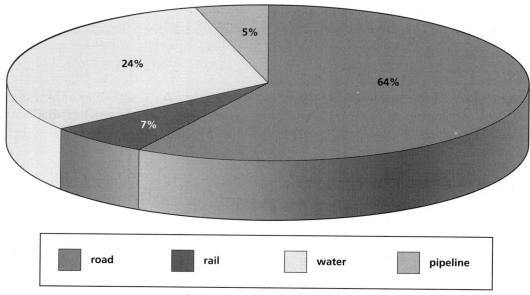

Source: www.transit.dtir.gov.uk

IMAGE 43.
Methods of transporting goods in Britain

Other forms of transport that may be used include air and sea. Transport by sea is rare within the UK but large ports such as Portsmouth in the south of England and Leith, in Edinburgh, still serve as busy areas for ships docking from all over the world.

Air transport is the most costly form of transport but in some cases it may be the only option where a delivery must be made quickly to the other side of the world. Large freight carriers have their own fleet of cargo planes although most other air carriers offer a freight service on their flights to almost every world-wide destination.

Prestwick International Airport in Ayrshire is the largest cargo airport in Scotland, dealing with freight from all over the world.

SCHEDULING

Scheduling is essential to any business operation. This is making sure that all the factors of production are taken into account and are working in harmony with each other. This ensures that, from initial production to final delivery to the customer, every operation works smoothly and delivery times are met.

CASE STUDY

Burns Express Freight Ltd

Burns Express Freight Ltd was formed in 1993 by Carolyn and Derek Burns after having been employed for several years in the Transport and Distribution Industry. The company is based in Paisley and initially started with three vehicles and attained a turnover of £267,000 in its first year. From then, it has attained an average 20% per year growth and now has a turnover of £1.3 million and a fleet of 15 vehicles.

The company's main expertise is in the 'sameday' delivery business or 'just in time' as it is also known. This entails collecting freight from a business address and delivering it to its designated destination in the shortest possible time. This type of business has dramatically increased over the years due to companies no longer wanting to hold on to expensive stock costing them money. They would rather deliver orders as quickly as possible. This could mean delivery in the local Paisley area or an urgent delivery to Europe or worldwide. In both cases, the criteria are the same and are treated in the same way by the company.

The company is also proud of its reputation for reliability and service and after only three years in business attained BSI 9002 accreditation. This is the British Industry standard qualification for Quality Management and means that the company has to adhere to certain rules and regulations and work to an agreed standard to continue to achieve this accreditation.

www.burnsexpress.co.uk
(With thanks to Carolyn and Derek Burns.)

TOPIC SIX: Types of production

There are basically three types of production:

- **job**
- **batch**
- **flow**

JOB PRODUCTION

Job production means that one 'job' is done at a time, through to completion, before another 'job' is started. This effectively means that one product is made at a time.

Examples of businesses that use job production are house building, bridge construction and designer clothing.

Job production is typical in smaller businesses which rely on individuality to sell their products.

BATCH PRODUCTION

Batch production involves all stages of the production process being completed at the same time. Products may be similar, although different ingredients may be used for different products.

A number of products, called a batch, will be produced at once and although each product in a batch is the same, the products may vary from one batch to another.

Batch production is most commonly found in the food business but it is also common in other businesses, e.g. construction, where a row of houses may have their foundations dug at the same time and then the kits to assemble the frame for the houses erected at the same time.

FLOW PRODUCTION

Flow production is common in a factory with a production line where the product being produced flows through various stages, with parts being added at each stage. This is common in almost all instances of mass production where a standard product is being produced.

Examples of this type of business include car production and magazine printing.

This type of production results in a continuous output of products which are essentially the same.

As with any type of production method, there are advantages and disadvantages. Some of these are listed in the tables below:

Job production	
Advantages:	Disadvantages:
1. Easy to organise production 2. 'One-off' orders can easily be accommodated 3. Workers will be involved in the entire production process from start to finish and see the results of their labour	1. Production costs are likely to be higher for job costing since there are few economies of scale 2. Production time may be longer than using other methods since individual requirements of the job have to be met 3. Capital investment may be higher since specialist machinery may be required

Batch production	
Advantages:	Disadvantages:
1. Allows flexible production 2. Stocks of partly finished goods can be stockpiled and completed later, allowing a quick response to new orders	1. Production runs of small batches may be expensive to produce 2. If production runs are different from each other there may be extra costs and time delays in setting up different equipment

Flow production	
Advantages:	**Disadvantages:**
1. Economies of scale 2. Automated production lines save time and money 3. Quality systems can be built into the production	1. A standard product is produced which may not suit all customers 2. High costs associated with set-up of automated production line 3. Work can be repetitive and boring for workers 4. If production runs are high, too much may be produced and supply will exceed demand

TOPIC SEVEN: Quality assurance and quality control

 Quality is an important factor to the consumer in today's competitive market. It is difficult to define and means different things to different people. It may mean the quality of fit and finish or the price paid for the goods. Some consumers will place greater value on the reliability and useful life of the product.

The producer of the goods may have different aspirations relating to quality, e.g. meeting specifications or having very few customer complaints.

Quality assurance aims to make sure that quality standards are:

- set
- agreed
- met

through the entire organisation.

Quality control and **quality assurance** are different concepts which are linked to the management of quality within an organisation.

Quality control is a historic concept and assumes that there will be a degree of waste, up to 25%, where an organisation has in place a system of quality checking at the end of the manufacturing process.

This type of 'control' can lead to significantly increased costs of production and often the goods that are tested for quality control purposes need to be destroyed.

This type of quality control has led to such syndromes as the 'Friday car syndrome' and does not ensure that all goods that leave the production line are of the highest quality.

Quality assurance assumes that the wastage caused by quality control can be prevented. This means that quality is checked at every stage of the process instead of just at the end. This reduces waste to levels as low as 5%. Most modern businesses now rely on a system of quality control through the use of quality assurance at each stage of production to produce a better product and reduce their costs of wastage.

TOPIC EIGHT: Quality standards

 If you were to ask anyone on the street for their views on quality, it is likely that they would at some point indicate a specification of standards that has to be met.

However, although there are quality standards in place, these are not widespread and may be limited to certain industries and may not even be a requirement for all businesses operating in a particular business sector. Measurements of quality can include appearance, safety, availability, value for money, consumer support and the overall reputation of the product and the company. A good example of perception of quality is to be found in the car industry. Some car producers have developed a reputation for quality based on the fit, finish and general feel of their products. For example, German car manufacturers such as Volkswagen, Mercedes and BMW have developed a reputation for quality cars, whereas manufacturers from the Far East such as Kia and Perodua have developed a reputation at the budget end of the market.

There is also the effect of legislation in the UK linked to the quality of products. Consumers have a right to expect that goods are of 'satisfactory quality' and that they are 'fit for the purpose for which they are intended'. Indeed, the UK courts have been quite liberal in their interpretation of legislation, falling more often than not firmly on the side of the consumer.

In a recent case in which the writer was involved, the failings of quality control were highlighted and the need to rely on current legislation was necessary. The facts were that the writer purchased a brand-new 'quality' German motor car. After 250 miles, there was a catastrophic failure of the turbo unit in the engine; a fault that had not been discovered at any point in the production process or in the subsequent inspections prior to the customer taking delivery. The writer had to use his statutory right of rejection as the car was not of 'satisfactory quality' taking into account the price paid and the age of the car. Subsequent delivery of the replacement car revealed poor quality in the panel fit of the bonnet and again the writer had to rely on his legal rights in order to have the problem rectified.

Over recent years the UK government has promoted the benefits of the British Standards Institute. The aim is to promote quality at all stages of the production. As previously mentioned, this is a move away from the more traditional approach of testing for quality at the end of the production process and merely trying to rectify faults at that stage.

The British Standards Institute is responsible for the control and operation of the main British Standard: BS 5750. Many companies will only deal with other companies that are certified to this quality standard.

Organisations which aim to achieve this standard have to go through a process of producing quality manuals to set out their policies and procedures for quality assurance and take part in inspections to ensure that these policies and procedures are being implemented. Once a certificate has been issued, it will be subject to further regular inspections to ensure that standards are maintained.

BS 5750 is the benchmark for quality in the UK. The international equivalent is ISO 9000 and is recognised in over 90 countries worldwide.

There are other organisations which offer quality assurance marks:

- **British Standards Institute Kite Mark**
- **Association of British Travel Agents (ABTA)**
- **Investors in People (IIP).**

 **CASE STUDY**

125 Years On: The Next Generation

In 1992, one year before the 125th anniversary of the founding of the business, Gordon handed over the Managing Directorship to his daughter Audrey and the fourth generation of Baxters took up the reins. Audrey had made a successful career for herself in the City with the merchant bankers Kleinwort Benson before succumbing eventually to the lure of the Highlands and the challenge of running the family business, helped by her two brothers Andrew and Michael.

With the support of their dedicated management team, the new generation was set to lead Baxters into the 21st century.

'Our goal', says Audrey, echoing her father, 'must always be to produce quality products, package them in a professional manner and tell the consumer about them.'

As well as these quality products, Baxters now boasts a thriving business in their busy Visitor Centre on the banks of the River Spey which draws close to 230,000 visitors each year and generates almost £2 million in income. In many respects, Audrey, Andrew and Michael and their management team run a company of which their great-grandparents could never even have dreamed. The sheer scale of the operation, the science and technology that underlies it, the sophisticated sales, marketing and distribution – these things are light years away from the business that was conducted in the little grocery shop in Fochabers.

But there is much that has changed remarkably little. The house of Baxter was built, above all, on a commitment to quality which remains as strong today as it has ever been.

Not so long ago, the chief executive of a famous world-wide retailer was visiting the Baxter factory. He stopped for a moment to talk to one of the quality controllers on the production line.

'You'll be the mannie from X', she said, with customary Highland directness. 'They say you're important.' 'Well, maybe', replied the VIP, 'but not as important as you.' 'You'd better believe it', she agreed. 'I don't let anything out of here that's not right up to scratch.' 'I can imagine', said the VIP with a smile. 'Well, I'd better not hold you up. Goodbye.'

'Cheerio then', she said, 'and mind and fill out an order form before you go.'

(*Source: www.baxters.co.uk*)

TOPIC NINE: Total Quality Management (TQM)

The aim of Total Quality Management is to produce a perfect product every time. This system was first seen in the UK over 20 years ago when it was adopted by the Ministry of Defence.

TQM uses the principles of quality assurance but the view of quality is such that the exact needs and requirements of the customer must be regarded above everything else. This means that there is a change in the focus of the quality culture from the manufacturer to the client. The client tells the manufacturer what they want and it is up to the manufacturer to use this as his benchmark for quality.

To achieve TQM, it is essential that quality is evident at every stage of the production process. When properly implemented, wastage can be reduced to less than 3%.

TQM therefore requires:

- a whole-company focus on quality
- a commitment from each individual in the company
- consultation with every employee at every level of the organisation in setting standards
- a focus on teamwork and the creation of a feeling of worth among the workforce
- viewing TQM as a long term concept
- the creation of a plan for quality
- training for employees
- constant checking and review of performance
- constant checking for improvement.

The introduction of a system for quality assurance or TQM requires four key elements to be managed:

1 The definition of quality at each and every stage of production.
   This depends on the requirements of the customer and their ability to provide detailed specification. This may take into account such factors as intended use, safety standards, efficiency, materials to be used and cost.

2 The commitment of all the workforce.
   This requires several important points to be taken into account:

   - a commitment from the organisation to quality; this should be included in its mission statement
   - the production of a quality manual
   - a clear definition of staff responsibilities within the organisation
   - established standard operating procedures
   - quality audits
   - use of benchmarking
   - use of quality circles.

BUSINESS DECISION AREAS

3 The operation of a system in which the established quality can be assured.
This includes:

- **systems to help in the definition and specification of products/services**
- **systems for checking and monitoring quality at all stages**
- **keeping records**
- **establishing a system of review, monitoring and feedback**
- **appraising staff**
- **setting targets.**

4 A measure of the ability to meet quality requirements.
This can be measured both quantitatively and qualitatively.

TOPIC TEN: Benchmarking

Benchmarking is a process of quality assurance which uses the best performers in a particular industry to set standards for others to meet.

This means that organisations from the same business sector can compare their performance to the market leaders in the same field.

The setting of benchmarked standards is somewhat subjective as it may be identified from sources such as customers, journalists and business analysts.

TOPIC ELEVEN: Quality circles

Quality circles are groups of people that meet regularly within the organisation to identify, discuss and resolve problems in the production process.

Members of the quality circle should include a wide range of people from the workforce from shop floor workers up to senior management.

They were first established in the Japanese car industry several decades ago and are well suited to production systems where there are a lot of individual processes.

CHAPTER SUMMARY

By the end of this chapter you should be able to:

- **Identify and describe the main elements in the operations function including purchasing, systems design, automation labour requirements and system operations such as stock control.**

- **Describe the different types of production (Job, Batch, and Flow) and identify in which situations they should be used.**

- Describe the factors that affect quality in operations including: quality control, benchmarking, quality circles, and Total Quality Management.

- Describe the operations process of input, process and output, and apply it to different types of production system.

- Identify and describe quality assurance, stock control, quality standards, purchasing function, and payments systems.

- Describe and analyse the distribution and delivery systems including, warehousing, transportation and scheduling.

PREPARATION FOR ASSESSMENT

HIGHER ASSESSMENT

What you are asked to do here will depend on the assessment you are given, however the questions and the answers will have to cover the PCs. Where asked, you should always try to use examples from the case study or stimulus material.

PC (a) – Analysis of the importance of purchasing to a business is accurate and makes reference to factors which influence purchasing decisions

This assessment has two parts. The first is on the importance of purchasing, and your answer should include the fact that the materials that you purchase will affect the quality of the final product, so the organisation must make sure that it gets the right quantities of materials at the right price, of the right quality, at the right time. Good purchasing can reduce the cost of production and so increase profitability, and make sure that the final products are what the customer wants, so reducing returns and complaints.

The second part is about the factors that influence purchasing decisions, including: how much to buy (this will depend on how much you can store, what discount you can get for bulk-buying, and the cost of holding stock); which suppliers should you use (are they reliable? can they guarantee quality?, etc.)

PC (b) – Analysis of factors affecting the quality of operations of an organisation is accurate with respect to organisational and customer requirements

This PC also has three parts. The first is concerned with why the organisation should be concerned with what the customer wants in terms of quality. Your answer could include the fact that customers can go elsewhere if they are not happy, and that having quality procedures will make sure that customers will receive what the organisation says they will get. You could also mention the fact that quality standards may encourage continuous improvement in the organisation's production, and that with high-quality products they may be able to target different market segments.

UNIT 2

The second is concerned with the organisation's requirements. Your answer could include the fact that the organisation has to provide products at the quality standards that it specifies; that this would mean making available the resources needed to achieve that level of quality; and that the organisation's requirements must be at least of the same quality level as customers would expect from their product.

The third part of the PC deals with the methods available to ensure quality operations. Your answer could include: **quality control** – checking the final product for faults; **benchmarking** – comparing the organisation against the best in the industry and setting standards to match the best; **TQM** – where the organisation has quality chains established, with every member of the organisation responsible for quality, and where quality is checked at every stage; **quality circles** – where groups of workers meet to solve production problems and try to find ways of improving the process.

PC (c) – Analysis of different types of production is accurate to the product or services provided

This PC is split into two parts. The first is about giving suitable examples of where job, batch and flow production are used. It may be from the text you are given or you may be asked to give your own examples.

The second part requires that you can show you understand what each type of production is. Job production is for one-off jobs, usually to the customer's individual requirements. Batch production is where products are produced in batches because demand for the product will vary but will be too much for job production. Flow production is used where there is continuous demand for the product, and economies of scale are available from mass production.

 ## INTERMEDIATE 2 ASSESSMENT
Explain the operations function in an organisation

This assessment will be based on a short case study or a piece of stimulus material. What answers you have to give will depend on which assessment you are given, however the information given below will apply for any of them. Your answer should give examples from the case study when you are asked to do so.

PC (a) – Elements of the operations function are accurately explained and related to suitable examples

Here you will be asked to explain each of the elements that make up the operations function. The first is **purchasing**, and you should explain the importance of buying the correct quality, the right quantity at the right price from a reliable supplier, and that you should try to get discounts and the best possible credit terms. The second is **systems design**, and your answer should include decisions about whether to use a capital- or labour-intensive system. Labour-intensive is best used where the level of production is low, for example making dresses for individual customers. Capital-intensive is best when you are mass-producing. You should also discuss designing a suitable factory layout, and the flow of work. The third element is **system operation**, and here your answer should be about stock control, deciding on stock levels, storage, security, etc. You may also be expected to write about **automation** – the use of robotics in production. You should be able to explain that machines can carry out very complicated tasks very quickly, and with a high degree of accuracy. This leads to less waste and a better quality of output. The main problem with robotics is that they are not very adaptable.

PC (b) – The different types of production are accurately explained and related to the requirements of the organisation

Here you will have to explain what is meant by job, batch and flow production, and be able to describe when each is used.

Your answer should include: 'Job production is used when individual products are being made to the individual requirements of a customer.' They can be large, such as the building of a house extension, or small, such as making a wedding cake. 'Batch production is used where a number of very similar or identical products are made at the same time.' An obvious example would be in a bakery where the term 'batch' is still used to describe a number of loaves of bread being baked at the same time. 'Flow production is where there is a continuous flow of inputs into the process and a continuous flow of outputs.' Flow production is used where there is constant demand for the product which goes through a number of different processes. A good example of flow production may be electricity where you can use the product 24 hours a day.

PC(c) – Explanation of ways to maintain quality is accurate and related to customer requirements

Here you will be asked about methods for making sure of the quality in production. Your answer could include **quality control** – checking the final product for faults; **quality circles** – groups of workers meeting to solve production problems and improve standards; **benchmarking** – finding the best in the industry and trying to copy what they do successfully – 'We want to be as good as them.' You could also talk about **quality assurance** – checking the product for defects at each stage of production.

How many different methods you have to mention will depend on the assessment you are given, however your answer should include the fact that quality is about meeting or exceeding the customer's needs with minimum cost.

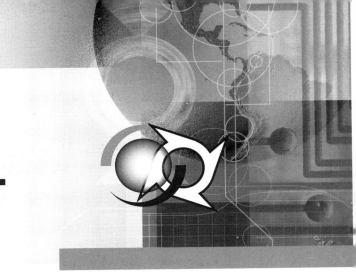

UNIT:3 EXTERNAL ASSESSMENT
PREPARING FOR THE EXAM

THE SYLLABUS

The Higher and Intermediate 2 Business Management examinations cover the whole syllabus, not just the Learning Outcomes which have been assessed throughout the course by internal assessments. A summary of the course syllabus is included in the next section.

There should be no unpleasant surprises if you make sure that your revision covers all aspects of the syllabus. The questions from past examination papers (Section 2) are arranged by Outcome – remember that in the external examination questions are 'integrated' – that means that one question (worth 25 marks) will be subdivided into three to five questions not all on the same Outcome of the course. It is important to get as much practice as you can in writing timed answers to extended response questions, as well as case studies (Section 1).

TIME MANAGEMENT

The examination is divided into two sections, the first consisting of a case study (stimulus material) worth 50 marks (25 marks at Intermediate 2), and the second offering a choice of two from five extended response questions worth 25 marks each. The exam at Higher lasts two and a half hours, at Intermediate 2 it lasts one hour 45 minutes. You need to do a lot of writing – be careful not to run out of time. Each section should take no longer than one and a quarter hours at Higher. You can do the sections in any order. Since the questions in the case study require a mixture of short and long answers, allocating your time might be easier if you start with Section 2 extended response questions and allow 35 minutes for each.

SECTION ONE – THE CASE STUDY

The case study will consist of stimulus material – which could be fictitious but it could also be based on a newspaper or magazine article about a real organisation which is undergoing 'problems'. This material provides the basis for the questions which follow, but you will not be able to answer all of them purely from the text of the case study. Be wary if using past MIS (Management and Information Studies) case studies for practice – they are dissimilar from those in the Business Management exam.

Usually there is a question about the problems facing the organisation, and sometimes one on identifying how to improve the situation. It is common for candidates to make the mistake of suggesting solutions (and gaining no marks) when they have been asked to identify problems – or to repeat problems (gaining no marks) in questions asking about solutions. Marks **are** available for showing exactly how a proposed solution would help solve the original problem.

Example

Question (from 2000 case study) for 8 marks:

'Identify four measures which could be taken to extend the life cycle of a product. Give examples.'

Candidates lost marks for writing about more than four measures but not illustrating them with examples. Some candidates wrote about one of the elements at length but ignored the other elements of the marketing mix.

A suitable answer:

'A firm might try to target a new market segment (1 mark) e.g. in advertisements, Kellogs has promoted cornflakes as something grandparents as well as children will enjoy eating. (1 mark)

A firm might repackage its product or give it a new name (1 mark), e.g. Opal Fruits' packaging changed and they were renamed Starburst to attract more customers. (1 mark)

A firm might employ a celebrity to endorse their product (1 mark), e.g. interest in Walker's crisps was revived by their TV campaign featuring Gary Lineker. (1 mark)

A firm might try to sell its products in different ways. (1 mark) e.g. the Body Shop Direct allow customers to see and try their products in a demonstration held in someone's home. (1 mark)'

SECTION TWO – EXTENDED RESPONSE

In general; the balance of the external examination paper reflects the importance given to the different topic areas (Outcomes) in the syllabus, proportionate to the amount of time recommended for each topic (Outcome).

Questions are 'integrated' i.e. each of them asks about more than one area of the syllabus. They are usually split into three to five parts. It is important to read through all the questions carefully before making a final choice. Try to make sure that you can attempt all parts of the question.

Attention to the words

'**Identify**' usually indicates a short answer, identifying, for example, a business term or part of a recognised business process (e.g. the decision-making process) or specific designations (e.g. different types of stakeholders). '**Suggest**' requires a little bit more, and can be more subjective. '**Describe**' requires a fuller answer, but a fairly straightforward one. '**Analyse**' and '**Discuss**' need a more sophisticated answer, usually making reference to pros and cons of an issue. '**Justify**' calls for an answer that gives a reason for the course of action suggested. '**Compare**' can cause candidates problems; some attempt should be made to **compare** rather than providing simple lists.

Example

Question (from 2000 paper Section two):

'Compare the objectives of a public limited company with those of a charity.'

Simply listing three typical objectives of each does not really answer the question. A better answer would be:

'A public limited company (plc) has profit maximisation as a major objective, as it has to satisfy the demands of shareholders for dividends (1 mark), but a charity's main objective is to help the cause it is associated with; it has no shareholders and raises funds only to benefit its cause. (1 mark)

The charity will aim to spread awareness of its cause (1 mark) whereas the public limited company wants to expand its market share. (1 mark)

The charity's ultimate objective may be to put itself out of existence once the problems it is dealing with are solved (1 mark) but the plc is more likely to want to survive against the threat of competition. (1 mark)'

MARKS

Be guided by the marks allocation. Generally, a valid point merits a mark. Marks can also be gained for developing a point, e.g. by explaining it in more detail (but beware of repetition of the same point just using different words), giving an example or illustrating it with a diagram.

Sometimes good candidates make only a few points, each developed at great length. Usually you are likely to score more marks if you make more points and develop each less thoroughly. Indeed sometimes the marking scheme may limit the number of marks allowed for developing a single point.

It is good practice to define terms mentioned in the question (although marks are **not always** available for defining/identification), e.g. '**de-layering** refers to the removal of layers of management from an organisation's hierarchy'. Even if marks are not given for such a definition, it is a good way to begin an answer as it focuses the question which is being asked.

Some candidates use bullet points. This is acceptable, but great care needs to be taken that you write in sentences after these. Lists of single word answers are unlikely to score highly.

UNIT:3 EXTERNAL ASSESSMENT
COURSE CONTENT

 INTERMEDIATE 2
Business activity in contemporary society

The business cycle	Wealth creation, production and consumption, satisfaction of human wants.
Types of business organisations	Self-employed, private limited company, public limited company, voluntary organisation, charity/public corporation, government-funded service provider, local authority-funded provider.
Sectors of activity	Primary, secondary, tertiary.
The role of the entrepreneur	Enterprise, identifying business opportunities, combining factors of production, risk-taking.
Objectives	Profit maximisation, survival, growth, social responsibility, provision of a service. Relate to types of organisation.
Stakeholders	Types: internal, external, owners, employees, customers, suppliers, community, government. The relationship of stakeholders to individual organisations and influence on organisational activity. Importance of stakeholders to private-sector and public-sector organisations. The effects of change in the business environment on stakeholders.
The changing nature of business	Factors which can cause change: **internal**, e.g. changes in costs, development of new products; **external**, e.g. changes in demand, changes in technology, changes in taxation, changes in the competitive market, changes in national and EU legislation. Importance of change to business, e.g. the need to respond to internal and external pressures. The need to ensure survival.
Changes in the business environment.	The increasing significance of multinationals; the greater business orientation in publicly funded organisations; changes in the size of firms, e.g. the importance of small firms, downsizing.

Key areas of business

INTERNAL ORGANISATION

Factors affecting internal organisation	Size, technology, market, product.
Limited company	Board of directors, managing director, shareholders, management.
Other types of organisation	Board of management, board of trustees, chief executive, etc.

MARKETING

The marketing concept	The role of marketing in different types of organisations, e.g. marketing in the public and private sectors, goods and services.
Market research	The assessment of customer requirements, e.g. surveys and sampling.
The marketing mix	Place, price, product/service and promotion.

HUMAN RESOURCES

Role of human resource management department	Maintenance of personnel information and records, terms and conditions of employment, monitoring of procedures, e.g. grievance and discipline, health and safety, awareness of legislative requirements (employment law, equal opportunities).
Changing pattern of employment within organisation	Trends towards greater use of part-time and casual staff and core labour force.
Recruitment and selection	Internal and external sources of recruitment. Methods of selection (e.g. application form, interviews, references).
Training and development	Reasons for training and development (e.g. flexibility, upgrading skills). Types of training (e.g. induction, staff development, national training schemes).
Employee relations	Interrelationships between employees and management (e.g. local and national arrangements, trade unions, works councils).

OPERATIONS

The role of the operations function	Purchasing (materials management), system design (automation, labour requirements), system operation (quality assurance, stock control).
Types of production	Job, batch and flow.
Payments systems	Time rates, piece rates, bonus schemes.

FINANCIAL MANAGEMENT

The role of the finance department	Payment of wages and salaries, payment of accounts, maintenance of financial records.
Financial information	Use and purpose of profit and loss, balance sheet, cash flow (FRS1).
Uses of financial information	Controlling costs and expenditure, monitoring performance.

Users of financial information	Management, owners, creditors, employees, citizens.
Sources of finance	Features, e.g. benefits and costs, internal and external; short- and long-term. Possible sources, e.g. banks, local enterprise companies (LECs), shares.

Information in business

Sources of information	Internal, external, primary, secondary.
Types of information	Written, oral, pictorial, graphical, numerical.
Uses of information in business	Monitoring and control, decision-making, measuring performance, identifying new business opportunities.
Evaluation of different types of information	Fitness for purpose, e.g. accuracy, completeness, method of presentation.
Types of IT	Mini computers, personal computers, multimedia, telecommunication systems (video conferencing, e-mail, etc).
Uses of IT	Decision-making, provision of information, maintenance of records, communications, etc.
Benefits of IT	Speed, flexibility, handling of complex information.
Business software	Manipulation of data using databases and spreadsheets to enhance decision-making.

HIGHER

Business in contemporary society

Structure of business organisations	Self-employed, private limited company, public limited company, voluntary organisation, charity; public corporation, government-funded service provider, local authority-funded provider. Above covers firms in all size ranges and national and international aspects of their operation, e.g. multinationals.
Sectors of activity	Primary, secondary, tertiary.
Objectives	Profit maximisation, survival, sales maximisation, growth, social responsibility.
Role of enterprise and the entrepreneur	Identifying business opportunities, combining factors of production, innovation, risk-taking.
Stakeholders	Shareholders, customers, employees, donors (for charities), management, government, suppliers, banks, taxpayers, community as a whole, local government.
Methods of growth or consolidation	Horizontal and vertical integration, diversification, merger and take-over, demerger, divestment.
Sources of assistance	Local enterprise companies (LECs), banks, local authorities via subsidised premises, etc. government help, e.g. grants and allowances, help for exporters through trade fairs, etc., advice and courses for small businesses, European Union (EU) grants.

UNIT 3

Factors affecting the operation of business	Business as a dynamic activity. The impact of changes in demand, demographic trends, competition, regional policies, structure of the labour market, local and central government, privatisation, EU, environment, technology. The above can be grouped under headings of social (e.g. changing tastes, population), technological (e.g. IT), economic (e.g. competition), political (e.g. government policy), competitive environment (e.g. new products introduced by domestic competitors, new entrants from other markets and/or other countries).

INFORMATION AND INFORMATION TECHNOLOGY

Types of information	Primary, secondary, internal, external, qualitative and quantitative.
Value of information	Accuracy, timeliness, completeness, appropriateness, availability, cost, objectivity, conciseness.
Examples of IT	Characteristics and uses of mainframe, mini computer, networks (Local Area Network – LAN, Wide Area Network – WAN, etc), telecommunications technology, e-mail, multimedia, CD-ROMs, etc.
Business software	Characteristics and use of business software such as databases, spreadsheets, decision-making packages. Awareness of data protection legislation.

DECISION-MAKING IN BUSINESS

Decision-making model	Identify the problem, identify the objectives, gather information, analyse information, devise alternative solutions, select from alternatives, communicate the decision, implement the decision, evaluate. SWOT analysis, the influence of information technology on decision-making.
Types of decisions	The nature of decisions. Types of decision – strategic, tactical and operational.
Problems of structured models	Time, ability to collect all information; problems of generating alternatives, lack of creativity.

Business decision areas

INTERNAL ORGANISATION

Grouping of activities	Function, product/service, customers, place/territory, technology, line/staff.
Functional activities of organisations	Marketing, human resource management, finance, operations, research and development.
Forms of organisational structure	Hierarchical/flat, span of control, formal and informal structures, awareness of organisation culture, matrix structure, the role and responsibilities of management, e.g. delayering, downsizing.
Nature of jobs	Authority, accountability, responsibility. Job specialisation and job definition.

MARKETING

The marketing concept — Marketing as a strategic activity. Marketing of products and services.

Market research — Techniques (e.g. survey, questionnaire, interview, test marketing), the assessment of customer requirements.

Target markets — Market segmentation, niche marketing, methods of segmenting markets, market share, market growth.

The marketing mix — Place, pricing strategies, product/service and promotion.

FINANCIAL MANAGEMENT

Cash flow — Use, purpose and interpretation.

Financial reporting — Description of components of and interpretation of balance sheet and profit and loss account.

Ratio analysis — Gross profit/sales, gross profit/cost of goods sold, net profit/sales, return on capital, current ratio, acid test.

Budgets — Uses of budgets (e.g. to monitor and control activity, gain information).

HUMAN RESOURCE MANAGEMENT

Changing pattern of employment within organisations — Trends towards greater use of part-time and casual staff, core labour force within organisations.

Recruitment and selection — Techniques: job analysis, job description, person specification, internal and external sources, selection methods, e.g. role of interview, application form, aptitude tests, psychometric tests.

Training and staff development — Costs and benefits to the organisation, induction, on-the-job, off-the-job.

Employee relations — Main institutions (ACAS, employers' associations, trade unions). Processes: negotiation, consultation, arbitration. Management of employee relations, e.g. single union deals.

Legislative requirements — An awareness of legislation relating to equal opportunities, employment and health and safety.

OPERATIONS

Input, process and output — Production systems in manufacturing, quality assurance, stock control, quality standards, purchasing.

Distribution and delivery — Warehousing, transport (road, rail, air, sea), scheduling.

Location of operations — Factors influencing location (e.g. proximity of market; labour supply, nature of product/service, availability of site, assistance packages)

UNIT 3

UNIT:3 EXTERNAL ASSESSMENT

EXAMINATION QUESTIONS

(arranged under Outcomes)

THE ROLE OF BUSINESS IN SOCIETY

1   Jill Royal is a fitness instructor who runs her own business as a sole trader. She
    needs to raise finance to expand the premises and to buy new equipment. Identify
    5 methods of raising finance.   (10 marks)

2   Explain the term '**franchising**' and name 3 franchises.   (5 marks)

3   Give **3 advantages** and **3 disadvantages** of franchising.   (6 marks)

4   List **4** objectives that a **charity** might have.   (4 marks)

5   Describe the role of the **entrepreneur** in setting up a business.   (4 marks)

6   Businesses constantly have to face up to **external pressures**, e.g. legal,
    environmental, social and technological pressures. Describe the effects these
    pressures could have on a business.   (6 marks)

7   Profit maximisation is often the main objective of private sector
    organisations. Name **3 forms of private sector organisation** and give
    2 advantages and 2 disadvantages of each.   (15 marks)

8   Identify **5 stakeholders** of a private sector organisation and give an
    example of how each may **influence** the way the organisation
    operates.   (10 marks)

9   Apart from financial **objectives**, e.g. profit maximisation, a business may have
    other equally important aims. Identify and describe **4 other** possible
    business objectives.   (8 marks)

10 Identify and describe **the sources of finance** available to someone who
    is setting up in business for the first time.   (8 marks)

11 The employees of an organisation are **stakeholders** of that organisation. Name 5 other possible stakeholders and state what their 'interest' might be. (10 marks)

12 Change (internal/external) affects businesses. Name the main areas where change can occur in business. (10 marks)

13 Supermarkets are often public limited companies. Describe the main features of a **plc**. (3 marks)

INFORMATION AND IT

1 Explain how a **multinational** organisation could make use of **electronic methods of communication**, and outline the **advantages** and **disadvantages** of electronic communication. (10 marks)

2 Managers use information to make effective decisions.
   (a) Identify **5 methods of presenting information** and give an advantage for each. (10 marks)
   (b) Give an example of how a supermarket chain might use each method you have identified. (5 marks)

3 Choose 5 types of ICT (including software) and explain how a hotel receptionist might use them. (10 marks)

4 Effective decision-making depends on reliable **information**. There are 4 sources of obtaining information:
   • primary
   • secondary
   • internal
   • external.
   Describe these and discuss their advantages and disadvantages. (8 marks)

5 **Information technology** can be an invaluable tool for decision-making. Choose **one** of the following and explain how it could be useful for **decision-making**.
   (i)   database
   (ii) Internet
   (iii) spreadsheet. (4 marks)

6 Any business implementing **IT** will experience **costs and benefits** in doing so. List 2 possible costs and 2 possible benefits. (4 marks)

DECISION-MAKING IN BUSINESS

1 Outline the stages of the **model** which managers should use to ensure effective decision-making. (5 marks)

2 Decisions made by managers may be strategic, tactical or operational. Describe each type of decision and give examples relating to decisions made within a large supermarket chain. (10 marks)

3 Identify and describe the 3 main types of business decisions. Give an example of each one. (9 marks)

INTERNAL ORGANISATION

1 (a) Describe the **features** of the following organisational structures:

    (i) **hierarchical structure**
    (ii) **flat structure**
    (use diagrams to illustrate your answer) (8 marks)

    (b) Explain why an organisation would decide to change from a hierarchical to a flat structure. (7 marks)

MARKETING

1 For each of the elements of **the marketing mix**, describe how a manufacturer could increase sales. (10 marks)

2 A car manufacturer is concerned that its supermini is about to go into the decline stage of the product life cycle. Explain the '**product life cycle**'. Use an appropriate diagram to support your answer. (8 marks)

3 Using each of the 4 elements of the **marketing mix**, describe how supermarkets compete in the market place. (12 marks)

FINANCE

1 Jill Royal is a fitness instructor who runs her own business. She prepares a **cash budget** at the beginning of each year. Explain why Jill does this. (5 marks)

2 Every business prepares **financial information**. List **5 users of financial information** (**stakeholders**) and explain how they would use the financial information. (10 marks)

3 Explain how a **computerised stock control system** could improve the **efficiency** of any organisation. (6 marks)

4 Organisations use financial information to aid decision-making. Identify **3 financial statements** that an organisation would prepare. Explain the purpose of preparing each of these statements. (6 marks)

5 Explain the uses of **4** of the following accounting ratios:
- gross profit margin (or percentage)
- net profit margin (or percentage)
- rate of stock turnover
- working capital ratio (or current ratio)
- return on capital employed
- acid test ratio. (8 marks)

6 Financial information is available to a number of users. Identify **3** of these users and explain how they would 'use' the information. (6 marks)

7 Explain the purpose of the **profit and loss account** and the **balance sheet**. (3 marks)

8 Identify **3 users** of a company's published accounts and explain how they could make use of the information in the accounts. (6 marks)

HUMAN RESOURCES MANAGEMENT

1 A business is introducing new equipment.
   (i) Identify and describe 2 approaches to **training staff** in the use of the new equipment. (4 marks)
   (ii) Give **one advantage** and **one disadvantage** of each approach. (4 marks)

2 A workforce may be unhappy with the idea of working with new equipment. Describe **3 forms** of **industrial action** that the workforce could take. (6 marks)

3 (i) Name and describe **2 pieces** of **employment legislation** that are designed to protect employees. (6 marks)
   (ii) What steps could an employee take if he/she felt that he/she had been **unfairly dismissed**? (5 marks)

4 An international hotel chain needs to recruit a head receptionist for one of its European hotels.
   (a) Outline the details that the **job description** and the **person specification** should contain. (8 marks)
   (b) A shortlist of candidates would be drawn up. Identify and describe **3 methods of selection** that the hotel chain management could use to appoint the right person for the job. (6 marks)

5 Describe a **recruitment procedure** which would ensure that the 'best' person for the job is selected. (10 marks)

6 Disagreements between employees and management may result in **industrial action**. Outline the probable effects of **industrial action** on employees, managers and other stakeholders. (5 marks)

OPERATIONS MANAGEMENT

1 A manufacturer of ready meals has had an increase in the number of customer complaints, which has led to a fall in sales. For example, a supermarket chain returned 1000 boxes of ready meals which were unsatisfactory. Explain how the manufacturer could **assure the quality** of its ready meals. (9 marks)

2 Explain how a **computerised stock control system** could improve the efficiency of any organisation. (6 marks)

3 Car manufacturers tend to operate a flow production system. Identify and describe **2 other methods of production**. Give examples. (6 marks)

4   Explain what problems a car manufacturer might have as a result of **overstocking** or **understocking**.   (6 marks)

5   Explain how **just-in-time production** could alleviate problems of overstocking. Identify any possible disadvantages.   (5 marks)

6   Describe the 3 main methods of production – **job**, **batch**, **flow** – giving an example of each.   (6 marks)

7   Explain what is meant by **quality control**.   (4 marks)

8   Identify the main **features** of a stock **control system**.   (6 marks)

UNIT:3 EXTERNAL ASSESSMENT

SOLUTIONS
 **(arranged under Outcomes)**

ROLE OF BUSINESS IN SOCIETY

1 • **Increase her capital** – put her savings into the business.
   • **Mortgage** – get long term loan (e.g. 20 years) to finance expansion of premises.
   • **Bank loan** – medium term loan (2–4 years) to finance purchase of equipment.
   • **Loan from family/friends** – needs to be paid back, but hopefully at lower rate of interest.
   • **Take on a partner** – he/she brings capital into business but gets share of profits.
   • **Government aid** – grant or loan.

2 Businesses run by one firm under the name of another; franchisee obtains a licence from the franchiser allowing them to sell goods/services under the franchiser's name.
   Examples: McDonald's, Kentucky Fried Chicken, The Body Shop.

3 **Advantages:**
   • Franchiser's name becomes better known as business expands.
   • New business benefits from the established reputation.
   • Franchisee selling a well-known brand name.
   • Every franchisee benefits from ideas (e.g. McDonald's Egg McMuffin).
   • Franchisee can contribute ideas to the business.

   Disadvantages:
   • Franchisee's reputation and profitability depend partly on the performance of the other franchisees.
   • Franchisee has to follow the regulations set down by the franchiser.
   • A percentage of the franchisee's sales/profits have to be paid to the franchiser.

4 • To relieve poverty.
   • To advance education.
   • To advance religion.
   • To carry out activities to benefit the community.
   • Growth.
   • Survival.
   • Improve/create good reputation.

5 • Developing the business idea.
• Organising the necessary resources.
• Financing (or arranging the finance for) the business.
• Being the risk-taker.

Examples – Richard Branson, Anita Roddick.

6 ## Political/legal
• HASAWA means businesses have to meet required Health and Safety standards.
• Ban on animal testing for cosmetics meant new Research and Development costs.
• Increase in tax would lead to lower profits.
• Local government may or may not grant planning permission.

Economic
• Changes in interest rates – higher means bigger loan repayments/consumers with less money to spend.
• Lower interest rates means firms have more money to invest/customers buy more products.
• Exchange rates will affect level of sales abroad.
• Competition will affect decisions, e.g. to reduce prices to compete.

Social
• Ageing population – products/services for older people.
• Firms may have more older workers.
• Changes in working patterns, e.g. flexi-time, home- and tele-working.

Technological
• Communications technology leading to faster communication (and teleworking).
• Worldwide markets available via Internet.

Environmental
• Effects of 'Foot and Mouth' disease, BSE, etc.
• Weather.
• 'Greenhouse effect'.
• Increased interest in organic food.

7 ## Sole trader
ADVANTAGES
• Easy and cheap to set up.
• Owner has complete control.
• Decisions can be made quickly.
• Owner receives all profits.

DISADVANTAGES
• Owner has unlimited liability.
• Can be difficult to raise finance.
• Responsibilities are not shared so owner has a heavy burden.

Partnership

ADVANTAGES

- Responsibilities of ownership are shared.
- More capital is available.
- Partners can specialise.

DISADVANTAGES

- Unlimited liability – except for the silent partner.
- Shared responsibility may lead to disagreements over the running of the business.
- Partners leaving/joining may result in a lack of continuity.

Limited company

ADVANTAGES

- Limited liability for shareholders.
- Shares can be resold on the Stock Exchange (plcs).
- Large amounts of capital can be raised (plcs).
- Privacy can be maintained as annual reports do not have to be published (private limited companies).

DISADVANTAGES

- Companies must be registered with the Registrar of Companies.
- Very expensive to set up a plc.
- Companies must publish annual accounts (not private limited companies).
- May become very large and so difficult to manage.

Franchise

ADVANTAGES

- Franchiser's name becomes better known as the business expands.
- The new business benefits from the established reputation.
- Franchisee benefits from the well-known brand name.
- Franchisee benefits from ideas from other franchisees, e.g. McDonald's Egg McMuffin.
- Franchisee can contribute ideas to the business.

DISADVANTAGES

- Franchisee's reputation and profitability depend partly on the performance of other franchisees.
- Franchisee has to follow the regulations set down by the franchiser.

8 Shareholders/Owners

- Ordinary shareholders can vote at the AGM and sell their shares.

Employees

- Can take industrial action, e.g. strike.

Suppliers

- Stop supplying the firm.
- Alter the period of credit.
- Alter the level of discount offered.

EXTERNAL ASSESSMENT

Customers
- Stop buying the product.
- Letters of complaint – to the organisation and the media.
- Carry out protests.

Banks
- Grant or withhold loans.
- Alter the rate of interest on loans.

Government
- Introduction of laws, e.g. HASAWA; Sex Discrimination Act; Equal Pay Act; minimum wage legislation etc.

9
- Growth.
- Survival.
- Social responsibility.
- Providing a service.
- Maximising sales.

10
- Own savings.
- Scottish Enterprise grant.
- Mortgage premises.
- Bank loan.
- Trade credit.

11
- Shareholders/owners – profits for dividends/salary.
- Managers – profits for salaries, job security.
- Suppliers – security of payment for goods supplied.
- Customers – quality of goods (value for money).
- Banks – security for loans.
- Government – ability to pay taxes, fund legislative requirements.
- Society – goodwill.
- Local community – job security.

12
- Technology – rapid changes in communications technology, production techniques and electronic components in recent years; resistance to change by workforce.
- Market changes – competition from new businesses, new markets opening up, single European market; must change tactics to combat these changes.
- Consumer tastes – fashions, effects of pressure groups (e.g. environmentally friendly 'green' views, GM foods, organic foods, low-fat foods, Greenpeace); manufacturers have to change, for example, ingredients, to retain customers.
- Legislation – e.g. taxation on pollution, EU regulations (e.g. for VDU users), working hours; businesses have to adapt to remain within the law.
- Changes in workforce – population changes (age and make-up of workforce); forces businesses to change recruitment policies.

13
- Limited liability.
- Board of directors.

- Shareholders.
- Dividends on shares.
- Stock exchange.

INFORMATION AND IT

1 E-mail
- E-mail to send and receive messages almost instantly – charts, graphs, pictures as well as text.
- Messages can be sent at any time and will be stored on the server.
- Messages can be stored and printed at both the sending and receiving ends.
- Passwords can be used for confidentiality.

Fax
- Can send an identical copy of a document in seconds.
- The document will be received even when there is no one in the office.
- Some fax machines have passwords to ensure confidentiality.

Internet
- The retailer could advertise and sell products on the Internet.

Video conferencing
- Video and audio links allow meetings to take place, saving time and money.

ADVANTAGES
- Communication is faster.
- Increases labour productivity.
- Increases administrative efficiency.
- Decreases customer complaints.
- Reduces staffing costs.
- Allows home-working.

DISADVANTAGES
- Price of equipment.
- Cost of staff training.
- Problems/blips in the system cause loss of working time.
- Health and Safety implications, e.g. anti-glare screens, breaks.
- Hackers may infiltrate the system.

2 (a) • Written – can be referred to again and again; can be kept as a record.
     • Oral – information can be received quickly; discussion and clarification is much easier.
     • Pictorial – it is a good way of stressing points; easy to remember.
     • Numerical – ideal for making comparisons with competitors; managers can identify what would happen if they took different courses of action (e.g. using a spreadsheet).
     • Graphical – good for displaying numerical information, e.g. sales figures as trends are easier to identify; comparisons can be made, e.g. sales of different products.
  (b) • Written – letters to suppliers; letters to customers; minutes of meetings; memos to staff; advertising leaflets.

UNIT 3

- Oral – telephone calls to staff/customers/suppliers; staff meetings; job interviews; staff appraisal.
- Pictorial – advertising leaflets.
- Numerical – use spreadsheet to find out what might happen to sales if prices increased; calculate the effect of increased wages on profit etc.
- Graphical – graphs showing sales figures for individual items; or total sales over the past three years etc.

3 Internet/E-mail
- Advertise special deals on the hotel website.
- Deal with on-line bookings.
- Send and receive e-mails to/from customers and head office.

Video conferencing
- Have meetings with receptionists from other hotels in the chain.

Databases
- Store information on rooms, e.g. special features, size, availability.
- Store information on customers.
- Use of mail merge to inform existing customers of special offers.

Spreadsheets
- Calculate customers' bills.

Word processing
- Letters to customers.
- Memos to deputy receptionists.

4
- Primary – first hand data that is tailor-made to a firm's own products, customers or markets; field research.
- Secondary – collected from second-hand sources such as reference books, government statistics or market intelligence; desk research.
- Internal – data collected from within the organisation; internal accounts or documentation.
- External – outwith the organisation; other companies' accounts, etc.

5
- Database – searching, sorting, manipulating, speed (quicker decisions).
- Internet – worldwide information, quantity of information gathered quickly, up-to-date, advertising/publicity, communication (e-mail).
- Spreadsheet – comparisons (predictions with actual), 'what-if?' statements, use of formulae, budgeting.

6 Costs:
- Training/loss of working time.
- Animosity/fears of staff.
- Financial costs of hardware/software.
- Amount of information available.

Benefits:
- Can handle difficult data quickly.
- Flexibility of integrated software.
- Improved presentation of data/documents.
- Amount of information available.

DECISION-MAKING IN BUSINESS

1   Decision-making model
- Identify the problem.
- Identify the constraints.
- Identify the objectives.
- Analyse the problem.
- Identify alternative solutions.
- Decide on the best solution.
- Communicate the decision.
- Implement the decision.
- Evaluate the decision.

2   Strategic decisions
- Concerned with the aims and objectives of the organisation (what the organisation wants to achieve) made by senior management, e.g. the Board of Directors; long term in nature, e.g. 3–5 years – examples.
- To become the number one supermarket in the UK; to maximise profits; to create a good reputation.

Tactical decisions
- Concerned with how to achieve the strategic decision made by senior and middle management – examples.
- Open more stores; provide better quality products; offer more products and different ranges; improve service, e.g. bag packing; home delivery; 24-hour opening; crêche facilities; increase advertising and promotion.

Operational decisions
- Day-to-day decisions (short term) – decisions made in response to changing circumstances made by junior management and supervisors.
- Examples – move staff from job to job when the store gets busy, e.g. from shelf stacking to checkout duty; redeploy staff if a member of staff is off ill.

3
- Strategic – long term aims and objectives, e.g. whether to sell off a poorly performing division or to invest extra capital to restore its competitiveness.
- Tactical – short term decisions about how objectives are reached (usually made by middle management), e.g. if sales are 4% below the annual forecast, the sales manager might decide to run a sales promotion or cut the price.
- Operational – day-to-day running of organisation (nearly all employees will be involved in these), e.g. daily decisions made by office staff on the delegation of work.

INTERNAL ORGANISATION

1   (a)   **Hierarchical**
- Traditional structure for medium and large organisations.
- Sometimes called a pyramid structure since it has few staff at the top of the chain of command and more further down the hierarchy.
- Many levels of authority, with those at the top of the hierarchy having more responsibility.
- Decisions and instructions tend to be passed down the structure and the many levels mean this can take time.
- Communications both up and down the structure tend to be slow.

Flat
- Very few levels of authority in the structure.
- Communication and decision-making are much quicker.
- Some large organisations are moving towards a flatter structure by removing some managerial levels (delayering).

  (b)
- To overcome effects of competition.
- Less employees means less salaries to pay.
- Improves communication – should be faster.
- Improves decision-making.
- Empowers staff to make decisions.
- Decisions are made more quickly so responses to changes in the market can be made more quickly.

MARKETING

1   Identify four Ps – 1 mark.

Product
- Introduce new **varieties** of ready meals, e.g. Italian, Indian.
- Introduce different **sizes**, e.g. meals for one.
- Introduce **complementary** products, e.g. naan bread for the Indian range.

Price
- Use promotional pricing on some meals, e.g. 20% off the Italian range.
- Use destroyer pricing to attract consumers away from the competition.

Place
- Increase sales outlets, have product in more supermarket chains.
- Introduce mail order or Internet selling.

Promotion
- Increase advertising – TV, magazines, etc.
- Use the pipeline promotion to increase sales outlets.
- Point-of-sale materials, sale or return agreements.
- Use out of the pipeline promotions to increase customer sales.
- Money-off coupons in newspapers, bonus packs, premium offers, sampling in supermarkets.

2   The product life cycle shows the length of time the product is on the market (when it appeals to customers). The life cycle commonly has four phases:
   - Introductory phase – product is recently launched and customers are becoming aware of the product; costs to the firm are high in terms of advertising and promotion.
   - Growth phase – sales rise quickly as more customers become aware of the product.
   - Maturity phase – the product is fully established and sales reach their peak.
   - Decline phase – competitors have entered the market and sales have started to fall.

   Some products will have a very short life cycle, e.g. fashion clothing, while others are much longer, e.g. Kellogg's Cornflakes.

3   Changes to
   - product
   - price
   - place
   - promotion.

   (References to supermarkets in competition with each other will attract marks.)

FINANCE

1   - To show the estimated figures of the cash position of the business over that period of time.
   - To highlight any cash shortages or surpluses that may occur.
   - To allow her to plan for cash shortages, e.g. arrange an overdraft.
   - To allow her to plan for surpluses, e.g. invest in new equipment.
   - To monitor the progress of her business.
   - To use it to show to a financial lender, e.g. bank or potential partner.
   - To allow her to compare the actual results with the estimated figures.

2   ### Managers
   - Evaluate how effective their decisions were.
   - Assist with decision-making for next year.
   - Need to maintain liquidity and creditworthiness.

   ### Employees
   - Assess job security.
   - Better pay and working conditions.

   ### Trade unions
   - Negotiate better pay and working conditions for members.

   ### Investors/potential investors
   - Look at the return on capital invested.

   ### Banks/suppliers
   - Find out how secure the business is to assess whether interest on loans would be paid/payment for goods supplied would be received.

   ### Government
   - Is the correct tax being paid?

UNIT: 3

General public
- Who controls the organisation?
- Issues such as pollution.

Competitors
- Compare financial information using ratios.

3
- Changes in stock could be recorded as they occur, giving a running balance total.
- Reduced need to physically count stock.
- Stock would be date labelled and the system would identify which stock should be issued next.
- Setting a maximum stock level would help control stock levels so that there was not too much stock being held.
- Setting of minimum and economic stock levels ensures automatic stock re-ordering.
- Just-in-time ordering of stock could ensure fresh stock and no storage costs.

4 **Trading account** – shows the trading activities of the organisation and calculates the gross profit (sales revenue minus cost of goods sold).

Profit and loss account – this shows the net profit (gross profit minus expenses) of the organisation so that corporation tax can be calculated. The net profit after tax is then available for distribution to shareholders and reinvestment.

Balance sheet – this statement shows the assets and liabilities of an organisation at a point in time. Allows the organisation to see what it owns (assets) and what it owes (liabilities).

Cash budget – this shows the estimated receipts and payments of the organisation for a specific period. It allows the organisation to see where there may be a deficit in order to arrange an overdraft; or a surplus – perhaps a good time to invest in new equipment.

5 ## Gross profit margin
Used to show the amount of gross profit to sales, e.g. a 40% margin shows that for every £1 of sales a gross profit of 40p is made. A fall in the ratio would have to be investigated, perhaps the cost of purchases has increased or goods have been stolen. Any fall would need to be reversed, e.g. by finding a cheaper supplier. Calculation: gross profit/turnover $\times$ 100.

Net profit margin
Used to show the amount of net profit to sales, e.g. a 15% margin shows that for every £1 of sales a net profit of 15p is made. A fall in the ratio may be due to increased expenses, e.g. wages or heat and light. The fall would need to be reversed by controlling expenses, e.g. switching off lights when not needed. Calculation: net profit/turnover $\times$ 100.

Rate of stock turnover
Used to show how long the business is keeping stock. Stock turnover is the average time stock is held in the business before it is sold. The figure will depend on the type of business, e.g. a greengrocer would have a high stock turnover figure, but a car showroom's would be much lower. Calculation: cost of goods sold/average stock.

Working capital ratio

Used to show if the business will have enough current assets to cover its current liabilities (pay its short term debts). Ideal ratio is 2:1. Calculation: current assets : current liabilities.

Return on capital employed

Used to compare the net profit to the amount of capital in the business. Shows the return shareholders will get on their investment. Calculation: net profit/capital employed $\times$ 100.

Acid test ratio

Similar to the current ratio but stock is removed since it is the least liquid asset. Used to show if the business will have enough liquid assets to cover its short term debts. Ideal ratio is 1:1. Calculation: current assets – stock/current liabilities.

6 ### Shareholders/owners

- To find out whether they should invest more or buy more shares.
- To find out if it is a good time to sell shares.

Managers

- To find out if it would be a good time to buy new equipment or expand in some way.
- To find out if it would be a good time to ask for more funding.

Employees

- To find out if it would be a good time to ask for a pay rise or improvement in working conditions.
- To check on job security.

Suppliers

- To help to decide whether credit should be given.
- To find out whether payment is likely to be received.

Banks

- To help to decide whether to grant a loan or overdraft.

Competitors

- To determine whether the rival organisation is a serious threat.
- To determine whether a buy out would be a good idea.

7
- Profit and loss account – calculate (net) profit.
- Balance sheet – show 'worth' of business on a particular date; shows assets and liabilities.

8 **Shareholders** – look at return on capital employed, decide whether to sell shares or invest more.

Suppliers – look at firm's ability to pay debts (current ratio).

Banks – will loan repayments be met?

Employees/trade unions – use information as a basis for wage bargaining.

Government – calculate Corporation Tax payments.

HUMAN RESOURCES MANAGEMENT

1 **(i)** ## On-the-job training
- Takes place at the place of work while employees are carrying out their job.
- Employee may watch an experienced worker doing the job ('sitting with Nellie').
- Uses actual equipment that will be used once training is completed.

Off-the-job training
- Takes place away from the place of work.
- May be during working hours or at another time, e.g. evening.
- May attend a college/training provider.

(ii)

On-the-job	
Advantages	**Disadvantages**
• Training takes place in familiar surroundings. • Cheaper for the organisation. • Uses the equipment that will actually be used. • Takes place during working hours.	• Employees not as productive while being trained. • Employees may pick up bad habits if 'sitting with Nellie'.
Off-the-job	
Advantages	**Disadvantages**
• No distractions since away from the workplace. • Training may be more structured. • May receive a recognised qualification once training complete.	• Costly – training course costs and supply staff costs. • Employees may have to carry out the training in their own time. • May not be using equipment exactly like they will use in the workplace.

2
- Work-to-rule – employees do only what they are contracted to do, e.g. no overtime.
- Strike – employees withdraw their labour so nothing is produced.
- Sit-in – employees will occupy their place of work to prevent any production from taking place.

3 **(i)** ## HASAW (1974)
- Provision of a safe work area with regard to machinery etc.
- Provision of training to ensure Health and Safety of employees.

Sex Discrimination Act
- Unlawful to discriminate in full- or part-time jobs or training.
- Equal pay for men and women.
- Protection against sexual harassment.

Race Relations Act
- Unlawful to discriminate against race.

(ii)
- Approach trade union rep.
- Go to employment tribunal.
- If this fails, appeal to court.
- Further appeal to House of Lords.
- Final appeal to European Commission.

4 (a) ## Job description
- Job title.
- Responsibilities of the job.
- Purpose of the job.
- Main duties involved.
- Department working in.
- Working conditions.

Person specification
- Qualifications/achievements.
- Skills.
- Physical characteristics.
- Hobbies/interests.
- Personality.

(b) ## Application forms
- Drawn up by the organisation so that all relevant information is requested.
- Information requested will include qualifications, work experience, hobbies and referees.

CVs
- Prepared by the job applicant to provide a summary for the potential employer.
- Information will include qualifications, work experience, hobbies etc.
- May not provide specific information that the organisation is looking for.

References
- These are comments on the applicant by someone who knows them.
- May be used to check the accuracy of the information given on the application form.
- A previous or current employer may be a referee.

Interviews
- Allows the organisation to find out more information about the applicant.
- The impression created at the interview will be important.
- Interview may be carried out by one person or by a panel of people.
- Interviews are usually face-to-face, but may be carried out over the telephone.

Testing
- Applicant may be given an aptitude test, e.g. a word processing or English test.
- Personality tests may be used.

UNIT 3

Presentations
- Applicants may be asked to give a presentation on a relevant topic.

5
- Advertise in appropriate places.
- Prepare job description and person specification.
- Send application forms.
- First interview.
- Draw up shortlist.
- Second interview.
- Use of tests.
- References.

6
- Bad publicity/bad image.
- Lose customers – fall in sales and profits.
- Suppliers don't want to supply.
- Industrial action, e.g. strike action, which may mean that contracts cannot be honoured.
- Loss of sales may result in redundancies.
- Fall in share price.

OPERATIONS MANAGEMENT

1 Quality control
- One method involves checking the final product at the end of the production process.
- Should result in less low-quality output to customers, but still some waste.

Quality assurance
- Quality checked at every stage of production process.
- Tries to create system of getting everything right first time.
- Should significantly reduce wastage.
- Also provides after-sales service and guarantees.

Total Quality Management
- Aims to produce perfect product every time in order to meet customer requirements.
- Based on principle of quality assurance.
- Uses the customer's definition of quality.
- Assumes that the next person in the production process is the customer.
- Each person in the production line is responsible for ensuring that their work is of the highest standard and quality.

Quality circles

Other factors
- Use better-quality raw materials.
- Use better equipment.
- Give staff better training.
- Recruitment of staff.
- Benchmarking.

2
- Changes in stock could be recorded as they occur, giving a running balance total.
- Reduced need for a physical stock count.
- Stock would be date labelled and the system would identify which stock should be issued next.
- Setting a maximum stock level would help control stock levels so that there was not too much stock being held.
- Setting of minimum and economic stock levels ensures automatic stock re-ordering.
- Just-in-time ordering of stock could ensure fresh stock and no storage costs.

3
Job production
- Single product made to specific requirements.
- Usually labour-intensive using skilled workforce so high-cost method.
- Workforce often very motivated.
- Examples: a designer wedding dress, a ship, a custom-designed kitchen.

Batch production
- A number of products or batches of similar products are made.
- Products are similar but different ingredients may be used for different products.
- Production can be divided into different operations where each stage is completed before moving on.
- Examples: bread, chocolate bars, canned soup.

4
Overstocking
- A large amount of cash will be tied up in stock.
- Storage costs will be high, e.g. insurance, heat and light, storage space.
- Stock may perish or become obsolete before it can be sold.

Understocking
- If there is not enough stock, production may have to be stopped so wages will be paid to staff who are not productive.
- If production is stopped then sales may be lost.
- If stocks are too low then the business would be unable to cope with unexpected orders; customers may see them as being inflexible and unreliable suppliers and again sales may be lost.
- Orders for materials may have to be placed more frequently; unlikely to get discounts for bulk buying.

5
Just-in-time production: Stocks arrive just before they are needed in the production process so:
- large amounts of cash are not tied up in stock
- waste is reduced since stock is not able to perish or become obsolete
- storage costs are reduced.

Disadvantages:
- relies on reliable suppliers
- may not be able to get supplies quickly enough to meet an unexpected order
- customers may be let down; sales may be lost along with the company's reputation.

6 Job, e.g. shipbuilding

Advantages:
- easy to organise production
- products can be tailored to customer
- workers more motivated.

Disadvantages:
- high production costs
- process may be lengthy
- equipment costs may be high.

Batch, e.g. bread

Advantages:
- can specialise on a stage
- batches tailored to customer
- stock of partly finished goods can be built up.

Disadvantages:
- small batches can cost more
- takes time to co-ordinate
- may need to use different machinery for different batches.

Flow, e.g. car production

Advantages:
- can achieve specialisation of work force and machinery
- easier to automate production
- can use just-in-time system into the production process.

Disadvantages:
- high start-up costs
- standardised produce may not meet needs of all customers
- work on the production lines tends to be boring and repetitive.

7
- Quality control – the process of checking the accuracy of work brought in or completed, usually carried out by quality inspectors, but sometimes employees do self-checking.
- TQM – checking at every stage of production should improve quality of finished goods; less customer complaints; more custom, less waste; improved motivation of employees.
- Quality assurance – extends beyond the production process, e.g. after-sales service and guarantees.

8
- Procedures need to ensure that stock is ordered, delivered and handled with efficiency.
- Customer demand should be met cost-effectively.
- Stock rotation.
- Stock recording based on maximum and minimum levels.
- Re-order level.
- Use of just-in-time production/stock-keeping methods.

UNIT:3 EXTERNAL ASSESSMENT

EXAMINATION QUESTIONS
(arranged under Outcomes)

THE ROLE OF BUSINESS IN SOCIETY

1   Socio–cultural trends can affect the operations of any business. Describe **3** socio–cultural trends which might affect the operations of a high street bank.   (6 marks)

2   Identify **5** stakeholders of a high street bank and describe how the interests of these stakeholders might differ.   (10 marks)

3   Franchising is a form of business enterprise. Identify the advantages of this for
    (i)   the franchiser
    (ii) the franchisee.   (9 marks)

4   How has the pattern of employment in the UK changed in the last 20 years?   (5 marks)

5   A retail group decides to divide into 2 companies – how could demerging affect different stakeholders?   (8 marks)

6   Additional finance may be necessary to launch a new product. Identify **2** suitable sources of finance. Justify your choices.   (4 marks)

7   Compare the objectives for a public limited company with those for a charity.   (3 marks)

INFORMATION AND IT

1   What legislation exists to protect people from information stored about them on computers being used inappropriately? How can a person find out what information is stored about them on computers and if it is wrong how can they get it altered?   (6 marks)

2   Carrying out market research does not necessarily guarantee success in the market.
    Why might information gathered by an organisation be of little use to them?   (10 marks)

3 The use of **e-mail** is increasing worldwide. Although it has many advantages, there are also disadvantages. Explain the drawbacks to an organisation of using this form of communication. (5 marks)

4 Multinational companies depend on effective communication. Using examples, discuss how technology is being used to improve global communication. (8 marks)

5 An organisation is about to change its old, stand-alone computer system for a modern, **networked** system with access to the Internet.
   (a) What benefits might it gain from this change? (8 marks)
   (b) What problems might arise from this change? (8 marks)

6 To make quality decisions you need **quality information**. Describe the features of quality information. (9 marks)

DECISIONS AND DECISION-MAKING

1 How could a **SWOT analysis** help the decision-making process in an organisation? (6 marks)

2 Identify a **strategic objective** of a bank and describe **2 tactical decisions** which could be made by the managers of the bank to achieve the objective. (3 marks)

3 A large burger chain has cultivated a strong corporate culture. If an organisation sets this as a strategic objective, describe the tactical decisions required to achieve it. (6 marks)

4 Identify the stages of the **structured decision-making model** and relate them to a school considering the purchase of a minibus. (10 marks)

5 What is the role of the manager in a high street retailer? How does this role contribute to the overall success of the business? (10 marks)

6 A large retail group decides to divide into two companies.
   (i)   What type of decision does this demerger represent? Justify your answer. (2 marks)
   (ii) How could an organisation find out whether the decision taken was the right one? (3 marks)

7 Discuss the factors which might affect the quality of a decision. (5 marks)

8 Identify the possible stages of a **structured decision-making** model and relate each stage to an organisation replacing an old, inefficient computer system. (16 marks)

INTERNAL ORGANISATION

1 A major high street retailer (Marks and Spencer) may decide to **de-layer**. What does this mean and what effects on the organisation does de-layering have? (8 marks)

2 An organisation may choose to organise its activities by function. Describe other organisational forms which may be used, making reference to the type of organisation for which each may be appropriate. (9 marks)

3   The larger burger chains have branches in most of our large towns. They operate within a centralised organisational structure. Describe the features of
(i)   a centralised structure
(ii) a de-centralised structure. (10 marks)

MARKETING

1   At Christmas time, toy manufacturers often face the problem of not being able to obtain stocks of the most popular toys (e.g. PlayStation 2). Toy manufacturers produce updated versions in order to extend their **product life cycle**. Identify and describe **4** other means of extending the life of a product. (8 marks)

2   Discuss the factors which would contribute towards a good **product mix** for an organisation. (5 marks)

3   How can the use of information and communications technology (ICT) support market research? (10 marks)

4   Discuss how the Scottish Tourist Board could make use of the Internet to 'market' Scotland. (9 marks)

5   Describe and justify the research method you would employ to find out if visitors to Edinburgh Castle were satisfied with their experience. Your answer should refer to the reliability of the information you have gathered. (10 marks)

6   Select **2** of the following methods of market research and describe each, discussing their advantages and limitations:
(i)   face-to-face interviews
(ii) postal survey
(iii) focus group. (8 marks)

7   Distinguish between **penetration** and **skimming** pricing. (8 marks)

FINANCE

1   The Managing Director of a public limited company, on looking at his cash budget, is concerned to see that the firm is facing a deficit of £10,000 next month because a plan exists for the cash purchase of a new machine.
Identify and justify **4** possible decisions the Managing Director could make to avoid this potential deficit. (8 marks)

2   Discuss the strengths and weaknesses of using **ratio analysis** to judge the performance of a business. (8 marks)

3   The following are examples of issues which might be identified by an organisation as the cause of a cash flow problem:
• an unexpected breakdown of machinery
• a rise in inflation

- a change in legislation requiring a product to be modified to make it comply with new Health and Safety regulations.

  (i) Describe the effects each issue will have on cash flow. (3 marks)

  (ii) What actions should the management take after a problem has been identified? (4 marks)

4 Identify the problems with accounting information which might hinder decision-making. (4 marks)

5 (a) A manager might use ratios to identify problems of:
- liquidity
- profitability
- efficiency.

Describe what these ratios would show about the organisation's performance. Your answer should refer to the relevant ratios. (9 marks)

  (b) Give examples of decisions which could be made as a reaction to poor performance identified by these ratios. (5 marks)

6 (a) Identify the parts of a **cash flow forecast** (cash budget). (4 marks)

  (b) Explain how a cash flow forecast might be used. (8 marks)

7 Identify 2 **liquidity ratios**, give the formula for each and explain the ways that they might be used. (8 marks)

8 How might the use of a **spreadsheet** help in ratio analysis? (5 marks)

HUMAN RESOURCES MANAGEMENT

1 Launching a new product or service may require the organisation's existing staff to undergo training.

  (i) Identify the objectives of such a training programme for the existing staff of an organisation. (5 marks)

  (ii) How does this type of training differ from an induction training programme? (5 marks)

2 (a) Describe how employees in a large manufacturing company might be involved in the decision-making process.

  (b) Analyse the benefits of this involvement for both the employee and the employer. (15 marks)

3 Some employees may feel that their employer is discriminating against them because all people doing the same job are not receiving the same pay. Explain the steps employees can take to have the situation remedied. (9 marks)

4 What measures might an organisation introduce to develop good working relationships with employees and trade unions? (6 marks)

5 Describe the constraints legislation may impose on an organisation. (10 marks)

6 Errors sometimes occur in manufacturing, e.g. a supermarket is unhappy about the quality of one batch of lasagne which has been distributed throughout the UK. Explain the role of the Public Relations Officer in dealing with this situation. (5 marks)

7 (a) Name 2 laws relating to health and safety in the workplace. (2 marks)
   (b) Describe the ways that health and safety laws affect most organisations. (7 marks)

8 When recruiting staff, what is the purpose of an **interview** and how should it be conducted to be as effective as possible? (10 marks)

9 In addition to an interview, some firms give applicants special **tests**. Identify and describe 2 such tests. (6 marks)

10 (a) Give examples of a possible key field in a staff database and explain how it might be used. (2 marks)
   (b) Explain the uses which a Human Resource department might make of a staff database. (7 marks)

11 Quality circles are an example of industrial democracy. What are they and how might they benefit an organisation? (6 marks)

OPERATIONS

1 Discuss the factors which must be considered when deciding on the most effective channel of distribution for a product. (7 marks)

2 A furniture manufacturer chooses to use the JOB method of production. Describe the advantages and disadvantages of this method over FLOW production for the furniture manufacturer. (6 marks)

3 Manufacturers have to transport goods to retailers. Describe the external factors which might result in transport difficulties. (4 marks)

4 The British Standards Institute (BSI) Kitemark is an indication of product quality
   (i) Name 2 other quality standards. (2 marks)
   (ii) Describe the benefits of a quality standard to both an organisation and its customers. (3 marks)

5 Describe the main factors which have to be taken into account by an organisation when choosing a **method of production**. (5 marks)

6 What steps can be taken in the manufacturing process to ensure a quality product is **produced at all times**? (10 marks)

7 Describe the factors influencing a purchasing manager's choice of suitable suppliers of materials and services. (10 marks)

UNIT 3

EXTERNAL ASSESSMENT

UNIT:3 EXTERNAL ASSESSMENT

SOLUTIONS

(arranged under Outcomes)

THE ROLE OF BUSINESS IN SOCIETY

1. • Increased access to technology – customers may choose to use telephone or Internet banking instead of visiting a branch; also increased use of ATMs for transactions.
   • Consumers make greater use of plastic cards instead of cash – payment for goods possible at supermarket checkout by card.
   • Growth of home ownership – banks have entered mortgage/home insurance market.
   • Growth of share ownership – banks may now act as stockholders.
   • Increased travel – need to provide currency, travellers' cheques, etc.

2. Stakeholders
   • Shareholders.
   • Management.
   • Employees.
   • Suppliers.
   • Customers.
   • Creditors.
   • General public.

   Conflicts of interest
   • Directors might want to raise profits/increase efficiency and may cut jobs.
   • Expenditure might be increased at the expense of shareholders' dividends.
   • Customers may face a rise in price if managers try to increase profits.
   • Wage rise may not be granted in order to increase profits.
   • Management may close a branch for reasons of efficiency at the expense of customer convenience.
   • Banks may face government restrictions, e.g. a maximum of £7000 to be invested in ISAs.

3. (i) The franchiser
   • Receives royalties.
   • Sees their business grow in the way they want it to as strict guidelines re layout and products sold are issued.

(ii) The franchisee
- Has the advantage of a well-known brand name/product which is less likely to fail.
- Benefits from promotions which affect all outlets.
- All franchisees benefit from the ideas of others, e.g. Egg McMuffin thought up by one McDonald's franchisee.
- Can trade on an established reputation.
- Competition may be restricted.
- Training may be carried out by franchiser.

4
- More part-time workers.
- More flexi-time.
- More temporary workers.
- More home-workers/teleworkers.
- More women.
- More self-employed.
- Number of hours being worked altered (EU directive on length of working week).

5 Shareholders
- If one area is more profitable than the other shares could be sold.
- Dropping the loser may increase share value of the more successful group.
- Smaller organisation may mean better management with tighter control.
- Less chance of diseconomies of scale.

Customers/general public
- A more efficient company should lead to cheaper product/better quality of product or service.
- Customers of different groups may have different needs which may be better served by controlling groups separately.

Employees
- A more efficient organisation may provide job security, wage increases etc.

Management
- More focused on one management area (one group) with a smaller area of control.
- Change in organisation structure may lead to promotion opportunities.
- More control in one particular area may mean they have more decision-making power which is more motivating.

6
- Bank loan – easy to obtain.
- Lease machinery – eases cash flow.
- Mortgage (if premises are required) – relatively easy to gain.
- Profit reinvestment – no interest payable, no collateral required.
- Sell assets – quick to raise money, no collateral required.
- Debenture issue – holders do not have control, large amounts can be raised.
- Share issue – large amounts can be raised.

EXTERNAL ASSESSMENT

UNIT 3

7 Objectives of public limited company
- To maximise profits.
- To grow.
- To survive.
- To create a good reputation.
- To maximise sales.
- To achieve objectives.

Objectives of a charity
- To provide a service.
- To achieve its objective, e.g. to provide aid for a starving population.
- To ensure business organisations are environmentally responsible (Greenpeace has charity status).

(Some attempt at comparisons, e.g. using examples, would be required.)

INFORMATION AND IT

1 Data Protection Act
- Organisations must register the purpose for which they hold the information.
- Organisations must not disclose the information in any way that is different from those purposes.
- Take appropriate steps to keep the information safe.
- Not hold the information any longer than is necessary.
- Individuals can request information held about themselves and have the information corrected or erased.
- Individuals can complain to the Data Protection Registrar if they feel information held about them is incorrect, inaccurate or misleading. The Registrar has the power to have the information corrected.
- Claims for compensation cam be made against an organisation if an individual suffers damage because of the loss, destruction, unauthorised disclosure or inaccuracy of personal data held.

2 Information of poor quality is of little use; information has to be:
- **accurate** – wrong information can lead to a wrong decision being made
- **timely** – must be available at the right time for the decision being made
- **up to date**
- **complete** – if information is omitted, inaccurate decisions may be made or there may be a delay in processing
- **available** – all the information needed may not be available
- **appropriate** – if information is not relevant to the issue, the decision-maker may be misled
- **cost-effeccive** – if information is too expensive to gather, there may be no cash left to take it any further
- **objective** – information must be free from bias
- **concise** – brief or less important facts may get lost.

3
- Information overload – if too much information is sent out, important messages may be overlooked.
- Staff need to be trained to use it.

- Constantly checking e-mail may mean a member of staff is wasting time.
- E-mail may be used for personal reasons — abuse of working time.
- Message may be deleted by mistake.
- Messages easily mis-addressed — problem of confidentiality.
- Hackers may access sensitive information.
- Legal problems — companies may reserve the right to read e-mail if they are concerned about litigation.
- Viruses.

4   Internet
- Allows on-line communication to take place at any time.
- Web page can be used to advertise goods.
- A vast source of information.
- Information is more likely to be up-to-date.
- Visual images can be transmitted — e.g. weather reports.

E-Mail
- Text, graphics can be sent between computers world-wide at any time of day.
- Confidentiality possible by use of a password.
- Speed of communication greatly improved.

Video-conferencing
- Video/audio links can be set up to allow a meeting to take place.
- Possible to link to computers now so becoming easier to organise.
- Interaction easy.
- Cost of travelling removed.

Fax
- Linked to telephone network — allows identical copy of document to be sent to recipient fax machine.
- Transmission time is fast — relatively cheap.
- Diagrams/charts can be sent.

Mobile/WAP/TV phones
- Person has easy access to telephone — no need for money, phone cards, etc.
- Person's office/family know where they can be contacted.
- Messages can be left.

Satellite links
- Allows visual images to be transmitted — may support, e.g. a news item.

5   (a) • Better communication.
- More efficient.
- Better profits.
- Superior quality.
- Improved image.
- More competitive.

(Examples should be provided.)

(b) cost of
- equipment
- training
- software
- maintenance/support.

6
- Relevant
- Accurate
- Sufficient
- Meaningful
- Timely
- Appropriate form
- Cost effective

(Examples should be provided.)

DECISIONS AND DECISION-MAKING

1
- Help to identify any problems.
- Help to identify objectives.
- Information can be gathered in SWOT then analysed.
- Alternative solutions can be devised/selected and the strengths and weaknesses identified.
- Implement decision – capitalise on strengths/opportunities and minimise weaknesses/threats.
- Evaluate decision – use another SWOT.

2 Strategic objective
- to make a profit
- to grow.

Tactical decisions
- raise prices
- cut back on expenditure
- take over/merge with building society.

3
- Introduce uniform/dress code.
- Introduce standard layout of premises.
- Insist on standard quality throughout the organisation – food quality, portion size, etc.
- Insist on staff having consistent attitude towards customers.
- Build up a sense of values.
- Special offers.
- Advertising decisions.

4

Identify problem	Pupils are unable to attend sports matches as a result of having no transport and the school is therefore not competing.
Identify objectives	To be able to transport pupils to sports matches.
Gather information	Availability of suitable bus, price, delivery time, safety features, availability of drivers etc.
Analyse information	Consider buses available, consider finance available/where to obtain finance etc.
Devise alternative solutions	Do nothing, use public transport, organise car rota (insurance problems?), purchase bus, lease bus.
Select 'best' solution	Either obtain bus or implement one of the other alternatives.
Communicate solution	Inform staff, parents and pupils of the decision.
Implement solution	As from the start of the new term, pupils will be transported in the minibus.
Evaluate	Are more pupils now able to attend matches?

5

ROLE	DESCRIPTION OF ROLE	ROLE APPLIED TO EXAMPLE
Planning	Looks ahead and sets aims and strategies	To increase branch sales by 15% next month
Organising	Arranges for the resources of the organisation to be in the right place at the right time	Appoints appropriate staff to the various departments
Commanding	Tells other staff what their duties are	Explains to floor supervisors what they are expected to do
Co-ordinating	Ensures that the staff work towards the same aims Ensures that the staff fit in with the work of the rest of the organisation	Ensures that till operators, canteen staff, cleaners, etc. perform their job so that the store can operate within its opening hours
Controlling	Measures, evaluates and compares results against plans and supervises and checks work done	Checks and compares the sales figures with the target set
Delegating	Makes subordinates responsible for tasks and gives them authority to carry them out	Human resources manager is asked to devise suitable training programmes
Motivating	Encourages others to carry out their tasks effectively	Sets up a system of team working

EXTERNAL ASSESSMENT

6   (i)   **Strategic** – as it affects the long term situation of the organisation. It is made by top management.

     (ii) Evaluate results – has the outcome been achieved? e.g. have profits risen? If not why not? Evaluation and decision-making can be continuous and the decision-making process may have to start again.

7   Accurate, timely, complete, appropriate, available, cost-effective, objective, concise information required. Ability to use techniques. Time taken to consider all the options. No snap judgements made. All the facts are gathered. All the alternatives considered. Level of experience of decision-maker. Ability to take risk. Self-interest.

8   • Identify problem.
     • Objectives.
     • Gather information.
     • Analyse.
     • Devise alternative solutions.
     • Select 'best' solution.
     • Communicate decision.
     • Implement decision.
     • Evaluate.

INTERNAL ORGANISATION

1   Definition: cutting out levels of management within the organisation to flatten out the structure.
     • Improves communication.
     • Speeds up decision-making – more responsive to changes in the market.
     • Reduces wage bill.
     • Empowerment – giving staff responsibility for their own work and decision-making by delegation, transfer of responsibility and greater access to information.
     • Additional work for remaining employees.
     • Cuts costs/increases profits.
     • Becomes more competitive and efficient.

2   (max 3 marks per heading)

     ### Product/service
     • Different products may require different approaches to production and marketing.
     • Each product can act as a profit centre – individual performance/profits measured.
     • Healthy competition can exist between products.

     ### Customers
     • Different market segments can be catered for.
     • Personal service possible.
     • Different groups of customers may have different needs, e.g. car fleet sales and individuals.

Place/territory
- Local needs may vary.
- Having a local manager may be helpful to communications as opposed to dealing with a regional manager.
- Competition between regions (branches) encourages improvements in performance.

Technology
- Staff training simplified.
- Staff can concentrate on one technological process (specialisation).
- Each process can be monitored.

3   (max 6 marks per section)

(i)   Centralised structure:
- Senior management have more control (strong top leadership).
- Procedures are standardised (e.g. buying). This leads to economies of scale and lower costs.
- Senior management sees the business as a 'whole'.
- Senior management should be more experienced in decision-making, leading to better quality of decisions.
- Communication improves with fewer decision-makers.
- External communications are in a standardised format.
- Easier to promote a corporate image.

(ii)   De-centralised structure:
- Empowers and motivates staff.
- Reduces workload of senior management.
- Able to respond better to local conditions and requirements of customers.
- Decision-making should be quicker.
- Prepares junior management for promotion.

MARKETING

1
- Change/modify product, e.g. diet drinks.
- Alter packaging.
- Alter channels of distribution.
- Alter price.
- Alter promotion methods.

(Examples should be provided).

2
- A range of similar products (e.g. washing powder, liquid, cleaning materials) allows manufacturer to distribute to the same retailers/wholesalers thus reducing transportation and distribution costs.
- Source of raw materials might be similar – benefits of economies of scale.
- Wide spread of product lines can be intentional – allows organisation to spread risk and enter new markets.

3
- Much wider scope of secondary information available, e.g. databases compiled by market research agencies.
- EPOS/loyalty cards allow shops to monitor spending patterns – who, when, how often?
- Using information from EPOS/loyalty cards, organisations know who to target with specific promotions and focus their advertising on – cheaper than targeting everyone.
- Internet/e-mail – can invite immediate response from user who may offer opinions.
- Information is more up-to-date.
- Information is easier to process – searching/sorting.
- Network links make sharing information easier.
- Interviewing may take place over the telephone, with data being keyed directly on to computer – cheaper and quicker than employing market researchers.

4
- Website could provide up-to-date information about the area – special events, current prices, weather, travelling conditions.
- Pictures of attractive areas can be shown.
- E-mail address can encourage users to request information – brochures/catalogues – less effort than writing.
- Interactive forms can be set up.
- FAQ section can be set up.
- Feedback can be obtained from customers who enter information – can improve customer service quickly.
- Much wider market.
- Could enhance Scotland's 'image' – modern, technologically advanced.
- E-commerce allows selling of tickets, merchandise, etc.
- Users may come across website simply by scrolling.

5   Questionnaire would most likely be used. A set of questions designed to obtain information would be directed at a sample of visitors (written/verbal) as they leave, so the experience is still fresh in their memories.

Justification:
- All visitors would be asked identical questions.
- Information is relatively easy to collate.
- Questions are designed to gather relevant information.

Reliability:
- Depends on size of sample.
- Depends on structure of sample, e.g. is there bias?
- How experienced is the interviewer?
- Were the questions leading?
- Were the questions confusing?
- Were the answers given truthful?

6

METHOD	ADVANTAGES	DISADVANTAGES
Face-to-face interview – a personal interview held in the street or home	• 2-way communication • Researcher can encourage respondent to answer • Mistakes and misunderstandings can be dealt with right away	• Personal interviews can be expensive – researchers have to be selected and trained • Home interviews are unpopular with consumers
Postal survey – market researcher sends questionnaire through the post	• Inexpensive – no trained interviewer needed	• Questions must be simple and easy to answer • The response rate is very low incentives are often needed to fill in and return the questionnaire (free gifts/ prize draw)
Focus group – specially selected groups of people, usually led by an experienced chairperson who puts forward points to encourage open discussion	• Qualitative information in the form of opinions, feelings and attitudes	• Can be difficult to analyse qualitative information

7   Penetration
   • Low price to gain entry into an existing market or for an existing product to gain entry into a new market for that manufacturer.
   • Attracts custom by breaking brand loyalty.
   • Once brand loyalty established, raise price to market price.

   Skimming
   • High price.
   • No competition.
   • Completely new product or new to the market.
   • When sales start to fall, price is decreased.
   • Sacrifice high sales for high profits.
   • High profits attract competitors.

FINANCE
1

DECISION	EXAMPLE OF JUSTIFICATION
Lease machine	This would spread payments and avoid the overdraft
Pay in instalments	This would spread payments and help avoid the overdraft
Do not buy machine at all	Firm would not face the overdraft (but production may suffer due to not having the new machine)
Cut some expenses	Leaves more funds available to finance machine
Increase income	Makes more funds available to finance machine

UNIT: 3

2 Strengths
- Shows how well the business is doing.
- Useful tool for evaluating accounts.
- Allows comparisons to be made between different companies.
- Comparisons can be made between actual and predicted results.
- Differences can be accounted for.
- Trends can be identified.
- Provides information for external users – banks, potential investors.
- Identifies movements of stock.
- Shows if debts are being collected quickly enough.
- Identifies if too much cash is tied up in unproductive assets.
- Gearing shows structure of funding to potential investors.

Weaknesses
- Do not mean much on their own – must be compared.
- May not take account of:
  - changes in accounting procedures
  - differences between firms
  - changes in business activities
  - general business conditions (e.g. recession)
  - inflation.
- Like must be compared with like – size, product, objectives.
- Some information may be estimated and therefore not be accurate (stock valuation/depreciation).
- Information is historic.
- Does not take into account factors like quality of workers, location of firm.

3 (i) An unexpected breakdown of machinery
Production stops therefore no goods to sell, income reduced (unless stocks are held). Repair/replacement costs money. Replacement is perhaps too much in a one-off, need to spread payment or lease. Workers, although idle, still require payment.

A rise in inflation
Costs of raw materials and overheads will rise. Selling price may have to be increased to cover rises. Wage demands may have to be met (spiral effect). Selling price rise may lag behind increase in costs, reducing profitability.

A change in regulations requiring a product to be modified to make it comply with new Health and Safety regulations
Product may require modification (e.g. when seat belts became compulsory in cars). Costs of new machinery or modifications to existing machinery. Training costs to use new equipment. More expensive raw materials may be required.

(ii) Management must:
- **Monitor** the situation, e.g. record the number of production hours lost.
- **Control** the situation, e.g. replace machine, train workers.
- **Plan** to prevent the problem from recurring, e.g. change production techniques.
- **Decide** the best course of action.

4 • Description of:
  – timely
  – accurate
  – complete
  – appropriate
  – available
  – cost effective
  – objective
  – concise.

  • Accounting information is historic.
  • Only provides quantifiable data – may not be relevant to issue being considered.
  • Effects of, e.g. inflation not reflected in comparative figures.
  • Some values are subjective (e.g. goodwill).
  • Non-financial information is not reflected in figures (e.g. staff morale, market share etc).
  • Information may not be in an appropriate form.
  • Different methods of stock valuation make comparisons difficult.

5 (a) **One mark for each ratio and one mark for what each tells the manager.**
  • Tells manager if the company is doing well or not in comparison to similar firms.
  • Tells manager if the company is doing well or not in comparison to previous years.
  • Tells manager if the organisation is meeting targets or not and by how much.
  • Helps identify why the above is happening.
  • Efficiency ratios show how well resources are being used – return on capital ratios.
  • Liquidity ratios show whether a firm can repay its short-term debts – current ratio, acid test ratio.
  • Profitability ratios show profit being made from sales – GP ratio, Mark-up, Margin.

  (b) The manager may choose to do the following:
  • Raise the selling price.
  • Look for a cheaper supplier to reduce cost of sales.
  • Choose to sell something else.
  • Try to reduce expenses.
  • Renew/set targets.
  • Discipline staff.
  • Introduce new machinery.
  • Renew faulty machinery.
  • Offer cash discounts to encourage debtors to pay more quickly.
  • Tighten debtor control.
  • Introduce special offers/promotion to increase stock turnover.
  • Raise profit margin on slow-moving items.
  • Introduce JIT.
  • Reduce liabilities (e.g. overdraft).
  • Reduce creditors.
  • Increase cash/bank (e.g. by selling unnecessary assets).

6 (a) • Opening balance(s).
  • Inflows.
  • Outflows.
  • Closing balance(s).

UNIT 3

(b) • Target-setting.
  • Identifying cash flow problems.
  • Taking action to avoid cash flow problems.
  • Comparing with actual cash flow.
  • Supporting business plans/applications for funding.

7 • Current ratio – current assets:current liabilities (1.5–2):1 good.
  • Quick ratio – current assets – stock:current liabilities (1–1.5):1 good.
  • Show ability to pay debts.
  • Poor ratios should be investigated.
  • Solutions. (max 3 marks)
  • Suppliers – before giving credit.
  • Banks – before giving loans.
  • Customers – before awarding long-term contracts.

8 • Fast/automatic calculations.
  • Faster reports and so faster decisions.
  • Formulae.
  • Guaranteed accuracy.
  • Graphs and charts.
  • What ifs.
  • Easier to understand for non-accountants.

HUMAN RESOURCES MANAGEMENT

1 (i) • To update skills.
    • To enable staff to know what they are doing – improve employee satisfaction.
    • To produce a more flexible workforce.
    • To allow change to be introduced successfully.
    • To improve image of organisation – organisations which offer good training programmes may attract new members of staff.
  (ii) • Induction training is for new staff. It is a means of allowing staff to see how the whole organisation operates. It is not job-specific, it gives information about organisation. It allows time for staff to settle in and put new employees at ease.

2 (a) **Description** of:
    • works council
    • quality circle
    • empowerment
    • employee share schemes
    • profit share schemes
    • job enrichment
    • job enlargement
    • joint consultation
    • Total Quality Management
    • employee director
    • suggestion box.

(b)
- Enhances dialogue between employer and employee.
- Increased responsibility – greater motivation therefore greater productivity.
- Increased loyalty to the organisation.
- Profit sharing – employees realise the need for efficiency and competitiveness.
- Employees feel valued.
- Closer to customer so customer receives better service.
- Quicker decision-making.

3
- Go to manager and discuss the problem.
- Manager to discuss problems with departmental manager.
- Issue discussed with HR manager.
- Issue discussed by Managing Director and trade union officials.
- If all internal procedures fail – ACAS involvement.
- Employment tribunal – consists of legally qualified chairman and two other people. They will hear the case and make a ruling. Less formal than a court.
- Employment Appeal Tribunal will listen to any appeals from tribunals – presided over by a judge.
- European Court of Justice hears cases and passes rulings for EU countries.
- Support may be available from EOC (Equal Opportunities Commission).
- Industrial action.

4 Works councils
- Consist entirely of workers' representatives.
- Have legal rights of access to information from management on a range of topics.
- Legal right to joint decision-making on matters affecting employees and levels of manpower.
- Social Chapter means works councils will have to be introduced to medium/large companies.
- Job rotation.
- Open door policy.

Single union agreements
- Easier for employer to negotiate with one union instead of several – reduces time, conflict.
- Easier to build up rapport.
- The greater the number of workers speaking with one voice, the more likely they will be listened to.

5 Additional costs:
- Equipment has to be purchased for lifting, etc.
- Protective guards have to be fitted to machines.
- Protective clothing may be required.
- Training may be needed, e.g. fire prevention, health and safety.
- Working Time Regulations.
- May need more workers.
- Increased number of breaks may affect productivity.
- Age regulations, e.g. under 16s cannot serve petrol.
- Health and safety implications for serving food.

- Packaging of food (sealed packets).
- Best before dates may result in dumping of food.
- Products may be affected, e.g. chocolate made in the UK has different cocoa/milk ratio than in Europe.

6
- Address a press conference to offer an explanation and apology.
- Issue a press release.
- Make a donation to charity to try and compensate the public.
- Respond to criticisms.
- Ensure no unfavourable press notices.

7 (a)
- Health and Safety at Work Act.
- Data Protection Act.
- VDU Regulations.
- COSSH Regulations.
- EU Directives.

(b)
- Compliance costs.
- Possibility of being sued/compensation.
- Safer/healthier working environment:
  - fewer accidents
  - fewer delays to production
  - better motivated workforce
  - better quality of output
  - increased productivity.
- Poor record affects recruitment.
- Image/reputation.

8 Purpose
- To judge applicants face-to-face.
- To get candidates' views/opinions.
- To compare with application form/CV and check references.
- Use of body language.
- For candidate to sell themself.
- For candidate to ask questions.
- To make comparisons with other interviewees.

Conduct
- Put interviewee at ease.
- Introduce yourself.
- Avoid interruptions.
- Don't rush.
- Have a list of questions.
- Get interviewee talking.
- Concentrate on areas outside application form.
- At end, ask if any questions.
- At end, tell interviewee when decision will be made, etc.
- Make up notes before next interview.

9 • Aptitude – problem-solving/copying/speed.
 • Attainment – skills.
 • Intelligence – mental abilities.
 • Personality/psychometric – traits/characteristics.

10 (a) • Employee number/NI number – unique identifier.
 (b) • Attendance.
 • Discipline.
 • Performance.
 • Communicating.
 • Selection of staff for:
   – promotion
   – training
   – teams
   – specific jobs.

11

QUALITY CIRCLES	BENEFITS
• small groups of workers • mainly shopfloor • identify any areas that could be improved • pay and conditions normally excluded • make suggestions • implement improvements • must have management and worker support	• degree of empowerment/industrial democracy • workers feel valued • improved productivity/quality • cost savings

OPERATIONS

1 • Nature of the product. Cost and speed of transportation to be considered; fresh product requires a short handling time technical/specialist products require specialist advice.
 • Number of consumers. Small number may be best met by direct selling. Large number requires the use of retailers to make product widely available.
 • Location of market. Is transport easily available to the consumer?
 • It may be desirable to keep product exclusive.
 • It may be desirable to retain high profit margins (lots of retailers may lead to competitive pricing).

2

JOB – single product to customer's specification	
Advantages	**Disadvantages**
• one-off orders to meet customer demand • high price can be charged • specifications can be changed by customers even if job started • workers likely to be skilled and motivated • supervision easy	• expensive due to high skills of staff • high research and development, administration and transport costs • wide variety of equipment/tools required • lead times can be lengthy

UNIT 3

| **FLOW** – process whereby production items move continuously from one operation to the next ||
Advantages	Disadvantages
• costs spread over large number of goods – economies of scale • bulk discounts likely to be achieved when purchasing raw materials • huge quantities can be produced • process is often automated which lowers labour costs	• huge investment to set up • individual customer requirements cannot be met • equipment use may be inflexible • worker motivation can be low because of repetitive nature of job • breakdowns can be very costly

3 • Weather.
   • Strikes.
   • Breakdowns.
   • Short term – use alternative method even if more expensive as this is better than losing sales – customers may go elsewhere.
   • Long term – review situation. How likely is it to recur? Consider purchasing own lorries etc.

4 (i) • ABTA symbol.
        • BS5750/ISO 9000.
        • AA/RAC recommendations.
        • Scottish Tourist Board star ratings.
        • Investors in People.
        • CE mark (an EU award).
        • The Lion Mark (British Toy and Hobby Association).

   (ii) • Customers are assured of a quality product/service.
        • Customer is considered in setting the definition of quality – what is it that the customer wants?
        • Symbol acts as a marketing tool.
        • Government may award contracts only to organisations which hold BS5750/ISO 9000.
        • A benchmark is established, thus continually improving the product/service.
        • Brand loyalty.
        • Repeat sales and fewer returns/complaints.

5 • Nature of the product.
   • Quantity to be produced.
   • Resources available.
   (Development of above necessary.)

6 Quality assurance
   • Standards are set, agreed and met throughout the organisation.
   • Process is based on prevention – steps taken to reduce errors.
   • Checking occurs at every stage.
   • Ensure quality of supplies of materials and parts.
   • Establish system of monitoring and controlling process.
   • After-sales service provided.
   • Ability to meet delivery deadlines.

- Commitment and skill of workforce.
- Aim for zero defects.

TQM
- Customer is important —produce what they want and quality they want.
- Quality chain — everyone and everything working to a standard.
- TQM must start from the top — resources must be provided.
- All workers must be concerned with quality.
- Checking of quality — whole process must be monitored.
- Constant search for improvement.
- Quality to be defined at each stage.
- Everyone accountable for their own performance.
- Everything must be controlled — quality of supplies, machinery, final output.

7
- Price.
- Terms.
- Quality.
- Quantity.
- Time.
- Place.
- Reliability.
- Flexibility.
- Reputation.
- Contactability.

(Expansion of above necessary.)

UNIT: 3

ACAS	Arbitration, Conciliation and Advisory Service. See **www.acas.org.uk** for more information.
Appraisal	Evaluation of staff performance and identification of training needs.
Aptitude testing	Tests carried out to assess a candidate's suitability for a position.
Arbitration	Where two opposing parties meet with an independent third party and agree to abide by the decision of the third party.
Articles of Association	This legal document applies to limited companies and lays out the terms of business for the company.
Augmented product	This is a product with additional features over the regular product.
Automation	The use of machines and technology in production.
Bar codes	A series of black and white vertical lines used to identify different products.
Benchmarking	Used in the area of quality control to establish an accepted standard.
Brainstorming	A method used to generate new ideas by taking note of all kinds of ideas at a meeting no matter how outlandish.
Branding	A method of attaching a 'persona' to a product based on an established make.
CAD	Computer Aided Design – the use of computers and computer software in the design process.
CAM	Computer Aided Manufacture – the use of computers in the manufacturing process.
Capital	Money invested in business by the owner(s) at the commencement of the business.
Capital-intensive production	Production of goods or services that requires large amounts of capital (money).
CBI	Confederation of British Industry.
Centralised structures	Businesses where the main functions are to be found in one central location.
Channel of distribution	The method by which the product produced by the manufacturer reaches the consumer or end user.

GLOSSARY

Collective bargaining	A system whereby negotiations are carried out on behalf of several parties instead of negotiating separately.
Consultation	A process of seeking and gathering information from interested parties.
Consumer trends	The general fashion that is followed by the general public at any point in time.
Core activities	The main commercial activities of a business.
Core product	The main product manufactured by a business.
Corporate advertising	Advertising carried out in the media by business.
Corporate culture	A phrase used to describe the atmosphere or feel of a business.
Corporate re-engineering	The complete redesign of the organisation to meet the needs of the market.
Customer grouping	Where an organisation organises itself around the different types of customers it has.
Cycle of business	The identification and satisfaction of consumer needs, only for more needs to be created.
De-industrialisation	The moving from a manufacturing economy to a service economy as the economy ages.
De-layering	The removal of layers of management to flatten the organisations structure.
Delegation	The transfer of responsibilities from a manager to a subordinate.
Demand-oriented pricing	This occurs when the price of a product is set according to the level of demand.
Demographics	The use of statistics for births, deaths, etc.
Desk research	Research that is carried out solely from a desk relying on information to hand e.g. in books and journals rather than collecting it from the field.
Destroyer pricing	This occurs when a business sets the price of a product so low that it destroys the market share of a similar product produced by a rival company.
Differentiated marketing	Offering different products to different groups of consumers in the market.
Disciplinary procedures	A set of actions that are followed when a member of staff breaks the accepted code of conduct.
Discrimination	Making a distinction on the basis of unjust grounds.
Division of labour	Breaking down tasks into smaller ones so that workers can become specialists.
Downsizing	Changing the size and focus of a business to a smaller scale.
Durable goods	Goods which can be used again and again.

GLOSSARY

E-commerce	Conducting business and accepting and making payments using the Internet.
Economic stock level	The level at which there is no excess or shortage of stock.
Emotional selling proposition	When consumers trust a brand or business, and so will return to buy again and again.
Employee relations	Referring to the relationship that exists between employer and employees.
Employment protection	Legislation which exists to protect the rights of workers.
Employment tribunals	A legal hearing heard by the Employment Tribunal Service for employees who have raised an employment law issue against their employer.
Empowerment	Creating a sense of worth and responsibility amongst employees.
Entrepreneur	A person who starts a business from their own idea with the intention of making a profit.
Entrepreneurial structures	Structures which are based around one or two key decision makers.
Equal opportunities	Employers must provide the same opportunities to all employees and potential employees regardless of gender and race.
Extension strategies	Ways in which an organisation can extend the life cycle of a product.
Factors of production	Land, labour, capital, and enterprise which are required for the production of goods or services to take place.
Field research	Research that is carried out away from the office.
Flat structure	Relating to the structure of a business where all people operate at the same level.
Flexi-time	Flexibility in working hours meaning that employees can start and finish work at different times so long as they complete a set number of hours each week.
Franchises	A business that is operated under the name of a parent business and the 'owner' effectively rents the name to trade under e.g. McDonalds and The Body Shop.
Fringe benefits	Extra benefits that employees receive from their employer or as a result of their employment over and above their salary.
Functional relationships	Relationships between the functional departments of the organisation.
Generic advertising	Advertising which promotes a whole industry such as the beef industry rather than individual producers' products.
Goods	Items which are produced by manufacturers.
Government-funded Service providers	Bodies which are set up and funded by the government.

Grievance procedures	A set of rules and regulations set up in a business to govern breakdowns in employee and employer relations.
Health and Safety	The protection of employees from risks through unsafe working environments.
Hierarchical structure	Relating to the structure of a business where it resembles a pyramid with those at the top (fewer) having more authority and in charge of those at the bottom (more).
Hierarchy of needs	The different needs employees need to have satisfied through their employment.
Hot desks	A desk reserved for use by part-time members of staff.
Induction training	Orientation training for new employees usually carried out before they start work.
Industrial action	Action taken by employees who are in dispute with their employer and often in the form of a strike.
Informative advertising	Advertising that conveys useful information instead of trying to convince you to buy a product or service.
Inputs	The factors of production which are put into the production process.
JIT – Just in Time operations	Operations set up to minimise stock and production levels to meet actual demand.
Job analysis	The process of identifying what vacancy might exist within an organisation.
Job enlargement	Creating extra tasks and responsibilities for employees.
Job enrichment	Allowing the job holder to develop their own specialist expertise.
Job rotation	Allowing workers to carry out a variety of different tasks.
Job specification	Details of what a vacancy will involve for the candidates in terms of tasks to be undertaken, responsibilities, etc.
Kanban	Stock record card system used in Just-in-Time production.
Labour	The mental and physical effort of the employees of the organisation.
Labour intensive production	Production where the cost of labour exceeds the cost of capital.
Land	The natural resources used in production, including all things grown on and extracted from the land, sea, and atmosphere.
Lead time	The time taken between placing an order for supplies and the supplies arriving.
Limited liability	Where the owners/shareholders of the organisation are only liable for the amount they invested in the business.
Line relationships	The relationship between superiors and subordinates within the organisation.

Line/staff grouping	Line employees are the core workers of the business, and staff are the employees that support the core activities of the organisation.
Local authorities	Local government bodies/the local council.
Market growth	When the sales and customers within a market increase.
Market orientation	When organisations base their operations on market research, finding what customers want, and then supplying it.
Market segmentation	Where organisations split the whole market into different groups who have similar wants and needs.
Market share	The share of the whole market (sales/customers) that one organisation has.
Memorandum of Association	A legal document required when setting up a limited company.
Merchandising	Methods of encouraging customers to buy at point of sale such as displays, posters, etc.
Minimum stock level	The least amount of stock a firm can hold without production having to be stopped before new stock arrives.
Mission statement	A document issued by an organisation detailing their strategic aims and objectives.
Motivation	The management skill involved in getting workers to work harder and/or better.
Multi-skilling	The development of a number of different skills amongst workers to enable them to perform a variety of jobs.
Negotiation	The process of coming to an agreement between employers and employees.
Non-durable goods	Goods which are used only once or twice and then have to be replaced e.g. food.
Off-the-job-training	Where workers are trained away from the workplace e.g. college.
On-the-job-training	Where workers are trained while they are doing the job.
Operational decisions	Routine decisions on the day to day running of the company.
Organisational charts	Diagrams which show the place of employees within the organisation in terms of their department, their level of authority, and their immediate superiors and subordinates.
Output	The product or service which the organisation produces.
Outsourcing	Arranging for outside suppliers to provide support functions which are not core to the business e.g. printing.
Overtime	Working beyond the normal contracted hours, usually attracting higher rates of pay.
Parent companies	A firm which owns all the shares in another firm.

Pay and conditions	The details which are contained in the contract of employment including rate of pay, hours to be worked, etc.
Payment systems	The different methods of paying production workers.
Penetration pricing	A low-price pricing strategy to allow a new product to the market to gain sales and market share.
Performance-related pay	Paying workers according to how well they work or rewarding them for achieving targets.
Person specification	Drawn up during the selection process to identify the qualities and skills the ideal candidate for the job should have.
Personality tests	Tests carried out during selection to establish the personality type of a candidate for a job, and how they would react in different situations.
Persuasive advertising	Advertising which attempts to persuade the customer to buy the product.
Pest analysis	Analysis of the external environment in which the organisation operates (Political – Economic – Socio-cultural – Technological).
Piecework	Where employees are paid by how many items they produce.
Place/territory grouping	Where the organisation is organised around the different areas of the country or the world where they operate.
Primary sector	Industry which is based around the exploitation of natural resources including farming, fishing, mineral extraction, etc.
Product concept	How a product will satisfy a variety of needs for the consumer.
Product differentiation	Where businesses use factors such as a brand name to make their product appear different to similar products on the market in the minds of consumers.
Product life cycle	The various stages a product will go through from introduction to growth to maturity to decline.
Product line	A range of similar products produced by an organisation with slight differences to appeal to different tastes and markets.
Product mix (range)	A range of different products produced by the same organisation at different stages in their life cycle, to spread risk, maintain profit levels, and to provided investment for new products.
Product orientation	Where an organisation concentrates on the production of new products rather than carrying out research to see what consumers want.
Product portfolio	*see Product mix.*
Product/service grouping	Where the organisation is grouped or organised around the different products or services that it provides.
Production planning	The process of establishing what is required in terms of land, labour and capital to meet consumer demand.

Production systems	The methods available to the organisation to produce goods and services.
Profit sharing	Where employees are rewarded with a share of the organisation's profits when they exceed certain levels.
Promotional pricing	A short term pricing strategy to lower price in order to boost sales.
Promotions into the pipeline	Promotions offered to companies to encourage them to buy more of a product for sale.
Promotions out of the pipeline	Promotions offered to consumers to encourage them to buy more of a product.
Psychometric testing	A tool used during the recruitment process to establish how each of the candidates thinks.
Public relations	The communications tool of the organisation when dealing with those outside the organisation including customers, the media, and the government.
Public sector	Here the organisations are owned by the government on behalf of the people.
Publicity	Planned or unplanned discussion in the media about the organisation.
Purchasing mix	Finding the best supplier in terms of price, reliability, quality, etc.
Pyramid structures	Organisational structures with few people at the top of the organisation and many at the bottom (hierarchical structure).
Quality circles	Groups of workers meeting to solve production problems and improve standards.
Quota sampling	A method of selecting the number and type of consumer to carry out market research on.
Random sampling	Random sampling involves producing a random list of individuals to survey.
Recruitment	The process of attracting the right applicants to apply for a vacancy.
Re-order stock level	The point at which new stock should be ordered to ensure that the stock level does not fall below the minimum stock quantity.
Re-order stock quantity	The amount of stock needed to bring the stock level back to the economic stock level.
Sampling	The process of selecting who and how many consumers should be selected for market research.
Secondary	Organisations who are primarily involved in the manufacture of goods or semi-finished goods.
Selection	The process of deciding on the right candidate for a job.

Services	Things that are done for consumers for a price such as banking, hairdressing, etc.
Shareholders	Private individuals who own a part or a share in a limited company.
Shortages/bottle necks	Problems in production when too few or too many items move from one part of the production process to the next.
Single union agreements	An agreement between the employees and the employers that all of the employees will be represented by one trade union.
Skimming	A short term high pricing strategy used when there is little competition in the market.
Sole traders	One person businesses where the owner takes all the profits and makes all the decisions.
Span of control	The number of subordinates a person has working directly for them in the organisation.
Staff authority	Areas where the staff or support departments have the right to tell the core departments what to do, e.g. human resources ordering health and safety checks.
Staff relationships	How the staff departments interact with the core departments.
Staff welfare	The responsibility of the human resources department to look after the employees within the organisation.
Stock control	The function in operations where the levels of stock are maintained in the most economic and efficient way.
Strategic decisions	The long term goals or aims of the organisation.
Subsidiary companies	Businesses which are wholly owned by another business.
Swot analysis	A tool used in decision making to look at the internal and external environment of the business.
Tactical decisions	Decisions about how the resources of the organisation are to be organised and used to achieve their goals or aims.
Target markets	Where organisations market their products or services at specific parts of the market rather than the whole market.
Tele-working	Information and communication technology used to allow employees to keep in contact with the organisation whilst away from the workplace.
Tertiary/service sector	The sector of industry which provides services to the consumer such as retailing, banking and insurance, etc.
Test marketing	A tool used in marketing where the product is released in one small market to gauge consumers reactions to it prior to the full market launch.
TUC	The Trade Unions Council is the parent body of all trade unions.

Undifferentiated (mass) marketing	Marketing directed towards all consumers in the market rather than targeting specific groups.
Unique selling proposition	Something about a product that makes it different in the consumers mind from similar products, e.g. the brand name.
VAT	Value added tax is a tax placed on the purchase of most goods or services.
Voluntary sector	This includes organisations such as charities who are not owned by government or private individuals.
Wealth creation	The process whereby the activity of organisations creates wealth for the whole economy.
Works councils	A group of representatives from the workforce who have the legal right to access information from management, and have joint decision-making powers on most matters relating to employees.

CHAPTER 1

1   Record company, recording studio, CD manufacturer, casing manufacturer, graphic designer, printer, music company, advertising agency, accountants, lawyers for contracts, etc.

2   As our economy matures, we demand more and more services and with that an increase in demand for information. Call centres provide a cost-efficient way of satisfying these demands.

   Our economy has seen a rapid decline in traditional areas of employment such as engineering and shipbuilding on the Clyde and coal-mining in Ayrshire, Fife, and the central belt. We have become much more reliant on service-sector employment to ensure the wealth of Scotland.

3   Any suitable example would be acceptable. One may be a local corner shop.
   Land – There is the land that it is built on, all the natural materials used in its construction, and natural gas supply.
   Labour – Would be the workers in the shop, including the owner(s).
   Capital – Would be the shop fittings, machinery such as tills, scales and vans.
   Enterprise – Would be the owner(s).

4   Will depend very much on the local area, but could include:
   Primary sector – Local farm, garden nursery, fishing business, etc.
   Secondary sector – Local manufacturers such as the local bakery, building firms, etc.
   Tertiary sector – Shops including national chains, garages, local health service, banks, hairdressers, etc.

5   (a) A legal firm will typically adopt a partnership as a suitable business organisation as this is a traditional approach that allows development of the firm (taking on new partners, etc.), although some firms have opted for a limited company organisation.
   (b) A window cleaner would be likely to set up as a sole trader, as there would be little expense involved in running the firm and large debts would be unlikely, so he or she would not have to worry too much about unlimited liability.
   (c) A garage repair and sales outlet would need a good deal of capital to set up, and buying cars for sale could put a strain on the cash flow of the business, so limited liability would be desirable. In this instance a private limited company would be the most appropriate business organisation.

6   (a) Universities are funded by central grants from national government, and by the fees they collect.
   (b) Local bus services were provided by local councils up to the 1980s; they are now provided by private firms.
   (c) The water supply is provided by three regional water supply companies funded by national government. Plans are underway to unite these to form one water company for the whole of Scotland. In England the water supply is provided by private companies.
   (d) Sheltered housing is mostly supplied by the local authority, although there are some private schemes as well. They are sometimes partly funded by national government for their own policy objectives

ANSWERS

(e) The letter postal service is provided by Royal Mail. It is currently a publicly funded business, although there are always plans around to privatise this service.

7 (a) Any three from socio-cultural, technological, economic, political, finance, methods of growth, competitive environment.
   (b) Examples of socio-cultural factors include changing tastes and fashions, lack of brand loyalty amongst consumers and changes in the population structure.
   (c) Examples of economic factors include the state of the economy, competitive environment and pressure groups.
   (d) Examples of political factors include the implementation of government policies and the effects of restraints on business.
   (e) A merger is when two businesses agree to join and act as one. A demerger is when two businesses that had previously merged agree to split up and operate individually.
   (f) Sources of finance and advice to businesses include LECs, banks and local authorities.
   (g) Divestment occurs when one or more subsidiary companies are sold off by the parent company.

8 Two business objectives of HBOS are increased returns for shareholders and growth.

9 A sensible answer would include the following points:
   • The BBC has a higher percentage of public funding, whereas Scottish Television is a commercial organisation.
   • The BBC exists primarily to offer a public service.
   • Scottish Television is a 'for profit' company
   • The BBC cannot generate revenue from advertising.
   • Scottish Television generates a high percentage of its revenue from advertising.

10 (a) Objectives help to identify the goals of the business, how these will be achieved and the end result.
   (b) Objectives may be general or specific.
   (c) Examples of business objectives are:
       • Survival
       • Growth and development
       • Profit
       • Social responsibility
       • Service provision

11 (a) Stakeholders are people who have a key interest in the business.
   (b) Examples of stakeholders include:
       • Owners
       • Suppliers
       • Employees
       • Committees
       • Community
       • Customers
       • Banks
       • Management
       • Donors
       • Shareholders
       • Investors
       • Local government

- Members
- Taxpayers

(c) Stakeholders will be able to exert influence on business according to the degree of involvement or interest in the business.

(d)

Type of business	Stakeholder	Interest
Sole trader	Owner	Maximise profit
Partner	Partner	Provide good service
Private limited company	Director	Growth
Public limited company	Shareholder	Responsibility to shareholders
Voluntary organisation	Volunteer	Providing service
Charity	Volunteer	Personal job satisfaction
Public corporation	Members of the public	Interest in activities
Government funded organisation	Government officer	International activities
Local government funded organisation	Local councillor	Local impact

CHAPTER 2

1 (a) Primary information is information collected by the company. It is usually verifiable and suitable for its purpose.
   (b) Secondary information is information that is not necessarily the most ideally suited for its purpose and may not be able to be traced back to its original source.
   (c) Internal information comes from within the business.
   (d) External information comes from outwith the business.

2 No answer required.

3 (a) Good information should be accurate, timely, complete, appropriate, available, cost-effective, objective and concise.

   (b)

Source	Purpose	High/ low	Reason
Personal Computing Magazine	To decide which computer to buy	High	Information source is specific to the need and is from a reliable source
The Internet	To find the latest weather forecast	High	Specific information can be found and it should be reliable and up-to-date
The Scotsman newspaper	To decide how to cast your vote at the next election	High	Information is informative although it may have a bias
Magazine advert for a new snack food	To decide whether or not to buy it	Low	Advertisement is likely to be persuasive in nature

Conversation overheard on the bus	To predict the winner of the Snooker World Championships	Low	Information is subjective and the outcome is uncertain
Scottish Qualifications Authority	To find out students' exam results from last year	High	Information is verifiable and comes from a reliable and traceable source
Telephone banking service	To find out the balance on your account	High	Information is reliable and secure
Horoscope in a magazine	To find out what will happen to you in the future	Low	Information is not verifiable and is a prediction of future events

4   (a) Examples of IT in use today:
- Computers
- Networks
- Email
- Internet

(b) A mainframe computer is a large and powerful computer used to carry out complex tasks and calculations. Its use in business today is not very common due to the development of the personal computer and network technology. The use of mainframes is restricted to organisations such as NASA and their cost is high.

(c) LAN stands for Local Area Network and is a collection of computers that are connected, usually by cables, over a small geographic area e.g. an office building. The LAN makes use of client-server network technology. WAN stands for Wide Area Network and is a collection of computers that are connected over a wide geographic area e.g. several towns or cities.

(d) Modern business may make use of client-server technology in the office and utilise a server connected to several personal desktop computers and other peripherals. When employees work away from the office, they may make use of laptop computers to record working activities or make presentations.

5   (a) The use of Internet banking has benefited Minola Smoked Products by expanding their market area and improving their cash flow through consistent receipts.

(b) Minola Smoked Products is able to operate in a global market through its website, offering secure payment facilities from anywhere in the world.

6   (a) ICT stands for Information Communication Technology and refers to the use of the Internet and electronic means of communication.

(b) Three examples of modern use of the telecommunications network are:
- Internet
- Email
- Fax

(c) This answer will depend on the answers given in the previous question.

(d) Advantages of email:
- Fast
- Cheap
- Reliable
- Unaffected by time zones

Disadvantages of email:
- Can be intercepted
- Email address is required to send and receive
- Emails can get 'lost' as they travel across the Internet

(e) Students will obviously choose their own example, however, the main points should remain the same.

A good example is how the airline industry has changed since the widespread use of the Internet made it possible to sell tickets online. The change in consumers from people wishing to visit a shop to those who now prefer to use the Internet from home or work to shop for goods and services has made this possible. Better security when paying for goods and services online has also increased the use of the Internet and e-commerce.

7 (a) Four types of business software:
- Word processing
- Spreadsheet
- Database
- Presentation
- Email
- Internet

(b) Any suitable answer.

(c) Any suitable answer.

(d) Any suitable answer.

(e) Any suitable answer.

(f) Decision-making software is usually used by large government operations.

8 (a) The Data Protection Act (1998) protects the rights of the individual by governing the collection, storage and use of information that is held in electronic or paper systems.

(b) Data Protection Principles include:
- Obtain and process data fairly and lawfully.
- Register the purpose for which the information is held.
- Not to disclose the information in any way that is different from those purposes.
- Only hold information that is adequate, relevant and not excessive for the purposes required.
- Only hold accurate information and keep it up to date where necessary.
- Not to hold the information any longer than necessary.
- Take appropriate security measures to keep the information safe.
- Give individuals copies of the information held about themselves if they request it and, where appropriate, correct or erase the information.

(c) An organisation must respond to a request for information within 28 days.

(d) An individual may be refused access to information about themselves e.g. where the information held is for the purpose of:
- preventing or detecting a crime,
- catching or prosecuting offenders,
- accessing or collecting taxes or duty,
- restrictions relating to information held by the Government departments of Health and Social Work.

CHAPTER 3

1 Employees have to be kept informed in order that they stay motivated and do not undermine the success of the decision. Shareholders have to be kept informed as they are the owners of the business and it is their investment in the business that allows it to keep trading. By informing all stakeholders there is a far greater chance of success, and less likelihood of complaints.

2 Internal constraints are:
   - Finance available
   - Company policy
   - Employees' abilities and attitudes

   External constraints are:
   - Government and EU legislation
   - Competitors behaviour
   - Lack of new technology
   - Economic environment

3 (a) They would only buy the most up to date machinery. They would develop a reputation for quality and a good delivery service. To trade in profit within three years of setting up. To employ only the best sales people.
   (b) They believed they would only be successful if they were able to offer a better product than their competitors.
   (c) Answers here will vary. However, it could include such things as to maximise profits (they achieved their target of trading within profit early). They may also have wanted to be the market leader in Aberdeen as this is what they appear to have achieved.
   (d) Clarion could identify one or two of their main customers and try to become their sole supplier. They could try to merge with one of the large printing companies in order to gain access to their technology. They could purchase the new technology themselves.
   (e) Answers will vary, however the most obvious answer would be to try to become a single supplier to one of the oil companies. This would give them a very large customer who would guarantee them a lot of business in the short term. It may be a problem in the long term as the oil company may decide later to switch to another printing company. Merging would mean a loss of control of the business although the owners would be well rewarded for their share. The cost of the new technology may be high and would require substantial funds through borrowing, which may cause problems for the firm in the longer term if they were unable to repay the loan.
   (f) Again, answers vary, however, if we were to take the example given, Clarion would have to spend time and money negotiating the deal with the oil company. They would have to meet the exact requirements of all their needs and this could mean employing new staff, purchasing new machinery, and dedicating a sales team to work with the oil company to meet their needs.
   (g) The choice here is to find another printer or to buy the business from the sub-contractor. If it is likely that he will sell the business to someone else, then that would be the preferred option, as the new purchaser could continue with the contract with Clarion and also carry the risk of running his or her own business.
   (h) Sales staff will have to work to ensure that Clarion continue to offer the best price and service, and that they continue to keep in touch with their customers to ensure that Clarion is meeting their needs, so they are unlikely to change suppliers.

(i) The first step would be to ensure that none of their staff are being head hunted by the multi-national. They could enter into pay and conditions negotiations, or carry out staff appraisals to ensure staff are happy. It is also important to find out what the Chief Executive of the multi-national wants, they may want to talk about a merger or some other form of business agreement which would be beneficial for Clarion.

(j) Staff should be advised of the current situation. Only if they trust the management of Clarion will they continue to be motivated to provide the best possible products. A staff meeting could be arranged with all the employees, or groups of employees, to tell them what is happening, and promise to let them know of any further developments. It would also be helpful to let them know they will be included in discussions regarding the businesses future so that they can have their say.

(k) The first step is to find out exactly what is wrong. Are they simply unsettled or have they been approached by the multi-national? It may be that some reassurance is required, or it may be that offering improved pay and conditions is needed if Clarion want to keep them. At the end of the day, it may be better to let them go if things do not improve.

4   (a) The interpersonal role, the information role, and the decision role.
    (b) Plan, organise, command, control and coordinate; and delegation and motivation.

5   (a) Profit maximisation, sales maximisation, social responsibility, to provide a service, to increase market share, growth, survival, creating a good reputation, etc.

    (b)

Shareholders/owners	Through decisions that are made at AGM, etc. To invest or not in the business, to withdraw their investment.
Managers	In the decisions that they make. In their need for financial and non-financial rewards, and in how hard they work.
Employees	In how much effort they put in, in their negotiations over pay and conditions, through their trade unions, and by how they represent the business.
Suppliers	By whether or not they supply the business, by varying their terms of credit, and by offering discounts.
Customers	By buying or not buying the product. By complaining about the product.
Competitors	By attempting to increase their own market share through varying price or advertising campaigns, or by bringing out new improved products.
Government	By introducing new laws, and by varying the rates of taxation.
Society	Through pressure groups, or through complaints to the press, or complaints to the local authority or government.

6   **Step 1 – Identify the problem** – Set the aims.

Step 2 – Identify the objectives – Managers have to decide on exactly what it is they want to achieve.

Step 3 – Gather information – The more information that can be gathered the better the chance of success the decision has. Extensive use of internal and external information is required.

Step 4 – Analyse information – Study the information you have collected.

Step 5 – Devise alternative solutions – Using the information you have collected, decide on a number of different courses of action you can take that will meet the aims.

Step 6 – Select from alternative solutions – From the alternative courses of action that you have devised select the one which you think will be most likely to meet the aims of the organisation under present circumstances.

Step 7 – Communicate the decision – All those involved must know exactly what is going to happen, what effects these changes will have, and why you have decided on this course of action.

Step 8 – Implement the decision – Arrange for the resources to be put into place. Issue appropriate instructions, and ask for feedback on how things progress.

Step 9 – Evaluate – Using the information you are collecting on how the process is going, compare this to what was expected to happen.

7　The skills of workforce and management, including its entrepreneurial skills, will be included in the study. How well the capital is being used to provide efficient production and distribution will be looked at, as will its financial performance and the range of products.

8　Political – Economic – Socio-cultural – Technological – Competitive.

9　
- The time it takes to complete.
- The ability to collect all the relevant information.
- The problems involved in generating alternative solutions.
- The lack of creativity involved (ignoring the gut feeling of experienced managers).

10　
- The time taken to collect, assess and analyse the information.
- The quality and quantity of information that becomes available to make a good decision.
- The ability to generate alternatives.
- The possibility of enhanced innovation and responsiveness.

CHAPTER 4

1　(a) Principal Teachers are experts in their own subjects and assessments and examinations. They know best how the subjects should be taught, and what should be taught at different levels; what pupils should sit which levels (e.g. Foundation, General or Credit; Intermediate 2 or Higher); and what resources are needed.

　(b) As with all organisations this will vary from school to school. They will decide how to spend their budget and what teachers should teach what classes. They will also decide when any assessments or tests should take place; what levels are offered (e.g. Intermediate 1 or Advanced Higher) but some of these decisions will be restricted by whole-school policies.

2　Departments could include bakery, butchers, household, delicatessen, etc.

3　Any employer with a large workforce would be acceptable. A good example would be the local council. They employ thousands of staff to do a wide variety of jobs with a wide variety of skills from solicitors and architects, to cleaners. They will need a large department to look after all these staff.

4　(a) The business is grouped around the main functional areas where departments are formed, e.g. marketing, operations, finance, human resources, etc.

(b) **Advantages:**
- The resources of the organisation will be better used.
- Staff will become experts in their own field.
- Career paths created within the departments.
- Communication and cooperation within the department are excellent.
- Team work improves.
- Decision making can be better.

Disadvantages:
- Staff become loyal to the department rather than the organisation.
- Communication barriers between the departments can be created.
- Response to changes in the business environment can be slow.
- Some decisions will take a long time to make.
- Some problem solving requires more than one department, making responsibility hard to identify.

5 (a) **Marketing** – concerned with market research, acquiring and keeping customers and achieving sales.
Finance – responsible for the flow of money in and out of the business, budgeting, obtaining finance, decision-making.
Administration – responsible for information systems.
Operations – responsible for purchasing of raw materials, the production of goods and services, and storage and distribution.
Research and Development – responsible for the development of new products and technologies.
Human Resources – responsible for recruitment, training, appraisal, etc.

(b) Marketing will work closely with Research and Development to develop new products that customers will want to buy. They will work with Finance on things such as pricing and advertising budgets. They will provide Operations with forecasted demand figures so that production will be planned.

Finance will draw up budgets for all departments, and will advise each on how the effects of decisions will affect profitability.

Administration will provide all departments with the necessary information systems to allow them to operate efficiently.

Human Resources will provide and recruit staff for the other departments, arrange staff training and appraisal, and will advise on employment law.

6 Rail, airline, financial services, cosmetics, etc.

Each product is very different in terms of production, marketing, distribution, etc. Each will attract a different market segment. An expert in the air industry would not have skills which could be easily transferred to cosmetics, and vice versa. It makes sense to keep these divisions independent, as they can offer each other very little.

7 It allows them to tailor their products for individual customer wants. They can respond quickly to the changing needs of their customers, and in being able to do so they can build up customer loyalty.

Disadvantages of customer groupings:
- Administration of such a grouping can be time consuming as individual customer needs take time and effort to meet.

- If staff change then the feeling of personal service can be lost.
- Again, there will be duplication of personnel and resources.

8 Shell will explore for oil, develop oil fields and set up refineries where it can do so profitably. Oil is only found in certain geological areas so Shell has to go there to get the oil. The fields will have a lifetime of up to 30 years, so it will set up long-term, large-scale operations.

Advantages of place/territory grouping:
- Local offices with local knowledge can cater for local clients needs.
- Local offices can overcome problems caused by different countries having language and cultural differences.
- Because the local office is accountable for that area, it can be held accountable for success/failure in that area.
- Customer loyalty can be built up through a local personal service.
- The local office is more responsive to changes in customer needs.

Disadvantages of place/territory groupings:
- Administration can be time consuming.
- If staff change then continuity of personal contact is lost.
- Duplication of personnel and resources.

9 W H Smith's three areas are very different in terms of how the products are marketed to three different groups or segments. Wholesale will be large-scale sales to a relatively small number of customers, with logistics (transportation, storage, distribution, import/export, insurance) being a very specialised area. Retail will be the sale of fast-moving consumer goods, and the operation and management of a large chain of shops will be very different to the specialisation of wholesale. Internet sales will require the continuous updating of technology and processes, which will again require very different specialist knowledge.

10 The core activities would be things like learning and teaching, and the development of new courses. Support activities could include administration, finance and human resources.

11 (a) A hierarchical structure is a tall structure, with many layers of management or authority. Decisions and instructions are passed down the structure and information is passed up.

   (b) **Advantages:**
   - Each member of staff will have a clearly defined role and level of responsibility.
   - It allows for specialisation of tasks.
   - The level of supervision can be very high.

   Disadvantages:
   Communication can be very slow.
   The organisation will be slow to respond to change.

12 (a) Flat structures have few layers of management or responsibility. Tall structures can become flat structures through de-layering.

   (b) **Advantages:**
   - The organisation can be quick to respond to changes in its market.
   - Communication can be much faster.

   Disadvantages:
   - The level of supervision may be reduced due to wider spans of control.
   - Who is in charge of and responsible for what may be confused at times.

   (c) **Empowerment**
   This is the delegation of authority to allow staff to make operational or sometimes tactical decisions as they work. This prevents delays, speeds up decision making, and motivates staff.

Delayering
This is the removal of layers of management or authority within an organisation to reduce costs and speed up communication and decision making.

13 (a) In a matrix structure teams are made up of staff from the functional areas, usually to work on projects.

   (b) **Advantages:**
   - Staff get the chance to develop skills in other areas.
   - They also get the chance to develop, increasing job satisfaction and motivation.
   - The organisation will work more closely with their customers.

   Disadvantages:
   - This is an expensive way of organising.
   - Duplication of resources is impossible to avoid.
   - The economies of scale available with a tall structure will not be available.

   (c) **Multi-skilling**
   This is where staff develop expertise in a number of areas, instead of specialising in just one area. This leads to much more flexibility amongst staff.

14 (a) An entrepreneurial structure is one where there are only one or two key decision makers. It is common in small businesses, however, as the business grows it is likely to opt for another structure as it places a lot of decision making responsibility on these individuals, so the stress levels are high. They are also used in areas where decisions have to be made quickly on a daily basis.

   (b) **Advantages:**
   Decision making is very quick, and is made by key individuals who have a great deal of expertise, so they should be accurate.

   Disadvantages:
   - It places too much stress on key staff.
   - There is little consultation of other staff.

15 (a) Centralised structures rely on a relatively small number of key decision makers, usually the senior managers of the organisation. Most decisions are made centrally and then communicated to the rest of the organisation.

   (b) **Advantages:**
   Decision making is quick, and should be accurate. It allows the organisation to present a common identity to their markets.

   Disadvantages:
   - There is little consultation so not all information is available for good decision making.
   - There is little opportunity for staff development or staff motivation through increased responsibility.

16 (a) De-centralised structures move many of the decision making powers away from the centre of the organisation. Local managers can make many local decisions to suit their own particular market.

   (b) **Advantages:**
   - It allows the organisation to be more responsive to changes in the market or environment in which it operates.
   - The quality of decisions should therefore improve.

- Delegation and empowerment of staff allows them to develop their professional skills and gives them greater opportunity to display their own abilities, increasing their motivation, making them harder working.
- Having the power to make decisions means that staff who are aware of their customers and market can prepare for possible changes in advance. This reduces the amount of negative impact on the organisation.

Disadvantages:
- Senior management lose some control over the organisation.
- Decision making may not be as accurate as it should be.
- Company policy may become blurred, or even in competition with local decisions.

17 (a) A tall structure. It is a large organisation, so it will need to be well organised so that management can keep control of the business. Also, its market is large and widespread.

(b) A flat structure. It operates in a local market, so control is already centralised. It will use a high degree of technology, so it will have few workers.

(c) A flat structure. It will have only a few employees, who will all be experts in their own field, so they will not need a lot of supervision.

18 (a) They are useful because:
- New members of staff can immediately see who they are responsible to, and identify other members of their department.
- Each member of staff is included, showing which department they work in, their job title, and who they are responsible to and for. It could also include telephone or room numbers and in some cases photographs may be used to identify key individuals.
- Customers or suppliers can easily identify the various functional departments, and identify who to contact in that department.
- Senior managers can have an overview of the whole organisation, identifying where problems with communications may occur either up and down the hierarchy or between departments. They will also be able to see the number of employees for whom each manager has immediate responsibility (**span of control**). This will allow them to identify possible problems with control, and appoint assistants if necessary.

(b) The span of control is the number of people any manager or supervisor has working directly for him or her.

19 (a) Staff, in the role of advising management on employment matters.
Functional, in working with other departments in recruitment.
Line, in ensuring implementation of employment legislation in other departments.

(b) Staff, as this is purely an advisory role.

(c) Staff, in a purely advisory role.
Line, as they may have authority to ensure all staff work within the law.

(d) Line, in charge of other mechanics.
Staff, in advising management on the effect of their decisions.

(e) Line, in charge of other sales staff.
Functional, in dealing with other managers within the organisation.
Staff, in providing sale information to senior management.

(f) Functional, in their work with other departments.
Line, in implementing marketing strategies throughout their stores.
Staff, in supporting supermarket branch managers.

20 (a) Will depend on student's own perceptions and experience.
   (b) Will depend on student's own perceptions and experience.
   (c) By implementing policies on homework, dress code, discipline, attendance, etc.
   (d) By creating a corporate culture, the company can influence the behaviour of staff in a positive way. It can create a positive corporate image for customers and suppliers to identify, and it can encourage cooperation and teamwork amongst staff.

21 (a) The most significant reason for change is to enable business to respond better to the constant change in their markets and business environment. They are also constantly looking for ways to improve their processes, to become more efficient and cost-effective.
   (b) **Outsourcing** is where part of the operations of the organisation is passed to an outside specialist who will be able to do the job better than the organisation itself, or at a lower cost.

22 Downsizing involves a reduction in the productive capacity of an organisation. This would inevitably lead to a reduction in the workforce. Unions would resist it because they would try to keep their members in employment, and experience has taught them that downsizing usually leads to a shortage of workers when the markets pick up. Workers could then be re-employed, but often on lower pay rates and less favourable conditions.

23 There are fewer levels of management, for example there are not Assistant Head Teachers. There are eight curriculum managers, who have replaced a usually higher number of PT's. Some departments have been merged, for example technology, ICT (computing) and business studies have become one department.

CHAPTER 5

1 Marketing is important because it allows for communication between producers and consumers. It allows them to identify consumers' needs, anticipate future needs and satisfy their needs.

2 Market research shows that tea consumption has fallen from 46 grams per person in 1989 to 32 grams in 2002, although it is still the UK's most popular drink, with 40% of the market. However, tea consumers tend to be older people, who will not be replaced by younger drinkers.

The tea industry has developed new products to appeal to a wider range of consumers.

It has decided that they cannot compete directly on low price. So it has opted for a high-price, quality market instead.

It has targeted 'up-market' establishments to sell its new tea concept.

It is promoting by using themed events as opposed to mass marketing techniques, and where advertising is used it is concentrating on advising consumers of the health benefits of tea.

3 To increase sales revenue and profitability. To increase or maintain market share. To maintain or improve the image of the business, its brand or its product. To target a new market or a new segment of the market. To develop new and improved products.

4 Product orientation is the concentration on the product and or the production process; market orientation is where the business constantly reviews the customers' needs.

Product orientation is only successful for a product which is so technically advanced, or has a sufficiently high novelty value, that the product will sell itself. The company may not provide what the consumers actually want, and so they will lose sales, and not keep up with new developments in the market.

5 **Goods** – These are products that we can see and touch. They may be durable, like mobile phones, televisions, motor cars, things that we can use again and again, or they may be non-durable such as burgers, stamps, or a newspaper.

Services – These are things that are done for us. We cannot see them but we should feel some benefit from having used them. Banking and finance, tourism, insurance, and education are some of Scotland's biggest employers, and these are all services.

6 Market share is the percentage of the total market sales that an organisation has achieved. Market growth is when the market as a whole grows, meaning that the number of consumers buying or using the product has increased.

7 **The Trade Descriptions Act** – The goods or services which consumers buy, must be what the advertising claims they can do.

Monopolies and Mergers Act – This protects consumers from organisations becoming so big that they can set prices higher than they should be, and can prevent new companies or products coming onto the market.

Fair Trading and Competition Acts – These Acts try to ensure that no businesses work to prevent competition in the market. Competition is thought of as being healthy for the market and for consumers, driving down prices and giving consumers a wider choice.

Consumer protection laws – These Acts work to ensure that the products that we buy are safe. They set minimum standards of safety for things like car tyres and furniture. They also ensure that a business is liable for any damage which its defective goods may cause to a consumer.

8 Unique selling proposition is something about a product that makes it different from the others on the market, in the mind of the consumer. Emotional selling proposition is an emotional bond between the brand and the consumer that creates strong brand loyalty.

9 Demographics – age, gender, social class, household income, location, lifestyle/tastes/fashions, personality, politics.

10 Businesses are able to use differentiated marketing by using market segmentation. This is when the whole market is split into different groups who will have similar wants and needs and so businesses can produce goods and services specifically for those groups. In doing so it can more closely meet the needs of those customers, and so is more likely to make sales.

11 The core product is the basic product that meets the needs of the consumer. The augmented product has additional features which can make it more attractive to the consumer, and can prolong its life cycle.

12 Having a wide range of products spreads the risk for the business. Here, the company is operating a number of different industries, so is not relying on one industry.

13 **Development** – The product is being designed and prepared for the market. There are no sales, costs are very high and no profits are being made.

Introduction – The product is launched on to the market. Sales are very low, advertising and distribution cost are high, and no profits are yet being made.

Growth – Consumer awareness begins to increase along with sales. Costs are still relatively high, however, it is likely that the product will become profitable during this stage.

Maturity – Here customer awareness and sales reach their peak, costs are comparatively low, and profits are at their highest. Competition is strong.

Decline – Sales start to fall, the cost of advertising is high, and prices may fall. Profits start to disappear.

14   •   Promoting more frequent use of the product.
      •   Developing new markets for existing products.
      •   Finding new uses for existing products.
      •   Developing a wider range of products.
      •   Developing styling changes.

15   A well known brand allows for instant recognition of the product by the customer, and this makes it easier for the buyer to choose that brand from amongst a range of very similar products.

      Because the consumer knows, trusts, and likes that brand, they will have brand loyalty which will lead them to buy that product again and again – repeat purchases. This leads to a stable level of demand for the product, which is good for the manufacturer and the retailer. For the manufacturer it allows for better production planning.

      Because of the level of trust the consumer has, it is very difficult to get them to change brands, or experiment with new brands. Consumers believe that the product will be better than its competitors, and so the manufacturer can charge premium (higher) prices.

16   **Low price** – A business may decide to charge a price lower than competitors where there is price elasticity of demand. This means that consumers respond positively to changes in price, and lower prices will result in much higher sales.
      Market price – Setting your price at the market rate means that your prices are broadly in line with those of competitors.
      High price – Is adopted in the long term by businesses offering high quality, premium goods and services where image is important, such as in perfumes.
      Skimming – This involves using a high price initially, usually for a new product where there is little competition.
      Penetration pricing – This involves setting a low price, sometimes at a loss, to attract customers to the product in an established market with strong competition. As the product becomes established in the market the business can increase the price.
      Destroyer pricing – Again this involves setting a price below those of competitors, but this time at an artificially low price so as to destroy competition. The business will probably be running at a loss in terms of its sales, however, as soon as the competition is eliminated the price will return to market price or above.
      Promotional pricing – This is used to boost sales in the short term by lowering the price of the product. It can also be used to create interest in a new product.
      Demand orientated pricing – Here, price varies along with the demand for the product.

17   •   The product
      •   The market
      •   Legal requirements
      •   Buying habits
      •   The business

18   •   Cost
      •   Target audience
      •   Competitors' advertising
      •   Impact required
      •   The law

19   **In to the pipeline:**
- **Dealer loaders** where, for example, the retailer is given six boxes for the price of five.
- **Point of sale displays, posters or video cassettes.** Video hire shops are given display material to encourage hires of new videos. Some stores run videos of new products for customers to watch.
- **Dealer competitions** where they can win prizes that would appeal to them.
- **Staff training** for the shops' staff in order for them to deal more effectively with customer enquiries.
- **Sale or return**, which is offered by most newspapers, where if the businesses do not sell all their newspapers they can simply return them without charge.
- **Extended credit**, where the shop does not have to pay for the products for some months, allowing them to take stock and receive payment for sales before they have to actually pay for them.

Out of the pipeline:
- **Free samples or trial packs** which are given away in store or with other products. Magazines are a common way of distributing free samples.
- **Bonus packs** where, for example, you may get 50% free. These are common with many convenience goods such as coffee or washing powder.
- **Price reductions** which are short term pricing strategies to encourage sales. For example a pack may carry '*50p off*' on its packaging.
- **Premium offers** where one product is given free when you buy another.
- **In store demonstrations** or tastings. Tastings are common in supermarkets where customers are allowed to taste and try new products.
- **Merchandising**.

20   Public relations is the communication of the organisation with consumers, society, the press, etc. It is generated by the organisation. Publicity can be generated from within the organisation or from outside the organisation.

21
- **Shape and weight** – These can affect how easy the product is to distribute and handle, which can lead to higher costs.
- **Protection** – The packaging must be robust enough to ensure that the product and its packaging are not damaged in transit or storage. The packaging must also protect the product from possible damage from light, heat and dust.
- **Convenience** – It is important that the packaging is easy for the consumer to handle. Awkward shapes and sizes will put the customer off buying.
- **Design** – The design should be eye-catching to allow it to be distinguished easily from competitors' brands. Colour may be important as, for example some foodstuffs and colours do not mix. As with Cadbury, the colour of the packaging may be used to promote the brand image.
- **Information** – Food products are subject to legal requirements about their ingredients appearing on the packaging, and some technical products, such as light shades, must show the maximum wattage of bulbs that can be used.
- **Environmental factors** – There has been a great deal of public concern regarding recyclable materials being used on packaging, coupled with a pressure to reduce the amount of unnecessary packaging.

22   **Random sampling**
Random sampling involves producing a random list of individuals to survey. Those picked for inclusion in the sample could be generated randomly, using a computer and the telephone directory or the electoral register.

Quota sampling

This type of survey is preferred when carrying out research. Here, those chosen to be surveyed are selected in proportion to the whole population by social status, gender, age, etc. Once they have reached the quota for, say, males aged between 15 and 21, then no more are surveyed.

23 The interview gets information from consumers on a wide variety of different information including what they own, what they would like to own, what they plan to buy, and about their values, attitudes and beliefs. Because of the two way communication, the interviewer can explain questions, encourage answers and ask follow up questions where appropriate. It also allows for more detailed responses than the questionnaire where answers will usually consist of no more than one or two word answers.

CHAPTER 6

1 (a) Financial information provides a history of the business and is the basis for internal control, internal reporting and external reporting to other agencies e.g. the Inland Revenue.

(b) A manager might use financial information in order to make an informed decision.

(c) Useful financial information should be:
- Relevant
- Reliable
- Traceable
- Free from bias and opinion
- Clear and understandable
- Be comparable
- Consistent
- Be presented in a reasonable time scale
- Have all irrelevant information removed

(d) Users of financial information include:
- Shareholders
- Potential shareholders
- Short-term creditors
- Long-term creditors
- Government and local authorities
- Competitors
- Employees
- Analysts
- Management
- Customers
- General public

(e) Any reasonable answer.

CHAPTER 7

1 • To promote a policy of continuous learning and staff development.
- To recruit, develop and retain people with the appropriate skills and attitudes required for present and future jobs.
- To manage employee relations, both on a one-to-one basis and on a collective basis, and maintain the commitment of the workforce.

- To design, implement and manage remuneration, reward and appraisal schemes, which motivate people towards achieving the organisation's objectives.
- To maintain and improve the physical and mental well-being of the workforce by providing appropriate working conditions and health and safety conditions.
- To take account of all government legislation relevant to human resource management.

2   The first is their physiological needs for things such as food, clothing, shelter and warmth. These needs are satisfied by wages and various financial bonuses high enough to meet weekly bills.

The second is their safety needs which can be satisfied through job security, their contract of employment, membership of a trade union, and protection of the various employment laws.

The third is their emotional needs for love and belonging. These can be satisfied through teamworking, job rotation and social clubs.

Esteem needs are the need for self-respect and the esteem of others. This can be done by recognition for a job done well, promotion, merit awards, job title, even the size of office or desk given.

Finally, self-actualisation needs are filled through self-fulfillment. They can be satisfied by promotion, more responsibility, ownership of company shares, or self-employment.

3   **Quality circles** are groups of between 4–10 workers who work for the same supervisor. They meet regularly to identify, analyse and attempt to solve work related problems. They increase the motivation of the workers by involving them in the decision-making around their own jobs, thus increasing efficiency and raising profitability.
Job-enlargement increases the number of tasks a worker will perform, making their jobs less repetitive and boring. It works best where the employees are organised into groups, where all the workers are trained in all jobs the group carries out. They use **job rotation** to allow workers to change the tasks they perform on a regular basis. It also allows for **multi-skilling**.
Job-enrichment involves giving workers some opportunities to choose how to complete a particular task, again usually working as a team.

4   There has been a large rise in the number of people in part-time jobs, and with organisations making more use of casual staff and contractual staff. The core workforce has been cut back, with many 'non-core activities' being outsourced.

5   Women are now making up a much larger portion of the workforce. Organisations tend to be male structures which work against the best interests of the female employees. Organisations will have to change the way they operate to allow women to be more effective.

6   Many firm have found that they will often suffer shortages in staffing and skills. As a result, they are having to re-employ workers they previously let go, and are spending more money on staff recruitment and training.

7   There are fewer people being born, which means we have an aging working population. There will be fewer young people to recruit and train, so other areas of the labour market will have to be investigated.

Secondly, it involves forecasting any possible future staffing needs of the organisation, including likely staff turnover, promotion of existing staff, retirements, and releasing surplus staff. This will be a continuing process as staff needs will change with the organisation's environment (political, economic, socio-cultural, technological and competitive). They will then compare this with the number of appropriately skilled workers who will be available.

Thirdly, they will have to look at support for staff development in training and motivation. This will include the establishment of a corporate culture.

Fourthly, they will look at any possible increase in workload, for example due to expected increased demand for the organisation's products, the development of new products, or the introduction of new technologies that will require new skills not available in the current workforce.

8 **Facilitator role** – This involves providing guidance and training to other managers within the organisation in all HRM policies and procedures and on practical aspects of their job such as interviewing for new staff and carrying out appraisals.
Audit role – This is the monitoring and reporting on all the HRM policies within the organisation, ensuring that all staff follow procedures.
Consultancy role – Here they provide managers with guidance and advice on specialist assistance to manage potentially difficult situations effectively, such as making staff redundant.
Executive role – HRM are the resident experts in all matters relating to HRM management.
Service role – Providing useful, up to date information, for example on new employment legislation.

9 Job analysis – job description – person specification.

10 INTERNAL RECRUITMENT
The costs involved in promoting internally are lower than recruiting externally. The person is already known to the organisation and so the risk of appointing the wrong person is reduced.

The existing employee will have benefited from the organisation's own investment in training and so this will not be lost if the employee has to leave in order to get promotion.

The prospect of internal promotion can be a strong motivator for employees, and helps in external recruitment where promotion possibilities are available.

Large organisations will use internal recruitment as they have a large pool of workers that they can pick from.

DISADVANTAGES IN INTERNAL RECRUITMENT
Firstly, it restricts the number of applicants for the post as the best person for the job, in the long run, may not yet work for the organisation. Secondly, new workers can bring new skills and ideas to the organisation, and thirdly, promotion will probably create another vacancy which will then have to be filled.

EXTERNAL RECRUITMENT
This has the benefit of attracting the widest range of interested applicants with the right qualifications for the post.

The new staff may bring new ideas to the organisation.

The new staff can bring in new skills to the organisation such as specialists in ICT.

DISADVANTAGES IN EXTERNAL RECRUITMENT
The costs involved are much higher, and the time taken for selection is longer.

11 APPLICATION FORMS
Application forms give applicants the same questions and opportunities to describe themselves. This makes it much easier to compare information from a large number of candidates.

The application forms will be compared to the person specification to see which appear to match. The HRM department will then look at all the applications and decide which applicants to reject at this stage.

From the applications that appear to be suitable, a decision must be made as to how many should be invited for interview.

INTERVIEW

It may be that the organisation selects a long-list of 10 or more candidates for a first interview, which will then be reduced to around five for a second interview, when a final decision will be made. Applicants under consideration should be invited for interview, and references sought from existing or previous employers or schools.

Interviews do help in the selection process in identifying the personality and characteristics of the applicant, and also gives some indication of how they react in stressful situations, however, some applicants may be highly experienced in interviews.

TESTING

Aptitude tests – These tests measure how good the applicant is at a particular skill such as mathematical skills, typing or shorthand speeds, driving ability, etc. These tests are objective in that each applicant's performance can be measured and compared.

Psychometric tests – These test are designed to measure the personality, attitudes and character of the applicant. They are timed tests, usually multiple choice, taken under exam conditions and are designed to measure the intellectual capability of the applicant for thinking and reasoning, particularly logical/analytical reasoning abilities.

Personality tests – These can give an indication as to whether they are a team player or not, and what team role or roles they perform best.

12   **Induction training** – Used for staff new to the organisation. Will include training in the organisation's policies and procedures.

On-the-job training – Training while you are actually doing the job, usually paired with a more experienced member of staff for close supervision and instruction.

Off-the-job training – Training away from the work area. Can involve courses on the premises or at another location, for example gaining qualifications at college. An organisation may use its own instructors or use outside specialists.

13   They identify future training needs, consider development needs for the individual's career, they can improve the performance of the employee, they provide feedback to the employee about their performance, they identify individuals who have potential for future promotion within the organisation, or who have additional skills which could be useful now or in the future.

14   ACAS, employers' associations such as the CBI, employees' associations, professional associations such as the Police Federation, the TUC and the various trade unions.

15   NEGOTIATION

The purpose of negotiation is to come to an agreement. Here employers and employees will meet to discuss issues that affect both parties to agree, plan and implement some changes in the workplace.

CONSULTATION

Consultation is enforced on employers under employment law for some changes within the organisation. No agreement is necessary and the employer is under no obligation to take account of the views of the employees.

ARBITRATION

Where no agreement can be reached between the employer and employees, and a dispute resulting in some form of industrial action is possible, an independent arbitrator such as ACAS may be called in to try to resolve the problem. The arbitrator is unbiased and neutral to the dispute, will listen to both sides, gather other evidence as appropriate and offer a solution.

COLLECTIVE BARGAINING

Collective bargaining is the process where the trade union or other body negotiates with the employer on behalf of the employees, usually on pay or changes that are proposed in the workplace. The process starts when either the employees' representatives or the employers propose some change to their existing agreement.

Once both parties have an agreement, the employees' representatives will then take the offer back to their members, recommending that they accept.

16 **Strike** – In a strike all or most of the workers stop working – they withdraw their labour.
Sit-in – Where workers occupy their workplace in an attempt to stop the employer closing the unit.
Work-to-rule – Where employees work strictly to their terms and conditions of employment.
Overtime ban – This is where workers refuse to do overtime.
Boycotts – Workers simply refuse to carry out certain duties or use certain machines.

17 Works councils and single union agreements.

18
- The job title.
- The specific rules and duties relating to the job.
- The pay scale and rate of pay.
- How they will be paid, for example weekly or monthly.
- The normal hours to be worked.
- The availability of and rate of pay for overtime.
- Holiday entitlement.
- Arrangements in the event of illness.
- Any pension scheme arrangements.
- Terms of notice required to be given by the employee and the employer.
- Details of the grievance procedure.
- Details of the disciplinary procedure.

19 The personal details of the employee, their employment history and appraisal records.

20
- Equal Pay Act 1970
- Anti-discrimination laws:
  - Sex Discrimination Act 1975
  - Race Relations Act 1976
  - Disability Discrimination Act 1996
- Employment laws:
  - Employment Act 1989
  - Employment Relations Act 1999
  - Employment Rights Act 1996
  - Working Time Regulations 1998
  - National Minimum Wage Act 1998
- Health and Safety at Work Act 1974

CHAPTER 8

1
- The nature of the product being produced.
- The size of the market for the product.
- The resources available to the organisation.
- The stage of development of the business.
- The mix of labour and machines to be used.
- The availability of technology — automation/robotics.

2
- Which of the alternative suppliers should be used.
- The delivery time, including reliability of the suppliers.
- The price charged, including discounts and credit facilities.
- The available quality.
- The quantity that should be bought.
- The size and suitability of storage facilities available.

3
- What the economic stock level should be.
- What the minimum stock level should be.
- What the re-order stock level should be.
- What the re-order quantity should be.

4 Barcodes are now the electronic language of business. They allow stock to flow from suppliers to manufacturers, and from manufacturers to consumers. Modern business would be very difficult without them.

5
- There is less capital tied up in stock, so money can be used for other purposes or removed entirely from the manufacturer's expenditure.
- The storage costs for space, equipment, warehouse and stores staff, services, etc. are reduced to a minimum.
- There is near to zero stock losses/wastage through theft, accidental damage, stock exceeding its shelf-life, stock obsolescence.

6
- **Employees** — Basic wage, piece rate, overtime, fringe benefits, profit sharing, bonuses and share save schemes.
- **Senior managers** — Fringe benefits, profit sharing, bonuses and share options.